TRADE, FINANCE
AND DEVELOPING
COUNTRIES

TRADE, FINANCE AND DEVELOPING COUNTRIES

Strategies and Constraints in the 1990s

Sheila Page

Overseas Development Institute, London

HARVESTER WHEATSHEAF

New York   London   Toronto   Sydney   Tokyo

First published 1990 by
Harvester Wheatsheaf
66 Wood Lane End, Hemel Hempstead
Hertfordshire, HP2 4RG
A division of
Simon & Schuster International Group

Printed and bound in Great Britain by
BPCC Wheatons Ltd, Exeter

British Library Cataloguing in Publication Data

Page, Sheila, *1946–*
Trade, finance and developing countries: strategies
and constraints in the 1990s.
1. Developing countries. Economic policies
I. Title
330.9172′4

ISBN 0–7450–0606–X

1 2 3 4 5   94 93 92 91 90

CONTENTS

TABLES

ACKNOWLEDGEMENTS

The five principal authors of the case studies, Mohamed Ariff, Supote Chunanuntathum, Juan José Echavarria, Peter Robinson and Jürgen Schuldt, contributed much more than their working papers and chapters to the study. Their views on the objectives of the research, on the problem of reconciling international comparison with national analysis and on the preliminary results immeasurably strengthened the final work. Although they will disagree with some of my conclusions (as they do with each other), I am deeply grateful for their comments and their support, and their tolerance of my severe abridgement of their papers.

During the research for this I have had advice and comments from too many individuals in academic research, governments and industry for me to be able to name all of them, and in many cases they would be unwilling to be named. I would like to thank particularly those who attended the six meetings in Bangkok, Bogota, Harare, Kuala Lumpur, Lima and London at which we presented the country and general results; the managers and government policy-makers who participated in the study of foreign investors which was one of the background elements of this research; and colleagues at the Overseas Development Institute who listened to early versions of the ideas presented here. Both the country authors and I must give special thanks to Margaret Cornell who edited and greatly clarified our papers.

I am grateful for financial support for the research to the Economic and Social Research Committee of the Overseas Development Administration, the Economic and Social Research Council (under award number B00232126), the International Development Research Centre of Canada and the National Economic Development Office. None of these has any responsibility for any of the views expressed here.

PART ONE

BACKGROUND AND ASSUMPTIONS

1

INTRODUCTION: THE CHOICES FOR THE NEW NICs

The first reaction to the success of the NICs (Newly Industrialising Coun-tries) in achieving rapid growth and the transformation of their economies was admiration, accompanied by encouragement to laggards to emulate them. In the late 1970s and early 1980s, some of the most obvious features of their economies, notably their success in exporting manufactures, were identified as explanations of their performance which could be suggested as policies to be followed by others. They remain the most recent examples of what an earlier generation of seekers for general explanations called 'take-off', and some observers still urge what were then identified as their strategies on other developing countries (cf. World Bank, *WDR*, 1987). But there is a growing perception that the performance of the top four countries was exceptional compared with other similar countries in the 1960s and 1970s, and that the 1960s and early 1970s were themselves an exceptional period in terms of overall growth and the relation of trade to output. This has led to reappraisals of the lessons to be drawn from the NICs, and of how their example can be followed by other countries in other conditions. The present study starts from the premise that it is necessary to reappraise the NICs' experience, and also to look at a broader range of middle-income developing countries which have the potential to be the next generation of NICs.

It therefore looks, issue by issue, at the experience of three levels of countries within what can be broadly classified as the upper middle-income developing countries (excluding the dedicated oil producers), at their individ-ual performance using aggregate data and, in order to examine the validity and the practical implications of general explanations, at fuller analyses prepared by economists in five of the potential NICs. Eight NICs, the five case-study countries and 13 countries in the next stage (listed in Table 9.1) are covered. These countries account for about 85% of exports of manufac-tures by developing countries, and similar shares of private and official financial flows from the developed countries to the developing. By taking this large sample, it is possible to examine general propositions about the different strategies, in particular *vis-à-vis* different domestic and external possibilities.

The countries that are normally classified as the NICs, those that now have manufacturing sectors of a similar relative size to those of the industrialised countries (more than a quarter of GDP), are in fact an extremely diverse group in terms of recent growth or other conventional measures of performance, as well as in industrial structure and non-economic characterisitics: Hong Kong, India, Singapore, South Korea, Taiwan, Argentina, Brazil and Mexico. If the potential members of the next group of industrialising countries are to be found among those whose manufacturing sector is now in the 20–25% of GDP range, they include Malaysia, Thailand, the Philippines, Colombia, Costa Rica, Chile, Uruguay, Peru, Egypt and Zimbabwe. Of these, Malaysia, Thailand, Colombia, Peru and Zimbabwe were chosen for our country studies. These studies which look at trading performance and financing in more detail, and in relation to other parts of the economy, government policy and particular country conditions, are especially important in analysing the choice of policies actually available and how decision-makers respond to economic opportunities or to policies.

The country studies, Part Two of the book, do not follow a common pattern because they are intended to bring out not only the different problems and how they can be met, but the different objectives and policy approaches. Part Three (Chapters 9–15) draws together their evidence with the trade and financing experiences in the large sample, with Chapter 15 assessing the essential characteristics and current problems of their external exposure. The remaining chapters, which make up Part Four, examine explanations and conclusions about the role of the external sector and how it relates to other aspects of the countries' development.

THE EXAMPLE OF THE NICs

The apparent association between high and rapidly growing exports and rapid growth of manufacturing suggested to many observers that a policy of opening an economy to external influences or even of deliberately biasing growth towards exports could improve rates of investment and growth and raise efficiency, not only through the conventional trade and multiplier effects on efficient allocation of resources and increased demand, but by increasing the flexibility of the economy and minimising the risks of wrong domestic policies (e.g. Bhagwati, 1978; Krueger, 1978; Balassa, 1981, 1982; Dell, 1982). This explanation was generalised to removing all controls and restrictions. The argument was that the general performance of individual firms and of the economy as a whole is improved by requiring them to meet changes in demand, particularly in external demand.

Examining this case requires testing each step of the argument and distinguishing between deliberate choices and chance, and between economic response and the role of government. The trade performance may result from countries' particular economic or other characterisitics. It may be that suitable domestic policies for successful industrialisation also contribute to export growth or that particular export opportunities existed which an already flexible or efficient economy could exploit. It is clearly wrong simply to take 'the growth rate of exports as a proxy for orientation' (Balassa, 1982: 51). In new circumstances, a flexible and efficient economy may find different paths of development, and recent research has suggested that the experience of the most recent successes was more complex than initial studies suggested (Bradford, 1986: 119). The detail of how the NICs have succeeded in practice suggests that the contrast between 'external' and 'internal' policies was never as great as some studies imply.

Chapters 16 and 17 of the present study examine how important various ways of improving external performance, including finding new export products, new markets, new sources of finance, or reducing dependence on imports, particularly of intermediate and capital goods, have been for the NICs' successes, and whether there are systematic differences between these successes and those of other countries. In looking at the NICs' possible examples for the next generation, it is necessary to try to identify the replicable elements of their achievement. Should their successors look for the same markets or products; or for different ones but using similar strategies; or simply for diversification?

In the 1980s, we are more aware of the issue of financial constraints on trade policies. Different types of long-term finance, especially the choices of official or private, loans or direct investment, offer different advantages and disadvantages other than the purely financial. But they may not all be available to a particular country, especially at present. Direct investment, in addition to offering a way of transferring to developing countries the increasing company profits in the industrial countries, may offer access to technical knowledge and other prerequisites specifically for industrialisation or access to export markets. This may make it more desirable, but it may be particularly difficult to integrate into a recipient country's own plans, or indeed may prove difficult to attract. The types of short- or medium-term finance available, and their cost, can affect the choice of trading and long-term financing by altering the costs of fluctuations in financing requirements. Loans on commercial terms have imposed long-term costs on the potential new NICs which are themselves a 'new' external condition. These financial constraints are considered in more detail in Chapters 14 and 15.

EXTERNAL STRATEGY

It is essential to take account of the particular objectives as well as the constraints on different countries. This is a neglected area in many general studies which, partly because it is readily comparable among countries, emphasise growth as the basic measure of success, with only the conventional provisos of a sustainable external position and low inflation. Particularly if growth is then measured in terms of external prices (again for comparability, but also as the conventional measure of efficiency – (e.g., Henderson, in Krueger, 1982) – it can reinforce the conclusions initially drawn from the experience of the NICs, namely, that good export performance is the driving force behind 'good' results. One of the first 'results' of collaborative research such as that followed in the present project is to show how inaccurate this is as a description of countries' own criteria, and therefore how misleading and inadequate such an approach must be.

The question of external strategy is closely linked to that of the degree and type of industrialisation to be undertaken. There may be a conflict between temporary rapid growth and constructing an integrated industrial structure, or each may depend on the existence of the other. Industrialisation may also be seen as a way of reducing vulnerability to external influences (particularly for countries which have been principally primary producers). Industrialisation must also, however, be treated as an end in itself, an essential component of development for most of the countries in this study.

The striking changes in the world economy suggest that countries that have remained relatively closed face a smaller change in the challenges they face in the 1980s, even if they experienced slower growth in the 1970s. This raises the question of the choice between high-risk, but possibly high-growth, paths and lower-risk ones, if these exist. The question of policy choice is frequently discussed in terms of selecting one plan. The problem of risk suggests, if it is possible without inconsistency, using more than one of the possible ways of improving external performance. Such a strategy may make the exceptionally good results of the best performers unattainable, but by reducing the risk of complete failure it may increase the 'expected' return, or at least reduce the spread of possible outcomes around it. For this reason, it is necessary to examine whether the risks of different choices have actually changed, and also how they appeared to the successes in the past and how they appear now to their potential followers; the perceived range of possible outcomes is different. The world economy may appear more risky than in the past simply because expectations must now take into account the much wider fluctuations that have been observed since 1970, or there may have been fundamental changes that affect the opportunities for new NICs. The latter question is addressed in the next chapter on current expectations.

In any decision, the weight attached to reduced risk should clearly not be 0. Therefore, showing that a particular strategy offers the opportunity for the highest gains is not a sufficient argument. But equally clearly, it should not exceed any other criterion, and it is therefore possible to suggest that some strategies are too averse to risk. The discussion in Chapter 17 of the lessons that the case-study countries themselves draw from past experience considers whether the unusually severe events of the 1980s have taught 'too great' an aversion to risk, and whether one contribution of policy might now be to reduce the constraints imposed by risk.

The value of diversification, however, may go beyond risk-reduction. A broad spread of products or markets or suppliers may offer the efficiency advantages, in the non-traditional sense, of raising skills and flexibility that have been attributed to export orientation. This issue is related to the role of industrialisation. How to achieve this type of efficiency increase, and how to change the way in which decision-makers respond, proves to be basic to examining what special contribution an externally-based strategy may make.

It is in the role of government that the intrinsically separable questions of which strategy should be chosen and whether the government or private decision-makers should make the choice must come together.[1] The value attached to risk-avoidance is close to the issue of the objectives of particular societies, and also to that of the role of governments. They may consider it their function to decide the acceptable degrees or types of risk that a country can incur. An external strategy may look more risky to a government if the world economy appears less predictable (or controllable) than the national, but a private decision-maker, for whom the government may also be a source of uncertainty, may attach different weights. Certain types of strategy, possibly including some types of diversification or spreads of activity, may require more (or different types of) government action than a price-based, export-led strategy to be fully successful. Some of the diversification advantages may be difficult for individual enterprises to internalise, so that government would have to intervene to promote such a strategy. Promoting certain sectors which are regarded as having special advantages may require more direct forms of government action. Different country attitudes to the acceptable limits on government action, or different practical constraints on it, may limit the choice of strategies. These are discussed in Chapter 18.

CURRENT EXPECTATIONS

The collapse of international growth, trade and capital flows in 1980–2, and of confidence in future trends, also spurred reappraisal of the relevance of the NICs. The performance of even the non-oil-exporting developing countries had actually improved during the 1970s in spite of the much less favourable world conditions. It was the realisation that this was the result of sharply differentiated performance between the NICs and the others that had been one of the reasons for the interest in and research on their performance. For most countries, the 1970s were a period of poor external performance and slow growth or stagnation. If good performance on the external account is crucial to development, the crisis of 1980–2 and the resulting expectations that the external climate would be even more unfavourable suggest that choosing the appropriate strategy for maximising the benefits to be gained from external influences could now be an even more important element in countries' performance. The two oil price rises of the 1970s and the debt crisis of the 1980s illustrated the vulnerability of all countries to external changes: minimising the costs of external exposure has, therefore, become a more important criterion than in the more optimistic 1960s.

The difficulties posed now by slow growth in the developed countries and the constrained financial situation are different from those of the 1970s and also from those of the recession of the early 1980s. The reduction in long-term expectations is new: throughout the 1970s each slowdown was taken by most observers to be temporary and the recession was not foreseen. Now, however, both private and public decision-makers in developed countries are taking slow growth and low employment of labour and capital (and natural) resources to be normal. The direct effects of slow growth on their demand for imports are therefore intensified by increasing unwillingness to undertake the domestic adjustments necessary to accommodate any rise in the share, or changes in the composition, of imports. Prospects for demand from oil producers, the major growth markets of the 1970s, are now poorer. The ability of developing countries to increase or even maintain their share of world trade is therefore increasingly questioned.

The poor growth prospects and the decline in world savings (because of the fall in the OPEC surplus) also reduce expectations for the quantities of investment and raise its likely cost. The ability of developing countries to share in the reduced supply of bank lending has fallen because the volume of past debts has brought many to the limits (and beyond) of their ability and willingness to borrow. Even if the problem of past debts is resolved, both countries and banks will be more cautious. The reduction in the OPEC surplus and the corresponding rise in incomes in the official and private sectors in industrial countries also change the composition of funds available: any transition has costs and uncertainties, and the ability of developing countries to attract funds from these sources is uncertain.

There is, however, a tension between taking such a general approach and looking at individual countries. What becomes immediately obvious is that for none of the countries studied here does 1980–2 appear 'the' turning point in the sense that it is for 'non-oil developing countries' in general, and industrial country performance and the aggregate supply of savings are only two among several significant changes in their prospects. For Peru, export and financing difficulties had come in the 1970s, while its growth in 1986 was 8%, well above its normal levels and the depressed general average for developing countries. Colombia had unusually good terms of trade in 1986, when commodity prices generally were lower than at any time since the Second World War, and it continues to receive unforced bank lending. Zimbabwe's external possibilities are bound up with the prospects for trade with South Africa. Growth in Asia means that the external prospects for Thailand and Malaysia are much more immediately favourable than for African or Latin American countries, but each faces particular problems for specific exports and for the domestic balances. All the country studies thus stress that each country had particular advantages and disadvantages that brought earlier or later crises, different turning points or opportunities. Two basic questions for the present study, therefore, are whether the choice of external strategy is the most important area for policy or concern and how dependent the choice of strategy and its success are on conditions in the world economy. They are raised in Chapter 3 on the objectives and conditions of the individual countries, as well as in Chapter 16. In the country studies, it is clear that other problems are seen as crucial by policy-makers and the individual authors.

The concluding chapter attempts to show how the three themes of the study interact. The countries' own objectives are national ones, economic and non-economic, and their actions, policies and domestic constraints are central to their performance and to the differences among them. The world economic situation influences and can set limits on all of these which go beyond, and are more complex than, a simple model of dependency. How economies react to any conditions and policies, particularly how developing economies behave, pushes economics to its very unsatisfactory borders with industrial and behavioural analysis.

NOTE

1. It is important to preserve a distinction between what governments do or should do and how efficiently they do it. All would argue for improvements in the latter; differences arise on the former.

2
EXTERNAL PROSPECTS FOR DEVELOPING COUNTRIES

The discussion of future strategies in the studies was based on agreed assumptions about medium-term economic conditions. We did not think it necessary to specify a detailed medium-term forecast. What was important was to take a common view of the most important features of the next five years, particularly the significant differences from the past, and of general expectations beyond this period. Against this, each country would assume, or plan, its potential path, to remove short-term constraints and achieve longer-term targets. Starting the country studies in early 1986, the researchers took the expectations of the international organisations in autumn 1985 (Page, 1985) as a guide, modified by the expected results of the fall in oil prices at the end of 1985 and early 1986. As developing countries in aggregate are largely self-sufficient in oil, even if the major oil producers are excluded, and in particular as three of the countries in this study – Peru, Colombia and Malaysia – are oil exporters, the major potential favourable effects of this come from the response of the oil-importing developed countries.

The first obvious difference from the 1970s is in the immediate background to the starting point. Until 1973, the world had enjoyed a quarter-century of almost uninterrupted growth of output and trade, with both developed and developing countries expanding rapidly and steadily: there was only one year with a fall in world trade (of about 1%), and the analysis of business cycles had changed to that of 'growth recessions'. Since the beginning of 1973, all the major industrial countries and most of the smaller, as well as most developing countries, have had their most serious recession for half a century, with prolonged periods of stagnation and actual falls in output and trade, not merely once in the mid-1970s but, after an apparent recovery, again and more seriously in the early 1980s. There is still controversy over whether the depth and extent of this prolonged depression were the result of an exceptional combination of causes: unrelated external events reinforcing planned or cyclical downturns in individual countries, or whether they mark some more permanent change, either in economic forces or political choices. What is important for the present study is that, under either explanation, past assumptions about what is a normal growth path and what is an inconceivable recession have been altered. The continuing difference of views creates a climate of uncertainty and lack of confidence in future prospects which alters the climate for private or public decisions, especially on investment; and the depression itself has had serious effects on the investment base on which the next 5–10 years can build. The financial 'crash' of October 1987 came after the country studies had been completed, and could have reinforced the uncertainty and loss of confidence.

The perceptions of risk are increased because the events leading up to the unprecedented 1973 rises in commodity prices and terms of trade, first traditional, then oil, and then the sharp falls in output and trade of 1973–5, and later to the depression of 1982–3 and the debt crisis of 1982–5, did not appear at the time to be unusual. Each of these crises was largely unforecast, although one response to the uncertainties of the 1970s had been an expansion in forecasts by the international agencies, focusing on the effect of events in the developed countries on the outlook for the developing countries. The recession after 1979 was not forecast in the preceding year, and during the next three years its continuation and deepening were not expected, and the recovery, particularly in forecasts taking a 5–10 year outlook, was persistently over-forecast.[1] The earliest forecasts published for such periods, at the end of the 1970s, had 1980–5 as their medium term. The forecasters' problem was to foresee that growth in the industrial countries would be slower not only than the 3.5% averaged in the recovery after the 1975 recession, but than the average for the whole period since the first oil price rise, 1973–80, namely 2.5%. None did so. Forecasts by the World Bank, the OECD, the IMF and the UN all assumed that performance would improve, although there were warnings from the GATT and the Bank for International Settlements in the late 1970s that growth would be slow.

On trade, the problem for medium-term forecasters in the late 1970s and early 1980s was to foresee that trade would grow not merely more slowly than in the past, but, in contrast to the traditional relationship, more slowly than output. The forecasts were too high, and higher than output. Developing countries grew by about 6% a year in the 1970s, not much below their rate in the 1960s and faster than industrial countries. The growth rate began to slow in 1979, declined to 2% a year in 1982–3, and the rise in 1984 to 4%, which was seen by the forecasters as the beginning of a recovery to a sustainable level, slightly above the rate of population growth, fell back to 3.5% in 1985. The World Bank forecast in 1978 had been 5.5% plus or minus half a point, which was reduced by 1980 to a range of 4.1–4.7%. In 1986, however, their growth recovered, equally unexpectedly, to 5–6%, and in 1987–8 growth in the developed countries recovered equally unexpectedly.

With the outcomes for many of the most important variables outside even the uncertainty range given for the forecasts, the results suggest that conventional forecasting does not provide a reliable basis for assessing medium-term external prospects for developing countries, at least in periods when there are large shocks to the international system, or for recognising turning points. The forecasts have also failed to warn of shocks: although all forecasters saw by autumn 1985 that the patterns of external imbalances and slow growth were unsustainable, none suggested that this would result in a collapse in oil and, later, other commodity prices. They are also inadequate in analysing how countries will respond to such shocks.[2] In 1986, the industrial countries grew less than expected after the oil price fall, and the developing countries grew more than had been expected even with the too-high forecasts for their industrial country markets. In 1987–8, the developing countries grew less than expected.

For the developing countries, identifying changes for interest rates and financing has become more important in recent years, both because of their increasing exposure to financial markets and because these also have become more variable. Fewer forecasters risk tackling these, but the large fall in external lending by financial institutions in 1982 was not forecast, and forecasts since then have tended to be over-optimistic on both capital flows and interest rates.

The lack of reliable medium-term forecasts for the international economy is clearly a serious problem in itself in a period when uncertainty and external exposure have increased. The inaccuracy of those by the major international institutions raises another set of problems because of developing country dependence on these organisations. Some countries now in difficulties might have followed different policies if the forecasts had indicated slow growth or high interest rates. Some may now wish to follow policies different from those recommended because they do not accept the present forecasts. Although the forecasts are described as scenarios, without official backing, this does raise questions about the proper role of a creditor or policy adviser who is also a forecaster. Some of the institutions themselves have raised doubts about whether their own forecasts are 'real' in the sense of presenting the forecasters' central or best guess about the future, or hortatory or minatory, i.e. designed to change countries' views and actions. This further complicates taking a view of the future and defining the obligations of the forecasters to those who are users of both their forecasts and their credits.

For the purpose of the present study, we agreed on two sets of forecasts, one to represent a consensus of current economic opinion, and a lower one, the outcome if all the major uncertain factors came in at the low end of expectations (Table 2.1). This was not intended to represent the lowest possible, or to include any international catastrophe of the scale of the 1980–2 depression, because forecasting the economic and policy reactions to these would have dominated the study. How countries should treat the uncertainty between these outcomes or the chances of events being much more favourable or unfavourable is itself a question of national strategy which the country studies consider, but all decisions must start from some 'most likely' outcomes. Particular assumptions made for individual countries about the external factors that most affect them were made on the same basis.

The forecasts for industrial country output assume a poorer performance than in the 1970s, and thus much poorer than in the decade before 1973.[3] The trade forecast derived from this does not assume a large change in elasticities, in spite of the doubts raised by the outcome of recent years. Excess capacity may reduce demand for imports and technology changes may alter patterns of international specialisation, with particularly severe effects on primary commodities and mass-produced manufactures. (These are discussed in more detail in the trade chapters.) Protection is known to be increasing again, particularly against the developing countries and the goods which they are most likely to produce (Page, 1987b). At the least, any increase in import elasticities seems unlikely, and (by assumption) there will be no stimulus from a demand external to both as there was from OPEC in 1974–8. How far new developing country exporters of manufactures can continue to out-perform the average, and the effects of the lower relative prices on exports of primary commodities, were questions for the study. The general assumption was that markets for both in the industrial countries would be growing slowly, with risks of protection and preference for established suppliers, so that increasing exports would be on average more difficult than in the past. The differences among industrial countries' performances were assumed to be smaller than in the past, but their direction, and the relative performance of different markets, was considered significant.

After the falls in commodity prices in 1986, these assumptions implied some improvement in the next few years, but that the levels would remain low, and the forecast rejects any expectation of a general boom. It does not, however, rule out large changes for individual commodities (as Colombia and Malaysia have already observed for coffee and tin), and that such moves could occur within a poor aggregate performance was an assumption of the study. The inflation and interest-rate assumptions for the industrial countries are lower and higher, respectively, than in 1970s, and the real interest rate assumptions are historically high. These imply that the costs of financing past and new borrowing will remain high, and that it will be more difficult to reduce their ratio to exports or output through real or nominal export growth.

Under these non-crisis scenarios there seemed no reason to reject the consensus forecasts of little change in the capital flows to developing countries as a group, which nevertheless means a large reduction compared with what was available in the 1970s. The average forecast can be taken to assume official flows that grow by rather less than output in the industrial countries (partly because of absolute declines from the OPEC countries), no significant medium-term private financial lending, and at best trend (3%) growth in direct foreign investment (Chapter 14 gives more detail). Access to finance, therefore, as well as its cost, is expected to remain more difficult, although, perhaps even more than trade, this is an area in which the conditions in individual countries can make their differences from the average much more significant than changes in the general situation.

The exchange-rate assumption was intended to be simply that: i.e. the type of assumption decision-makers must make, but with the range of past movements and fluctuations, and their implications for future uncertainty, clearly more important than the particular point. The fall by early 1986 in the oil price was assumed to have brought it closer to a reasonable relationship with supply and demand conditions than had been the case as late as the first half of 1985. The assumption was that it would remain subject to the same constraints of secular weakening of demand and over-supply as other commodity prices. Again, uncertainty was considered an important element of the forecast.

Because of the possibility of changes in the structure of industry and of demand, the relationship between external constraints and growth in developing countries is not mechanical in the medium term: this is a theme of the present study. It was, therefore, inappropriate to adopt in advance a forecast for developing country output. The forecasts used for developed countries suggested about 5% for the 'principal' and 3% for the 'low'. This is slightly lower than the 6% of the 1970s, which itself embodied a decline from 6.5% in the first half to 5.5% in the second, although it is considerably better than the 2.5% of 1980–5.

The change in the early 1980s applied to all areas, but especially to the South-East Asian countries and Latin America. Output there grew by 5–6% a year during the 1970s, but fell to 1% in the first half of the 1980s. Growth in Africa followed much the same pattern but at much lower levels, declining from around 4% to near 0 in the 1980s. The general consensus of the forecasters, that output in the Asian countries would continue to be higher than the average, in Latin America slightly lower and in Africa significantly lower, was accepted. This assumption of strong area differences is important in considering the role of intra-regional trade in an external strategy. Although all three areas would face poorer performance under the 'low' assumptions, and the ranking would not be changed, Latin America would be most seriously affected because of its vulnerability to changes in the costs and availability of financing.

Thus the background against which present decisions in developing countries must be made is one of little rise in output overall since 1980 in most countries, with only two years of apparent recovery, 1984 and 1986, separated by the disappointment in 1985. This makes it increasingly likely that there has been a decline in medium-term potential because of the prolonged period of low investment (even below replacement level) in many countries.

Expectations for the rest of the world, especially for the trade and financing flows with direct impact on developing countries, are significantly poorer than in the 1970s.

NOTES

1. The forecasts are summarised and compared with outcomes in Page (1984–7, 1984b).
2. Llewellyn et al. (1985) find some improvement in computing international shock transmission, but confirm that this remains a weakness.
3. It is sufficient, however, to give rising standards of living in the industrial countries, which therefore do not face the acute pressure to improve performance seen in the developing countries.

Table 2.1 Scenarios assumed: Average rates over five years, with the additional assumption of no major change in economic conditions or expectations for the 1990s, but the risk of some change (in either direction)

	Principal[b]	Low[b]
GDP industrial countries	3	2
US	3	2
Japan	4	>2
Europe	2.5	<2
World trade	5	3
Inflation, industrial countries	4	4
Exchange rates	no change	no change
Interest rate[a] (three months LIBOR)		
real	4	6
nominal	8	10
Prices in trade (nominal)		
manufactures	4	4
oil	$18	$15
other prices	4	1

a. Countries may pay different differentials on this.
b. The assumptions are meant to represent:
    Principal: consensus of economic opinion.
    Low: The uncertain forecasts all emerge at the low end of expectations, but no catastrophe.

3

NATIONAL GOALS AND EXPECTATIONS

The general outlook outlined in the previous chapter suggests that, in the absence of significant policy changes, developing countries can expect a further decline in their economic performance after already suffering falling growth in the second half of the 1970s, and a serious recession in 1980–5. The purpose of the country studies presented in the following five chapters is to identify the type of strategy which could improve this discouraging outlook and the implications for policy for the external sector. Expressing this as a simple numerical target, $n\%$ extra GDP growth, was rejected. A common quantitative target would not take account of other objectives or of the different dimensions of the problem in each country. What was important was to improve performance in terms of the set of objectives that countries would have chosen in the absence of unfavourable changes in the external situation. None of the countries was likely to be unaffected by the new external constraints (and some would have had difficulties in meeting their objectives without the changes).

The effect went further, because the series of unfavourable external shocks suggested that reducing vulnerability or increasing flexibility in reacting to them should now have a higher priority than in the past. If professional forecasts do not provide a desired reduction in uncertainty, greater autonomy, which could attenuate a country's link to slow external growth, may be a possibility. The arguments for export-led growth saw this as promoting efficient responses to changes in demand, with flexibility as one element of this. It is not clear, however, whether flexibility is the result of a particular strategy, and if so whether this must include export promotion, or a characteristic that makes certain policies workable. The country studies therefore included identifying what types of flexibility are needed, what induces it and where it might conflict with other goals. This is one element of choosing a strategy under conditions of uncertainty. In terms of the comparison with the old NICs, it means asking whether there was an association between fast export growth and flexibility of response, and whether this was because flexible countries are better able to export, or chose to export in the 1970s, or because exporting itself improves flexibility.

Although this study focuses on a period of roughly five years into the future, the 'better performance' was taken to include not only 'satisfactory' performance within this period, but establishing a base and a strategy consistent with good performance judged by longer-term criteria. Some policies may need to be adjusted more or less urgently to meet present problems, but we would argue that the period is also one in which all countries need to initiate changes in direction that will only have their full effects over a longer timescale. This is true even for countries that see favourable elements in the present situation. The fall in oil prices is taken by Thailand and Malaysia as presenting a window of opportunity to undertake policies that might not have been possible at the previous price, while the recent high price of coffee offers Colombia a temporary opportunity to rearrange its strategy at a time when its external position is not under intense pressure.

Identifying the most important problems facing the countries, where these are not on the external side, is clearly important in setting the effects and potential contribution of the external sector into context, and later in considering how useful general policy discussions that start from it can be. The primary focus of the general study, however, is on the effect of the changed external circumstances and how to respond to this, and how far the countries have a real choice of external strategies, given their own structural or political constraints and the international assumptions.

Malaysia's commitment to shifting a high proportion of income, capital and jobs to the Malay part of the population, without worsening the position of other groups, and while reducing the proportion of the population living in poverty, the New Economic Policy (NEP), made attainment of rapid growth, with a target of 8% a year, essential in the 20-year period from 1970 to 1990, but not the sole measure of success. Ariff and Semudram argue that the employment and ownership targets, and the regulations aiming to achieve them, restricted growth. The NEP was introduced following severe communal rioting in 1969, at a time of high unemployment. It gave public spending and government intervention an explicitly redistributive role, as well as that of promoting growth. Employment as a target influenced the choice of the composition of industry, specifically the promotion of labour-intensive exports in the electronics sector. By 1985, the ownership targets were already running behind, and not reaching the poorest. Even in 1975–80, growth had not reached 8%, although it remained high until 1984. Malaysia as an oil producer and exporter did not suffer as severely as many countries in the early 1980s, and it has not been unable to borrow. But the cost of servicing its debt has risen sufficiently to alarm the government, and its exports have grown unusually slowly and its imports rapidly. The economy stopped growing in 1985, and remained depressed in 1986. Since then the government has chosen to concentrate on growth, deferring the NEP targets. The country study adopts this change to growth as the most important immediate target (while maintaining the objects of the NEP as long-term goals), but even with reforms it can forecast only 3–4% growth, well below the original target of 8.5%, or even the 1986 plan target of 5%. It thus considers that the change in Malaysia's situation has been so serious that it cannot be restored to the previous path.

Zimbabwe is another country where redistributive targets have been important and are expected to remain so. Conflict among economic groups is a major constraint. One of the government's objectives, although not an overriding one, is to limit the share of one of these: foreign companies. In the long run, one policy is to restructure the economy into a socialist economy. Robinson argues that, while not an immediate objective, this must be a constraint on the range and type of policies to be considered. Arguments for reducing government intervention in order to improve growth prospects would not be as acceptable as they are in Malaysia. He includes consumption and employment as additional target variables together with GDP, and looks for a strategy that redistributes income and employment while reducing external dependence.

Zimbabwe suffered stagnation in output in the second half of the 1970s, after growth of 6% in the first half, then had two years of exceptional growth in 1980 and 1981, and little growth on average since then, with only one good year (1985). The official target of 5% is thus for an improvement on past performance. Robinson considers this unrealistic, given the expectations outlined in the previous chapter. The alternative strategies developed are, therefore, ways of improving performance on all the criteria suggested, but they still fall well short of the plan's 5%, and are little different from the average for the last five years. The study argues that the deterioration in Zimbabwe's performance is not particularly associated with changes at the world level, although exports have been affected by the changes in terms of trade and there have been outflows of capital. Rather it results from domestic problems and more specific external problems – the political and military situation of southern Africa.

Thailand has suffered a falling growth rate, particularly in the 1980s when it fell to 4–6% (although without the large fluctuations observed in Malaysia and Zimbabwe), from 7% in the 1970s and 8% in the 1960s. Growth in 1985–6 was particularly low. This was associated with a large deterioration in the terms of trade, so that Thailand matches the conventional developing country model more closely than the other countries in this study. It is still mainly a commodity exporter and has, therefore, been badly affected by the fall in prices. The objective of the government is to recover from this low growth, but Chunanuntathum, Tambunlertchai and Wattananukit argue that the problems lie more in the composition and efficiency of production than in the effects of the external situation. They argue that in the next few years it is more important to improve efficiency, including opening up to external markets, but also through domestic measures, than to increase growth. Like Malaysia, Thailand is reluctant, because of the cost and risks, rather than unable, to continue to increase its foreign private borrowing.

Echavarria in the *Colombia* study sees the country's immediate problem as a structural one of altering its dependence on coffee. The economy has grown in the last five years, although the rate fell to about 2% from about 5% during the preceding two decades. Colombia's position as an oil exporter meant that it did not face serious problems from rising import prices in the early 1980s, and the rise in coffee prices in 1986 protected it from the consequences of the fall in the oil price. Although its access to bank finance diminished when other Latin American countries went into crisis, it has been principally affected by the increase in its cost. A cautious policy on demand is considered appropriate. Within this, direct government spending is expected to need to concentrate on alleviating the very unequal income distribution, and specifically on combating the current rural violence. For this reason, other tools have to be found for implementing the external strategy.

Peru, like Zimbabwe, has the objective of altering the nature of its economy, unlike the other countries in this study which, broadly at least, accept the present capitalist structure. Schuldt emphasises that the present government's strategic planning has been in contrast to past policies. In analysing these, he stresses how the governments have responded to different short-term interests within the economic system rather than to a commonly accepted, medium-term set of objectives. The long-term goal is to move away from 'dependency' on the international system, with redistribution of income and decentralisation leading to a reorientation towards domestic markets and the use of domestic savings. The programme for managing the current debt crisis, although seen as the most urgent problem, has to take account of this long-term plan. The 'heterodox' theoretical assumptions behind the current government's strategy suggested that faster growth, redistribution and better external balance need not be seen as in conflict (unlike the assumptions for Malaysia, Thailand and Colombia): growth could be combined with shifts of consumption away from imports through redistribution (the strategy seen as possible only in the long run for Zimbabwe) within the Five Year Plan. The country's political and social instability has meant that taking simple conspicuous actions has also been an objective (for instance, the limit on debt repayments and the nationalisation of private banks). An improvement in performance is particularly urgent for Peru. After growing at 5–6% in the 1960s and early 1970s, it had little growth in the second half of the 1970s, culminating in a fall of over 10% in 1983. After two years of slow recovery, it grew by over 8% in 1986 (the first year of the Garcia government), faster than in its own history (or expectations) or than the rest of Latin

America, but this did not continue into 1987–8. Even after the 1986 recovery, income per capita remained lower than 15 years before; the immediate goal is therefore to restore the 1976 level.

Thus, growth is seen as the most important immediate target for only three of the countries studied, but even for these it is regarded as a means to other objectives, which constrain how it is pursued. Four have important re-distributional goals. Three have a strong emphasis on restructuring their economies, and the changing nature of their vulnerability to external forces is an important element. In these countries, the external sector is seen as an important constraint on development, while for Malaysia and Thailand it is an important part of the development strategy. For all, the performance of the external sector is crucial to the development strategy, but not itself an objective.

PART TWO
COUNTRY STUDIES

Chapters 4–8 are based on papers published as ODI Working Papers:

No. 20: 'Colombia, 1970–85. Management and consequences of two large external shocks', Juan José Echavarria, 1987.

No. 21: 'Trade and financing strategies: a case study of Malaysia', Mohamed Ariff and Muthi Semudram, 1987.

No. 22: 'Trade and financing strategies for Thailand in the 1980s', Supote Chunanuntathum, Somsak Tambunlertchai and Atchana Wattananukit 1987.

No. 23: 'Trade and financing strategies for the new NICs – the Zimbabwe case study', Peter B. Robinson, 1987.

No. 28: 'Trade and financing strategies for the new NICs – the Peru case study', Jürgen Schuldt, 1988.

4

MALAYSIA

MOHAMED ARIFF and MUTHI SEMUDRAM

INTRODUCTION

During the 1970s, the Malaysian economy had the characteristic features of a small open economy exposed to cyclical changes in world economic activity. Given the small domestic market and a comparative advantage only in primary exports, its ability to obtain stable foreign-exchange earnings to finance development is still limited. The economy is very dependent on the fluctuating fortunes of its trading partners, particularly in the OECD countries. In the 1970s the external sector was an important contributing factor to cyclical economic instability. In the 1980s, countercyclical stabilisation policies and export booms and recessions have had a smaller influence on growth rates.

In the market-oriented economy of Malaysia, where the private sector remains dominant, development planning can only indicate the directions in which sectoral developments are expected to proceed. Economic planning has been a hazardous exercise because of the high risk of plans being derailed by external forces. For example, the Fourth Plan (1981–5), an important link in the 20-year Outline Prospective Plan (1971–90), had anticipated soaring oil prices and generally high commodity prices, and envisaged an average real GDP growth rate of 8% p.a. in the first half of the 1980s and 8.5% in the second half. Instead, the growth rate has continued to decelerate; in 1985 it fell to −1%. A major turn-around is not likely to occur until the late 1980s. Commodity prices are also unlikely to pick up significantly in the foreseeable future. The implications for the growth of exports, savings, investments and income are serious. The mid-term review of the Plan, which was released in 1984, scaled down the planned targets in the light of the ongoing recession.

The current Fifth Plan (1986–90) became obsolete before it was launched. Although sober and modest in contrast to the Third and Fourth Plans, its target of 5% average annual growth is clearly over-optimistic. It is noteworthy that development expenditure in the Fifth Plan is 8% lower than in the Fourth.

Recession alone cannot be blamed for the derailment of the Plans. There are also structural problems which the Plans have failed to address. The unwillingness or inability of the industrialised countries to bring about structural adjustments in their economies has created problems for countries like Malaysia, so that they must take a hard look at their economic objectives and strategies. We do not suggest that Malaysia should reverse its outward-looking policy, for such a reversal would not be in its long-term interest, given its factor and resource endowments and the constraints of the domestic market. But there is certainly a need for it to restructure its economy in line with the shifting pattern of comparative advantage and to seek new markets for its products so as to reduce its over-dependence on the markets of the industrial countries.

When the first oil price rise occurred Malaysia was still a net oil importer. The oil shock had deflationary effects on the economy but these were cushioned by the general commodity boom of 1973–4. At the time of the second oil price rise, in 1979–80, it was still experiencing boom conditions largely supported by rising prices for agricultural commodities. In addition, it was by then a net oil exporter. So, in fact, it benefited from the second oil shock. The oil account trade balance steadily increased from M$607m. in 1976 to M$3.4bn in 1980; crude petroleum exports grew by 29.5% and their share in total commodity exports increased to 25%. The surpluses continued to exist despite an oil depletion policy which slowed the rate of domestic extraction during 1979–80.

In the early 1980s, the government pursued countercyclical domestic policies to protect incomes and employment levels from the unstable external conditions. These policies were based in part on a view that the recession would be short-lived as in the past. Expectations were that the turn-around would begin by about mid-1982. But the recession continued and, with declining revenues and the increased cost of borrowing, constraints on the government's financial position reduced its capacity to continue the counter-cyclical policies.

The expected turn-around in the economic growth of the industrialised countries, particularly the United States, came around mid-1983.World trade began to expand, led by exports to the US, which in Malaysia's case increased by 22.7% between 1983 and 1984. From 1985, it became clear that US policies were proving detrimental to domestic industries and calls were made for increasing protectionism. Outright protection was rejected in favour of lowering the value of the US dollar.

Malaysia's budgetary problems continue to persist although strong meas-ures were taken to reduce public expenditures. In 1986, for the first time in the country's history, it experienced a deficit on the operating account (M$1.3bn) resulting in an overall budget deficit of M$8.8bn. Financing a deficit of this magnitude will impose pressures on liquidity and interest rates if further domestic borrowing is attempted. Monetary management will be tested to the full when a reduction is made in foreign borrowing, and this will reduce the balance-of-payments surplus given the ever-increasing services deficit.

Economic restructuring has become necessary to promote growth. The private sector has been given the main role in reactivating the economy. Various incentives have been provided to stimulate private investment, but to date no significant changes have occurred.

The New Economic Policy (NEP) objectives will not be realised by 1990, and a more realistic framework is called for. There are some signs of a decrease in inter-ethnic economic disparities which is the major objective of the NEP. But there is also disturbing evidence that intra-ethnic income inequalities are growing and need to be arrested. The NEP's stringent requirements have resulted in huge economic rents accruing to the Bumiputera elite; the 20-year timescale is too short and the benefits of the NEP are not being evenly distributed.

EXTERNAL SECTOR

Structure of exports

The vulnerability of the economy to external influences is exacerbated by high export concentration. The new commodities whose shares have increased, e.g., palm oil, saw logs and petroleum, are just as prone to price fluctuations as the traditional items like rubber and tin. There was a real export growth of 16–18% during the three boom periods of the 1970s, giving a surplus except for a brief period between 1973 and 1974 when the real export index flattened against that of imports. Stronger manufactured export bases were also established, notably in electronics and textiles. Manufactured export earnings, particularly from electronics, rose sharply from M$200m. in 1973 to M$2,832m. in 1980. The share of manufactured exports increased from 20% in 1976 to more than 30% in 1980.

In the primary sector, expansion in some sub-sectors has been extremely erratic. Production is sometimes stepped up in the wake of falling prices to neutralise their effect. Producers also tend to go to extremes in their response to rising commodity prices. To make matters worse, there is increasing competition from other countries. Malaysian policies themselves may have been responsible for this phenomenon to some extent. Large-scale acquisition of foreign interests in the plantation sector, for example, may have encouraged foreigners to step up their investment activities elsewhere. The country may also be losing its competitive edge in some traditional export items, owing to rising production costs and falling productivity. Lack or inadequacies of R & D activities may also contribute to the erosion of its comparative advantage in some areas.

In the manufacturing sector bottlenecks tend to thwart expansion. Industries catering for the domestic market are already experiencing market saturation, while export-oriented industries are beset by the current global slowdown and protectionist barriers. The ambitious drive towards heavy industrialisation, launched in the early 1980s, has aggravated the situation not only by diverting scarce resources away from other industries but also by imposing additional constraints and costs on the economy.

General trends in exports can be seen in Table 4.1. Most major commodities have lost share. Singapore remained the largest outlet for rubber, but the volume diminished. There was an upsurge in exports of petroleum and petroleum products in 1975–80, mainly destined for Japan and Singapore, but in 1983 they fell slightly. Tin has performed particularly badly; most is exported unprocessed to the Netherlands and Japan with increasing quantities now going to the USSR. In recent years, palm oil exports have shifted towards developing countries such as Pakistan and India. Exports of copper are small. Electrical machinery explains the rise in the share of manufactures.

Structure of imports

The history of imports during the period 1970–84 (see Table 4.2) can be broken down into four phases, as follows:

1. 1970–5 import substitution;
2. 1976–80 boom conditions and general rise in imports;
3. 1980–4 continued import rise;
4. 1984–6 a general decline.

During 1970–5, imports of capital goods rose rapidly to meet the high investment demand generated particularly by the public sector through implementation of the NEP. Intermediate goods also grew marginally faster than GNP, while consumer goods imports lagged behind. During the boom period of 1976–80, all three categories grew significantly and well ahead of GNP. This continued in the 1980s, in the face of international recession, until 1985, when total imports declined by 7.3%, followed by a further decline of 8% in 1986.

Consumer durables have a very high income elasticity. Intermediate goods also have an elasticity higher than 1, due to their share in manufactured exports. During 1984–5, food and consumer durable imports declined by 2.3% and 6.1% respectively, and are still declining. There were significant drops in imports of capital goods in 1985 (11%) and in 1986, largely reflecting cutbacks in government and private investment.

Manufactured goods have consistently accounted for around 16% of total imports over the period 1975–83, with machinery and transport equipment making up the largest share. Japan, the United States, Singapore and West Germany continued to be the major suppliers, in that order. Chemical imports averaged about 8.3% of the total during 1975–83, mainly from the same four suppliers. Imports of food and live animals, mainly from Thailand and Australia, have shown a gradual decline.

Trade balance

This mix of agricultural, energy and manufactured goods ensured the Malaysian economy a high and rising trade share in the 1970s. In contrast, the 1980s, in the face of recessionary pressures, experienced a fall in export volume, while imports continued unabated; import volumes rose a third faster than exports. The import/export ratio increased from 0.9 to 1.16 in 1982, largely because of capital imports. The countercyclical policies pursued stimulated domestic absorption, and a substantial part of the growth generated was translated into imports which external revenues could not sustain.

The current account surpluses, particularly in the late 1970s, had been the result of the large trade surpluses arising from high commodity prices. In the 1980s, these surpluses were trimmed by high import volume, the significant drop in commodity prices and also sizeable increases in services payments. The current account went into deficit for the first time in 1980 and continued in 1981–3, financed by extensive foreign borrowing. Despite the drop in the oil price in 1986, Malaysia was in trade surplus from 1983 onwards, but the deficit on the services account increased markedly (see Table 4.4).

Investment income and services

Investment income is one of the largest components of the invisibles deficit, more than 50% in 1985. Net payments increased from M$1.8bn in 1980 to about M$5.6bn in 1985. Before 1980, these payments were mainly retained profits and dividends on foreign investments, but after that date the largest component was the interest payments on the public sector's external borrowings.

The increase in profit remittances has been offset to some extent by the restructuring of a large number of companies, which led to foreign ownership of corporate equity being reduced from about 60% in 1970 to about 40% in the early 1980s. Nevertheless, repatriation of profits has risen, mainly because of foreign investment in manufacturing and petroleum.

Freight is the second largest source of payments abroad, reflecting the inadequate progress made by Malaysian shipping and air companies. Only 15% of exports are transported in Malaysian vessels, less than 4% of the trade with Japan and nil in that with the United States and West Asia. The Malaysian share is significant only to Europe, at 18%. It has been the practice for importers of Malaysian goods to nominate their own shipping vessels. To change this would require massive investments in the shipping industry.

Investment flows

Foreign investment in Malaysia consists of both direct and portfolio components. External linkages established by direct investment are much stronger and more lasting. Direct foreign investment may be further categorised into:

1. joint ventures;
2. wholly foreign-owned projects;
3. turnkey operations;
4. licensing and franchising operations; and
5. management contracts.

Joint ventures account for the bulk of the investment, but licensing and franchising arrangements and management contracts are growing in importance.

Singapore, Japan and the United Kingdom are the most important sources of foreign investment, jointly accounting for about 66% of gross foreign capital investment and more than 59% of foreign fixed assets in 1983. There have been shifts in the sectoral allocation in favour of export-oriented industries in recent years, in line with the shift in industrial policy towards exports.

Table 4.3 provides some comparative statistics by industry. These show that Japanese investment has centred on textiles and the electrical and electronics industries, the two most important export-oriented and also most labour-intensive manufacturing activities in Malaysia. Investments from Singapore and Britain, on the other hand, have gone mainly into import-substitution activities. US investment also seems to focus on activities catering for the domestic market, with the notable exception of investment in the electrical and electronics industries in the Free Trade Zones which are completely export-oriented. One should not, however, jump to the conclusion that Japanese investment has a stronger export orientation than American. Not all investment in apparently export-oriented activities (e.g. textiles) can be regarded as 'outward looking', since a substantial proportion of their output is also marketed locally. In fact,there is some evidence to the contrary: it appears that Japanese affiliates in Malaysia sell the bulk of their output in the local market, while US affiliates export the bulk of their output. Moreover, Japanese firms export much less to Japan than the American firms do to the US.

Some general observations are worth making. First, although the share of private flows in total foreign resource flows has been increasing, the proportion of direct investment in total private capital flows has declined because of the rise in borrowing. Second, the share of direct foreign investment in gross domestic investment also appears to be declining from 4.5% in 1972–6 to 2.5% in 1977–81. Third, the number of technology agreements with foreign companies has increased from 16 in 1970 to 49 in 1976 and 131 in 1983. In this context, it is of interest that technical assistance and know-how agreements accounted for over half of such agreements during the period 1970–83, most of them with Japan, the UK and the US. All these are indicative of the shift away from the traditional foreign investment package towards 'new' forms involving greater unpackaging of foreign capital and technology.

Malaysia has actively sought foreign investment for a number of reasons and through a variety of incentive schemes. Modernisation of the economy, diversification of the production structure, employment creation, technology transfers, industrial dispersion and export orientation of the manufacturing sector have been some of the important policy objectives. The contribution of foreign investment in these areas has been somewhat limited, presumably because of a built-in bias in favour of large-scale, capital-intensive projects.

Although it calls for reduced (to 30% in 1990) foreign equity participation, the NEP strategy requires substantial injections of foreign capital and technical and managerial know-how to smooth the restructuring of society through the rapid expansion of national resources rather than through disruptive redistribution of the existing national 'cake'. The contradiction is partly resolved by resorting to new forms of foreign investment.

Foreign borrowing

To understand the role of external debt in the Malaysian economy, one needs to take a systematic look at its structure and profile. According to the Treasury records, the earliest foreign loan secured by the federal government was US$4.5m. from the World Bank in 1965 to finance the first phase of the Muda Irrigation Scheme in Kedah and Perlis. Prior to that, Malaysia had relied largely on direct aid, mainly from Britain. By the end of 1985, the World Bank had given Malaysia 44 loans totalling US$1.26bn, going to agriculture (US$700m.), education (US$230m.), transport and communications (US$206m.), industry (US$61m.), public utilities (US$39m.), and health (US$22m.). Indeed, these projects provide outstanding examples of how properly managed foreign loans can benefit the recipient country.

The Asian Development Bank (ADB) has been the second major multilateral source of foreign loans: 49 loans totalling US$1.174bn were given during the period 1968–85 for projects in agriculture (US$376m.), transportation (US$225m.), energy (US$217m.) and water supply (US$90m.). Bilateral loans have also contributed significantly to the financing of development programmes. Japan tops the list with loans amounting to M$3.11bn during 1968–85. Other lending countries are the United States (M$408m.), France (M$356m.), Saudi Arabia (M$256m.), West Germany (M$187m.), Kuwait (M$139m.), Sweden (M$57m.), Canada (M$31m.), Australia (M$4.2m.), Austria (M$2.1m.) and Holland (M$1.4m.). The bulk of Japanese loans (most of them under yen credit agreements) have been used to finance transportation, electricity, oil and gas, ports and roads, broadcasting and telecommunications. These official loans had concessional interest rates, varying from 5.5% to 11.6% on World Bank loans and from 3.25% to 5.75% on Japanese yen loans.

The point has now been reached at which it has become increasingly difficult for Malaysia to obtain loans at concessional rates. The country is no longer regarded as poor. Its needs have also changed considerably. Increased emphasis is now placed on industrial projects rather than on basic sectoral developments, and multilateral institutions do not provide loans for such purposes. The consequence has been a dramatic increase in commercial borrowing, associated with greater government involvement in the economy under the NEP through off-budget agencies (OBAs), some of whose market loans have government guarantees. Direct government commercial borrowing increased sharply from M$1.35bn in 1975 to M$15.46bn in 1985, and loans obtained with government guarantees increased from M$588m. in 1975 to M$9.1bn in 1985 (see Table 4.6). The ratio of commercial loans to total external debt increased from 50% in 1975–9 to 65% in 1980–5. About 75% are denominated in US dollars; the other currencies include the yen, pound sterling and Deutschmark.

Interest payments on government loans amounted to M$4.3bn in 1984; this figure increased to M$4.7bn in 1985, with total debt servicing standing at M$5.5bn in 1984 (about 22.5% of export earnings). For long-term debts, however, the debt-service ratio was only 12.3% in 1984 and 14% in 1985, a fairly small burden in comparison with that of many other developing countries. With export earnings falling and the ringgit depreciating against the major currencies, the ratio exceeded 20% by the end of 1986. Government external borrowings in 1984 were just over half the US$2.619bn borrowed in 1982. External debt increased by 7% in 1985 compared to 31% in 1983 and 18.2% in 1984. However, external debts incurred by off-budget agencies and guaranteed by the government continued to rise sharply. Total debt (both public and private) was M$40.2bn at the end of 1985 (55.6% of GNP, as against 50.6% in 1984).

The rising level of debt servicing in the face of weak export earnings has been a major concern in recent years. It is mainly this concern which led the government to seek refinancing in 1984 and 1985, to take advantage of more favourable terms as well as to avoid the potential 'bunching' of loans in the late 1980s: US$2.6bn syndicated loans were refinanced resulting in savings of

M$217m. The government's net external borrowings in 1986 have been estimated at M$2.8bn, of which only M$1.3bn constituted new loans.

Other debt-management measures include diversifying the currencies, instruments, markets and sources of external loans. In November 1984, a US$600m. Floating Rate Note was secured, most of it to refinance existing US dollar-denominated loans with shorter maturities and higher margins. In March 1985, another US$600m. was obtained, pegged at a rate never before offered to any developing country and to be repaid in 15 years – the longest maturity period ever secured by a developing country from private financial institutions.

The FRN market is no longer offering the terms of 1984 and 1985, partly because Malaysia's credit rating has become somewhat tarnished. Moreover, it is not keen on the long-dated issues which Malaysia is seeking. In 1986, therefore, Malaysia turned to the more costly syndicated loans markets. Over-subscription of its first issue may mean that it is still considered a low-risk country.

TRADE AND INDUSTRY POLICY

The New Economic Policy

The NEP was adopted after the communal conflicts of 1970. It is a 20-year, poverty-eradication programme, aimed at changing the pattern of employment, ownership and control in the economy to reflect the country's racial composition. Legislation and guidelines on ownership and employment have been introduced and a number of public enterprises set up to hold in trust the required Bumiputera (indigenous Malay) share of the equity.

Total investment in the Amanah Saham Nasional (ASN) – a unit trust scheme set up to increase the Bumiputera stake in the economy – had reached M$2.28bn by the end of June 1985, while about M$753.8m. had been redeemed. The 1.73 million ASN investors represent only 35% of eligible Bumiputeras, and nearly 74% of them have a stake of 500 units or less each, far below the 50,000 units targeted. The implication is that the benefits of the NEP are not trickling down fast or far enough. Bumiputera corporate ownership measured in terms of paid-up capital was estimated to be more than M$14bn as at the end of 1985, which falls short of the 2.1% target under the mid-term review of the Fourth Plan.

While the NEP's objectives are laudable, it has imposed constraints on business activities, especially with respect to employment and ownership, which have tended to inhibit some sectors. The implications of the NEP were particularly adverse for foreign investors. The foreign share of the country's corporate wealth has to be reduced from more than 60% to 30%. Foreign investors have found it difficult to comply with the NEP guidelines, especially with regard to Bumiputera equity involvement in their business ventures. Shortage of skilled manpower and the low propensity to save in the Bumiputera community have tended to thwart attempts to achieve the NEP goals. It is now evident that these will not be achieved by 1990 and the NEP will almost certainly continue beyond that date under a new label. New targets and strategies for implementation in the 1990s are now being studied.

There are clear signs that the government wants to be pragmatic about the NEP. It has relaxed the rules governing foreign equity. Any company set up with foreign capital between October 1986 and December 1990 will be permanently exempted from the need to restructure its equity along NEP lines, provided it exports or sells at least 50% of its output to FTZ firms or licensed manufacturing warehouses, and it employs at least 350 full-time Malaysian workers in proportions corresponding to the racial composition of the country. In addition, a company with a paid-up capital of US$2m. will qualify to employ at least five expatriates. The new concessions are also extended to existing companies which are wholly or partly foreign-owned if they expand their operations. The NEP stipulations with regard to employment still remain in force, however.

Import substitution

Malaysia began to adjust its industrialisation policy from import substitution towards export orientation in the early 1970s. Several factors were responsible. First and most important was the failure of the earlier policies to generate growth of manufacturing output and employment. Second was the spectacular success of export-led industrialisation in the Asian NICs. Third, there was a change in the intellectual climate towards greater emphasis on exports and a growing belief in an association of exports with efficiency and import substitution with inefficiency. It would be inappropriate to characterise the Malaysian experience as 'export-led' industrialisation. The growth rates of manufactured exports, although impressive, pale in comparison with the spectacular track record of the Asian NICs.

However, export orientation did not mean an abandonment of import substitution. Both have been pursued in parallel, although with a stronger emphasis on the former, especially for new investments. Investment incentives were restructured to offer a variety of export incentives, including export allowances and accelerated depreciation; tax holidays, investment tax credits and other fiscal incentives were aimed increasingly at export-oriented industries. Pre-shipment and post-shipment export credit refinancing facilities at concessionary rates of interest were also introduced. The establishment of Free Trade Zones (FTZs), discussed in the next section, were another positive measure.

Notwithstanding the successful initiation of export-oriented industrialisation, there has been growing scepticism about the future prospects of manufactured exports, which questions both the desirability and feasibility of such an industrialisation strategy. Admittedly, there is no empirical or theoretical basis which suggests that export-oriented industrialisation is more conducive to economic growth than import substitution. However, there are suggestions in the current literature which point to the superior performance of the outward-looking strategy (Krueger, 1978: 283–96).

Nevertheless, it is possible to overdo export promotion; deviations towards 'excessive' export promotion are as undesirable as those in the opposite direction. One aspect which has been much criticised is the FTZs. While these criticisms are mainly directed at non-economic issues such as labour conditions and life-styles, an important economic consideration is whether the substantial public investment in FTZs can be justified in conventional cost-benefit terms. However, it may be argued that such excesses are less likely in an outward-looking regime because the costs are more visible, and also that the dynamic gains of export promotion tend to exceed the static losses from misallocation of resources.

The impact of export-oriented industrialisation on employment, wages and income distribution is hard to assess. Although theory tells us that trade benefits the abundant factor (Stolper–Samuelson theorem), it does not necessarily follow that export-oriented industrialisation in the labour-surplus Malaysian economy will bring about a better income distribution than import substitution does. In practice, the relationship is far more complex. Much depends on such factors as the product-mix, technology and intersectoral linkages. Generous incentives may tend to reduce the share of income accruing to both government and labour, while fiscal incentives may encourage excessive capital intensity. There is some evidence to support this: the incentives are often beyond the reach of the labour-intensive, small-scale firms. It is, however, conceivable that, under dynamic conditions, demand for both capital and labour will increase.

There is some evidence showing favourable effects on employment. Employment coefficients based on input–output tables show that exports from the typical FTZ sector are more labour-intensive than manufactured exports as a whole (Van Dijck and Verbruggen, 1983). The coefficients are also higher for total manufactured exports than for total manufactured production.

Another issue is that of linkages and externalities. There is frequent criticism that export manufacturing activities have very few linkages with the rest of the economy. This is true for FTZs, but it does not apply to all export-oriented industries. There is evidence to suggest that production- and employment-spread effects are significant for Malaysian export-oriented activities, especially for the natural resource-based industries (ibid.). However, high linkages *per se* are not necessarily desirable. While high externalities in the form of technology and skill diffusion are important, high linkages in the input–output sense may be indicative of a more closed, inward-looking economy.

Free Trade Zones

FTZs have duty-free access to imported inputs and machinery, while at the same time enjoying a wide range of investment and export incentives. The fragmented statistical evidence suggests that nearly 75% of the FTZs in Malaysia are foreign-owned, but wholly foreign-owned firms account for more than 90% of their total direct employment.

The overall contribution of the FTZs to labour absorption appears to be limited. Employment in the 11 FTZs amount to less than 100,000 persons, or only about 11% of the manufacturing workforce or 1.6% of the total labour force.

There is heavy concentration on certain industries. Electronics and textiles account for more than 70% of FTZ employment and 95% of FTZ exports. Over 80% of the country's textiles exports come from the FTZs (Ariff and Hill, 1985).

Wages and working conditions in FTZs have attracted much attention as the zones are an important focus of the export drive. However, no major differences are apparent in a comparison of wage levels in the zones with those in the rest of the manufacturing sector. Trade unions are virtually excluded and there is some evidence to suggest that labour regulations concerning minimum wages and working hours are violated to some extent (Datta-Chaudhuri, 1982). However, comparison of wages and conditions in the FTZs and elsewhere must be interpreted with great caution. Not all the variables in the comparison are standardised. Moreover, female workers account for 90% of total unskilled employees. Both these factors tend to depress wage levels relative to other activities. Although labour regulations are often violated, there is no evidence to suggest that this occurs on a wider scale in FTZs than elsewhere in the economy. The fundamental question is whether labour would have been better off in the absence of export manufacturing activities. There is no evidence to suggest that this is so.

Net foreign-exchange earnings relative to total exports are low because about 97% of FTZ raw material inputs and about 80% of their capital goods are imported. Linkages in the sense of the wider benefits from local procurement, technology, skill dissemination and other spill-over effects appear to be minimal, since FTZ activities consist primarily of labour-intensive assembly operations. Other externalities, such as those resulting from increased knowledge of and contact with international markets and technologies, are likely to be more beneficial.

FTZs have probably made a positive net contribution to the Malaysian economy. For an economy where there is a glut of labour, employment considerations tend to outweigh all others in evaluating their role.

Structure of protection

There is no doubt that industrialisation was facilitated to a considerable extent by the protective system, although the protective measures were rather mild in nominal terms (NPRs) by modern standards. Average effective rates (EPRs), on the other hand, have been significantly high. The system has undergone substantial changes in both nominal and effective terms.

There was a general upward trend in NPRs in the 1970s, the average NPR for all sectors increasing from 16% in 1970 to 22% in 1978. However, the pattern of nominal protection did not change significantly. The proportion of industries receiving NPRs of less than 40% declined marginally, from 92% in 1970 to 88% in 1978 (Hock, 1984). In general, effective protection exceeded nominal protection. The average EPR increased from 25% in 1965 to 39% in 1978. However, the peak, at 44%, was in 1970, suggesting that average effective protection declined during the 1970s.

Nevertheless, there have been major changes in its structure. In 1965, 39% of manufacturing industries had negative EPRs, while only 8% had EPRs of more than 100%. The proportion with negative EPRs was reduced to 31% in 1970 and 14% in 1978, while those with EPRs exceeding 100% increased to 16% in 1970 but subsequently declined to 10% in 1978. Moreover, both NPRs and EPRs have exhibited wide dispersions, as shown by the coefficients of variation. In the case of NPRs, the latter show no obvious trend. By contrast, the EPRs show a clear downward trend in dispersion, with the coefficient falling from 102 in 1963 to 60 in 1973, with a marginal increase in 1978.

Marked changes in EPRs for the major product categories are also apparent. Effective protection for consumer durables increased sharply from 5% in 1965 to 173% in 1978, with non-durable consumer goods ranked second. Intermediate products with a lower level of fabrication have obtained much less protection than those with a higher level. Effective protection for beverages and tobacco, despite the high average NPR of 147 in 1978, has been eroded by high tariffs on inputs.

The system has tended to be biased in favour of import replacements and against export activities. This is largely attributable to the *ad hoc*, case-by-case approach which has characterised Malaysian tariff administration. These biases have caused great distortion in the manufacturing sector. On the whole, there appears to be a bias in favour of consumer goods industries at the expense of producer goods industries. Several export activities suffer from negative protection. Even for those industries with positive and sizeable

EPRs, the anti-export bias tends to be strong since the value-added of export sales is often less than that of domestic sales. The implicit penalty on manufactured exports has been aggravated by exchange-rate over-valuation.

The incompatibility of the protection structure with the strategy of export-oriented industrialisation is readily clear. The implicit penalty on manufactured exports has been mitigated to some extent by countervailing subsidies in the form of various export incentives, such as export allowances and export credit facilities at concessionary rates of interest. But these have been inadequate. Moreover, countervailing subsidies are undesirable as a policy instrument.

Exchange-rate policy

Since September 1975, the ringgit has been tied to an unspecified basket of currencies. Unofficially it has close ties with the Singapore dollar because of the historical links. Up to the end of 1984, a strong link with the US and Singapore dollars had been the norm. The authorities then adopted a more flexible policy in response to sluggish economic activity and an overvalued (by 20% by the end of 1984) exchange rate (Institute of Strategic Studies, 1985).

There was an appreciating real effective rate during the period 1975–84 as a result of the export boom. A large proportion of export earnings was spent on non-tradeable goods (construction, fuelled by the rapid expansion in development expenditure, services, etc.) whose relative prices rose, exerting pressure on wages.

ROLE OF GOVERNMENT AND AGGREGATE DEMAND

Expansion, 1979–84

The role of fiscal policy needs to be evaluated in the context of the impact of the external sector on the government budget. Investment in fixed capital is needed to transform a rural agrarian economy into an industrial one. Investment (private and public) was therefore accorded high ranking in all Malaysia's development plans, and outpaced total demand and growth in GDP in every period. The nature of public demand changed significantly from the early 1970s onwards. The NEP introduced specific social and political dimensions to public spending. At the beginning of the 1980s, countercyclical expansionary domestic policies were employed to stabilise the economy against external influences.

The government's commitment to a programme of accelerated development largely stemmed from the commodity boom of the late 1970s, and the substantial growth of oil exports after 1977. During the period 1979–83, the federal budget remained highly expansionary; total federal government expenditure rose by 129% from M$11.7bn in 1978 to M$26.8bn in 1981. This was a major factor boosting the economy in the initial phase of the current recession (see Table 4.5) but the results tended to be destabilising. Revenues remained marginally higher than operating expenditures, and both increased in line with GNP, but development expenditures rose to 14% of GNP in 1980 and reached a maximum of 20.5% in 1981; they then declined.

Stimulating total demand at a rate which could not be financed by higher levels of savings meant a widening of the resource gap. Invariably, other sources of financing have been needed, resulting in higher domestic and external debt. The financial repercussions of the countercyclical measures were quickly apparent and the fiscal brakes were applied towards the end of 1982. As a result, the public deficit was reduced from 24% in 1982 to 12% in 1985, public consumption, which averaged 16% growth during 1979–82, fell to roughly 3% in 1982–5, while investment growth sank from 33% to a mere 3%.

The new fiscal strategy was effectively laid out in the 1984 budget in which the government attempted to reduce the budget deficit as a proportion of GNP from 19% in 1982 to about 6% by 1985. Sharp cutbacks in development expenditure brought it down to 7.9% in 1985, but recessionary conditions and declining tax buoyancy meant an upward surge in 1986.

In value terms, the overall deficit declined from M$11.3bn in 1981 to M$7.5bn in 1985, but rose to M$12.5bn in 1986. Financing of this deficit called for foreign borrowing, which averaged 5% of GNP during 1981-5. The period of high external deficit corresponded to a large savings–investment gap. In 1978, savings exceeded investment by 4.7% of GNP; from 1980, however, there was a deficit, amounting to 13.4% of GNP in 1983.

Fiscal restraint (1985–6)

Malaysia's economic growth rate, averaging 7.3% during 1980–4, had been the envy of many Third World countries. The crunch came in 1985 when the economy rapidly decelerated to register a fall of 1% in real GDP. The balance of payments had shown signs of strain even earlier. For a country which had become used to substantial trade and overall payments surpluses and rapid economic growth, the slowdown was difficult to tolerate.

In the past, policy-makers had responded to downturns by adopting countercyclical monetary and fiscal measures with some degree of success. This time round, however, there was a major policy departure; there was considerable reluctance on the part of the government to resort to deficit measures, because it did not have the resources to spend its way out of the recession. Countercyclical policy will work effectively if reserves built up in boom years are run down in lean years. This obviously has not been the case in Malaysia. Malaysian planners have shown a strong tendency to get carried away in good times, as evidenced by many ambitious programmes in the early 1980s. The heavy industrialisation programme, on which more will be said later, is a classic example of the draining away of scarce resources. The financing of prestigious projects like the Penang Bridge, the activities of Non-Financial Public Enterprises (NFPEs) created under the NEP and the outflow of foreign exchange to finance the acquisition of foreign equity interests in plantations are cases in point.

The upshot of all these has been that the government had no means to counteract the current recession. Expansionary fiscal policies were ruled out, as they would have meant increased external borrowing. Expansionary monetary policies were postponed because of fear of unleashing inflationary forces. Instead, the government resorted to a belt-tightening exercise. There was a sense of withdrawal and retreat in its responses. Development targets were adjusted to changing circumstances without new targets being sought. The public sector was assigned a low profile and the task of pulling the economy out of the recession was left to the private sector. No private sector response was forthcoming, however, since the environment was not congenial. Economic recession, financial scandals and political uncertainties hardly constitute a climate in which the private sector can strive or thrive. Budgetary policy was under another constraint, namely political expediency; with a strong possibility of snap elections, it was not able to address the recession squarely.

Once the general elections were out of the way, significant fiscal changes were expected in the 1987 budget, but again there were constraints. The private sector was in such poor shape that it could not withstand tough fiscal measures; the budget therefore contained no major tax increases, and adjustments were made mostly on the expenditure side. The 1987 budget turned out to be yet another austerity budget. Government revenue was estimated to have fallen in 1986 by M$2bn. Even with operating expenditure slashed by M$1.4bn there was an estimated budget deficit of M$1.3bn. Total government expenditure for 1987 was estimated as M$27.4bn, 11% less than for the previous year. Operating expenditure was expected to be trimmed down by a further 6% to M$20.7bn and development expenditure by 25% to M$6.6bn. Notwithstanding these cutbacks, the deficit was expected to double to M$2.7bn. It can be argued that this austerity drive is a good thing, given the severe resource constraints. But it cannot be denied that it has tended to have a deflationary effect.

The Central Bank's policy of keeping interest rates low was in conflict with its interventions in the foreign-exchange market to prevent the depreciation of the ringgit. It appears that there has been too much government interference and that the Central Bank has not been free to follow what it considered to be the best policy. It is this lack of autonomy which seems to have led to much of the confusion characterising Malaysia's monetary policy in recent times.

The country has been denied the reflationary measures that could have provided the tonic which it badly needs. The authorities seem to be worried about the impetus such policies might give to imports and the consequent strain on the balance of payments. They also appear apprehensive of the possible inflationary consequences. These risks are real but they seem worth taking to counter the recessionary spell. A current account deficit could be accommodated without much difficulty: Malaysia retains a fairly good credit rating. Consumer price indices have remained so flat that a mild increase might have a stimulating effect on the economy.

The government has acted out of a strong desire to restrain public expenditures, particularly those of the NFPEs whose capital spending served to exacerbate the difficult budgetary situation. Since 1984, the NFPEs have come under the scrutiny of the Treasury and have suffered drastic cuts in their expenditures, while some of them are being privatised.

The effect of the public sector on investment

Government participation in the economy has increased rapidly. Public sector expenditure, for instance, increased from 28% of GNP in 1975 to the peak of about 36% in 1982. It fell slightly, however, to 33% in 1984.

Gross investment contributed roughly about one-third of the GDP growth experienced over the decade 1975–85. Between 1975 and 1980, for example, it averaged 12% p.a. growth and contributed about 3% of the 9% of GDP growth. In the second half of the decade this figure was reduced to roughly 2% out of 6% growth overall.

With the rapid changes in public sector spending, private investment became more volatile than consumption and for the first time in recent years it fell in 1981–2. From an average increase of 8% during 1983–4, it slumped by about 20% in 1985, and this declining trend continued in 1986. Statistical analysis of the determinants of private investment suggest that the direct impact of an increase in the share of the government has had a moderate effect. According to estimates, private investment increased by 0.3% for every 1% increase in government investment. The linkage is reduced by direct leakages in the form of capital and intermediate imports.

Revenue effort

For many years, public savings have been buttressed by tax revenues from petroleum and this has obscured the underlying deterioration in the balance between current revenues and expenditures. The depletion of petroleum and timber resources by 1990 suggests that measures must be taken to augment revenues.

By Asian standards, and even those of the industrialised countries, the revenue effort in Malaysia is respectable (see Table 4.7). Nevertheless, tax revenue is still insufficient to meet current and future requirements. Furthermore, revenue buoyancies have diminished in recent years with the greatest decline occurring in indirect taxes. Several factors are responsible for this trend: (a) the fall in export prices; (b) changes in the structure of import duties and the extension of liberal exemptions, although there was an increase in duties on luxuries in 1984; (c) the reduction in the number of excise taxes in 1982; and (d) liberal exemptions for corporations, leading to reductions in the number of firms subject to corporation tax.

POLICY OPTIONS

Short- and medium-term economic prospects are by no means promising. The current difficulties cannot legitimately be attributed entirely to depressed external demand, since there are also structural problems on the supply side which have contributed to the production glut. Our projection of a positive growth in real GDP is based on a number of premises. First, demand for primary commodities may respond positively to the fall in their prices. Second, the fall in the price of oil will stimulate growth in the industrialised and newly industrialising countries, resulting in increased demand for raw materials. Third, expansion in other sectors of the economy may be able to more than compensate for the contraction in the commodity sector. Fourth, government policy to stimulate output and employment may help to alleviate the problem. Finally, there are clear indications that the Consumer Price Index will remain remarkably stable.

Unemployment was a serious problem in 1986–7, and was expected to remain so. It is concentrated in certain categories of workers, including about 60,000 Malaysians who were made unemployed in Singapore and workers affected by retrenchment in the electronics and tin industries. About 20,000 tin mine workers have become jobless as more than 100 mines went out of production in 1986. An additional 200,000 school leavers joined the labour force early in 1987.

Export prospects

The situation is likely to improve gradually from 1987 onwards. Oil prices may rise to a slightly more comfortable level and manufactured exports, notably electronics, textiles and wood products, are likely to rise, albeit slowly, with increased demand in developed countries. Ringgit depreciation is likely to make Malaysian manufactured exports competitive in traditional markets. Commodity prices are, however, likely to remain depressed for some time and no major turn-around is expected in the immediate future. However, much depends on the economic performance of the US, Japan and the European Community.

It is extremely difficult to forecast movements in individual primary commodities, as there are far too many elusive determinants. Prospects for tin exports remain bleak because of the uncertainties following the suspension of operations by the International Tin Council (ITC). Rubber prices have been in the doldrums since early 1984 with prices plunging to the lowest level for ten years. However, the medium-term outlook for natural rubber is somewhat better than that for tin. The ratio of buffer to commercial stocks is much smaller in the case of rubber. Palm oil, Malaysia's 'golden crop', is undergoing a depressed spell. Cocoa prices have been tumbling. Pepper seems to be the only exception to the all-round decline in recent times.

The medium-term prospects for manufactured exports are not bad. With lower interest rates and lower oil prices, consumer demand in industrialised countries is picking up. There was a rebound in the semiconductor and textile industries after 1986. Malaysia was already the world's third largest producer and exporter of semiconductor components. Electronics exports estimated at M$5bn in 1985 account for 38% of the country's total manufactured exports.

Trade and industry policy

The Industrial Master Plan (IMP), released in February 1986, places high expectations on the manufacturing sector. It envisages a 6.4% annual GDP growth with total investment growing at the rate of 5.7% p.a. The target growth rate of the manufacturing sector is 8.8%. The IMP expects that 705,400 new jobs will be created, bringing the total labour force in manufacturing to 1.5 million by 1995.

The Plan singles out several industries. It aims to make the rubber products industry one of the leading sectors in the expansion of the resource-based industries, by raising local consumption from 65,000 to 308,000 tons by 1995, and to develop the industry into an export-oriented one. The tyre industry is to be the priority.

The IMP also stresses the development of downstream palm oil and palm kernel oil-based products such as oleochemicals. Food processing has also received attention, the main focus being on cocoa products and animal feeds. Exports of processed foods are projected to grow by 6.8% p.a. from 1986 to 1990 and 7.8% p.a between 1990 and 1995. The IMP plans to transform the wood-based industry into a major resource-based activity by concentrating on the production of downstream products mainly for export.

The strategy for non-ferrous metal products is import substitution for aluminium and copper, and export orientation for tin. Products with growth potential in the non-metallic minerals industry include cement, glass and ceramics.

The IMP laments the heavy import content of electronics products and the industry's heavy dependence on external resources. None the less, it expects employment in the industry to double and exports to triple by 1995. The IMP calls for a rationalisation of automobile manufacturing and assembly, so that there will be only three manufacturers in the country by 1995, with an upgrading of plants and scale.

The overall message is loud and clear: Malaysia must resort to large-scale manufactured exports in order to maintain high industrial growth. The IMP strategy consists of the following:

1. balanced incentives for import substitution and exports;
2. a free-trade regime applied to all exporters regardless of products; and
3. application of the 'market principle' in the choice of activities to be undertaken by individual firms.

The main drawback is that it does not take full cognisance of the fact that the economy is unlikely to register the growth rate envisaged of 6.4% on average over the period 1986–95. It may be less than 4%.

We have no quarrel with the IMP objectives. The accent on export-oriented resource-based industries, in particular, is well placed, as they have potential comparative advantage. But the timing seems to be wrong. The problem of market access for these products has not been fully addressed. Given the protectionist trends in developed country markets, it will be difficult to export resource-based manufactured products, since the higher the degree of processing and fabrication, the greater are the protectionist barriers.

The economic planners ambitiously identified the 1980s and 1990s as the decades of heavy industrialisation for Malaysia. It was felt that a fairly rapid growth had been achieved in the 1970s and that the time was ripe to take the economy further into an advanced stage of industrialisation. Apparently, the planners were swept off their feet by the Korean experience.

The establishment of the Heavy Industries Corporation of Malaysia (HICOM) marked the launching of the heavy industrialisation programme, yet another manifestation of active state participation and intervention in the country's industrial development. The term 'heavy industry' is hard to define precisely. In the Malaysian context, 'heavy industrialisation' has meant the setting up of iron and steel plants, petrochemical manufacturing units and the manufacturing of motor vehicles. It now appears that the decision in favour of heavy industrialisation was made too hastily, without regard for market size and scale economies. The fact that some of these industries are based on domestic resources, i.e. oil and natural gas, cannot compensate on its own for other shortcomings such as the limited domestic market and inadequate technical skills.

The steel industry is already in deep trouble and is saddled with excess capacity. The problem is that it produces too many bars and wire rods and too few billets for the domestic market. There are six steel mills in operation in the country. The current slump in world steel prices has brought ex-Malaysian post-delivery prices to new low levels. HICOM is now lobbying hard for tariff protection and for a subsidy to cut down its huge electricity bills which form 22% of production costs.

Local steel consumption is projected in the IMP to grow at between 7.5% and 10% annually in the next ten years. Given the protracted economic slowdown, a growth rate at the lower end is more likely. Moreover, there seems to be little immediate prospect of steel exports, given current world production and low prices. There is no way that Malaysian exports can become competitive in the foreseeable future. Production costs will rise, as local producers increase the domestic content by using domestically-produced billets following plans to raise the tariffs on imported ones. The country would have been far better off had it concentrated on expanding and modernising existing iron and steel facilities set up almost two decades previously, instead of establishing new modern ones under the patronage of HICOM.

The production of the national car represents another 'milestone'. 'Proton Saga' hit the road in September 1985. In the first production year, only 7,500 units were produced. Production in 1986 stood at 40,000 units and is expected to increase to 67,000 units in 1987 and 105,000 in 1988. Given the slow growth of domestic demand, the projected expansion is unlikely to materialise.

The first batch of cars incorporated 16 types of locally manufactured components, which put the domestic content at 38%. By the end of 1986, there were 52 types of local component. By the end of the sixth phase there will be a grand total of 147 local parts for the national car. The Ministry of Trade and Industry has produced a list of 102 types of component that can be manufactured locally with various incentives. To date, a total of 282 such components have been identified. How many of these can be produced economically is, of course, a different story. However, more than 50 local firms have already sent their applications to MIDA to take advantage of the tax incentives.

The government had bulldozed the project through, believing that, despite its heavy cost, it was necessary to provide the propulsion to launch Malaysia into the heavy industry orbit. The argument that motor car manufacturing is a must for heavy industrialisation is not at all convincing, however, nor does it make economic sense. The car costs twice as much to produce at home as, say, in Japan. Increased volume of production in the future is unlikely to reduce the unit cost substantially, as the domestic market is not large enough to exploit economies of scale fully. Moreover, gains from scale economies are likely to be offset by higher costs arising from increased local content.

Exchange-rate policy

Exchange-rate policy has to be balanced in terms of several objectives: export growth and the adjustment of the balance of payments, the effect on domestic inflation and the long-term process of industrial development. The real effective exchange rate appreciated by 10% from the second quarter of 1981 to the fourth quarter of 1984 and began to depreciate marginally in early

1985, finally registering an effective depreciation of almost 9% by the second quarter of 1986. By early 1987 it appeared to be at the 1973 level. Given the present economic circumstances, it is hard to judge the appropriate level, but indications are that the depreciating ringgit has helped the manufacturing sector since 1986.

By maintaining an undervalued exchange rate, Malaysia can redirect resources from imports to exports and import-substitution activities. If it does so, this will justify the cost of this protection. The exchange rate is an important instrument of macro-policy for long-run industrial strategy as long as some target real rate is adhered to for a long period.

Foreign investment

Much as Malaysia might like to reduce the ownership or equity component of foreign investment, the current trends in the balance of payments may well render such a policy extremely undesirable. Moreover, the new accent on 'heavy industrialisation' will tend to increase dependence on foreign investment, at least in the short and medium term. One thing seems clear: the country will have to rely on direct foreign investment, not only to inject greater dynamism into the economy but also to solve the balance of payments problem. Foreign debts cannot provide long-term solutions, as these need to be serviced regardless of the country's export performance, whereas foreign investments in export-oriented activities must generate foreign-exchange earnings before profits can be repatriated.

However, it is difficult to ascertain whether the various incentives given to foreign investors are really necessary. Conditions differ greatly among industrial projects and among industrial locations, but there obviously are enormous social costs in the tax concessions and exemptions. Although tax incentives are seldom cited by investors as the main reason for investing in the country, it does appear that they are viewed as compensation for costs or inconvenience associated with politically engineered regulations. Thus, one might argue that less regulation or deregulation would make a lot more economic sense than increased tax incentives.

External borrowing

Much of the external debt problem is closely associated with the OBAs. It is now apparent that many of them are in such bad shape financially that they can hardly repay the loans guaranteed by the government. In addition, some of the programmes which the government has mounted, especially the heavy industrialisation projects which have been financed mainly by borrowed money, have turned out to be inefficient and non-viable.

The current abhorrence attached to external debt is thus mainly the result of the ways in which external debts have been abused in recent times. The government seems to have grown wiser and is now keeping a close watch on the activities of the OBAs. But it also seems to have developed such a phobia against external debt that it no longer dares to use external loans to fight economic downswings, although there is no economic rationale for this. Malaysia enjoys a good credit rating internationally and, provided loans are productively used, they can be self-liquidating. Unfortunately, at present the authorities seem more concerned with what is needed to service the debt rather than with what external loans, if prudently applied, might do for the sagging economy.

Regulation and intervention

Government intervention in general and regulation in particular are pervasive in the Malaysian economy. Much revolves around the NEP. As a result, the extent of direct government involvement in the economy has increased dramatically since 1970. The role of the state seems to be changing, however. It is increasingly regarded as one of facilitating and promoting private sector activities. The reigning philosophy thus seems to favour no more than minimal government participation in business. But there has been very little attempt to deregulate the economy so far, apart from piecemeal privatisation efforts.

Public enterprises were the main instruments of direct government involvement. With the worsening economic conditions and budgetary constraints, the burden imposed by their losses became excessive. As a consequence, during 1984–5 it was announced that a number of public sector activities were to be privatised.

There is no doubt about the government's seriousness in disposing of its stake in business. It sold 15% of its shares in the Malaysian Airline System in 1984, reducing its stake to 55%, and it plans to divest further to 30%. Next in line for government divestment is the Malaysian International Shipping Corporation. The Telecommunications Department has been privatised and plans are under way to privatise the postal services.

Privatisation in the Malaysian context means not only the conversion of public enterprises into private ones but also the entry of private enterprises into industries which were hitherto government monopolies. An example of the latter is the private television network, TV3, which competes with the two government-owned networks. Negotiations are under way for the establishment of a number of private radio stations in the country.

The Industrial Co-ordination Act (ICA) of 1975 represents the most important piece of regulatory and licensing regulation governing the industrial sector. It requires, among other things, all manufacturing companies with a paid-up capital of M$250,000 or more to obtain a licence from the Minister of Trade and Industry who is empowered to refuse a licence in the national interest, and may impose any condition (including compliance with the 30% Bumiputera share in line with the NEP) before a licence is issued or renewed. Provisions such as this are described by businessmen as 'too restrictive'.

More recently (in 1984), the government tightened the Companies Act 1965 with 73 amendments, one of which provided for a panel to administer, supervise and control takeovers and mergers. Another requires companies to disclose shareholdings of 5% or more in order to improve the relevant authorities' surveillance of predatory moves.

Although the new regulations are designed not to stifle the activities of private enterprises, there are areas of some concern. In particular, the wide-ranging powers of the Registrar of Companies and the functions of the proposed panel on takeovers and mergers, whose decision is final and cannot be challenged in a court of law, would have serious implications. The spate of legislation has caused the business environment to take on a highly regulated look. Other government interventions seem to have increased recently, apparently prompted by the economic slowdown, for example the measures taken to prop up the local stock market. The Finance Ministry has also exerted pressure on the commercial banks (through the Central Bank) to channel funds into certain sectors and to adjust their lending and deposit rates.

While there are sound economic justifications for some of the regulations, and political pressures render others necessary and inevitable, some are so complex that they cannot be effectively enforced, while others are implemented on an *ad hoc* basis. One consequence of the regulatory system is that it creates incentives for corruption, especially where the officials have substantial discretionary authority. The very complexity of the system causes uncertainty and unpredictability. Businessmen often encounter lengthy delays in obtaining approvals. Bureaucratic red tape can be extremely frustrating. Worse still, off-the-cuff press statements by cabinet ministers are often interpreted as policy guidelines by the bureaucrats, causing much confusion. In short, the environment is not conducive to undertaking large-scale ventures with long gestation periods.

That the private sector in Malaysia has grown in strength and size is undeniable and government contributions to its development cannot be ignored. But the character of this development has been tainted by the very nature of the government support. First, the private sector has grown so used to this support that it finds it difficult to operate independently of it. This is particularly so in Bumiputera enterprises which have been 'pampered' by the NEP concessions.

Second, under the import-substitution industrial policies, private sector enterprises have become so inward-looking that they tend to shy away from venturing out into international and regional markets. The anti-export bias created by the protection regime is largely responsible for this.

Third, the export-oriented industrialisation strategy of the 1970s stimulated multinational corporations, especially those located in the FTZs, while local private enterprises remained insulated. The enclave nature of FTZ operations meant an absence of domestic linkages which would have provided a fillip to local enterprises and reoriented them towards the global market.

Fourth, it appears that export incentives have failed to entice local private enterprises into exporting. Many Malaysian manufacturers who were eligible for export incentives did not avail themselves of the facility either because of ignorance or owing to the cumbersome procedures (Ariff *et al.*, 1984). Moreover, as noted earlier, the subsidies implicit in the export incentives were insufficient to offset the anti-export bias created by the protection regime.

Last but not least, the system of incentives has favoured large-scale industrial units with enormous capital and has left to one side medium- and small-scale enterprises. Although investment incentives in general, and export incentives in particular, did not openly discriminate against local enterprises, it is foreign investors who have benefited most from them by virtue of the fact that they had more capital to invest. Medium- and small-scale enterprises lacked the necessary technological know-how.

In summary, the system of incentives has rendered the local enterprises essentially inward-looking, catering for the domestic market. However, recent changes in the domestic economy have helped to reorient them. The domestic consumer market, already hit by the recession, has been diminished further by the deflationary influences of the government's austerity drive, thus forcing manufacturers to seek export outlets for their products. This process has been facilitated by the depreciation of the ringgit.

None the less, the system of regulation and intervention has tended to produce impediments to private sector initiatives. A good deal of the time and resources of private enterprises has been dissipated in circumventing regulations, and many are technically operating in breach of the law. Such a climate is not conducive to the growth of entrepreneurship. Local enterprises tend to spread their resources thinly in view of this uncertainty. They are so preoccupied with local regulations that they can hardly afford to venture out into the regional market. In addition, direct involvement in the marketing of their manufactures abroad means encounters with regulations in other countries, with which they are completely unfamiliar, and for which, unlike the multinationals, they possess neither the resources nor the expertise. Nevertheless, the degree of over-regulation is relatively mild compared with several other countries in the region.

CONCLUSION

During the period 1975–80, the Malaysian economy experienced unprecedented growth. The first half of the 1980s, however, witnessed lower average growth, with the lowest ever recorded growth rate of −1% in 1985.

Part of the explanation is the worldwide recession which led commodity prices to fall to very low levels. Ironically, the government's macroeconomic policies have caused the recession to last longer than it would otherwise have done.

Given the world economic environment and the prospects for growth in the industrialised countries, the short- and medium-term prospects for the Malaysian economy do not appear promising. At best, it may have bottomed out and the worst may be over. The growth rate may climb to 3–4% for the rest of the 1980s. This growth is largely expected to come not only from firmness in commodity prices, but also through foreign investment in the manufacturing sector encouraged by the provision of incentives. The lower oil prices and the resultant improvement in growth prospects in the industrialised countries are expected to generate demand for commodities. The government has taken several steps to stimulate growth through export promotion, but this may not be sufficient to absorb the number of unemployed estimated to be in the region of 450,000 or 8.2% of the labour force.

Export orientation must continue to ensure greater efficiency in resource allocation. Given the small domestic market, import substitution will impose heavy costs under heavy protection.

The economy appears to be over-regulated. Some deregulation is necessary so that the business environment can become more conducive to private sector initiatives. The government should go slow on the NEP. Its objectives can only be achieved through economic growth. With a stagnant economy new targets and new timetables must be introduced.

There is need for tariff reform especially to reduce tariff escalation and to reduce the anti-export bias. Although the system of protection appears to be less severe in Malaysia than in other countries, it has tended to penalise export activities with a bias in favour of import replacements.

Given the present economic environment, a second hard look at the heavy industrialisation programme is needed. Phasing the programme out now may be uneconomic as a lot of capital has already been sunk into it, but it is important to inject no more capital into the unprofitable industries, and not to start up new ones. Efforts must be made to reorient the heavy industries towards the export market or at least the ASEAN regional market.

Malaysia has been actively seeking foreign investment for a number of reasons and through a variety of incentive schemes. Its emphasis on direct foreign private investment would not only help promote growth but also help alleviate balance-of-payments problems.

External borrowing needs to be watched carefully to ensure that the debt burden does not get out of hand. There is, however, no logic in turning one's back on external debt if it can be productively used.

Since 1986, the exchange rate has been more flexible and has begun to depreciate effectively, and this trend has helped the manufacturing sector. A liberal exchange-rate system is desirable, with intervention in the market in times of excessive speculation, but maintaining a long-term trend rate conducive to the promotion of exports.

Free Trade Zone areas have played a useful role. Some of the criticisms levelled against them seem misplaced. Of their very nature, FTZ industries cannot have extensive linkages or substantial technological transfers. Their main objective was employment creation in which they have succeeded. None the less, there is a need for another look. There is overconcentration in electronic components, and a need for greater diversification. Efforts must be made to encourage local as well as foreign companies to participate in the FTZ operations.

Table 4.1 Exports, principal commodities and markets (percentages)

	1970	1975	1980	1983
Primary products				
Rubber	40.20	23.80	19.70	11.80
China			5.90	6.30
Germany, Fed. Rep.	6.20	7.10	6.40	
Korea, Rep.				5.80
Singapore	25.30	25.70	25.90	18.60
USSR	11.10	8.30	6.70	6.80
United Kingdom	8.90	6.90		
USA	11.60	11.20	7.60	11.10
Wood & cork	19.90	13.10	17.00	13.60
Australia	4.30			
China	45.10	40.90	46.80	44.70
Hong Kong	13.60	10.30	7.90	10.50
Japan		10.20	7.30	8.50
Korea, Rep.	12.80	13.20	7.30	6.50
Netherlands	4.80	3.70	9.30	10.40
Petroleum & products	8.50	11.40	29.40	27.50
Australia	16.00			
Japan		36.20	41.60	22.30
Philippines	18.80	12.40	4.10	2.50
Singapore	46.30	29.30	23.30	45.80
Thailand	7.10	11.10	3.10	13.10
USA			26.90	
Tin	23.40	14.20	10.70	5.60
Canada	3.30			
India		2.70		
Italy	6.50	3.00	3.20	
Japan	26.90	13.60	26.20	30.30
Netherlands	8.40	31.00	32.50	43.80
USSR		6.20	9.30	10.70
USA	36.80		15.20	

Table 4.1 (continued)

	1970	1975	1980	1983
Palm oil (*crude*)	6.20	12.90	3.90	4.60
India			12.40	19.60
Iraq	17.10	8.00		7.10
Japan			12.70	7.40
Netherlands	8.30	17.00	14.90	
Pakistan		6.50	13.00	22.00
Singapore	30.60			
USSR				12.10
United Kingdom	22.10	17.00	9.40	
USA	5.30	26.80		
Manufactures				
Cork & wood products	2.00	2.40	2.00	1.60
Japan	20.00	18.80	7.30	7.30
Singapore	7.50	16.80	33.00	39.10
United Kingdom	27.30	21.40	13.20	14.90
USA	29.10	14.20	13.20	10.90
Textile, yarn & fabrics	0.40	0.90	1.70	1.20
Australia		12.60	8.80	7.50
Canada				5.50
Germany, Fed. Rep.		15.50	6.60	
Hong Kong			11.60	13.00
Japan			9.40	7.60
New Zealand	4.00	8.90		
Philippines	7.70			
Singapore	27.40	17.40	7.10	9.20
United Kingdom	17.10			
USA	15.00	11.00		
Non-ferrous metals	23.50	14.20	10.80	5.80
Japan	26.80	13.50	25.90	29.60
Netherlands	8.40	30.80	32.10	42.40
USSR		6.10	9.10	10.40
USA	36.70	29.40	15.00	4.00
Electrical machinery	0.30	3.60	10.90	13.50
Germany, Fed. Rep.		3.50	7.30	6.30
Hong Kong		3.50	7.10	5.50
Indonesia	5.80			
Iraq	11.90			
Japan		6.60	4.80	6.60
Saudi Arabia	9.20			
Singapore	34.80	18.90	14.50	10.50
Thailand	9.30			
USA		54.60	53.20	58.20
Articles of apparel	0.40	1.20	1.40	1.60
France		17.60	12.60	5.30
Germany, Fed. Rep.		25.10	23.30	15.50
Netherlands		9.30		
USA	64.2	12.7	20.2	45.7

Table 4.2 Import structure and sources, 1970–85 (percentages)

	Rates of growth			Proportion of total imports				
	1970–5	1976–80	1980–5	1981	1982	1983	1984	1985
Consumption goods	9.1	22.2	8.7	20.0	19.2	18.9	19.7	21.6
Food	7.0	13.7	9.5	6.0	5.9	5.6	5.7	6.1
Consumer durables	16.4	47.7	8.6	4.1	3.8	3.9	4.9	4.9
Other	9.2	20.8	8.4	9.9	9.5	9.3	9.1	10.6
Investment goods	25.1	25.9	6.0	28.2	31.1	31.8	32.7	31.3
Machinery	18.9	33.4	4.6	10.8	10.9	10.7	11.0	10.8
Transport equipment	2.7	45.1	7.1	3.6	5.5	5.4	4.1	4.3
Metal products	15.4	39.1	−0.4	6.5	7.1	6.7	6.3	5.7
Other	60.5	9.0	13.7	7.3	7.6	9.0	11.3	10.5
Intermediate goods	22.1	35.2	3.5	50.3	48.1	47.6	46.5	46.3
Manufacturing	17.0	36.8	5.7	27.4	26.8	28.4	30.1	29.4
Construction	33.1	24.2	9.3	3.5	4.4	3.9	3.7	3.0
Agriculture	17.9	26.8	−2.2	2.8	2.2	1.9	2.3	2.5
Crude petroleum	70.0	34.3	−7.0	7.7	5.0	5.3	3.9	3.6
Other	20.3	49.2	7.4	8.8	9.7	8.1	6.5	7.8
Total imports	16.5	28.3	5.0					
GNP growth rate	13.7	16.9	6.5					
	(1970)	(1975)	(1980)					
Principal sources of imports:								
Machinery and transport								
Germany, Fed. Rep.	10.4	9.8	8.5			7.5	5.2	5.8
Japan	26.2	28.3	35.1			37.0	37.8	33.0
Singapore						7.2	8.6	10.5
USA	18.3	18.3	25.6			26.2	24.8	24.0
All imports								
Japan	17.5	20.1	22.9			25.3	26.3	23.0
Singapore	7.5	8.5	11.7			13.9	13.0	15.9
UK	13.5	10.0						
USA	8.6	10.7	15.0			16.1	16.3	15.2

Sources: Economic Reports, Ministry of Finance; *Quarterly Economic Bulletin*, Bank Negara.

Table 4.3 Foreign investment in companies in production by selected country and industry, as at 31 December 1983 (percentages)

	Singapore	Japan	UK	USA
Food manufacturing	21.7	10.6	21.3	5.1
Beverages & tobacco	5.9		16.2	23.0
Textile & textile products	5.8	31.9	1.0	2.4
Leather & leather products	0.4			
Wood & wood products	4.5	9.5	0.8	1.2
Furniture & fixtures	1.1	0.2		0.2
Paper, publishing & printing	1.6		0.4	0.2
Chemical & chemical products	4.7	2.8	16.4	36.5
Petroleum & coal			15.6	
Rubber & rubber products	1.9	1.7	3.0	4.5
Plastic products	0.6	1.7	0.1	
Non-metallic mineral products	14.3	7.6	6.0	0.4
Basic metal products	11.4	6.9	2.6	
Fabricated metal products	3.2	2.7	4.0	0.7
Machinery	0.7	2.8	2.6	3.0
Electrical & electronics	6.1	15.5	5.5	15.6
Transport equipment	4.6	3.2	3.9	2.2
Scientific & measuring equipment		0.3		1.8
Misc. manufactures	0.1	1.6	0.6	2.9
Hotel & tourist complexes	11.1	0.7	0.1	
Total	100	100	100	100
Share of total	32.9	17.3	15.9	5.0
Total value, M$m	1337	704	645	227

Source: Calculated from unpublished data provided by Malaysian Industrial Development Authority MIDA.

Table 4.4 Balance of payments – current account, 1978–85 (M$ million)

	1978	1979	1980	1981	1982	1983	1984	1985
Exports (fob)	16,932	24,060	28,013	26,900	27,946	31,762	38,452	37,585
Imports (fob)	13,242	17,152	22,775	27,143	29,704	30,760	31,466	28,709
Trade balance	3,690	6,908	5,238	−243	−1,758	1,002	6,986	8,876
Net non-factor services	−1,621	−2,867	−3,993	−3,476	−3,867	−4,890	−5,558	−4,931
Freight & insurance	−1,061	−1,318	−1,781	−2,008	−2,154	−2,132	−2,120	−1,732
Other transportation	143	21	−56	7	154	53	−99	−28
Travel	−324	−553	−885	−672	−775	−1,104	−1,249	−1,392
Govt transactions (nie)	5	−13	−7	7	59	35	23	27
Other services	−384	−1,004	−1,264	−810	−1,151	−1,742	−2,113	−1,806
Net factor services	−1,756	−1,991	−1,820	−1,836	−2,679	−4,208	−5,255	−5,665
Net investment income	−1,756	−1,991	−1,820	−1,836	−2,679	−4,208	−5,255	−5,665
Net services – total	−3,377	−4,858	−5,813	−5,312	−6,546	−9,098	−10,813	−10,596
Net transfers	−104	−17	−45	−78	−75	−21	−90	−130
Current account balance	+209	+2,033	−620	−5,633	−8,409	−8,117	−3,917	−1,795
CA as a percentage of GNP	0.69	4.58	1.20	10.13	14.09	12.46	5.28	2.50

Source: Bank Negara, *Quarterly Economic Bulletin*, various issues.

Table 4.5 Federal government finance and savings–investment balance, 1976–86 (% of GDP)

Item	1976	1977	1978	1979	1980	1981	1982	1983	1984	1985	1986
Revenue	22.8	25.0	24.4	24.4	27.8	29.1	28.5	29.0	28.0	29.4	29.0
Operating expenditure	21.6	23.8	22.2	23.3	27.4	28.9	28.5	28.6	26.7	27.9	31.1
Surplus or deficit	1.2	1.2	2.2	1.1	0.5	0.2	0.03	0.4	1.3	1.5	2.0
Development expenditure	8.6	10.1	10.2	9.6	14.7	20.5	19.1	14.7	10.9	9.4	11.4
Total expenditure	30.6	33.9	32.5	32.9	42.1	49.5	47.6	43.2	37.6	37.4	42.5
Overall surplus or deficit	7.4	8.9	8.0	8.6	14.2	20.5	19.1	14.3	9.5	7.9	13.4
Public sector overall surplus or deficit						20.4	18.9	17.0	13.2	10.5	18.9[a]
Gross national savings	29.2	28.3	28.8	32.8	28.3	24.0	23.2	25.0	26.8	27.1	
Gross domestic investment	22.7	24.8	27.9	28.1	29.5	34.4	37.0	36.7	32.6	29.6	
Current account deficit	6.5	3.5	0.9	4.7	−1.2	−10.4	−13.4	−11.7	−5.8	−2.5	

Note: a. 1987: 13.9.

Sources: Bank Negara Malaysia, *Quarterly Economic Bulletin;* Department of Statistics.

Table 4.6 Federal government outstanding foreign debt (M$m.)

Year	1975	1980	1981	1982	1983	1984	1985
External market loans							
USA	982	1,409	4,023	8,126	10,332	12,008	11,234
UK	250	109	109	177	177	243	447
West Germany	70	131	123	115	201	200	1,376
Others	46	535	542	582	1,561	2,201	3,242
Subtotal	1,348	2,184	4,797	9,000	12,271	14,652	16,299
External project loans							
USA	126	210	54	51	38	45	49
UK	105	173	172	165	165	163	123
Japan	341	845	953	1,044	1,237	1,738	2,448
World Bank	330	703	900	1,088	1,230	1,316	1,381
Asian Development Bank	91	512	620	741	855	925	982
West Germany	34	129	128	111	91	74	42
West Asia		34	52	96	141	166	214
Others	50	57	92	81	118	245	449
Subtotal	1,077	2,663	2,971	3,377	3,875	4,672	5,688
Suppliers' credit				119	754	820	825
IMF			510	662	828	703	263
Total	2,425	4,847	8,278	13,158	17,728	20,847	23,075

Source: *Economic Report*, various issues.

Table 4.7 International comparison of revenue effort (% of GNP)

Country	Average 1979–83
India	12.9
Sri Lanka	22.6
Pakistan	15.8
Indonesia	23.7
Thailand	14.6
Philippines	12.3
Malaysia	27.7
Korea	19.3
New Zealand	34.1
UK	36.3
Australia	25.8
USA	20.5

Source: *International Financial Statistics*, IMF.

5

THAILAND

SUPOTE CHUNANUNTATHUM, SOMSAK TAMBUNLERTCHAI and
ATCHANA WATTANANUKIT

GROWTH AND STRUCTURAL CHANGE
IN THE ECONOMY

By any international standards of comparison, Thailand had achieved a
relatively rapid economic growth rate for the decade and a half up to 1985.
The annual real economic growth rate fluctuated between 4% and 9% during
the period 1969–80, an average of 7%, but for the more recent period,
1981–5, the average fell to 5%. Even this remained relatively satisfactory by
international standards. At the same time, however, there was an increasing
international trade deficit which is becoming an urgent issue for Thailand in
its medium-term development. There is a need to seek new policy options
with respect to trade and financial strategies.

Real GNP per capita grew by a simple annual average rate of 4.5% during
the period 1969–80. It then declined to 3% p.a. during 1981–5, a reduction of
a third. Table 5.1 gives the structural change in GDP for 1969–85. The
share of primary products fell from 34% in 1970 to 25% in 1985, with a
particularly sharp decline for the agricultural sector. The share of the
manufacturing sector, on the other hand, rose almost continuously, from
around 16% in 1969 to approximately 21% in 1985. Sectors whose share also
rose strongly included banking, insurance and real estate, and electricity
and water supply. Construction fell. Other sectors showed no perceptible
trends.

The current balance of payments and sectoral balances

Export volume quadrupled between 1969 and 1985, while imports doubled.
Though the growth in exports was much higher, their unit value, with the
exception of the years of 1972–4, grew much less, by 170% as compared with
360% for import unit values. Thus the international terms of trade deterior-

ated substantially (again with the exception of the years 1972–4) by 41% between 1969 and 1984.

The ratio of the commodity trade deficit to GNP therefore rose substantially, fluctuating between 3% and 10% during 1969–85 (see Table 5.2), as compared with about 3% during 1961–6. The service trade surplus as a percentage share of GNP was quite low in all years after 1975 as compared with 1969–75, and although it improved slightly in 1983 and 1985, it in no way offset the high merchandise trade account deficit. The current account deficit as a share of GNP remained high in 1983 and 1984 and was still 4% in 1985.

The detailed balance of payments is presented in Table 5.3. The move into deficit occurred even before the 1973 international oil price hike. The surplus during 1972–4 was mainly explained by commodity prices, especially for rice. Although Thai production fell in line with the world crop failure in 1972–3, and severe export taxes as well as quantitative restrictions (including bans on exports) drastically reduced rice export volumes to only 0.8m. metric tonnes in 1973 as compared with 2m. metric tonnes in 1972, the value of exports in 1973 was down by only 19%, and with rice prices remaining high in the first half of 1974, the export volume of 1m. tonnes that year fetched a peak value 172% higher than that of the previous year.

For the 17-year period 1969–85, the balance of payments showed eight surplus and nine deficit years. Net reserves as a proportion of GNP declined from 14% in 1969 to 7% in 1985, while the coverage of imports also fell from an average of 8.6 months in 1969 to 1.9 months in 1984, recovering to 3.5 months in 1985.

Net investment income has been significantly negative since 1976 reaching Baht 38bn in 1985. Although there was a large positive net inflow of other service income in the 1980s (this includes, of course, the factor income of labourers employed in the Middle Eastern countries), net factor income still remained a very large negative item. This resulted from heavy external borrowing to finance the basic trade account deficit. Direct foreign investment fell as a proportion of total capital movements, from an average of 42.5% during the period 1969–74 to as low as 3% in 1979, although it picked up to about 11% in 1980 and 1981. External borrowing in the form of loans and credits, with both short-term and long-term maturities, increased in relative importance in the country's international capital flows after 1974.

It can be argued that in a still relatively low-income and fast-growing developing economy, as Thailand was in the 1970s and 1980s, there is bound to be a deficit in the current account. Specifically in the Thai case, this deficit indicates a desire for domestic investment and a domestic savings gap, which has to be filled by foreign borrowing.

Table 5.4 shows the sectoral balances for 1969–84. The net foreign investment column is conceptually equivalent to the country's current account position. The private sector saving–investment balance was negative only in 1969. Positive saving by the private sector fluctuated, and the figure in 1982 corresponded to an economic recession with a GNP growth rate of 3.63%. Private investment was then low with no corresponding reduction in private savings. The government sector, on the contrary, and with the exception of 1974, had a deficit throughout the period. In the sharp recession of 1982, the shortfall in revenue collection was large, due to the high share of indirect taxation in total taxation, while expenditures remained at a high level; this was the peak public deficit in the period, at 6% of GNP. There was also a large deficit for government enterprises in 1982, giving an external deficit despite the large positive private surplus.

The deficit in the public enterprise sector increased after the mid-1970s, and began to exceed the central government deficit in 1978. The surplus from the private sector was inadequate to finance the combined deficits of the other two sectors. There was a continuous inflow of net foreign investment throughout the period and government enterprises relied heavily on foreign savings after 1975.

The balance of payments and the monetary system

A deficit in the current account is equal to the building up of claims by foreigners or the reduction of foreign assets. The change in net foreign assets is, in turn, linked to the working of the monetary institutions. There were ten years of lending by the non-bank private sector during the period 1969–84. In some of these positive years, the net lendings by the private sector through the banking system were inadequate for government borrowing, for example, in 1969, 1971 and 1976. This resulted in a reduction in net foreign assets along with all the other years of net borrowings by the private sector.

The government also borrowed directly and indirectly from the rest of the non-bank private sector. Even though recorded direct lending tends to be negligible because of the small domestic capital (equity and bond) market, the government regularly borrows (through bond selling) from the Government Savings Bank. In certain years this borrowing was large, helping to reduce the deficit financing by the banking system. There were, thus, increases in net foreign assets, for instance during 1980–2 and 1984. Nevertheless, it can be concluded that credit-creation by the monetary institutions accommodated the overspending in the overall economy in a number of years, given the deterioration in the international terms of trade. This resulted in the reduction of previously accumulated net foreign assets in the years of balance-of-payment deficits.

The external value of the Baht declined, therefore, with a number of devaluations during 1969–84. It was devalued officially by 7.9% in December 1971, and by 10% in February 1973 to keep its original parity with the US dollar. There was, however, a minor revaluation by approximately 4% in July 1973 because of the continued depreciation of the US dollar in that year.

Exchange-rate policy was altered from the traditional single peg to the US dollar to a basket peg in March 1978. This system lasted only about six months, after which the so-called daily exchange rate fixing system was put into force. In July 1981, however, there was a 8.7% devaluation, and the exchange rate was again officially pegged to the US dollar. A further devaluation by 14.8% followed in November 1984 after the imposition of other austerity measures including an 18% ceiling on commercial banking credit. The Bank of Thailand then adopted a discretionary floating policy with the Baht linked to a basket of major trading partners' currencies.

IMPORT GROWTH AND STRUCTURAL CHANGES

The changing structure of production away from an agriculture-dominated economy has been accompanied by a change in the country's trade structure. The past growth in the manufacturing sector was based on production for the domestic market, consisting mostly of import substitution of consumer goods. In the first stages of industrialisation, domestic producers were able to secure adequate demand for their output under a heavy protectionist regime. However, by the end of the 1970s, the domestic market seemed to be exhausted and ceased to contribute to industrial growth as before.

The Thai economy moved towards industrialisation partly in order to cope with the balance of payments problem, but imports of manufactured goods continued to grow. The industrialisation process over the last two decades seems to have worsened the country's balance of trade, especially following the first oil price shock. The proportion of imports to GDP up to then was 18–20%. After 1973, this increased rapidly, reaching 28% by 1981 following the second oil shock.

During 1960–70, the average annual rate of growth of imports was 10%. The oil shocks of the 1970s caused further sharp increases up to 27% in 1976–80. The rate decreased between 1981 and 1985 mainly due to much slower growth at home and worldwide economic recession.

Non-oil imports rose sevenfold from 1970 to 1985, more slowly than oil during the 1970s, but this situation was reversed by 1985. Oil imports fell mainly because of partial domestic gas and oil substitution, beginning in 1981–2.

The share of consumer goods, as shown in Table 5.5, declined from 35% in 1960 to 20% in 1970 and 10–14% during 1980–5. The first stage of Thai industrialisation in the 1960s focused mainly on import substitution; industries producing previously imported consumer goods, especially non-durables, grew very rapidly. Later, the rate began to slow down, since domestic markets were relatively small and opportunities for import substitution tended to be exhausted. For durable consumer goods, import values remained at their 1960 level of 8% of total import values until 1969, going down to 5.6% in 1985. Three major groups of durable imports which showed a slightly decreasing trend were household appliances, electrical appliances and cycles and motor cycles. This sequence was similar to the experience of most other developing countries, since import substitution of non-durable consumer goods was easily established as a driving force for the first stages of industrial development. Income rose and the range of products which could be competitively produced for the domestic market expanded. On top of that, protectionist policies were followed to encourage import-substitution industries.

The share of intermediate goods and raw materials in total import values increased from 18.5% in 1960 to 25.5% in 1970 and has remained at that level. The import-substituting industrial policy pursued in the past has not thus succeeded in reducing Thailand's imports but only in changing the import structure. Imports of capital goods also increased from 25% of total imports in 1960 to 35% in 1970 and have been maintained at 30% since 1983. The largest items in this group are non-electrical machinery and spare parts, which account for almost half the total. Possibilities for import substitution thus still remain in intermediate, capital and durable consumer goods. These industries are much more difficult to establish. With some indigenous natural gas and oil production which came on stream at the end of 1981 and 1982 respectively, the oil import share was reduced to 23% in 1985.

Reference to the Thailand input–output table for 1975 and 1980 sheds some light on the import dependence of the manufacturing sector. Computed proportions of imports to total supply higher than 15% are presented in Table 5.6 by industrial sub-sectors. The sub-sector with the highest import dependence was petroleum and natural gas, but recently, since domestic production has developed, this has decreased. Many sectors, including machinery, aircraft, synthetic resin, artificial fibre, and other chemical products, scientific equipment and secondary steel products, showed a high and increasing trend of import dependence. Sectors showing a high but decreasing trend included raw materials for textiles, office and household machinery and appliances, fabricated metal products and motor vehicles. Some sectors including motor vehicles, motor cycles and bicycles, office and household machinery and appliances, drastically reduced their imports.

Thailand is still mainly dependent on imports from two countries: Japan and the United States. Their combined share still accounts for nearly 40% (see Table 5.7). The European Community's share decreased from 19% in 1974 to 12% in 1984 and 14% in 1985. Within this group, West Germany and the UK are Thailand's most significant trading partners. Imports from the Asian NICs increased considerably in the past decade, from 6% of the total in 1974 to 14% in 1984. Within this group, the two most significant countries are Singapore and South Korea. But if oil imports from Singapore are excluded, total imports from the NICs amounted to only 5–6% of the total until recently, when the share increased to 9%. Between 1974 and 1980, the share of imports from the Middle East reached as high as 17%, but dropped to 9% in 1984 and 8% in 1985.

Table 5.8 provides information on imports from the major suppliers by commodity groups disaggregated by an economic classification. During 1977–85, imports of capital goods from Japan constituted a significant share of total Thai imports, followed by intermediate goods and raw materials, reflecting the industrialisation process. Against the trend for the total, imports of durable consumer goods, including electrical appliances, household goods and cycles, increased. The question is whether Thailand is capable of reforming its attitude in favour of imported goods, or of efficiently producing these products up to international standard without heavy protection.

The picture for the US is similar. Imports have mostly consisted of capital and intermediate goods and raw materials. However, it is interesting to note that, since 1979, imports of arms have increased to the same level as imports of electrical machinery and spare parts.

Imports from the EC followed the same pattern, with machinery and intermediate products, especially chemicals, constituting a large proportion, followed by food and beverages, basic metals, fertilisers, vehicles and spare parts, and arms. Excluding oil imports, major import items from the Asian NICs consisted of non-electrical machinery and spare parts for industrial use, most of which came from Taiwan and recently also from Korea. However, imports of final consumer goods especially clothing, footwear and electrical appliances, also showed an increasing trend.

A number of studies confirm that the Thai manufacturing sector as a whole has been heavily and discriminatorily protected. Trairong Suwankiri (1970) found the structure of protection biased in favour of the production of consumer and intermediate products rather than capital goods. Narongchai Akrasanee (1973) showed that the effective rates for export industries were all negative. Among import-competing industries, consumer and intermediate goods enjoyed heavy protection.

A recent study (Chunanuntathum, Mongkolsmai and Tambunlertchai, 1985) compared the effective rates for 1975 and 1982. In both years value-added in exportable activities was generally taxed more than that in importable activities. The rice milling sector experienced an effective protective rate (EPR) of −83.77% in 1975 and −28.07% in 1982. Other exportables with negative rates of protection in both years included tapioca milling, grinding of maize, sugar, sawmills, rubber sheeting and block rubber, and non-ferrous metals. Excluding rice milling, the EPRs of these exportables ranged between −48.93% and −14.93% in 1975 and −21.94% and −14.89% in 1982. ˙

The manufacture of importables tended to have positive protection, but there were many cases with high negative rates in 1975. In 1982, when nominal rates on their outputs were much higher, the EPRs for these importables were also much higher, with nearly all of them becoming positive. A few examples may be cited. Monosodium glutamate had an EPR of −21.64% in 1975 and 444.13% in 1982. Distilling and spirits blending and breweries had a positive protection of 10.59% and 7.49% respectively in 1982, as compared to −22.38% and −41.85% in 1975. For the motor vehicle sector, the EPR was equal to 308.16% in 1982.[1]

Setting aside three cases in 1982 in which the EPRs were negative, the effective rate for the manufacturing activities producing importables ranged between 2,948.47% for flour and other grain milling and −30.30% for fertilisers and pesticides, thus reflecting a wide variation among different importables.

Given the negative EPR for the exportable category, it can be concluded that effective protection for manufacturing discriminated against manufactured exports to a greater extent in 1982 than in 1975. There is also evidence from the calculation that the EPR exhibited greater variation among different industries in 1982 than in 1975.

EXPORT GROWTH AND STRUCTURAL CHANGES

Export performance

Thailand's share in world exports amounted to only 0.4% during 1980–4, slightly higher than the average of 0.3% in the 1970s. Significant export expansion came in the 1970s. In the early 1970s, there was a commodity boom in the world market, and the prices of Thailand's major export items, including rice, rubber, tin, maize and sugar, increased substantially, offsetting to a significant extent the impact of the oil price increase on the country's external balance. Furthermore, starting from around 1973, exports of manufactured goods expanded rapidly, despite the turbulent trading environment. Thailand seemed to benefit from being a marginal supplier in the world market for various manufactured products, and the protectionist practices in the major importing countries did not impose too serious a constraint on Thai exports during the decade. Since the early 1970s, there have been only two years when exports fell: 1975 and 1983. There was a drought in 1975 together with severe recession in the industrialised world following the first oil price hike. Despite a relatively good crop year in 1983, there was again a deep recession in the major importing countries. The pace of export expansion in the 1980s was much slower compared with that of the previous decade. However, the average growth rate was still over 10% a year.

The manufacturing sector has become more export-oriented. Table 5.9 indicates that the ratio of exports to output increased from 13.8% in 1975 to 20% in 1980. Highly export-oriented industries include rubber products and non-ferrous metals (mainly tin), food, textiles, leather products, plastic products, ceramics and earthenware, fabricated metals and 'other' (mainly jewellery).

Food comprises about half of total exports (see Table 5.10). The share of raw materials has declined significantly, from over 40% of total export value in the early 1960s to around 10% in recent years. The combined share of manufactured exports, SITC 5–8 goods, has shown a significant increasing trend, and by 1985 reached 41%. Manufactured products like other exports showed slower growth in the 1980s as compared with the earlier period, especially in SITC 6.

Table 5.10 tends to understate the importance of manufactures, since a significant proportion of food products have been exported in processed form. The share of exports from the agricultural sector declined from 82.7% in 1961 to 38.3% in 1985, while the share from manufacturing rose from a negligible 2.4% in 1961 to surpass agriculture with 50% in 1985. Fishery products also showed a marked increase during the 1970s. Mineral products fell, due largely to the fall in tin exports. The importance of forestry products also declined steadily and by 1985 their share in total exports dropped to only 0.2%.

These figures, however, although revealing the increasing importance of manufactures, also show the importance of primary-based commodities in Thailand's exports. The combined share of agricultural, fishery, forestry and mineral products, although decreasing, still constituted 50% of total exports in 1985. The importance of the primary sector therefore cannot be overlooked, even at this stage when the country is emerging as a new generation NIC.

Table 5.11 shows that the principal manufactured exports are processed food, textiles, garments, electronic goods (mainly integrated circuits) and jewellery, together accounting for over three-quarters of the country's manufactured exports. Other important manufactured exports which showed high growth rates in the 1970s were footwear, wood products and furniture, leather, rubber and plastic products.

There has been a degree of diversification in primary exports. Maize and tapioca products have emerged as the major export commodities since the early 1960s. Other agricultural and fishery products whose export values increased rapidly are mung beans, prawns and cuttlefish, and among processed foods are various types of canned food, sugar and vegetable oils. If we define principal exports as those commodities whose export value exceeded 1% of total exports, there were only five in 1960, namely rice, rubber, maize, tapioca products and tin. Their combined share was 98.4%, with rice and rubber accounting for 75%. In 1965, prawns, sugar and mung beans entered the list. In the 1970s, many more commodities qualified and by 1984, there were 18 principal export items. Rice, while still remaining the most important export item, has significantly decreased its share; rubber has also dropped, to less than 10%.

The major export destinations are the industrialised countries, with Japan, the United States and the European Community taking about half. But there has been significant market diversification over the last two decades or so (see Table 5.12). Japan's share has shown a declining trend over the last decade, and in 1984 exports to the United States exceeded those to Japan for the first time. Some 'other' countries absorbed an increasing amount. Excluding Singapore, Hong Kong was the most important market among the Asian NICs, but its importance has been declining steadily and in recent years its share was only around 4–5%. Taiwan and South Korea are still small markets, but their shares have improved recently.

Since the 1973 oil price increase, exports to the Middle East and other oil exporters have risen considerably, with Saudi Arabia as the most important market, followed by Iran and Nigeria. Exports to these three countries comprised 5–6% of toal exports in recent years, with the Iranian market expanding at a rapid rate. Bearing in mind the recent decline in oil prices and therefore in purchasing power of the Middle East countries, it is doubtful that exports to these markets will expand as fast in the future.

Although Thai exports still rely heavily on developed country markets, some of the small markets, such as in Africa and Oceania, have increased in recent years.

Exports to Japan mostly comprised animal products, processed foods and plastic and rubber products; jewellery, frozen chickens and prawns and other seafoods are among the rapidly growing exports to the Japanese market over the past 7–8 years. But Japan has not absorbed much of Thailand's manufactures. It has been a much smaller market for textile products than the United States and the EC, and at present textiles comprise only 2–3% of exports to Japan. Japanese importers have long affiliations with producers in South Korea and Taiwan, and it is difficult for Thai products to penetrate the Japanese market. The rapid increase of textile exports from China to Japan in recent years should, however, give some indication that it is not impossible for a new textile exporting country to break into the Japanese market. With the appreciation of the yen, more Thai exports could be promoted. Preliminary statistics for 1985 and the beginning of 1986 already indicated high growth rates for a number of Thai exports to Japan, including tapioca products, jewellery and garments.

At present processed foods and textile products are the two most important groups of exports to the US market, and they have grown rapidly in recent years. In view of the recent depreciation of the US dollar and increasing US protectionism, the prospects for further growth will not be as good in the near future, particularly for textiles and garments which have already been subjected to severe restrictions.

Exports to the EC, mainly tapioca, tin, textiles and garments, have increased significantly since the early 1970s. The Netherlands is the most important trading partner, mainly because of tapioca; other important EC importers are West Germany, the United Kingdom, Italy, France and Belgium. The prospects for further expansion are not very good, particularly for tapioca and textile products,which are restricted by import quotas or 'voluntary' export restraints. For tapioca, the quota is approximately equivalent to the average over the past ten years. For textiles and garments, the quotas for most items in which Thailand has a competitive edge have been almost fully utilised. Strenuous efforts must therefore be made to promote other exports. The recent trend for jewellery, canned food and some other new manufactures seems to be encouraging. However, as these are much smaller items, it is unlikely that Thailand will maintain its past growth records.

ASEAN countries as a group absorb around 15–20% of Thai exports, with Singapore the most important importer, followed by Malaysia and Indonesia. In the early 1960s, Malaysia absorbed nearly 20% of Thai exports, with rice, tin concentrate and rubber the most important items. But since the establishment of a tin-smelting company in Thailand in the mid-1960s, export of tin concentrate to Malaysia for smelting has stopped. Rice and rubber exports have also declined in importance, as markets for Thai rice became more diversified and Malaysia emerged as the world's leading rubber producer. (The volume of trade between Thailand and Malaysia could be significantly understated due to under-reporting of the border trade between the two countries.) Singapore's importance also declined during 1965–70 due to the diversification of Thai rice markets, but the increased export of manufactures to this market enabled Thailand to maintain its export share to Singapore at around 8–10% for the last decade.

Export policy and prospects

The international economic environment facing Thailand in the 1980s is quite different from that in the previous decade. The world prices of its major export commodities have mostly been declining, and some export commodities have been restricted by quotas. There is also increasing competition in labour-intensive exports from lower-wage developing countries like China and Sri Lanka. It is therefore expected that the rate of Thai export expansion will slow down in the 1980s. We shall now look at the trend for some of the principal export commodities.

For *rice*, the major traditional markets are Hong Kong, Indonesia, Malaysia and Singapore. But in recent years exports to Indonesia have decreased significantly, as Indonesia has become self-sufficient in rice production. On the other hand, some Middle East and African countries, including Iran, Nigeria and Senegal, have become important markets. In fact, despite their declining share in the country's total exports, rice exports have expanded considerably over the last decade and Thailand has become the world's largest rice exporter. The world price has dropped significantly, however, particularly since the promulgation in December 1985 of the Farm Act in the United States which gives a substantial subsidy to American rice exporters. It is expected that some Thai rice markets, particularly in Europe and South America where Thailand has a disadvantage in transportation costs, will be lost to the United States. The medium-term prospects for Thai rice exports are thus not very good.

Like rice *rubber* has suffered a downward trend in price in recent years. With the decline in the price of petroleum products, it is expected that the price will be further depressed. *Maize* exports have not expanded much over the last few years. Japan used to be the biggest importer, but it has now turned to imports from the United States and other countries. Over 80% of Thailand's *tapioca* products have been absorbed in the EC market, where they are now subject to voluntary export restraints. Thai exporters have therefore been trying to diversify their markets but with only limited success. Tapioca has also suffered a downward trend in price.

In addition to these four agricultural commodities, another primary product, *tin*, has fared even worse in the world market since its price has been falling steadily following the collapse of the International Tin Council's buffer-stocks in 1985. The value of Thailand's raw tin exports reached a peak in 1980 at Baht 11,347m. and was down to Baht 5,280m. in 1984. It is not likely that tin exports will increase much in the near future. Thailand will thus face serious constraints in further export expansion of major primary products. But there are some other *less important primary commodities* which have shown high growth rates during the past decade and their prospects for further growth have not been seriously threatened. Among these are frozen prawns and chickens, cuttlefish and a variety of fruits and vegetables (which at present remain minor export items).

If, however, Thailand is to maintain a reasonable rate of export growth, the major emphasis will be on manufactures. Some of these have also suffered from stagnation or even decline in their export values. *Sugar* has shown the largest decline, from Baht 12,932m. in 1982 to Baht 5,222m. in 1984. Since the mid-1970s, there has been a clear downward trend in sugar prices due to the shift in demand to substitutes. The prospect for further expansion is thus not good.

For other manufactures, such as textile products, jewellery and integrated circuits, past export growth has been impressive. Thailand exported less than Baht 100m. worth of *textile products* in 1970; by 1984 textile exports reached Baht 19bn with garments comprising 64% of this. Over half have gone to the two largest markets: the EC and the United States. But textile exports to other countries such as Kuwait, Saudi Arabia, Singapore and the United Arab Emirates have also grown rapidly over the last 6–7 years. There will be serious constraints on further expansion since quotas in the two largest markets have mostly been filled, and the economic growth rates of countries in the Middle East will be slower. Thai textiles, particularly garments, will nevertheless still enjoy rapid growth in other markets such as Japan, Canada,

Australia and the Scandinavian countries. Since these are much smaller markets than the United States and the EC, the overall growth will inevitably decelerate in the future.

Exporting *jewellery* started in the 1960s but the amount was very small. At present, however, jewellery accounts for around 3–4% of total exports. Major importers include the United states, Japan, Hong Kong and West Germany. Since jewellery is a labour-intensive product and requires good craftsmanship, Thailand will still have a comparative advantage, but the recent trend of exports seems to indicate that future growth will not be as high as in the past.

Since 1972, a few multinational firms have come to Thailand to assemble *integrated circuits* exclusively for export. By 1984, IC exports amounted to 4.3% of the country's total exports. But the local value-added for these products is very low. IC products are sent mainly to Singapore and the United States for further processing. Thailand could probably enjoy a comparative advantage for IC assembly for a few more years, but it may lose this as wage rates increase.

Besides the major items, other Thai manufactured exports are in general less restricted by protectionist practices. Among those registering rapid growth over the last decade and which may continue to grow at respectable rates is a variety of canned foods, toys and other plastic products, artificial flowers, ceramic products and leather goods. These are minor items, however, and, despite their high growth rates, the overall growth of exports will substantially decelerate as major items are subjected to the various restraints discussed above.

Despite this decelerating trend, exports will still grow at a higher rate than GDP. Continued export expansion is necessary for the economy to maintain a reasonable growth rate. In addition to income and foreign-exchange earnings considerations, the promotion of exports will also be helpful for employment absorption, as Thailand's exports, particularly of manufactures, are mostly labour-intensive commodities. In the 1970s manufactured exports grew at a very rapid rate from a small base. Although Thai exports at present still comprise only a very small proportion of world exports or even of exports from developing countries, their volume is now over four times and their value around 12 times that in 1970. Their absolute growth is thus much larger, despite the much reduced growth rate.

As the principal exports will be more severely constrained, diversification in both commodities and markets will have to be contemplated. Past records on diversification have been quite satisfactory, and further diversification, although more difficult than in the past, is by no means impossible. Increasingly, fruit and vegetable items have been entering the export list recently as a result of improved preserving and packaging techniques. There are also a greater variety of canned fruit, vegetable and marine products. Textiles and leather products, among others, are industries which have moved from import substitution to become increasingly export-oriented, and more varieties have been added to the product list. Ceramic products, plastic wares and toys, artificial flowers and some automobile parts and components (in very small amounts) have also been exported, together with some electronic goods, such as radio and television sets. If productivity could be improved and the incentive system made more conducive to exporting rather than producing for the local market, more import-substituting items could be moved into exports. Considering the country's resource endowment, however, further export expansion is likely to rely more on resource-based products, particularly various food items. In many cases these do not compete with domestic industries in the importing countries, and hence are less subject to protectionist restrictions. Competition from other developing countries is also likely to be less severe as compared with other traditional labour-intensive items such as clothing and footwear. In any event, more strenuous promotion efforts will be needed if the pace of export expansion is to be continued.

Thai exports mostly comprise resource-based and labour-intensive products, which are consistent with the country's perceived comparative advantage. The lag in the development of manufactured exports, compared with the Asian NICs, could be due to the fact that Thailand was relatively rich in natural resources. It was not until 1960 that industrialisation by means of import substitution began to be seriously promoted by the government. During the 1960s, there was little concern for the promotion of manufactured exports. In fact, Thailand was able to develop its industries during the 1960s without much foreign-exchange constraint, since foreign-exchange earnings in service income, direct investment inflows and inflows of foreign aid and loans more than offset the trade deficits resulting from increasing imports of capital and intermediate goods. By the 1970s, however, the growth rates for a number of import-substituting activities decelerated. The balance of payments was also in deficit during 1969–71 after a long period of surpluses. It was during this period that promotion of manufactured exports was seriously considered by the economic planners, and various incentives for manufactured exports were devised in the early 1970s.

The major incentive is the rebate of import duties and business taxes on material imports used in the production of exports. The Bank of Thailand has also offered rediscount facilities with preferential interest rates through commercial banks to provide short-term loans to exporters. In 1975, an Export Service Centre was established to provide information to both Thai and potential foreign exporters. The previous year, the Board of Investment (BOI) extended promotional privileges, with tax and other incentives, to trading companies engaged in exporting. These measures were all geared toward the promotion of manufactured exports. Overall, however, the incentives have been rather modest, compared with those in other developing countries, particularly when higher incentives for local sales through high import tariffs on industrial products are taken into consideration.

Exchange-rate policy

Developments in the world currency market in the 1970s were helpful in correcting the over-valuation of the Baht. The policy of pegging the Baht to the US dollar resulted in its *de facto* devaluation against other major currencies. This may well have helped the competitiveness of Thailand's non-traditional exports since the early 1970s. From 1979 to 1985, however, the situation changed in the opposite direction, as the US dollar appreciated and Thailand's export competitiveness was correspondingly eroded.

The change in exchange-rate policy in 1984 was a major step towards correcting the over-valuation. Since November 1984, the rate has fluctuated around 26–8 Baht to the dollar. It seems that the competitiveness of exports has been a major concern of the Bank of Thailand, as the value of the Baht has not increased much against the dollar even when this was very low.

EXTERNAL FINANCE AND DEBT

Direct foreign investment

Foreign resources in the form of direct investment are usually preferred to loans, for at least two reasons: the cost of servicing is linked to the outcome of the investment and profits may be ploughed back; and secondly, the major movers of international direct investment are multinational firms, which tend to possess certain advantages, particularly in terms of technological knowledge in both production and marketing. Easier access to the markets of the developed world is said to go along with foreign direct investment in export-related activities. Foreign direct investment can also be induced, by means of government-imposed and distorted incentive schemes, into the various import-substituting forms of production. In such cases, the benefits, especially net foreign-exchange saving, may not be apparent.

The recent net inflow of direct investment in Thailand is not impressive. It was an important contributor to net foreign-exchange receipts from the mid-1960s to 1974, but fell to a low point of 3% of capital inflows in 1979. It then recovered to approximately 11% in 1981–2. Its share in the total capital inflow was only 8.5% in 1985.

The principal suppliers are Japan, the United States and the EC, but US investment showed some decline especially during the period 1976–80. In constrast, the share of the Asian NICs, especially Singapore and Hong Kong, became quite large (see Table 5.13). But more important than the source of external finance is, of course, the activities to which the investment has been attracted. Manufacturing activities have been most significant, accounting for nearly one-third of the total (see Table 5.14). Textiles, electrical and electronic goods, chemicals, machinery and transport equipment are among the industries with substantial foreign investment. Other economic sectors with a significant amount are commerce, construction and mining (mainly oil and natural gas exploration).

Much of the investment in manufacturing was made under the official promotion programme. Under the investment promotion law, very generous incentives have been offered to foreign investors. These include tax holidays ranging from three to eight years, exemption from import duties and business taxes on machinery and capital equipment, and reduction of import duties and business taxes on raw materials and intermediate products. There are also additional incentives to export industries and industries located in provincial areas in order to attract foreign as well as domestic investment into these priority sectors. Furthermore, there is a guarantee against nation-alisation, and permission for Board of Investment-promoted foreign firms to own land and to bring in alien skilled workers in excess of what is allowed under the immigration law. Remittance of profits and other foreign-exchange payments have also been freed from restrictions.

Over the past few years, the BOI has been very active in promoting the inflow of foreign investment into certain activities. Compared with other countries in the region with a similar income level, Thailand possesses relatively abundant natural resources and a cheap labour force. Until re-cently, however, direct foreign investment has mostly been made in import-substituting activities. The response of foreign investors to the export pro-motion campaign was unenthusiastic in the 1970s. In recent years, however, more promoted firms have engaged in export activities.

As of the end of 1985, 1,670 firms had been granted investment pro-motional status by the BOI. Of these, 809 had varying degrees of foreign equity participation, but only 48 were wholly foreign-owned, the rest being joint ventures between Thai and foreign investors. Foreign equity accounted for 28% of the total registered capital in BOI-promoted industries, with Japan being the most important investing country, followed by the United States and Taiwan. Promoted activities with a significant proportion of foreign investment include oil and gas exploration, textiles, chemical prod-ucts, rubber, plastic and glass products, iron and basic metals, fabricated metals and machinery, electrical and electronic products, and transport equipment.

Borrowing

The state enterprises and the government itself became major borrowers in the international market around the middle of the 1970s. Their combined share in total capital flows jumped to around 30% in 1975 as compared with generally less than 16% before that date, reached 75% in 1978 and then remained at not less than 50% until 1982. Thereafter it declined somewhat but still averaged about 38%. State enterprises accounted for a large proportion of this public sector borrowing.

The government has generally refrained from direct participation in manufacturing and commercial undertakings since the beginning of the 1960s, confining its intervention to taxation and investment promotion. The public sector provided a basic infrastructure to promote a favourable atmosphere for investment by the private sector. Much of this was financed by external borrowing. Table 5.15 provides statistics of public sector external borrowing by economic activities under the different national economic development plans.

In the early stages of development external funds were relatively small as the government limited external borrowing to US$50–60 million p.a. Its role became significantly more pronounced following the Third Five-Year Social and Economic Development Plan (1972–6). This increase corresponded to the start of the economy's active phase of economic growth. About 33% of external resources went into the energy sector during the period 1961–83, followed by the transport sector. On average, their combined share accounted for about 60% of the external loans, reaching a peak of 80% during the Second Plan period. External loans for military activities increased considerably under the Fourth Plan, from $45m. during the Third Plan period when such borrowing began to $869m. This was even higher than for agriculture.

Table 5.16 provides the proportion of public and private outstanding debt and debt services. In the past public sector debt-service payments were consistently lower than private sector. Before 1980, the debt-service ratio was never as high as 5% of total export earnings. In the four years 1980–3, the public debt-service ratio was successively 5.3%, 7.0%, 8.9% and 10.2%. Since then, the problem of debt payments has adversely affected the whole economy, and led to a significant reduction in government spending and investment.

Outstanding debt for both the public and the private sector expanded from $405m. in 1965 to $1.4bn in 1975, and reached $9.5bn in 1983. In the private sector, it increased from $150m. in 1965 to $736.2m. in 1975 and $2.6bn in 1983, and in the public sector it increased from $255m. in 1965 to $623m. in 1975 and $6.8bn in 1983. Within the latter, state enterprises' debt guaranteed by government increased from $167m. in 1965 to $366m. in 1975, and rapidly expanded to $4.4bn by 1983. Expansion of public utilities in the latter half of the 1970s, especially in electricity, energy and transportation, was the major cause of this.

The increase in state enterprises' outstanding debt reflects:

1. the existence of a growing savings–investment gap in the state enterprise sector;
2. as stated in the Fifth Plan, the urgency of investment projects providing public utilities in various parts of the country, especially.in the rural sector, and

3. in addition to externally financed investment projects, the reliance of state enterprises on foreign resources for use as Baht counterparts in operating those projects.

During the period 1976–83, the amount of external borrowings used in this way showed an increasing trend, and the loans came from private foreign financial institutions under relatively more restricted lending conditions, e.g. at high interest rates with short grace periods.

The savings–investment gap in the state enterprise sector has been attributed partly to inefficient administration in the sector itself. However, it cannot be denied that government policy on price control for some utilities kept their prices unreasonably low. The tariff structure of the State Railway Authority, for example, was kept constant for almost two decades before 1975.

Table 5.17 shows that public utilities were the main borrowers, headed by the Electricity Generating Authority of Thailand (EGAT). Others which also showed an increasing reliance on foreign borrowing were the Telephone Organisation of Thailand, the Provincial Electricity Authority, the Metropolitan Waterworks Authority and the State Railway of Thailand. External resources channelled to state enterprises engaged in manufacturing have shown an increasing trend since 1978, due to the requirements of the National Gas Development Project. The external borrowings of the Petroleum Authority of Thailand (PTT) during 1978–83 totalled $1.23bn making PTT the second most important borrower after EGAT. A significant amount of foreign borrowing for state enterprises engaged in trade and service activities in the years 1977, 1979, 1981 and 1982 can be explained by the external borrowing by Thai Airways International.

At present, state enterprises depend mainly (about 80%) on foreign finance for their development projects. Although this is not a bad thing in itself, and is perhaps unavoidable, it may be appropriate, at present, to slow down some projects where the economic and financial rates of return are questionable, in order to avoid the problem of debt payments in the future. At the same time, the improvement of administrative efficiency should be considered as well as pricing policy in order to narrow the savings–investment gap.

Table 5.18 classifies foreign debt by sources. Over the two decades covering the First up to the Fourth Plan, external borrowings from official lenders, including the World Bank, the Asian Development Bank and foreign governments and agencies, accounted for 64% of total foreign borrowings; of this 37% came from international financial institutions and 27% from the governments of Japan, the United States and West Germany. Private lenders supplied the remaining 36%; of this, about 90% came from private financial institutions and the remaining 10% was suppliers' credits. During the Fourth Plan, there was increasing reliance on private lenders, up to 42% of the total.

This had important implications for the debt burden and debt-service payments because the terms of the loans were not, in general, attractive compared with those of the official lenders.

Reliance on foreign resources is perhaps unavoidable in the process of development for a country like Thailand. The appropriate level of foreign borrowing can facilitate economic growth and investment as well as macro-adjustment. On the other hand, over-spending through incurring debts can have an adverse impact on long-run economic growth and the liquidity of foreign reserves. Huge outstanding debt and service payments mean that resources may in future drain away to the creditor countries. In addition, they may delay certain macro-adjustments needed for long-run sustainable growth.

In the case of Thailand, net resource transfers (disbursements less debt-service payment) in the public sector have shown a positive sign throughout and slightly increased during the years 1979–81. After 1981, the net transfer showed a declining trend; disbursements decreased whereas debt-service payments increased. Net resource transfers in the private sector have in the past shown both negative and positive signs. There may be a negative net resource transfer in future unless cautious consideration of debt policy is undertaken.

The last few years have seen a deterioration in the Thai government's fiscal and financial position. It has been forced to cut back on budgetary outlays and to delay some rural job-creation projects for fear of facing the debt crisis experienced by many other developing countries. This may be a move in the right direction, though it may well affect short-run economic growth and adjustment.

CONCLUSION AND SOME POLICY OPTIONS

Thailand achieved rapid economic growth and development in the period 1969–85. In this process, the openness of its economy substantially increased. The current account deficit as a percentage of GNP also rose during most years in the period 1969–85, and was not adequately offset by the net inflow of foreign capital. There was a balance-of-payments deficit in 1969–71, 1975–9 and 1983. The most recent current account shortfall can be traced to the rapid rise in aggregate domestic overspending. The savings–investment gap for the state enterprises and the Treasury deficit were significantly higher from the middle of the 1970s onwards. Net domestic credit-creation by the banking system helped to finance much of this over-spending.

A strategy of reducing the domestic savings–investment gap has, therefore, become essential and should be undertaken along with the external trade and financial strategies. In particular, the income and expenditure of the state enterprises should be closely examined and decisions regarding their prices and investment, as well as on new undertakings, should be based more firmly on economic realities and potential. The government has adopted several measures in the last few years to reduce its own budget deficit, along with a restriction on the expansion of overall banking credit and the devaluation of the currency in 1984. Nevertheless, the deficit has remained high. It is for the Treasury to continue to try to reduce the budget shortfall.

Though the over-spending of the economy in relation to income may be essentially of a macroeconomic nature, the deterioration of the external account deficit is aggravated by the microeconomic problem of the government's own industrialisation policy of protection against imports. Thailand has experienced relatively rapid industrial progress since the 1960s. Although the private sector makes the investment decisions on most under- takings, the government has provided a favourable basis for industrial development by establishing the infrastructure as well as various incentive systems. At the same time, world economic growth and rapid trade ex- pansion were also quite favourable to developing countries like Thailand, especially in the context of trade liberalisation in the 1960s and 1970s. This favourable environment has changed, however. With the return to a histori- cally normal real income growth in the industrialised countries of around 2.5–3% per annum, Thailand's exports may well be affected, since its major trading partners are still the developed industrialised countries. Moreover, there is an increasing trend towards protectionism in many industrialised countries and this has already affected a number of its major export items. Despite these increasing external constraints, it is important for a small country like Thailand to try to adjust to the changed world environment. In the last decade and a half it has achieved an adjustment, which has resulted in a satisfactory increase in export diversification, in terms of markets as well as products.

There is a need to rationalise policies on trade and industrialisation. There has been distorted industrial growth as a result of heavy import taxes and restrictions on consumer products. Despite increasing attempts to promote exports by reducing taxes on various products, and especially import taxes on tradeable inputs used in export production, overall investment and commercial policies have still been biased towards import substitution. There are high and discriminatory effective protection rates for the import-substitut- ing sectors, together with escalating protection rates for intermediate and capital goods as well as consumer goods.

Such a policy has led to an increasing balance of trade deficit, growth of GDP at a lower rate than that of imports, and a lower rate of employment- creation than of manufacturing output. Protectionist policies may well stimulate growth in the manufacturing sector, reduce imports and improve the balance of trade situation in the short run. But in the long run, heavy protection distorts resource costs and the resource allocation of the econ- omy. It may well not be efficient and may in no way reflect the country's comparative advantage and resource endowment. Its continuing application may then delay structural readjustment for efficient industrial growth. In the 1960s when industrialisation was initiated, import substitution, along with excessive protection, was an easy way to start industrial development, especially in the production of consumer goods, the aim being to build up potential for further industrial growth at a later stage of development. Industrialisation has continued now for more than two decades, and the problem is that most import substitution has turned out to be poorly conceived and has failed to achieve foreign-exchange savings as well as efficient resource allocation. Thailand is endowed with plentiful labour and natural resources but has scarce capital resources and these have been attracted into industrial activities with excessive effective protection and away from other sectors, especially the agricultural sector. Export production has been penalised. An industrialisation process based on import substitution may well be interrupted once the domestic market becomes exhausted, and this leads to a slowdown of industrial and economic growth.

Little in the way of real liberalisation has occurred in tariff and non-tariff control measures. This is due, first, to the fact that import tariffs have been a major source of government revenue. Second, high protection is a quick way of establishing industries, especially those engaged in consumer goods production. Third, trade liberalisation may make the balance of payments more vulnerable in the short run.

Because of the unfavourable world economic situation and the increasing trend towards protectionism, a country like Thailand may face two alternatives if it is to maintain a high industrial growth rate: either moving to the second stage of import substitution or turning to the export of manufactured production. Second-stage import substitution encourages domestic production of intermediate goods and consumer durables. The basic characteristics of these activities are that they tend to be highly capital-intensive, and dependent on sophisticated technology and economies of scale. In a situation of scarcity of capital, low technology and a relatively small domestic market, further inward-oriented strategies require intensive efforts and, perhaps, more protection. At the same time, foreign-exchange savings will be small because of the need to import materials, machinery and technology. Heavy protection for such industrial activities leads to further discrimination against other manufactured and primary exports. A shift should be made in the protection structure in order to obtain less distorted growth in the manufacturing sector. Pursuing a policy of second-stage import substitution now will further misallocate scarce resources and impede the already required macroeconomic adjustment of aggregate overspending in the domestic economy.

The government should seize the opportunity of the current lower real price of oil, which is expected to continue at least for the medium term, and should venture into tariff rationalisation. Formal tariff rates, particularly on imports, which are usually adopted in an *ad hoc* way with varying objectives, have given rise to a highly variable effective rate of protection among the different economic sectors. A change in international trade taxation, giving a lower and more uniform effective protection, should be adopted.

NOTE

1. Since there has been an import ban on passenger cars, buses and trucks since January 1978, the average tariff for this sector in 1982 used in our calculations referred to the rate for vans and pick-ups.

Table 5.1 Composition by sectors of real gross domestic product at 1972 prices, 1970, 1975, 1980, 1985 (percentages)

	1970	1975	1980	1985
Primary products	33.90	31.73	26.49	24.79
Agriculture	32.20	30.50	24.85	23.21
Crops	23.68	22.43	18.50	17.61
Livestock	3.35	3.62	3.08	2.93
Fisheries	3.31	2.82	2.14	1.92
Forestry	1.86	1.64	1.13	0.75
Mining and quarrying	1.70	1.22	1.63	1.59
Manufacturing	15.54	18.08	20.69	20.84
Construction	5.80	4.18	5.66	4.65
Electricity and water supply	1.09	1.56	1.90	2.34
Transportation and communication	6.13	6.61	6.42	6.93
Wholesale and retail trade	17.67	17.58	16.47	15.71
Banking, insurance and real estate	3.87	4.73	5.95	7.76
Ownership of dwellings	2.00	1.75	1.54	1.48
Public administration and defence	4.31	4.11	4.24	3.93
Services	9.69	9.68	10.64	11.58
Gross domestic product (GDP)	100.00	100.00	100.00	100.00
Plus: Net factor income payments from the rest of the world	−2.44	−0.09	−2.83	−4.67
Gross national product (GNP)	97.56	99.91	97.17	95.33
Per capita GNP (Baht)	4025	4856	6126	7038

Source: National Economic and Social Development Board, *Nation Income of Thailand*, various issues.

Table 5.2 Shares of merchandise trade, services and current account deficit in GNP, 1969–85 (percentages)

Year	Merchandise		Trade balance	Services balance	Current account balance
	Exports	Imports			
1969	11.07	19.85	−8.78	4.62	−3.24
1970	10.46	19.43	−8.97	4.42	−3.81
1971	11.54	18.41	−6.87	3.74	−2.51
1972	13.24	18.65	−5.41	4.00	−0.65
1973	14.46	19.46	−5.00	3.16	−0.46
1974	18.01	23.26	−5.25	2.79	−0.66
1975	14.86	21.61	6.75	2.06	−4.14
1976	17.95	21.24	−3.30	0.49	−2.67
1977	18.02	24.57	−6.55	0.62	−5.73
1978	17.71	23.85	−6.14	0.92	−5.05
1979	19.56	28.17	−8.61	0.59	−7.79
1980	19.64	28.26	−8.62	1.66	−6.31
1981	19.64	28.26	−8.61	0.79	−7.33
1982	19.18	23.58	−4.40	1.07	−2.82
1983	16.14	26.07	−9.93	1.86	−7.37
1984	18.08	25.25	−7.17	1.58	−5.15
1985	18.97	25.07	−6.10	1.51	−4.15

Source: Bank of Thailand, *Monthly Bulletin*, various issues.

Table 5.3 Balance of payments, 1969–85 (million Baht)

	1969	1970	1971	1972	1973	1974	1975	1976	1977
Trade balance	-11,310.7	-12,244.8	-9,940.9	-8884.6	-10,802.4	14,302.2	-20,161.2	-11,084.9	-25,598.8
Exports	14,254.2	14,269.7	16,692.1	21,750.2	31,252.5	49,002.4	44,364.5	60,361.2	70,462.8
Imports	-25,564.9	-26,514.5	-26,633.0	-30,634.8	-42,054.9	-63,304.6	-64,525.7	-71,446.1	-96,061.6
Net service balance	5,954.4	6,036.2	5,404.1	6,583.0	6,836.4	7,600.7	6,160.8	1,642.5	2,405.2
Net freight, insurance and other transportation	219.9	222.7	283.5	458.5	548.4	899.8	1,032.8	1,096.9	1,219.2
Net travel	766.5	902.6	914.4	1,431.2	1,944.4	2,171.1	1,746.9	108.7	1,423.2
Net investment income	226.1	379.3	29.6	-327.3	-424.3	-14.3	111.1	-847.5	-1,479.4
Net government services	4,591.2	4,444.5	4,115.2	4,925.7	4,589.5	3,919.8	3,216.1	1,595.7	633.0
Other services	150.7	87.1	61.4	94.9	178.4	624.3	53.9	-311.3	609.2
Net goods and services balance	-5,356.3	-6,208.6	-4,536.8	-2,301.6	-3,966.0	-6,701.5	-14,000.4	-9,442.4	-23,193.6
Transfers	1,187.2	1,011.7	904.1	1,238.8	2,968.8	4,916.9	1,632.1	464.5	801.9
Net private	89.2	57.4	131.1	630.7	2,398.9	4,375.6	1,134.5	100.8	443.3
Net government	1,098.0	954.3	773.0	608.1	569.9	541.3	497.6	363.7	358.6
Current account	-4,169.1	-5,196.9	-3,632.7	-1,062.8	-997.2	-1,784.6	-12,368.3	-8,977.9	-22,391.7
Capital movements	2,897.6	2,478.8	1,733.1	3,643.2	2,937.6	9,054.7	7,754.7	9,263.6	13,966.9
Direct investment	1,057.5	890.5	808.4	1,427.1	1,604.9	3,836.3	1,744.8	1,614.1	2,163.8
Private long-term	1,399.7	1,252.1	499.9	1,670.4	-987.2	2,833.4	1,351.2	667.8	970.7
Loans and credits	1,299.2	1,007.7	397.0	1,392.5	-1,199.0	2,637.1	1,316.7	689.3	867.2
Portfolio and others	100.5	244.4	102.9	277.9	211.8	196.3	34.5	-21.5	103.5
Private short-term	186.0	183.4	154.8	309.1	1,292.4	1,131.3	2,600.3	2,778.5	5,226.1
State enterprises	272.2	90.7	60.2	338.3	372.7	1,173.9	2,203.0	1,839.3	4,767.3
Long-term	272.2	90.7	60.2	338.3	372.7	1,173.9	2,203.0	1,839.3	4,767.3
Short-term	0.0	0.0	0.0	0.0	0.0	0.0	0.0	0.0	0.0
Local & central government	-17.8	62.1	209.8	-101.7	654.8	79.8	-144.6	2,363.9	838.7
SDRs	0.0	0.0	298.2	320.7	0.0	0.0	0.0	0.0	0.0
Net errors and omissions	357.7	66.1	1,266.2	1,090.3	-1,076.2	741.9	1,755.6	-368.5	886.9
Overall balance	-913.8	-2,652.0	-335.2	3,991.4	864.2	8,012.0	-2,858.0	-82.8	-7,537.9

Table 5.3 (continued)

	1978	1979	1980	1981	1982	1983	1984	1985
Trade balance	−28,540.0	−47,053.1	−57,984.8	−65,781.9	−36,136.7	−89,237.1	−68,795.8	−61,671.5
Exports	82,250.8	106,881.2	132,040.5	150,218.2	157,203.4	145,076.1	173,520.0	191,703.0
Imports	−110,790.8	−153,934.3	−190,025.3	−216,000.1	−193,340.1	−234,313.2	−242,315.8	−253,374.5
Net service balance	4,279.1	3,237.9	11,144.9	6,042.4	8,795.0	16,758.4	15,199.5	15,284.2
Net freight, insurance and other transportation	833.8	1,079.2	1,589.7	1,570.3	2,562.2	3,614.4	4,641.4	4,914.5
Net travel	5,315.5	6,584.2	12,776.5	15,428.3	17,727.7	17,154.3	20,026.9	24,146.1
Net investment income	−4,811.7	−9,105.1	−11,685.4	−20,726.8	−24,982.7	−23,749.7	−30,219.0	−38,177.8
Net government services	813.2	1,142.7	1,795.1	688.8	731.8	1,134.8	1,302.3	1,940.5
Other services	2,128.3	3,536.9	6,669.0	9,081.8	12,756.0	18,604.6	19,447.9	22,424.9
Net goods and services balance	−24,260.9	−43,815.2	−46,839.9	−59,739.5	−27,341.7	−72,478.7	−53,596.3	−46,423.3
Transfers	816.0	1,224.0	4,430.5	3,690.2	4,203.5	6,376.6	4,128.1	4,494.1
Net private	128.0	461.9	1,529.9	1,100.8	1,723.4	3,517.9	1,407.3	1,273.6
Net government	688.0	762.1	2,900.6	2,589.4	2,480.1	2,858.7	2,720.8	3,220.5
Current account	−23,444.9	−42,591.2	−42,409.4	−56,049.3	−23,138.2	−66,102.1	−49,468.2	−41,929.2
Capital movements	14,858.3	33,766.8	50,736.6	55,130.2	38,345.2	34,497.2	58,365.0	51,468.8
Direct investment	1,010.8	1,047.7	3,816.0	6,363.2	4,338.6	8,008.3	9,624.6	4,379.2
Private long-term	888.3	8,460.3	14,861.0	19,076.7	9,971.7	5,087.3	25,577.5	7,585.0
Loans and credits	689.3	6,314.5	13,708.4	18,948.0	9,066.7	4,956.9	24,947.5	3,269.0
Portfolio and others	199.0	2,145.8	1,152.6	128.7	905.0	130.4	630.0	4,316.0
Private short-term	1,696.2	3,567.2	6,846.9	−4,379.6	2,960.4	4,987.5	6,949.9	7,657.9
State enterprises	5,170.8	12,143.6	19,003.1	26,044.4	13,477.6	10,325.2	10,547.4	12,806.9
Long-term	5,170.8	12,143.6	18,184.4	19,173.3	15,478.6	12,372.2	11,665.0	16,482.0
Short-term	0.0	0.0	818.7	6,871.1	−2,001.0	−2,047.0	−1,117.6	−3,675.1
Local & central government	6,092.2	8,548.0	6,209.6	8,025.5	7,596.9	6,088.9	5,665.6	19,039.8
SDRs	0.0	493.6	506.4	488.0	0.0	0.0	0.0	0.0
Net errors and omissions	−4,711.4	405.8	−3,654.3	2,962.3	−11,892.7	13,526.9	1,691.2	2,924.3
Overall balance	−13,298.0	−7,925.0	5,179.3	2,531.2	3,314.3	−18,078.0	10,588.0	12,463.9

Source: Bank of Thailand, *Monthly Bulletin*, 1969–85.

Table 5.4 Sectoral balances, 1969–84 (million Baht)

Year	Private sector $(S_p - I_p)$	Govt enterprises $(S_{gp} - I_{gp})$	Govt sector $(T - G)$	Net foreign investment[a]	Statistical discrepancy
1969	−161	−2,022	−2,809	−4,156	836
1970	187	−1,344	−5,481	−5,197	1,441
1971	2,020	−877	−7,281	−3,267	2,871
1972	11,542	−2,136	−7,674	−1,063	−2,795
1973	12,850	−762	−4,874	−997	−8,211
1974	2,056	−1,341	2,006	−1,785	−4,506
1975	2,008	−3,633	−6,730	−12,368	−4,013
1976	14,927	−6,389	−16,155	−8,978	−1,361
1977	5,719	−10,899	−12,458	−22,392	−4,754
1978	9,769	−14,983	−12,715	−23,445	−5,516
1979	2,456	−21,315	−13,154	−42,591	−10,578
1980	27,997	−34,853	−25,658	−42,409	−9,895
1981	29,496	−38,531	−21,360	−56,049	−25,654
1982	51,952	−31,988	−41,120	−23,138	−1,982
1983	14,914	−36,467	−22,824	−66,102	−21,725
1984	15,214	−44,865	−33,183	−49,450	13,384

[a] Minus signs indicate inflows from abroad.

Source: Bank of Thailand, *Monthly Bulletin*, various issues.

Table 5.5 Share of total imports by economic classification (percentages)

Type of import	1960	1969	1970	1975	1980	1981	1982	1983	1984	1985
Consumer goods	34.97	26.97	19.91	12.65	10.22	10.60	11.57	12.55	13.03	13.86
non-durable	26.58	18.91	12.91	7.70	6.49	6.28	6.61	6.78	7.21	7.94
durable	8.39	8.06	7.00	4.95	3.73	4.32	4.98	5.77	5.82	5.91
Intermediate products and raw materials	18.15	20.80	24.90	24.10	24.01	24.72	24.72	25.16	25.10	26.31
chiefly for consumer goods	10.71	13.79	15.32	15.44	14.93	15.56	15.48	15.72	15.92	16.49
chiefly for capital goods	7.44	7.01	9.58	8.66	9.08	9.16	9.24	9.44	9.18	9.82
Capital goods	24.60	30.94	34.70	33.27	24.42	26.19	24.30	29.31	29.54	29.56
machinery	14.08	17.44	22.74	22.00	16.75	16.93	16.37	20.70	21.17	19.67
others	10.52	13.50	11.96	11.27	7.67	9.26	7.93	8.61	8.37	9.89
Other imports	22.28	21.29	20.49	29.98	41.34	38.48	39.40	32.97	32.32	30.27
vehicles and parts	7.85	9.42	8.16	6.80	3.66	4.41	3.91	4.82	4.83	3.70
fuel and lubricants	10.65	8.77	8.62	21.30	31.12	30.03	30.91	24.12	23.39	22.58
other	3.78	3.10	3.71	1.88	6.55	4.04	4.58	4.03	4.10	3.99
Total imports	100.0	100.0	100.0	100.0	100.0	100.0	100.0	100.0	100.0	100.0
(million Baht)	9,622	15,433	27,009	66,835	188,686	216,746	196,616	236,609	245,155	251,169

Source: Bank of Thailand, *Monthly Bulletin*, 1975, 1980, 1985.

Table 5.6 Ranking of import dependency by industries, 1975 and 1980

1975		1980	
Sector	Imports/ total supply	Sector	Imports/ total supply
More than 50% import dependency			
Petroleum and natural gas	100.00	Petroleum and natural gas	99.89
Wood and metal machines	75.19	Wood and metal machines	77.62
Raw materials for textiles	67.14	Synthetic resin, plastic and	
Aircraft	65.97	artificial fibre	74.38
Synthetic resin, plastic and artifi-		Aircraft	68.80
cial fibre	65.38	Chemical products	65.65
Office and household machinery		Basic industrial chemicals	65.13
and appliances	61.78	Fertiliser and pesticides	59.70
Special industrial machinery	60.02	Scientific equipment	59.41
Fabricated metal products	59.74	Special industrial machinery	57.79
Chemical products	58.09	Electrical industrial machinery	54.74
Fertiliser and pesticides	58.08	Engines and turbines	53.84
Other petroleum products	55.41	Fabricated metal products	52.30
Engines and turbines	54.63	Photographic and optical goods	52.09
Photographic and optical goods	54.10	Secondary steel products	51.41
Electrical industrial machinery	53.23	Raw material for textiles	50.35
Other electrical apparatus and			
supplies	53.08		
Motor vehicles	50.75		
30–50% import dependency			
Scientific equipment	47.98	Watches and clocks	46.97
Basic industrial chemicals	45.69	Electrical apparatus and supplies	46.50
Mining and quarrying	40.85	Mining and quarrying	45.05
		Other rubber products	20.70
		Dairy products	20.24
		Livestocks	18.55
		Glass and glass products	18.30
		Insulated wire and cables	16.92
		Non-ferrous metals	16.40

Source: Calculated from Thailand Input–Output Tables.

Table 5.7 Share of imports by countries, 1974–84 (percentages)

Country	1974	1975	1977	1980	1984	1985
USA	13.49	14.01	12.29	14.42	13.33	11.32
Japan	31.39	31.55	32.35	21.19	26.95	26.51
EEC	19.01	17.06	14.46	13.15	12.07	14.39
Malaysia	0.28	0.42	0.95	1.80	4.86	5.90
Singapore	1.57	1.96	2.96	6.50	7.90	7.46
Taiwan	2.41	0.96	1.15	0.95	1.24	3.10
Hong Kong	1.35	0.96	1.15	0.95	1.24	1.17
South Korea	0.61	0.66	1.02	2.14	2.75	2.02
Middle East	16.66	17.62	16.04	16.89	9.12	3.67

Source: Bank of Thailand.

Table 5.8 Imports from major suppliers by economic classification, 1977 and 1984 (percentages)

	Japan		USA		EC		NICs	
	1977	1984	1977	1984	1977	1984	1977	1984
Consumer goods	12.32	15.38	10.52	10.00	24.07	23.69	22.43	15.83
Clothing & footwear	2.23	2.47			0.57	0.96	8.86	7.93
Elec. appliances	3.35	7.04	1.21	1.17	1.78	0.84	3.00	2.86
Intermediate & raw materials	33.30	26.70	39.15	24.73	31.60	30.68	20.05	16.48
Chemicals	11.59	9.09	9.35	10.57	21.55	20.21	5.63	5.43
Iron & steel	16.74	13.64			2.63	4.56	3.86	3.06
Capital goods	31.47	40.87	39.84	47.53	34.11	35.01	18.51	25.20
Metal mfrs	2.29	2.29	2.83	1.79	2.17	2.19	1.55	1.50
Non-elec. mach.	19.04	24.11	14.98	14.16	14.79	16.76	10.11	12.74
Elec. mach.	4.70	8.06	8.04	17.61	7.95	7.07	2.59	5.18
Scientific inst.	0.95	1.78	2.37	3.14	1.45	3.18	0.82	0.86
Other imports	23.06	17.05	12.48	17.75	10.22	10.62	39.00	42.49
Vehicles & parts	21.63	15.14			5.41	3.15	0.32	0.18
Fuel and lubric.	0.48	0.69	1.10	0.56	1.16	0.42	36.16	40.45
Munitions			8.25	13.66	1.22	5.46	0.83	0.37

Source: Customs Department.

Table 5.9 Export/output ratio by industry, 1975 and
1980 (percentages)

Industry	Export output ratio	
	1975	1980
Food	21.8	32.0
Beverages	0.1	0.6
Tobacco	7.1	7.9
Textiles	8.1	13.7
Leather	5.8	22.6
Wood & wood products	17.1	8.8
Paper & paper products	1.3	1.7
Basic industrial chemicals	1.2	8.7
Chemical products	2.5	2.9
Refineries & petroleum products	1.5	0.2
Rubber & rubber products	58.9	80.4
Plastic products	5.6	11.5
Ceramic and earthenware	4.4	16.4
Glass and glass products	2.2	6.4
Other non-metallic products	15.4	1.1
Iron & steel	1.6	9.3
Non-ferrous metal	57.7	82.9
Fabricated metal	5.1	14.5
Machinery	1.7	5.1
Electrical industrial machinery and appliance	10.9	33.2
Transport equipment	0.2	0.3
Other manufactured products	19.0	49.1
Total	13.8	20.0

Source: Thailand Input–Output Tables, 1975 and 1980.

Table 5.10 Distribution of exports by SITC commodity group (percentages)

SITC	Commodity	1960	1965	1970	1975	1980	1984	1985
0	Food	46.45	53.61	48.82	60.35	45.50	50.26	45.19
1	Beverages & tobacco	0.29	0.71	1.45	1.31	1.07	0.98	0.86
2	Crude materials	51.09	39.09	29.91	15.44	14.64	10.97	10.23
3	Mineral fuels & lubricants		0.32	0.32	0.56	0.06	0.24	1.28
4	Animal and vegetable oils and fats	0.02	0.06	0.10	0.09	.0.17	0.25	0.30
5	Chemicals	0.09	0.12	0.23	0.55	0.72	1.27	1.27
6	Manufactured goods	1.14	4.74	15.35	14.56	22.60	16.96	18.71
7	Machinery	0.01	0.07	0.11	1.30	5.84	6.95	8.86
8	Miscellaneous manufactured goods	0.17	0.22	0.41	3.59	6.49	11.37	12.54
9	Miscellaneous transactions and commodities	0.72	1.06	3.31	2.23	2.89	0.75	0.75
	Total	100.00	100.00	100.00	100.00	100.00	100.00	100.00

Source: Bank of Thailand, *Monthly Bulletin*, various issues.

Table 5.11 Shares and growth of principal exports (percentages)

Commodity	Distribution				Average annual growth rate		
	1970	1975	1980	1984	1970–5	1975–80	1980–4
Rice	23.55	17.39	19.75	19.75	18.39	27.23	7.37
Rubber	20.89	10.33	12.51	9.90	9.25	28.87	1.29
Maize	18.43	16.96	7.39	7.73	23.71	5.05	8.58
Tapioca products	11.45	13.66	15.07	12.64	30.32	26.49	2.76
Prawns	2.09	2.65	1.98	2.13	31.80	17.09	9.30
Tin	15.14	6.68	11.49	4.02	6.79	38.24	−17.41
Sugar	0.88	16.93	3.01	3.98	127.24	−12.18	15.10
IC products			6.23	5.60			4.54
Textile products	0.90	5.91	9.76	14.59	83.36	37.11	18.72
Precious stones	1.22	2.33	3.28	4.67	43.28	32.78	12.27
Footwear	0.002	0.04	0.36	1.56	130.81	88.61	54.73
Tobacco leaves	1.84	1.69	1.39	1.25	23.63	19.22	4.55
Mung beans	2.59	1.38	1.46	1.35	12.77	25.50	5.27
Canned pineapples	9.51	1.03	1.45	2.17	44.46	32.85	18.73
Canned fish			0.61	2.81			57.34
Canned crustaceans			1.00	1.64			21.65
Fresh cuttlefish	0.36	1.52	1.45	2.17	68.29	29.53	18.73
Wood products	0.34	1.48	1.38	1.25	69.05	22.35	4.83
Combined shares of principal exports[a]	97.00	99.94	98.98	99.21	26.33	2.31	28.35
Other exports	3.00	0.06	1.02	0.79	−45.75	145.66	−6.69

a. Items of which export value exceeds 1 per cent of total exports.
Source: Bank of Thailand, *Monthly Bulletin*, various issues.

Table 5.12 Distribution and growth of exports to major importing countries
(percentages)

Country	Annual average growth rate				
	1970	1975	1980	1985	1980–1
USA	13.4	12.6	12.6	19.7	17.69
Japan	25.5	31.5	15.1	13.4	5.14
Netherlands	8.6	11.5	13.2	7.1	−4.83
Singapore	6.9	10.3	7.7	7.9	8.32
Malaysia	5.6	5.3	4.5	5.0	10.00
Hong Kong	7.5	6.9	5.1	4.0	2.94
West Germany	3.6	2.8	4.1	3.7	5.53
Saudi Arabia	2.2	1.5	1.7	2.3	13.56
China		0.9	1.9	3.8	23.82
UK	2.1	1.3	1.8	2.4	13.54
Italy	1.9	0.6	1.9	1.7	4.45
France	1.0	0.9	1.6	1.9	10.40
Iran	0.2	0.9	1.6	0.9	−3.66
S. Korea	0.3		0.7	1.9	28.81
Australia	0.5	1.8	1.1	1.7	18.69
Taiwan	4.9	1.1	1.3	1.6	11.81
Belgium	6.7	2.7	2.5	1.2	−6.81
Nigeria		0.08	1.1	1.0	6.00
Indonesia	2.3	2.1	3.6	0.6	−24.6
Philippines	0.05	1.8	0.3	0.8	24.76
Brunei		0.3	0.1	0.2	15.35
Others	11.7	22.6	14.41	17.2	9.36
Total	100.00	100.00	100.00	100.00	7.74

Source: Bank of Thailand.

Table 5.13 Net private direct investment by country, 1971–85

Country	Amount (million Baht)			Percentage distribution		
	1971–5	1976–80	1981–5	1971–5	1976–80	1981–5
Japan	2,485.3	3,063.0	8,975.3	26.38	31.73	27.28
USA	3,762.5	2,398.5	10,593.5	39.94	24.85	32.20
UK	531.8	611.3	1,689.0	5.64	6.33	5.14
West Germany	71.9	597.0	782.2	0.76	6.18	2.38
France	251.4	17.5	292.1	2.67	0.18	0.87
Netherlands	245.3	107.5	2,072.4	2.60	1.11	6.30
Italy	87.1	517.1	243.0	0.92	5.36	0.74
Switzerland	178.3	200.3	405.6	1.89	2.08	1.23
Canada	48.6	−118.5	225.7	0.52	−1.23	0.69
Australia	67.0	41.9	287.5	0.71	0.43	0.87
Hong Kong	932.8	1,327.1	2,797.3	9.90	13.75	8.50
Singapore	496.7	668.3	1,180.2	5.27	6.92	3.59
Malaysia	100.5	158.8	217.5	1.07	1.65	0.66
Philippines	43.0	−0.6	26.7	0.46	−0.01	0.08
Taiwan	37.7	0.9	257.2	0.40	0.01	0.78
Others	81.6	62.3	2,852.0	0.87	0.65	8.67
Total	9,421.5	9,652.4	32,897.2	100.00	100.00	100.00

Source: Bank of Thailand.

Table 5.14 Net inflow of direct investment by economic sector, 1971–85 (million Baht)

Economic sector	1971–4	1975	1980	1985	Total (1971–85) Amount	%
Finance	1,623.0	392.9	−223.9	−1,279.3	1,889.7	3.64
Trade	1,308.9	545.4	745.2	1,061.2	9,814.5	18.88
Construction	767.4	168.6	782.6	1,584.8	7,980.5	15.35
Mining & quarrying	1,446.1	62.3	590.7	515.9	9,706.5	18.68
Oil exploration	1,362.6	33.7	440.9	430.0	8,556.5	16.46
Others	83.5	28.6	149.8	85.8	1,149.9	2.21
Agriculture	25.1	2.1	209.8	76.9	439.5	0.85
Industry	2,058.5	582.1	1,014.8	1,355.6	16,773.6	32.28
Food	281.9	82.3	91.2	393.3	1,223.4	2.35
Textiles	1,023.9	192.6	−1.5	58.9	2,794.4	5.38
Metal-based and non-metallic	140.4	22.1	47.8	−125.7	1,529.6	2.94
Electrical appliances	222.8	110.1	448.2	280.0	4,588.4	8.83
Machinery & transport equipment	50.9	1.8	92.2	32.0	1,328.6	2.56
Chemicals	203.4	91.6	213.4	488.4	2,185.5	4.21
Petroleum products	17.9	43.4	2.2	—	2,170	4.17
Construction materials	46.3	7.0	1.4	38.3	13.7	0.03
Others	71.0	31.2	119.9	190.4	937.0	1.80
Services	446.8	−8.6	696.8	1,063.5	5,366.0	10.32
Transportation & travel	208.5	−21.7	214.9	197.9	2,215.8	4.26
Housing & real estate	91.2	0.1	150.9	305.5	788.8	1.52
Hotels & restaurant	79.7	13.6	87.7	222.9	769.9	1.48
Others	67.4	−0.6	243.3	337.2	1,583.4	3.05
Total	7,675.8	1,744.8	3,816.0	4,379.2	51,970.2	100.00

Source: Bank of Thailand.

Table 5.15 External loans to public sector by economic activities (percentages)

Economic activities	The First Plan (1961–6)	The Second Plan (1967–71)	The Third Plan (1972–6)	The Fourth Plan (1977–81)	Plans 1–4 (1961–81)	1982	1983
Energy	18.0	54.6	26.0	38.1	36.2	37.0	25.1
Transportation	46.9	25.6	22.2	24.9	25.3	31.7	23.7
Agriculture	13.0	8.8	17.8	8.8	10.3	12.2	14.2
Manufacturing	6.7	7.6	7.7	2.6	3.6		7
Public utilities	13.5	2.2	5.7	4.1	4.6	1.2	
Social developement	1.9	0.3	1.6	4.5	3.8	1.0	1.1
Education			5.5	0.7	1.4	3.6	
Health				0.7	0.5	0.1	0.6
Military			3.4	12.1	10.0	6.0	7.5
Others		1.0	10.1	3.5	4.2	7.1[a]	18.3[b]
Total	100.0	100.0	100.0	100.0	100.0	100.0	100.0
(million dollars)	323	335	1,304	7,182	9,143	2,100	1,183

a. Included Structural Adjustment Loan (SAL) of 150.0 million dollars.
b. Included Structural Adjustment Loan (SAL) of 175.5 million dollars.
Source: Pranee Tinnakorn and Direk Pattamasiriwat, 'External debt of developing countries: a case study of Thailand's external debt', paper prepared for the Symposium on the Debt Crisis of the Thai government, 1985.

Table 5.16 Distribution of outstanding debt and debt-service payments in private and public sectors (percentages)

	1970	1975	1980	1984
Outstanding debt	100.00	100.00	100.00	100.00
Private	53.55	54.15	30.45	27.92
Public	46.45	45.85	69.55	72.08
Government's debt	23.56	17.34	25.45	25.84
State enterprises' debt with government guarantee	18.27	26.91	42.24	46.20
Public debt without government guarantee	4.62	1.60	1.86	0.04
Debt-service payments	100.00	100.00	100.00	100.00
Private	74.52	71.12	64.10	47.17
Public	25.48	21.53	35.90	52.83
Government's debt	9.05	7.71	16.29	21.10
State enterprises' debt with government guarantee	14.09	11.95	19.02	31.69
Public debt without government guarantee	2.34	11.87	0.59	0.04

Table 5.17 Foreign borrowing of state enterprises by economic activities, 1974–83 (percentages)

Year	Public utility	Infra-structure	Manu-facturing	Trade and service	Finance
1974	100.00				
1975	91.29				8.71
1976	100.00				
1977	42.52		0.93	34.86	14.68
1978	67.58	17.09	3.78	11.55	
1979	42.42	4.83	19.66	27.44	5.65
1980	69.14	6.52	22.28	0.80	1.26
1981	62.00		29.28	7.57	1.15
1982	26.86	9.71	49.31	12.89	1.23
1983	66.94	8.96	8.31	2.28	13.51

Source: Calculated from the data from BOT.

Table 5.18 Distribution of external borrowing of public sector by sources of fund (percentages)

	Outstanding debt			New borrowing			
	1970	1980	1983	1972–6	1977–81	1982	1983
Official lenders	89.1	52.7	60.1	89.0	58.1	69.7	80.7
International financial institutions	48.3	24.4	33.2	60.2	31.0	34.6	45.9
IBRD				37.7	19.6	29.3	32.5
IDA				2.4	1.3	—	—
ADB				20.1	9.0	3.3	10.4
IFAD				—	0.4	—	1.7
OPEC				—	0.6	—	1.3
Foreign governments	40.9	27.8	26.9	28.8	27.1	35.1	34.9
USA				6.7	5.9	4.5	7.8
Germany				1.9	2.3	1.0	2.3
Japan				18.1	15.9	23.3	23.6
Other[a]				2.0	3.1	4.3	1.1
Private lenders	10.9	47.8	39.9	11.0	41.9	30.3	19.3
Financial markets	0.7	45.1	36.7	11.0	38.9	28.3	19.3
Suppliers' credits	10.1	2.7	3.2	—	3.0	2.0	—

a. Including United Kingdom, Canada, Denmark, Switzerland, Kuwait, France, New Zealand, Belgium, Saudi Arabia and Australia.

Source: Pranee Tinnakorn and Direk Pathamasiriwat, 'External debt of developing countries: a case study of Thailand's external debt', A paper prepared for the Symposium on Debt Crisis of the Thai government, 1985.

6

COLOMBIA

JUAN JOSÉ ECHAVARRIA

Colombia emerges as such a shining example of growth and pragmatic and successful macromanagement . . . that it is tempting to suggest that here is a country that has really managed to mesh short-term adjustment with its long-term development strategy: Brazil, but without the inflation. (Thorp and Whitehead, 1987: 330).

EXTERNAL SHOCKS

The international environment faced by the different countries of Latin America was similar in many aspects, but the magnitude and consequences of the external shocks faced in the 1970s and 1980s were different. For Colombia, coffee was a special commodity in the 'commodity lottery'; exports of drugs contributed heavily to foreign-exchange earnings; and the country has always been more or less self-sufficient in oil. Colombia also followed a very conservative economic policy, especially on the external front: it never borrowed heavily abroad, and its pragmatic fiscal and monetary policies were always governed by fear of inflation. Even more important, most of its policy-makers were always sceptical about the positive contribution of the international mobility of money. Some financial liberalisation occurred in 1974 and 1978, but it was mainly domestic, and financial flows into and out of the country were always well controlled.

This chapter reviews the effect of two external shocks on the economy, the macroeconomic policies adopted in reaction to them, and their ultimate effect on growth. Comparisons are made with other Latin American countries and with other coffee producers in order to highlight particular aspects of the Colombian case.

Terms of trade

Latin American terms of trade in the first part of the 1980s were the lowest since the 1930s. Their index in 1986 was roughly half the average for the 1950s – their highest level. The decline began (Echavarria, 1982c; CEPAL, 1986) during the 1960s, and after a small improvement in 1970–4, started to fall again, dropping 20% between 1981 and 1986.

Colombian terms of trade behaved very differently. They improved in the second part of the 1970s, and in 1986 were 13% higher than in 1981. Coffee prices in 1977 were the highest ever recorded, and the level reached in April of that year (US$3.20/lb) represented nearly five times the maximum price registered in the previous 'bonanza' (1950–5) (Junguito et al., 1977: 218) and seven times the 1960s maximum. They dropped between 1979 and 1984, but their level in 1984 was not historically low (see Table 6.1). The new coffee 'bonanza' of 1986 was again untypical. Terms of trade for non-coffee exports were comparatively stable, but the importance of coffee in total exports was (and is) so high that the aggregate terms of trade behaved similarly to coffee.

Coffee prices were highly unstable after 1970. Only sugar, oil and cocoa were more unstable between 1970 and 1980 (see Table 6.1). This was especially important for Colombia, as coffee represents more than half of its total exports, a figure unusual even by Latin American standards. Excluding the exceptional case of Venezuela (oil), only Chile (copper) presents similar levels of concentration (see Table 9.8).

Foreign borrowing

International prices, total exports and oil imports were only marginally influenced by government policies. One might therefore say that some countries did better just because they were luckier. However, foreign borrowing was under government control. The supply of foreign funds was almost 'unlimited' in the 1970s, when petro-dollars were internationally recycled. Each country 'decided' how much it 'wanted'. Again, Colombia presents a very different case, largely because of the behaviour of coffee exports, the fear of inflation,[1] the absence of projects ready to be undertaken by the government and the fear of state interventionism in the economy. The country did not want to 'dance' with foreign bankers. It borrowed US$1,249m. in 1970, US$2,348m. in 1975 and US$3,343m. in 1979. Its stock of debt in 1984 was US$7,541m. (Berry and Thoumi, 1985).

We can distinguish five periods in this foreign borrowing:

1. 1970–2, fast growth;
2. 1972–8, when the stock of total debt decreased more than 20% in real terms, with private borrowing tightly controlled;
3. 1979–82 when debt increased at rates similar to the rest of Latin America and private borrowing increased even faster;[2]

4. 1982–5 when Colombia was one of the few countries in Latin America able to obtain fresh loans for both the private and public sectors. The ratio of the stock of debt to exports in 1985 was the highest since 1970, and the situation is even worse if we consider the ratio of interest payments to exports.
5. In 1986 Colombia did not need new loans. Nominal interest rates doubled after 1978/80 (to 13% from 7%); they decreased after 1982, but rose in real terms. Average maturity of the loans decreased between 1970 (21 years) and 1978 (14 years) to remain fairly constant thereafter. The average grace period has been stable.

Compared with other Latin American countries, Colombia had the lowest ratio of debt to GNP or exports in 1979 (except for Venezuela) and in 1986 (except for Paraguay).

Balance of payments

In Latin American terms, the two most distinctive characteristics of the Colombian foreign sector are, first, the low weight of oil imports; 30% of Brazilian exports are committed for payment for oil imports. Second, the country did not 'adjust' as the other countries did, at least not until 1984. At the beginning of the international crisis its international reserves were much higher than those of the average Latin American country (in terms of GDP and imports), but this was no longer true in 1984, when it was in a comparatively weak position.

Colombia's international reserves suffered major fluctuations during this period (see Table 6.2). From low (and unstable) levels in 1970–4 (equivalent to three months of imports in 1974), they jumped to US$5bn (14 months) in 1980. They began to decrease in 1982, fell by a half in 1983 and 1984, and only recovered in 1986.

The real deficits in the trade account and surpluses in the capital account during the first half of the 1980s were much larger than in any year of the 1970s, and tended to balance each other throughout the period considered. The ratio of interest payments to GDP was one quarter of that for Latin American oil-exporting countries, and one-fifth of that for the oil-importing countries. Capital inflows had been large at the beginning of the 1970s when the current account was highly negative, and decreased when it improved. They were modest in 1975–8. In 1978–9, Colombia borrowed abroad when its reserves were rising, and this was seen as a sign of incoherent policy, although *ex post*, when the unforeseen international recession arrived, this could be justified. Short-term borrowing has always been a minor portion of the capital account; the increase in capital borrowing in 1979–84 was in long-term borrowing. Direct investment in 1981 and 1982 was higher than in any year of the 1970s, but still represented less than 25% of long-term borrowing.[3] On the current account, interest and amortisation payments (most of the difference between the trade and current balances) were high both between 1970 and 1973 and after 1982.

The significant deterioration of the current account from 1980 to 1984 was the result of a fall in real exports (up to 1983), and increases in imports (up to 1982). Among exports, coffee, drugs and 'non-traditional' exports were of roughly similar importance.[4] However, the evolution of total registered exports was determined mainly by coffee; 'non-traditional' exports did not show large fluctuations. The year 1975 marked the end of a decade in which growth was based on non-traditional exports. They represented 60% of total exports in 1974, but then decreased year by year to traditional levels.[5] The important point is that the crisis in minor exports did not start in the 1980s. Manufactured exports increased much more than those of any other Latin American country between 1970 and 1974,[6] but then decreased in real terms and even in nominal terms after 1980.

Colombia was a net oil exporter in 1973, 1975 and 1984, and net oil imports in the intermediate years never represented more than 13% of total exports. Its import volume was not reduced drastically during the 1980s. Investment was not restricted by foreign-exchange constraints. Capital goods imports grew more than consumer or intermediate goods. Colombia shows the typical developing country import structure, with capital goods imports being more than 40% of the total and manufactured imports 65%.

In 1985, some tough, very 'orthodox' and *ex post* rather unnecessary policies were followed; no doubt similar policies would have been applied in 1986. Colombia would then have had the typical Latin American adjustment with a delay of three years. But sudden and unforeseen changes in some important economic variables made things easier. The new coffee 'bonanza' of 1986, and the external impact of the tough policies adopted in 1984/5 brought in foreign exchange; this and the good long-run prospects in the coal sector convinced international bankers, the IMF and the World Bank to treat Colombia as a special case (see below). New loans made the external situation even better. The adjustment process thus lasted only one year and was remarkably mild.

We have already hinted at the problems of predicting the Colombian balance of payments. The economy depends too heavily on a single, very unstable commodity. Nobody was able to forecast the coffee bonanza of 1975–9 or the new boom of 1986. In 1975–9 the subsequent fall was not expected. Some economists began to discuss 'structural' world developments (wars in Africa and Central America) which could keep coffee prices high. In the future, the problems of prediction will worsen: the Colombian foreign sector will depend increasingly on oil and coal exports, two other very unstable commodities.

However, we must make our best guesses. It is relatively clear that the economy will not face another coffee bonanza as large as that of 1975–9, which was much larger than any previous 'bonanza'. Junguito *et al.* (1977)

conclude that very large booms occur every 25 years. The boom of 1986 was very mild. According to World Bank predictions, real coffee prices in 1990 will be similar to those in 1983 – a bad year – being relatively constant in the second half of the 1980s (Thomas, 1985: 34).

Based on the agreed assumptions, Table 6.3 presents some guesses about the future of the balance of payments.[7] There will be large and increasing current account deficits for the rest of the 1980s, particularly after 1988, as trade surpluses will be insufficient to pay for services and transfers, which in 1988 and 1989 will be equal to total coffee exports. However, relative to exports or GNP the deficits will not be comparable with the worst years, 1982 and 1983. The ratio of debt to exports has been falling since its peak in 1985, and this trend will continue during the rest of the decade.

The present combined share of oil and coal is 15%, and will jump to 36% in 1990. This means both good and bad news. A larger percentage of revenue from these exports than from coffee will go directly to the state, and it is likely that the combined price of the three commodities will fluctuate less than the price of coffee alone. But the price of coal is tied to the price of oil, and both activities are very capital-intensive and create few jobs.

SAVINGS AND INVESTMENT

1970–85

Levels of savings and investment are very low in Colombia compared with other countries,[8] but also very stable, because fluctuations in external and public savings have been mutually offsetting. However, the aggregates hide the crucial fact that the private and public sectors behave very differently: the public sector saves much less than it invests, and the difference is becoming more conspicuous as private investment has been falling (and public investment rising) (Table 6.4).

This has been used to argue that government expansion has produced 'crowding out'; the private sector does not have enough resources to invest, but this must be examined. In order to prove that crowding out has occurred, it must be shown that the private sector would invest more if additional resources were available.

Some characteristics of the economy mentioned above indicate that crowding out is not important: most public investment is in infrastructure and 'public' goods, and now mining; the economy is not at full capacity; the private sector does not seem to react very strongly to the availability of additional resources or to lower interest rates. Firms have not considered credit availability a binding constraint, at least since 1979. Finally, at a more theoretical level, in an open economy with 'flexible' exchange rates like Colombia, government expansion could crowd out the external sector (by lowering international reserves) and not just private investment.

Until we get further evidence, then, it appears that the public sector's role has been one of stabilisation complementing private investment. By playing a compensatory role in relation to external savings, it has made total savings much more stable. Public savings increased in those periods when external savings were decreasing (1974–7); stayed at high levels when external savings were low (1975–80); and decreased again in the final period analysed.

The adjustment of 1980–4 in Latin America

Latin American countries have normally used foreign savings to finance domestic investment. Imports of goods and services have been higher than exports, and the difference was financed by long-term foreign loans. But the situation became much more difficult when new foreign loans vanished after 1982. Exports had to increase (or imports decrease) to service the debt. Internal savings had to rise if the level of investment was to be sustained, but the opposite happened. Economic recession lowered levels of internal savings and a great deal of the adjustment came through huge reductions in investment.

Latin American external savings became negative in 1983 and 1984, due mainly to very high interest payments abroad (2.2% of GNP in 1980; 6.6% in 1984), but also to the important 'adjustment' in the foreign sector after 1982. Exports were increased and imports reduced. Colombia was one of the few countries which continued to be able to import more than it exported; interest payments abroad were very low in relative terms.[9] External foreign savings were not larger than in the 'typical' Latin American oil-importing country, but much larger than in the oil-exporting countries. On average over the whole period, external savings were nil for the oil-exporting countries, and positive for Colombia (3.5%) and the oil-importing countries.

In aggregate, Latin American domestic investment fell because both external and national savings declined. The fall in Colombia's national savings was less dramatic. It was the only country among seven studied (IDB, 1985) where total investment did not fall between 1980 and 1984 (although it did in 1985–6), mainly because of the compensatory role of public investment, which did not occur in the other countries. Even more impressive, the size of its public deficit was not large, 2% of GNP in the worst years (1983 and 1984), as compared with 4.5% and 3.9% in the oil-importing countries. Altogether, it seems that the government played a very important role in the economy: deficits were not as explosive as many people thought, and total government expenditures included a large proportion of investment. Unfortunately, we do not have comparable figures for 1985 and 1986 when, it seems, public investment decreased markedly, and the public sector did not continue to show the healthy characteristics just described (*Coyuntura Economica*, October 1986).

ECONOMIC POLICY

Some authors like Ocampo correctly stress that Colombian policy-makers do not follow long-term policies, being distinguished simply by their prudent (and conservative) management of the economy (Thorp and Whitehead, 1986). This is one of the reasons why Colombian policies during the 1970s and 1980s appear so 'wise' today: in a very unstable international scenario prudent policies usually pay.

In this section we want to explore a complementary thesis. Long-term objectives were sometimes present, as revealed in the four-year Economic Plans, but the severe instability of the foreign sector forced governments to sacrifice them in order to achieve short-term targets. Under López the economy was 'blessed' with large amounts of foreign exchange. Under Betancur, especially after 1983, foreign exchange disappeared. In the first period all economic instruments were aimed at the single objective of controlling 'imported' inflation. Under Betancur all available instruments were devoted to controlling the bank crisis (first), and the fall in international reserves (thereafter).

Long-term economic policy[10]

Since 1972 there have been four presidents. During the government of Misael Pastrana (1970–4) inflation escalated to 25% or more, and the supply of foreign exchange and the size of fiscal deficits became so high that they were complicating factors in the control of inflation. At least up to 1974 the government assigned higher priority to economic growth than to stabilisation. Long-term policy focused on urban building as the main source of growth and employment creation,[11] and in order to obtain the resources needed to finance such activity important financial innovations were introduced. The UPAC ('constant purchasing power financial paper') was created, and was the pioneer of financial instruments with positive interest rates.

President López (1974–8) inherited a booming economy with high international reserves, but also inflation rates which were high by Colombian historical standards. The main goals were control of inflation and improvement in the highly unequal distribution of income, for which Integrated Rural Development Plans and Food Nutrition Programmes (supported by the World Bank) were adopted. An important tax reform was undertaken. The government tried hard to liberalise the domestic capital market, and most financial assets were 'freed'. López criticised the former administration for what he considered incompetent management of the economy, mainly in the area of prices and inflation, arguing that price increases hit the middle and poor groups of the population hardest and ought to be stopped immediately. Then, in 1975, the economy received the mixed blessings of the largest coffee exports ever recorded which, in turn, caused the highest inflation rates suffered by any Colombian government this century.

The Turbay government (1978–82) presented the National Integration Plan whose main emphasis was on public infrastructure: better roads between the three main cities, Bogota, Medellín and Cali. The Plan also aimed to increase regional autonomy and political decentralisation, in order to develop the energy and mining sectors and to reduce inefficiencies in government expenditures. At least during the first two years additional foreign reserves were not a target; the memories of the coffee bonanza remained. Later, however, many in the government began to argue in favour of growth and government expenditure, even at the cost of higher inflation.

In summary, some people see the Turbay Plan as nicely rounding off the set of priorities presented by the different governments. The sum of different unbalanced Plans could amount to a long-term balanced growth strategy. We might even argue that the separate sub-plans could achieve the same goals more effectively, by concentrating attention on a limited number at any one time: a creative disequilibrium, the outcome of Hirschman-type bottlenecks, if not a strategy.

In his four-year Plan 'Cambio con Equidad' (Change and Social Justice) President Betancur (1982–6) emphasised the construction of low-income housing. Distributive issues were now more important than under Pastrana, the only other conservative president in the period. Public sector construction had to increase even more than originally planned, in order to compensate for the lack of dynamism of the private sector, with important consequences for the size of the fiscal deficit. But government expenditures were also important for the 'Peace Strategy' adopted by the government; any economic strategy combined with peace efforts had to contemplate massive expenditures in guerrilla zones. The rapid decline in international reserves of 1982 and 1983 threatened these goals.

The initial actions of the administration concentrated on the 'rescue' of the financial sector, and an 'economic emergency' was decreed in October 1982. The government and the Central Bank behaved as 'lenders of last resort', and many banks and financial institutions, including the largest financial conglomerate in the country, the Grupo Gran Colombiano, were nationalised or subjected to government intervention. Schemes to refinance private foreign debts and large 'non-recoverable' domestic loans were also implemented (Ocampo and Lora, 1986: 20–1).

Coffee policy

The main external shocks to long-term policies came through the coffee sector. The huge increase in the international coffee price after 1975, caused by the severe Brazilian frost of July 1975,[12] combined with inappropriate management of the coffee sector produced a transformation in the

Colombian economy which could only be compared with that at the beginning of the century.

Coffee production had been stable in the 1950s and 1960s (7,000–8,000 bags a year) but increased to 12,300 bags in 1978 and a peak of 13,037 bags in 1980 (see Table 6.5). The transformation originated mainly from improvements in productivity – there was no net increase in total land under cultivation during the period – with the adoption of a highly profitable new variety of coffee ('caturra'), first commercially available in Colombia in 1975.[13] The evolution of coffee exports can thus be divided into two periods. The first (1975–9) with dramatic increases in international prices, production and real exports; and the second (1979–85) when exports moved with international prices, production and real exports remaining relatively constant. The Colombian share in world coffee exports doubled between 1976 (10.1%) and 1979 (19.1%), with a fairly constant share (about 14%) in the 1980s. Coffee's shares of GDP, agricultural GDP and agricultural exports reached their highest values in 1977 for the first two variables (9.6% and 32.5%) and in 1978 for the third (85.4%).

Coming back to the issue of economic policy, there are three possible ways of neutralising the influence of large inflows of foreign exchange into the economy:

1. keep foreign resources outside the country in the hands of private exporters;
2. mobilise them as domestic savings by
   (a) taxing them or
   (b) transferring them to the National Coffee Fund (FNC);[14]
3. if foreign exchange is already monetised, 'sterilising' it through
   (a) open market operations; or
   (b) other 'unorthodox' compensatory policies: fiscal surpluses; increases in 'import deposits', etc.

Alternative 1. keep foreign exchange outside the country, was never seriously considered as it would have completely eroded Colombia's long (since the 1930s) and successful tradition of exchange control. Once dismantled, it would have been almost impossible to reintroduce after the bonanza. 1975–9 was a period of high domestic profitability, international interest rates were not especially high and the nominal devaluation of the exchange rate was low (Echavarria, 1982b).

Alternative 2.(a), tax the additional resources and keep them in government hands, was not easy to implement on equity grounds or on political considerations. Coffee producers are a very homogeneous group of low- and middle-income farmers, and more than 300,000 families depend on coffee earnings; why should they pay higher taxes than other wealthier groups in the country? On the political side, the FNC, unlike the African coffee producers or Brazil, is a private sector agency representing the interests of the coffee growers and exporters, perhaps the most powerful pressure group in the country (Urrutia, 1985). This does not mean, of course, that it is impossible to tax resources away from the coffee sector. But under President López, it was explicitly decided that the coffee bonanza belonged to the growers and exporters. Equity does not always coincide with proper macroeconomic management.

It is completely rational to impose export taxes and quotas in large coffee-growing countries like Colombia, because private entrepreneurs simply will not do what is socially convenient; an export tax will allow the country to exert the monopoly power available, and to follow an optimal pricing policy. On the other hand, in times of large accumulation of stocks, higher production simply means higher unsold stocks, and the only social benefit could be the potentially higher export quotas in future international negotiations; stocks are one of the additional variables considered. This argument does not imply that the state should keep the taxes, which could instead be returned to the FNC (alternative 2.(b)).

There are three important aspects of coffee policy which ultimately determine how much of the international coffee price goes into the economy, and the distribution of the benefits (among the government, the FNC, the coffee growers and the coffee exporters):

1. *Effective international price.* The government fixes the effective international price, the price paid to the private exporter which will enter the economy. This depends on the exchange rate,[15] the ad-valorem tax and the international price.
2. *Domestic price paid* to the grower (by the FNC). If the difference between (1) and (2) is small, private exporters will not export, and the FNC will have to handle all the exports. It seems easier to control foreign exchange in the hands of the FNC, as the government has a voice inside the institution.
3. The government can transfer additional resources to the FNC away from growers and exporters, through the *retention quotas* (payable to the FNC by other exporters) and other taxes.

Table 6.5 shows some of these variables. The ad-valorem tax was not used properly during the bonanza period. Instead of raising it to 'sterilise' resources, it was lowered, especially in 1977 and 1978, and again in 1982 at a time when the government desperately needed money; it was then at its lowest level ever.

The share of the world price received by the grower did fall when the world price rose, but the magnitude of the changes was not as significant as was desirable. Three-fifths of the variations in the international price are normally passed through to the domestic price, and the period of the coffee bonanza was no exception. For most of the period the domestic price paid to the private producer represented between 50% and 55% of the international price (45–50% during the bonanza).[16]

There were enormous variations in the share exported by private exporters. They exported 60–80% of total exports in 1975–8, with much lower percentages in the years following the bonanza. (In 1980 they were banned from exporting.) The FNC obtained a large share of the bonanza revenues through important increases in the retention quota. Total 'savings' (the last column of Table 6.5) increased during the bonanza mainly because of the evolution of this quota.

Reactions to the external shocks

Economic policy, 1975–80. Fighting inflation. Between 1952 and 1980 the economy behaved like a standard semi-open economy: an increase of 10% in high-powered money could explain a 5% rise in the rate of inflation and some reduction in the level of foreign reserves. Regression analysis does not prove causality, and some authors argue that the relation between these variables is the opposite. In a recent study, however, using more sophisticated statistical techniques, Leiderman (1984) 'proves' that in 1953–78 there was no important monetary 'accommodation' to inflation and output growth. In Colombia money played an active role in causing price increases. For our purposes we need only say that money matters in the medium and long term, and even more when the economy is suddenly hit by unexpected increases in foreign reserves. How was inflation fought in the period of the coffee bonanza?

The impact of the foreign sector was certainly large. The average change in the monetary base between 1971 and 1974 was C$3.5bn/year, less than 10% of the current account surplus in 1977 and 1978. In other words, the monetisation of the current account surplus would have increased the monetary base by ten times the average for the previous period. And even the inflation rates under the Pastrana government had been considered unacceptable by López.

The public sector contributed more than any other factor to 'sterilise' the increases in the monetary base in 1975–8, mainly in 1976 and 1978; credit from the private sector to the government was never important in relative terms, and it had the wrong sign during the bonanza. The government made a serious effort to control foreign borrowing by the private sector and its impact. Finally, Central Bank credit to the private sector was expansionary during the coffee bonanza.

All the effects described, when combined, produced the changes in the monetary base. Given the size of the external shock, it is remarkable that the monetary base increased only 37% in 1975–8, in comparison with more than 20% under the Pastrana administration. The difference is even lower if we compare the changes in money supply (M2); 25% for 1971–4; 29% for 1975–8, indicating important reductions in the money multiplier, thanks to a complex scheme designed to avoid secondary money expansion (including a marginal reserve requirement of 100% from 1977).

There were other variables and policies controlling inflation during this period. In 1975–9 C$36bn were kept outside the economy, 32% of total exports and 25% of M2. These figures are similar to those for 1971–4 and 1980–4, not, as they should have been, much higher. Coffee exporters and the FNC brought back their resources.

Inflation rates were extremely high in 1977 and 1979–81,[17] but much lower than changes in money supply; only in six out of the 14 years studied were the figures comparable. Wages, the exchange rate and interest rates somehow contributed to reduce the impact of monetary growth on prices during the coffee bonanza. The increase in real wages between 1975 and 1980 was comparable with the historical increase in labour productivity (3%) and with no compensation for the drastic real deterioration of the previous period. The nominal devaluations in the exchange rate in 1977 and 1978 (6%) were the lowest recorded in the whole period analysed, despite high domestic inflation. Subsidies were substantially reduced in 1974. The combined effect was a serious revaluation of the real effective exchange rate: 13% in 1977. Finally, the evolution of nominal interest rates also contributed to the control of inflation during the period. In 1977 they fell 5% when the inflation rate rose from 20% to 33%, producing a negative rate of −6%.[18]

The changes in these three cost variables helped to control inflation, but precluded the achievement of some long-term objectives stressed by President López. The evolution of real wages ran counter to improvements in income distribution,[19] the evolution of the real exchange rate counter to his intentions of seeing Colombia as a 'new Japan in South America',[20] and the evolution of interest rates counter to positive interest rates reflecting scarcities in the economy. Direct price controls and subsidies (housing, cotton, consumption goods, i.e. milk, sugar and coffee) were introduced in 1975–8, although the President had attacked repressed prices as 'political prices' in his election campaign.

But other policies were adopted to control prices which should not have been used for these purposes in 'normal' times. Colombia has used trade controls in a pro-cyclical manner, partially because trade policy is used for stabilisation purposes in response to coffee export booms and busts; partially because the availability of foreign exchange allows the authorities to relax controls (Cuddington, 1986: 7).

On the tariff front the López government announced an important 'rationalisation' in the first months of 1975, which was never implemented. In the first months of the Turbay administration significant tariff reductions were announced (to increase imports and reduce reserves and the money supply) but pressures from important economic groups were strong enough to prevent them. It was not until 1981 that major reductions were adopted. But non-tariff barriers were reduced consistently throughout the bonanza (Cuddington, 1986), until the foreign situation started to deteriorate after 1981.

Thus the design of a more rational tariff structure, aiming at long-term industrial – and agricultural – growth, never materialised. Non-tariff barriers were reduced mainly to fight inflation. Import deposits were re-established to gain additional control of the money supply (Echavarria and Garay, 1978).

Economic policy, 1980–5. Acquiring foreign exchange[21]
The three most significant external shocks in the period 1980–5 were the collapse of the coffee market from the middle of 1980, the debt crisis of 1982, and the Venezuelan devaluation of the bolivar in 1983. These shocks forced some changes in domestic policies, but policies also changed for other reasons.

First, the *external situation* changed over time as described on pages 93–5. The first two years of the 1980s were still years of increasing reserves, but they began to decrease in 1982, and in 1983 fell by half. New inflows of capital were not enough to offset the deterioration in the current account, and decreased in 1982–3. New loans were obtained but repayments were also higher.

Second, *economic objectives* and priorities also changed. Fighting inflation was the main priority in the second half of the 1970s. In 1979–82 the situation of the foreign sector was still favourable, and discussion centred on the determinants of poor growth performance. The behaviour of the foreign sector was the main issue after 1982, or, more accurately, the interrelation between public deficits and the foreign sector.

It is interesting to analyse the transition from one priority to another. Four reasons appear plausible.

1. The new government simply changed priorities: the newly elected Turbay administration put more emphasis on growth and less on the control of inflation.
2. New, more traumatic problems appeared: the behaviour of the foreign sector after 1983 could be placed in this category.
3. The aim of controlling inflation was considered more costly than had originally been thought: after 1982 it was argued that inflation was much more difficult to control because expectations were now playing an important role. In a similar vein – looking now at benefits – the over-enthusiastic approach towards the advantages of large fiscal deficits to increase demand was followed by a much more cautious one.[22]
4. It was still felt that the problem was important, but it was similar, or more intense, in other Latin American countries. Inflation was high, but look at our neighbours; the economy did not grow, but we did not have negative rates like our neighbours . . . .

Ocampo has divided economic policy in the period into three main phases: 1980–2 (increasing disequilibrium and economic recession); 1983–4 (hetero-dox management of the economy); and 1984–5 (orthodox phase). The main elements of each phase were as follows.

1980–2. In the last two years of the Turbay administration the new strategy combined an expansionist fiscal policy, a contractionary monetary policy, and an important import liberalisation process. A fiscal deficit was seen as the instrument for building infrastructure; public goods should be built by the state and financed by long-term credit. This was not available domestically; international loans were seen as the solution. Import liberalisation was seen as one way to control the inflationary impact of the fiscal deficit. The deterioration in the foreign sector which began in 1980 was not perceived until 1982. But not all the deficit can be explained by investment. The fiscal 'counter-reform' of 1979, negligent tax collection and increases in current government expenditures explain most of it. Tariff reforms were important in the period, and in 1982 more than 70% of all tariff items were in the list of 'free imports' (compared to 30% in 1974 and 54% in 1979).

1982–4. The new Betancur administration initially agreed with most of the previous diagnosis, but its forces had to be directed to the control of domestic financial panic. Rumours had started in the last months of the Turbay administration that the banks were mismanaged and that the new government was planning to intervene in the Gran Colombiano financial group. Reactivation of the economy was the central issue, and to that end private credit and export subsidies were increased, and import liberalisation stopped. Housing construction was seen as the other tool to reactivate demand. Important measures were adopted (unsuccessfully) to help the private sector in servicing its foreign debt. It soon became clear that the room for manoeuvre was not unlimited, especially after 1983 when the external sector deteriorated rapidly. Deflationary demand policies were, however, never seriously considered.

1984–5. Some policies adopted in this phase were in line with those of the previous phase, [23] but the diagnosis changed significantly. Excess domestic demand was now seen as the main reason for the external disequilibrium. This was even more emphasised when the government became involved in negotiations with the IMF and the World Bank. It was necessary to reduce public expenditures (both current expenditures – real wages – and public investment). The most significant change on the foreign front was the agreement with the international agencies to return in 1985 to the real exchange rate of 1975 – an unprecedented real devaluation of 30%. Finally, the government agreed to liberalise imports gradually. At the beginning of 1985 tariffs were reduced on inputs for exportables and in mid-1985 all tariffs were reduced. New similar measures were adopted at the beginning of 1986. The negotiating stance adopted was radically different from that followed by other Latin American countries. Private bankers finally accepted 'monitoring' by the IMF instead of a normal agreement with the Fund. (*Ex-post*, however, there was not much difference between the two positions.)

GROWTH

Economic growth in the 1970s and 1980s

In the 1970s Colombia's economic record could be considered 'average' for Latin America. Compared with other Latin American countries it did well during the recession of the 1980s; only Brazilian growth was comparable (CEPAL, 1986: Table 2).[24] But growth in the 1980s was the lowest since 1925 (see Table 6.6).

Over a longer period (1913–50) the economy showed one of the highest per capita growth rates (though modest by post-World War II standards), and in 1950–80 growth accelerated much less than in other fast-growing countries (Syrquin, 1986: 3). GNP per capita represented 21% of that of the United States in 1950, and 24% in 1980.[25]

Four important points emerge from analysis of sectoral growth in the period. First, agriculture did much better than industry in the 1970s and 1980s, an important break with the past. Second, the poor industrial growth in the second part of the 1970s was not common to other Latin American countries, where overall it was higher than in any previous period (Echavarria, 1986: 2). Third, neither industry nor agriculture was the leading sector in the 1970s or 1980s. The fastest growing sectors in 1970–5 were: public utilities (11.16%), personal services, transportation and communications, and government services (6.0%), and in 1975–80, financial services (11.0%), government services and construction (5.6%). This unhealthy pattern will have important consequences for future growth. Fourth, the economy grew at its fastest historical rate between 1967 and 1974.

What are the main explanations of sectoral and aggregate growth? We do not have *the* answer, but some elements could be considered.

Capital and labour
For the Colombian economy as a whole McCarthy *et al.* (1985) find that capital and labour account for nearly 70% of growth between 1963 and 1980, and more than 85% if the period 1967–74 is excluded. The importance of the 'residual' jumped in 1967–74, with the 'healthy winds of greater international competition'. The contribution of capital is always larger than that of labour, but labour's importance has increased over time.

For industry, there are more complete studies (Echavarria, 1986: 14–19) which show:

1. The stock of capital grew faster in industry than in the rest of the economy during the last decades: in 1925 the capital–labour ratio was lower than average in industry; in 1967 it was 30% higher in industry than in the rest of the economy.
2. Employment and labour productivity were equally important in the explanation of growth in the whole period 1950–83. But the large change

in labour productivity occurred in the 1950s and 1960s; it remained constant after 1972.

3. The residual is more important in industry than in the economy as a whole, its weight oscillating between 30% and 50% depending on the sub-period, but its importance fell drastically after 1970.

These figures just quoted indicate the structural problems in Colombian industry during the 1970s. Labour productivity did not increase after 1972. The crisis of the 1980s thus hit an industry which had already been sick in the 1970s. The crisis in industrial production, in turn, is not due to lack of investment or employment.

Syrquin (1986: 448) finds something similar for the other Latin American economies, and not just for industry:

> growth in Latin America after 1973 cannot be described as having been 'savings-constrained' or 'trade-constrained'. Reduced growth cannot be explained as being due to a failure of resource expansion: rather, it was due to the low efficiency in the utilisation of internal and external resources.

He also finds that the slowdown in labour productivity since 1973 originated outside agriculture, primarily in industry.

Demand

The impact of different types of demand varies among groups. Depressions in the external sector which mainly hit rural groups are compensated for by expansionary fiscal policies which, in turn, benefit *urban* groups. It is paradoxical, but probable, that crisis in the external sector actually benefits urban groups. The growth of exogenous demand, exports plus government spending, decreased after 1974 affecting urban production. Aggregate demand dropped drastically between 1980 and 1983 contributing to one of the largest industrial crises in Colombian history. But the worst years are now over, and since 1983 the evolution of demand has been relatively favourable to industry. Industry grew by more than 8% in 1986.

Dutch disease[26]

A revaluation of the exchange rate (produced by a commodity boom) hits the production of tradeables, which are mainly industrial goods in countries like the Netherlands or Britain. Colombia has been cited frequently as one of the examples of Dutch disease. It is true that the industrial crisis started in 1974/5 when the real exchange rate began to rise (see Table 6.7). It is also claimed that the disease hit agriculture, a highly traded sector. But there are problems in this explanation.

1. In Colombia the industrial sector can be more closely identified with non-tradeables, and the agricultural sector with tradeables.[27] The Dutch disease model does not produce conclusive results for non-tradeables, and as a consequence it cannot explain the Colombian industrial crisis. In the

'tradeable' sector, agriculture, growth rates were unusually high between 1972 and 1978, when the Dutch disease should have appeared. It cannot be argued that the agricultural crisis was due to the influence of relative prices after 1979, when the agricultural and industrial sectors were in crisis in every Latin American country.

2. In a recent study on the 'Colombian Dutch disease', Kamas (1986) concludes that some of the elements of the disease were there, although 'the econometric estimates only weakly confirm that the real exchange rate affects domestic sectoral production in the way predicted by the model'. She also finds strong evidence for a significant output response to fiscal and monetary policies. The relative price of non-tradeables increased after the bonanza but did not decrease thereafter, indicating important rigidities in the economy; the disease model assumes price flexibility and mobile resources. Finally, for 32 sectors of the economy Kamas finds no clear relationship between growth rates and the share of traded goods; instead, the more traded sectors grew faster.[28]

Future growth and economic strategy

Foreign-exchange bottlenecks

Foreign exchange as well as savings will be required for future growth. Current account deficits will be with us for the rest of the decade, and foreign capital will be needed to meet interest payments and transfers. The worst years (1982 and 1983) are over but things will not be easy in the near future. The international situation will become increasingly complex: the problem of past debt remains unresolved and new loans are difficult to obtain in Latin America; the international economy is stagnant and protectionist pressures are multiplying. Two-gap models are once again attracting attention, after being considered only by 'heretics' in the 1970s. What can be done?

Since 1974 Colombia has been losing ground as an exporter of manufactured goods; slow international growth cannot explain this relative decline. Rather, it seems that a weak export promotion effort is responsible; the exchange rate has not been found to be a key variable in empirical studies.[29] But much more study is required. Understanding this phenomenon is particularly important for Colombia, since the success in 'minor' exports between 1967 and 1974 was associated with 'cheap' growth (which did not require much additional investment) and, at the same time, with a major investment boom.

International markets are extremely competitive in manufactures and 'marketing' is as important as any other input. This means that for them a *long-term* strategy has to be designed to regain our relative position. For other non-traditional (mainly agricultural) exports, prices are the relevant variable, but the close relation between food prices and the general price level calls for a cautious strategy on that front.

Other areas are more difficult to explore. Political considerations and inertia from the past seem to be crucial variables .in explaining foreign investment, and Colombia's recent experience in the area is not very encouraging. Measures were taken after 1982 to attract foreign capital (Echavarria, 1986: 168–72), without significant results. The political and social conditions of the country are not the most favourable to attract foreign investment.

'Export-processing zones' have been used by Colombian producers mainly to import goods into the country, with frequent complaints about smuggling. A few foreign companies operated in the zones in the 'golden' period of 1967–74 but decided to quit relatively quickly. Their main complaints were related to the quality of the labour, and to infrastructure. The fundamental fact, however, was that Colombia was not a country with extremely low paid labour (like Haiti) or important geographical advantages (like Mexico) (Echavarria, 1979).

Import substitution must therefore make the main contribution to removing foreign-exchange bottlenecks in the future.

Domestic factors
Although foreign exchange will be important for future growth, it is not the decisive element. Colombian long-term growth has been very stable, despite the extreme volatility of the external sector. Indeed, at times, adverse external conditions 'produced' structural modifications in the economy which benefited long-term growth (e.g. industrialisation in the 1930s). Internal factors, productivity, demand and structure, have played a crucial role in Colombian capital accumulation up to now, and something should be said in very broad terms about these factors. Most of this refers to industry since information and research on other sectors is not as complete.

Which sectors?

Agriculture and industry played the central role in developed countries' accumulation of capital and there is no reason why Colombia should be an exception. Growth episodes based on other sectors, particularly on the financial sector, should be seen as short-term phenomena which, by themselves, will not guarantee long-term growth.

The new resources from coal and oil must be considered in this light. They represent one of the few opportunities the country will have to invest massively in key objectives, and it would be wrong not to learn from neighbouring countries which have remained under-developed in spite of possessing the same resources. Regional conflicts could be acute, but they must not be allowed to be an important obstacle; special programmes designed for poor areas which are rich in natural resources could be arranged.

Every effort should be made to diversify out of coffee. Colombia did better than other countries in the 1980s while also being more specialised in a single commodity. The wrong conclusions could be drawn from this. To set all one's hopes on one single, highly unstable commodity is totally wrong, and it is difficult to understand how some writers can still ask for even greater dependence on the international coffee market. It is also wrong to treat the FNC as a fund only for the benefit of the 'cafeteros'.

The economy did well in the 1980s, through excessive specialisation in coffee, but what matters is the long run, and in the long run other countries did much better. Colombian long-term growth is not satisfactory, either in comparison with other Latin American countries like Brazil (which has diversified more from coffee), or in comparison with the South-East Asian countries. In his classic 'Typology of economies exporting raw materials', Furtado (1976) does not recognise coffee as one of the commodities able to generate the best conditions for growth.

Agriculture and industry are not doing well. The industrial 'crisis' started in Colombia in 1974; the country must regain the long-run rates of the past. Agricultural production grew more in the 1970s than in previous decades, but this was still not satisfactory. Low growth is only partially the result of international variables. The two sectors must be seen as complementary. Low prices for wage goods mean larger demand for industrial products and lower labour costs. Agriculture produces inputs required by industry, and generates savings to finance aggregate investment. Even if industry were to be preferred in a long-term strategy, the political and social conflicts specific to the country call for massive investments in the rural areas in order to buy peace.

We still do not have the studies required to say something conclusive about which sub-sectors to promote. The static concept of comparative advantage is of no help in the discussion, simply because future comparative advantages are acquired by present policies. If Japan, South Korea or any other of the successful NICs had followed the rules of static comparative advantage they would not be producing today steel, refined oil, petrochemicals, cars and other products for which income elasticity of demand is large, and in which technology and labour productivity change fast. Kaldor's laws represent additional elements in favour of industry (see Thirlwall, 1983); higher industrial growth will produce higher aggregate growth (1st Law); higher growth of industrial labour productivity (2nd Law); and of labour productivity in general (3rd Law).[30]

In agriculture Eduardo Sarmiento found, in 1982, that a devaluation of just 10–15% was all that was required to allow domestic production to be competitive. He also identified certain products (e.g. maize) in which it would be almost impossible to compete. More of this kind of studies should be undertaken.

In the area of manufactures we can be more specific. Echavarria *et al.* (1983) find a very biased industrial structure, favouring beer, processed food, tobacco and textiles, with large deficiencies in all the other more advanced sectors (SIIC 34–9). The methodology utilised shows that other countries of similar market size have been able to generate larger production in those sectors. If market size is not the main constraint on production, the explanation of the bias must be related to economic policy – or its absence. This does not mean, of course, that every 'advanced' sector should be promoted. In some sub-sectors it is impossible to do anything simply because technological constraints and barriers to entry preclude it.

The authors tried to rank sectors according to four alternative criteria: labour intensity (+), static comparative advantage (+), linkages (+) and import intensity(−). They found that metal products, machinery and equipment presented the most favourable characteristics, although with very negative elements for some of its sub-sectors like computing machinery and cars, among others. Basic metals also seemed desirable, and chemicals were clearly undesirable. We must reiterate that this study simply represents a line of research which could be fruitful for the future. It also calls for the promotion of medium-size firms which are simply non-existent in Colombia.

The role of the state
The main role of the state in the process of growth is to increase, or use available, taxes in order to invest in areas where the private sector does not want to invest, or should not do so. To treat any public investment and consumption as equivalent is simply wrong; efficiency and the kind of expenditure both matter.

There is a significant policy difference between coffee and the two new commodities available to the country, coal and oil, because the latter belong to the state, not to private producers. This will permit policies that were unthinkable in the past, but will also mean that more resources could be lost through inefficient utilisation.

Among the main future tasks for the state are the following:

1. To buy peace in the country, investing massively in agriculture, agrarian reform and infrastructure. The share of agriculture in total public investment has decreased from 25% in 1970 to less than 7% in 1982, and this trend has to be reversed.
2. To keep a stock of well-designed and essential projects. We saw how important this was after 1980 when public investment helped economic growth.
3. To complement private investment in industry. The industrial strategy proposed here requires the promotion of 'advanced' sectors in general. The private sector will undertake production in those labour-intensive sub-sectors which do not have important economies of scale; the state will

undertake production in bulky sub-sectors with large economies of scale. If both types of investments are not done simultaneously, both will fail.

LESSONS OF 1975–85 AND STRATEGY FOR THE FUTURE

Colombian policy-makers face a difficult scenario in the near future. There is not enough debate inside the country on topics which will be central to future capital accumulation. Urban unemployment is greater than ever, and income distribution is one of the worst among the developing countries; it certainly did not improve during the 1970s, although it may have done in the 1980s. Social and political conflicts are already extremely acute, and the final outcome in these areas will depend mainly on future economic growth and its distribution. Economic policy and the development strategy it reflects will be decisive in this respect.

Why did Colombia do relatively well in the first part of the 1980s? Its international reserves were very high at the beginning of the international crisis, and inflation rates modest by Latin American standards. These were two important assets with which to fight the international recession of the 1980s. Large international reserves allowed the country to import as much as was needed, especially capital goods bought by the public sector. Better co-ordination with the private sector might have allowed less traumatic consequences for national industry; nevertheless it was good policy to use scarce foreign exchange for capital goods imports instead of for consumption.

Public and private investment stagnated together in most Latin American countries, but in Colombia the favourable evolution of the public sector played an important compensatory role up to 1984. That this took resources from the rest of the economy does not necessarily mean that 'crowding out' can explain the lack of dynamism of private investment. International comparisons are revealing in this area, as private investment was even more stagnant in other countries, despite the additional resources 'released' by shrinking public investment. Public investment decreased drastically after 1984.

The government played another important role as public savings partially compensated for the extreme instability of external savings, making total savings and investment more stable. An especially encouraging aspect is that it was done without large public deficits, at least in comparison with the oil-importing Latin American countries.

How does one evaluate economic policy when the international situation is so volatile and unpredictable? The amount of foreign exchange inside the country is never known, given the size of the 'underground' economy. At the beginning of 1987 most analysts in the country were of the opinion that foreign exchange would not be a constraint in the coming years, with future coffee prices around US$2/lb. From that perspective, the adjustment policies followed in 1984 and 1985 seemed unnecessarily tough. Three months later coffee prices plunged to less than US$1/lb, and it seems that the future will be less favourable than predicted. The adjustment policy followed in 1984–5 now looks wiser.

1. Coffee prices, coffee production, and coffee policies must be seen as an essential part of the package of available macroeconomic instruments. The most important macroeconomic policy adopted during the López administration was to allow the coffee bonanza to benefit the coffee people, but it was too costly. This seems to have been understood by the coffee people and the government in the 1986 bonanza.

2. Economic policy was very efficient in controlling inflation. President López was right in saying that inflation had important distributive consequences which had to be fought, and the low levels of inflation at the beginning of the crisis of the 1980s proved to be one of Colombia's main assets.

3. In a very unstable international economy conservative and cautious policies always pay. There is no room for experiments or 'risk' lovers. Colombian policy-makers were always risk-averse and, *ex post*, it paid off. Many Latin American countries experimented with 'new' ideas in economics and had almost a decade to prove that they worked, but positive results never materialised. Domestic interest rates did not follow the predicted pattern and remained incredibly high. The experiments produced disastrous results in terms of growth and employment. Latin American economists in general are coming back to a pragmatic neo-structuralism which can avoid many troubles in the future (see Fishlow, 1985), and Colombian economists seem to show this kind of pragmatism.

4. Colombian policy-making seems wise (*ex post*) in comparison with other Latin American countries. But even better policies could have been implemented. With negative interest rates it would have been good policy to obtain foreign loans in the 1970s, but bad policy to invest those resources in the way they were invested in other Latin American countries. Best policies would have required every dollar to be invested in export-oriented activities (Syrquin, 1986). Other heavy borrowers like South Korea did exactly that, and they are not living with the extreme bottlenecks of Colombia's neighbours. Even without new loans, would it not have been better to permit imports or to import directly – capital goods mainly – in order to take advantage of the high exchange rate? The above arguments assume that we have *ex post* information. Could the state have borrowed from the private sector and invested?

5. Colombia was very cautious in borrowing abroad and in opening the economy to international financial flows, but that does not mean that there was no economic policy. On the contrary, the country has a long tradition of intervention, mainly on foreign variables, and it was used most of the time. Given the magnitude of the external shocks of 1975–85,

it seems good policy to fight with all available tools for one or two main objectives. Even tariff policies had to be used to fight inflation in the second part of the 1970s, and this was done successfully. Long-term growth, stability and distribution are the main objectives of economic policy, and at least in the area of growth Thorp and Whitehead (1986) show that the more heterodox and interventionist Latin American countries, Brazil and Colombia, show the best record.

In summary, given that there are no policies which could radically change future perspectives in the foreign sector, we should turn our attention to the domestic side. The main emphasis should be given to agriculture and industry, trying to promote a shift of resources out of coffee, oil and coal.

NOTES

1. Even in the worst years, the country's inflation rates were among the lowest in Latin America.
2. The share of Colombia in Latin American total debt (private and public) decreased from 6.8% in 1973 to 3.5% in 1979, and remained constant until 1982 (Villar, 1984: 227).
3. Illegal capital flight in and out of the country does not seem to have acquired the magnitude it had in Mexico, Argentina and Central America (Thorp and Whitehead, 1987: 303–4).
4. Nobody will ever be able to estimate exactly the importance of illegal exports (mostly drugs). Junguito and Caballero consider that marihuana and cocaine exports increased from US$1 million in 1970 to US$500m. in 1977 (one-third of coffee exports). Ruiz (1979) and Ruiz and López (1981) give higher figures: US$1.5bn in 1978, and 2.6bn in 1979, representing 126% of coffee exports in the latter year. They estimate that marihuana exports were much higher than cocaine exports at that time, but it is likely that the situation is the opposite today. Most probably, illegal exports are recorded as services in the capital account of the balance of payments, or as errors and omissions.
5. After a growth rate of 5% a year in constant prices during 1970–5, non-coffee agro-based exports grew only 1.7% in 1975–83 (Thomas, 1985: 9). Manufactures (mainly textiles, fibres and manufactured metals) represented 8% of total exports in 1970 and 20% in 1975; only 16% in 1983 (Echavarria, 1986: 60).
6. They represented 8.7% of total exports in 1970, and 21% in 1974. Manufactured exports are much smaller than 'non-traditional' exports.
7. The figures shown represent the averages of two recent estimates made separately by Fedesarrollo and the National Planning Committee (DNP). See Ocampo (1986: Table 2) for a discussion of the figures given by each Institution.
8. Among nine countries analysed in a recent World Bank document, Colombia and Peru had the lowest savings ratios (World Bank, 1986): share of GNP: 1980–4.

	Savings	Investment
Colombia	16.8	19.7
Peru	16.7	16.1
Paraguay	18.0	27.7
Ecuador	24.4	22.3
Brazil	20.3	20.4

	Savings	Investment
Mexico	28.7	23.3
Thailand	20.3	23.8
Malaysia	29.2	32.3
South Korea	25.3	28.4

9. The ratio of interest payments to GDP in Colombia was one quarter of that for Latin America oil-exporting countries, and one-fifth of that for the oil-importing countries.
10. This section relies heavily on Berry and Thoumi (1985).
11. The Plan cited four strategies, but really focused on only one: urban building. Rural–urban mobility was seen as desirable, or at least unavoidable, and leading to higher labour productivity for the country as a whole. Rural migration had to be absorbed by industry and modern activities in the cities.
12. The frost was more severe than any other in the post-war period. It reduced the production of the state of Parana (the most important coffee state in Brazil) to 10% of previous levels. Even worse, it also destroyed the trees, with important consequences for future production. A Producers' Pact failed to materialise in 1975, and the 'New International Coffee Pact' which was due to come into operation after October 1976 never worked out. A new agreement on coffee export quotas, the first since 1972, was signed only in September 1980.
13. Caturra produces 2–3 times more than the traditional technology – per unit of land – but with much higher inputs of fertiliser and labour.
14. The government has a large influence inside the FNC, a private non-profit-making federation of coffee producers that engages in commercial activities and has been the main body charged by the government with administering coffee policy in the country. The federation is responsible for the management of the National Coffee Fund (NCF), for the provision of technical assistance to the industry, for the control of domestic and export marketing, and for advice on the setting of certain rates of taxation and prices which affect the industry.
15. In 1977, the government introduced what were called exchange certificates which in practice reintroduced a multiple exchange-rate system. The certificates could only be redeemed after some days which meant that the value was reduced.
16. Davis (1983: 123, Table 4) provides useful information as to who benefited from the bonanza: the producer, the central government or the commodity organisation. The government obtained only 10–12% of export receipts between 1975 and 1977, when the figures for the other coffee countries analysed oscillated between 20% and 30%. The FNC got the largest share. The share of the government in total coffee taxes was 30% on average during the period of the bonanza, a decrease from 35% and 38% in 1974 and 1975 (Thomas, 1985: 216). The decreasing level is even clearer in terms of exports. From a level of 20% in 1974, it fell to 16% in 1978, then to 12% in 1981, and 6.5% in 1983. Most of the coffee countries analysed by Davis (1983: 129) had a larger deficit in 1978 than in 1975 because of the lagged impact of spending plans conceived at the height of the boom. Public capital expenditures also grew more than current expenditures. This did not happen in Colombia.
17. Not in comparison with other Latin American countries. This was an important Colombian asset at the beginning of the crisis of the 1980s.
18. The decrease in interest rates was due not only to direct controls, but also to the effect of the increases in money supply. Some authors like Fernandez and Candelo (1983) (see also Echavarria, 1982b) argue that the Colobian financial market is very segmented and isolated from the international financial market.

19. Miguel Urrutia (1983) shows that middle groups were badly hit by lower wages, while the lowest and higher income groups benefited in relative terms. (See also Echavarria *et al.*, 1983.)

20. 1975 marked the end of a very important experiment in export diversification which started in the mid-1960s. There are many factors which explain the low dynamism of minor exports after 1975, the evolution of the exchange rate being one of them, but not the most important one (see Echavarria, 1982b; Villar, 1984).

21. Based on Ocampo and Lora (1986).

22. Cf. different issues of *Coyuntura Economica* after 1982. In the earlier issues it appeared that all that was needed to reactivate the economy was a larger fiscal deficit to compensate for the deterioration in effective demand from the external sector. The deficit increased year after year and the economy continued to show slow growth rates.

23. At the end of 1984 an additional across-the-board tariff of 8% was imposed on imports.

24. We exclude Cuba, a country which grew four times more than any other Latin American country during the period.

25. Comparative figures for Brazil are 14% of US income in 1950, 28% in 1980.

26. The following paragraphs draw heavily on Edwards (1985, in Thomas). See also Edwards and Aoki (1983); Edwards (1985); Harberger (1983); Dornbusch (1974); Corden and Neary (1982).

27. The industrial sector is protected by heavy non-tariff barriers.

28. Kamas (1986) argues correctly that what should be measured is not growth but changes in growth, and she finds that the negative changes observed were stronger for the most open sectors. But neither industry nor agriculture was among them. Most of the tradeable sectors considered were 'advanced' and unimportant (in terms of weight) industrial sub-sectors: paper, machinery, transport materials, etc.(also mining and coffee).

29. Echavarria (1982b) and Villar (1984) do not find that the exchange rate had important effects on minor exports, and even less on manufactured exports. Like Echavarria, Edwards in his recent study (in Thomas, 1985) gives most emphasis to the international economy, but he finds a larger price elasticity than the other two studies. There is a fundamental flaw in Edwards' study so his results should be taken with reservation. The relation between the Colombian and the US dollar is not the relevant exchange rate as there were some years during the period under consideration when exports to Venezuela accounted for most minor exports.

30. For more on this line see Echavarria *et al.* (1983) and Thirlwall (1983).

Table 6.1 Commodity prices: growth and stability, 1970–86

| | Annual growth (%) | | | | Index of instability (Coffee = 100) 1970–80 |
	1970–4	1974–9	1979–84	1984–6	
All products	20.59	4.63	−2.29		63.34
Food	30.36	−3.61	−0.87		80.61
Aluminium	5.65	15.94	−4.83		76.98
Bananas	2.61	12.10	2.54	10.50	41.89
Bauxite	14.02	16.26	1.57	0.39	0.00
Coal	20.66	13.54	0.65		50.87
Cocoa	23.32	16.13	−6.17	−2.99	118.74
Coffee	8.23	18.72	−4.69	25.15	100.00
Copper	7.36	3.78	−6.22	0.72	58.80
Cotton	23.21	1.42	1.87	−12.34	70.34
Iron ore	5.67	4.29	0.44	−2.26	46.13
Meat	4.91	12.77	−4.64		64.80
Nickel	8.01	9.29	−4.48		44.30
Oil	65.79	12.10	10.53	−25.46	148.60
Sugar	68.02	−20.24	−11.69	10.94	233.84
Tea	6.32	9.11	9.90		67.42
Tin	22.76	12.50	−4.28	−33.18	80.55
Zinc	22.53	1.08	5.73	−13.90	57.51

Source: IMF, *Int. Fin. Stat.* Supplement on Trade Statistics.
Methodology:
The Instability Index was calculated as: II = SER/MP.
II: Instability Index.
SER: Standard error of the regression between prices and time (log-log).
MP: Mean of the dependent variable (log of prices).

Table 6.2 Balance of payments, 1970–85 (US$m)

	1970	1971	1972	1973	1974	1975	1976	1977
Current account balance	-293	-454	-190	-55	-350	-109	207	440
Trade balance	-14	-148	130	280	-16	293	578	734
Merchandise exports, fob	788	754	979	1,262	1,495	1,717	2,243	2,713
Merchandise imports, fob	-802	-903	-849	-982	-1,511	-1,424	-1,665	-1,979
Other goods, services and income	-315	-340	-355	-370	-386	-446	-432	-353
Credit	231	243	250	325	453	503	632	801
Debit	-546	-583	-605	-695	-839	-948	-1,063	-1,153
Private and official transfers	36	34	35	35	52	44	60	58
Capital account	327	346	246	147	272	182	196	-27
Direct investment and long-term capital	227	195	264	286	229	295	104	230
Direct investment	39	40	17	23	35	35	14	43
Other long-term capital	188	154	246	263	194	260	90	187
Short-term capital	100	151	-17	-139	43	-113	92	-257
Other	20	1	20	10	4	11	24	14
Net errors and omissions	-18	90	104	69	-17	10	211	159
Total changes in reserves	36	-17	180	170	-91	93	638	586
Total reserves								
Stock	206	188	326	528	441	540	1,151	1,750
Annual variation (%)		-8.95	73.66	62.14	-16.42	22.41	113.04	52.04

COUNTRY STUDIES

Table 6.2 (continued)

	1978	1979	1980	1981	1982	1983	1984	1985
Current account balance	322	491	−159	−1,895	−2,896	−3,003	−1,401	−1,390
Trade balance	642	510	−238	−1,544	−2,190	−1,494	246	−21
Merchandise exports, fob	3,206	3,506	4,062	3,219	3,216	2,970	4,273	3,713
Merchandise imports, fob	−2,564	−2,996	−4,300	−4,763	−5,406	−4,464	−4,027	−3,734
Other goods, services and income	−393	−120	−86	−594	−875	−1,673	−1,946	−1,833
Credit	924	1,345	1,800	1,795	1,757	1,133	1,055	1,111
Debit	−1,317	−1,465	−1,886	−2,389	−2,632	−2,806	−3,001	−2,944
Private and official transfers	73	101	165	243	169	164	299	464
Capital account	86	885	847	1,967	1,981	1,429	940	1,857
Direct investment and long-term capital	95	725	798	1,623	1,610			
Direct investment	68	105	48	212	338			
Other long-term capital	28	620	750	1,410	1,272			
Short-term capital	−9	160	49	344	371			
Other	103	53	393	298	330	93	−849	NA
Net errors and omissions	19	68	375	316	64	−271	−76	−535
Total changes in reserves	530	1,497	1,456	686	−520	−1,753	−1,166	−917
Total reserves								
Stock	2,360	3,875	5,056	5,002	4,013	2,260	1,094	NA
Annual variation (%)	34.85	64.18	30.50	−1.08	−19.77	−43.68	−51.59	NA

Sources:
1970–82. IMF, *International Financial Statistics*, Supplement on Balance of Payments.
1983–5. IMF, *International Financial Statistics*.

Table 6.3 Projections of Colombian balance of payments, 1986–1990 (US$m)

	1986	1987	1988	1989	1990
1. Exports	5,604.5	5,967.0	6,181.5	6,670.5	7,037.5
Coffee share %	51.0	40.0	31.0	30.0	30.0
Oil and coal %	15.0	27.0	36.0	37.0	36.0
Others %	34.0	32.0	33.0	33.0	34.0
2. Imports	4,067.5	4,431.0	4,788.5	5,230.5	5,702.0
A. Commercial balance (1-2)	1,537.0	1,536.0	1,393.0	1,440.0	1,335.5
B. Services and transfers	−1,232.5	−1,651.5	−1,843.5	−2,055.5	−2,037.0
Current account	304.5	−115.5	−450.5	−615.5	−701.5
Debt/exports %	1.8	1.6	1.6	1.5	1.5

Source: Ocampo (1986, Table 2).
Methodology: Arithmetic average of DNP and Fedesarrollo's projections.

Table 6.4 Savings and investment in Colombia, 1970–83 (percentage of GDP)

	1970	1971	1972	1973	1974	1975	1976	1977	1978	1979	1980	1981	1982	1983
Gross investment (I + II)	20.23	19.42	18.13	18.27	21.46	16.99	17.56	18.77	18.28	18.15	19.07	20.62	20.49	19.37
I. Fixed net investment	18.02	17.51	16.06	15.80	16.39	15.34	15.89	14.53	15.38	15.42	16.77	17.65	17.46	16.89
A. Types of investment														
Construction	9.31	8.99	8.20	8.51	8.62	7.83	7.83	7.78	8.08	7.80	8.63	9.40	9.53	9.37
Plantations	0.86	0.77	0.77	0.73	0.62	0.55	0.47	0.41	0.44	0.44	0.43	0.44	0.48	0.37
Transport equipment	2.39	2.84	2.17	1.80	1.92	2.07	2.67	1.89	2.17	2.43	2.47	2.44	2.48	2.03
Machinery	5.44	5.71	4.93	4.77	5.23	4.89	4.92	4.53	4.77	4.76	5.24	5.37	5.86	5.12
B. Institutional sectors	18.02	17.51	16.08	15.80	16.39	15.34	15.89	14.53	15.38	15.42	16.77	17.65	17.46	16.89
1. Public sector	5.24	5.56	5.93	5.43	4.67	5.19	5.40	6.33	5.20	5.35	7.00	7.35	8.09	8.26
Public firms	2.07	2.47	2.71	1.80	1.49	2.60	2.77	3.49	2.52	2.58	3.25	3.24	4.32	4.73
Public administrations	3.17	3.09	3.21	3.63	3.18	2.59	2.63	2.84	2.68	2.76	3.75	4.11	3.77	3.53
Central government	2.36	2.48	2.59	2.69	2.05	1.66	1.65	1.85	1.81	1.55	2.27	2.45	2.29	2.14
Others	0.81	0.61	0.62	0.94	1.13	0.93	0.99	0.98	0.87	1.22	1.48	1.66	1.48	1.39
2. Private sector	12.77	11.95	10.15	10.37	11.72	10.15	10.49	8.20	10.18	10.07	9.77	10.31	9.37	8.62
Firms	8.31	7.69	5.01	5.10	6.26	5.31	5.86	3.75	5.12	5.14	4.97	5.42	4.65	3.56
Financial institutions	0.30	8.48	8.58	0.40	0.53	0.51	0.35	0.37	0.41	0.42	0.60	0.78	0.58	9.76
Households	4.08	3.78	4.57	4.78	4.94	4.32	4.28	4.08	4.65	4.51	4.28	4.19	4.14	4.31
II. Inventory changes	2.22	1.90	2.05	2.47	5.86	1.66	1.67	4.24	2.90	2.73	2.29	2.97	3.02	2.48
Coffee	0.19	0.21	-0.53	0.69	-0.63	-0.33	0.85	2.21	1.06	-0.16	-0.25	0.47	0.34	0.57
Others	2.03	1.69	2.58	1.78	5.69	1.99	1.63	2.03	1.84	2.89	2.55	2.50	2.69	1.91

Gross savings (−I+II)	20.40	19.09	18.37	18.82	21.68	17.90	17.68	19.34	19.05	18.01	20.06	22.12	22.51	22.48
I. Foreign savings (current account)	−4.07	−5.80	−2.19	−8.53	−2.83	−0.83	1.35	2.26	1.38	1.76	−0.48	−5.21	−7.43	−7.13
II. Gross savings	16.33	13.29	16.18	18.28	18.85	17.07	19.03	21.60	20.44	19.77	19.58	16.91	15.08	15.27
1. Public sector	4.43	3.33	3.04	3.14	4.04	4.89	6.74	7.42	6.85	4.65	4.61	2.82	1.84	8.09
Public sector firms	1.68	1.45	1.58	1.38	1.34	1.21	1.36	1.64	1.21	1.14	1.48	1.55	1.47	1.29
Public administration	2.83	1.88	1.46	1.76	2.71	3.68	5.37	5.78	5.64	3.51	3.13	1.27	0.37	−1.28
2. Private sector	11.98	9.96	13.14	15.14	14.81	12.17	12.38	14.16	13.59	15.12	14.98	14.89	13.24	15.18
Firms	3.84	4.08	3.51	3.81	4.17	2.88	3.29	3.12	3.29	4.31	3.93	3.89	3.50	4.33
Financial institutions	0.95	0.83	0.80	1.15	1.35	1.34	1.88	1.12	1.34	1.44	2.85	2.15	1.59	1.26
Households	7.11	5.05	8.83	10.18	9.28	7.96	7.92	9.95	8.96	9.37	8.99	8.84	8.15	9.59
Net balance (savings − investment)														
I. Public sector	−0.81	−2.23	−2.89	−2.29	−0.63	−0.38	1.33	1.09	1.65	−8.70	−2.40	−4.53	−6.25	−6.17
Public sector firms	−0.47	−1.02	−1.13	−0.42	−0.15	−1.39	−1.41	−1.85	−1.32	−1.44	−1.78	−1.69	−2.85	−3.45
Public administrations	−0.35	−1.21	−1.76	−1.87	−0.48	1.89	2.74	2.94	2.96	0.74	−08.62	−2.83	−3.408	−4.73
II. Private sector	−0.87	−2.00	2.99	4.78	3.09	2.83	1.81	5.98	3.41	5.04	5.20	3.78	3.87	6.56
Firms	−4.47	−3.61	−1.50	−1.29	−2.08	−2.43	−2.57	−0.64	−1.83	−0.83	−1.04	−1.52	−1.15	0.77
Financial institutions	0.57	0.35	0.22	0.67	0.83	0.82	0.73	0.75	0.93	1.82	1.45	1.45	1.01	0.58
Households	3.03	1.27	4.26	5.40	4.35	3.64	3.64	5.87	4.31	4.06	4.79	3.86	14.01	5.28
III. Foreign sector	−4.07	−5.80	−2.19	−0.53	−2.83	−0.83	1.35	2.26	1.38	1.76	−8.48	−5.21	−7.43	−7.13

Source: DANE, National Accounts.

Table 6.5 Coffee figures (percentages)

	Production, exports and stocks (000 Bags)[a]					Share in:			Prices		Taxes (%)		
	Production	Exports	Stocks	Stocks/exports	Private/Total exports	GDP	Agricultural GDP	Agricultural exports	World real 1975=100[b]	Domestic/international[c]	Ad valorem	Retention quotas	Total savings (all taxes + retention)
1958	7,442	6,431	114	1.8							13.6	0.0	16.0
1960	7,500	6,043	1,081	17.9							12.6	8.3	24.6
1961											12.3	8.7	24.6
1964	8,547	5,743	3,589	62.5							0.0	5.8	20.5
1969	8,266	6,874	5,583	81.2		6.5	23.9	82.2			18.7	15.3	34.1
1970						5.0	19.6	79.2	124.8	58.0	18.2	15.6	33.9
1971						5.3	20.2	73.5	102.6	59.0	17.6	16.0	33.6
1972						5.7	21.3	78.2	107.2	57.0	16.5	14.9	31.5
1973						4.2	16.0	73.0	120.2	53.0	18.5	16.7	35.2
1974	7,981	7,542	2,400	31.8		5.0	18.7	67.2	105.8	51.0	15.9	19.3	35.2
1975					60.0	7.5	27.2	78.3	100.0	50.0	16.7	17.6	34.3
1976					79.0	9.6	32.5	80.9	190.3	47.0	15.7	25.7	41.3
1977					70.0	7.7	29.1	85.4	263.8	38.0	13.6	31.2	48.6
1978	12,300	11,431	4,870	42.6	36.0	6.7	25.3	84.0	176.7	47.0	14.1	38.5	59.7
1979	11,848	11,540	3,450	29.9	23.0	5.8	25.2	78.6	154.1	43.0	15.7	37.9	60.0
1980	13,037	9,031	5,978	66.2	2.0	3.8	18.7	70.7	137.4	48.0	15.1	31.2	50.4
1981	12,893	8,990	8,289	92.2	38.0	3.6	18.1	76.0	97.4	63.0	11.2	9.4	20.7
1982	12,810	9,174	10,230	111.5	43.4				109.9	58.0	8.8	19.6	28.5
1983	13,464	9,966	12,175	122.2	42.7				104.8	59.0	NA	NA	NA
1984	10,700	9,600	11,900							51.6	NA	NA	NA
1985	11,900	11,500	10,300							54.0			
1986	11,000	10,500	8,800							74.3			

Source: Thomas (1985: 102–14); and Table F-4; *Coyuntura Economica*, December 1986, Tables II-1 and II-2. Some figures are estimated.

a. For the 'coffee year' 1 Oct.–30 Sept.). Then, instead of 1964, it should be 1964/65, etc.

b. Quoted prices, not actual sale prices for Colombia. Deflated by a US dollar price index of manufactured exports from developed to developing countries.

c. Ratio of the nominal domestic price paid by the Federation for Pergamino to coffee farmers, divided by the nominal world price of green coffee.

Table 6.6 Colombian economic growth, 1925–84 (percentages)

	Agriculture (1)	Industry (2)	(1)+(2) (3)	GDP (4)
1925–31	3.09	2.10	2.98	4.41
1931–39	3.42	12.40	4.70	5.04
1941–49	3.34	7.26	4.22	4.59
1951–59	4.09	7.30	5.13	5.21
1941–59	3.00	7.50	4.22	4.75
1960–67	3.09	5.49	4.02	4.73
1967–74	4.20	8.07	5.88	6.37
1974–78	5.03	4.20	4.64	4.90
1979–84	1.19	0.74	0.98	2.26
1925–84	3.14	6.49	4.01	4.64
1980	2.21	1.22	1.75	4.09
1981	3.20	−2.60	0.52	2.28
1982	−1.90	−1.40	−1.68	0.90
1983	1.80	0.50	1.15	1.00
1984	1.10	8.00	4.55	3.20
1985	1.80	3.00	2.40	2.00

Sources: CEPAL, 'El Crecimiento Económico de Colombia', Anexo Estadístico.
DANE and Banco de la República, 'Cuentas Nacionales de Colombia'.
Coyuntura Económica, March 1986, p. 11.

Table 6.7 Real exchange rate and export subsidies, 1973–85

| | Weighted real exchange rate | | | | Weighted real exchange rate (includes subsidies) | | | | Export subsidies (%) | | | |
| | 22 Countries | | Latin American Countries | | 22 countries | | Latin American Countries | | | | | |
	Minor exports	Imports	Minor exports	Imports	Minor exports	Imports	Minor exports	Imports	Cat. or cert.	Proexpo	Plan Vallejo	Total
1970–3	94.66	96.17	102.73	105.98	112.82	114.61	122.44	126.31	22.00	1.00	1.90	24.90
1975	100.00	100.00	100.00	100.00	100.00	100.00	100.00	100.00	2.20	1.20	1.40	4.80
1977	83.99	85.76	84.27	83.97	87.43	89.28	87.73	87.41	4.10	3.00	2.00	9.10
1979	82.49	84.01	78.39	82.93	85.71	87.30	81.46	86.17	3.50	3.00	2.40	8.90
1980	83.40	83.26	82.78	86.66	92.08	91.92	91.39	95.67	9.40	3.20	3.10	15.70
1981	79.65	78.18	85.76	88.39	90.21	88.55	97.14	100.11	11.70	4.20	2.80	18.70
1982	75.06	72.86	80.05	73.48	86.02	83.49	91.74	84.21	12.00	6.00	2.10	20.10
1983	72.98	76.35	67.80	68.28	87.46	91.51	81.25	81.84	18.70	4.90	2.00	25.60
1984	76.48	83.18	67.80	74.09	94.43	102.71	83.71	91.48	21.70	5.10	2.60	29.40
1985	80.73	87.43	70.45	73.74	100.30	108.62	87.52	91.62	22.40	4.10	3.70	30.20

Source: Coyuntura Económica, October 1985, p.77; March 1986, p. 65.
Methodology: The exchange rate for 1973 was modified with the subsidies for 1973.

7

PERU

JÜRGEN SCHULDT

Since 1945, Peru has suffered five general economic crises (1948–9, 1957–9, 1967–8, 1975–8 and 1983–4), each one more serious than the previous one. Over and above the purely economic crises, and also increasing in scale, there have been sharp social and political conflicts (strikes in the 1970s and terrorism in the 1980s). In each case an 'orthodox' process of economic stabilisation became necessary because of a severe 'external constraint'; recovery then came from a sharp rise in exports rather than (and even in spite of) the adjustment policies followed. For this reason, it is not surprising that Peru was the first and most frequent Latin American client for the IMF's conditional lending. The 1985–7 economic recovery will probably again be followed by drastic cuts in the standard of living. This sequence of crises makes it imperative to propose, analyse and then implement alternative economic policies and legal, institutional and administrative reforms, in order to achieve greater economic (and political) stability in the medium term.

THE POLITICAL RATIONALE FOR ECONOMIC POLICIES

Populism and manipulation of relative prices

The cycles in the Peruvian economy since 1945 can be explained basically by the conflict between the groups which were politically powerful (developmental and populist alliances), which supported import substitution, and those with economic power (the exporters and those allied to them). Each cycle (lasting on average 6–10 years) starts with an expansion in which real wages and the relative prices of the secondary and tertiary sectors all rise, until the increase in imports (given a constant exchange rate) hits the external constraint. Following this, the primary exporting sector forces a devaluation, which lowers real wages and puts the brake on industrial growth. Once the balance of payments has recovered and inflation has been reduced, a new cycle begins.

This pendulum movement is not only a fundamental characteristic of capitalism; it has been reinforced by the socio-political characteristics of the country, at least since World War II. It was then that the 'new social forces' appeared, which questioned the power of the landowners and of the primary exporting bourgeoisie (and its industrial, financial and commercial allies), which had been solidly entrenched up to that point and whose economic policy had corresponded almost perfectly to textbook neo-classical liberalism. This alliance saw its economic and political power gradually reduced and we then begin to see a situation of 'shared power'. The 'grande bourgeoisie', the national and foreign industrialists, the lower middle class and the working class formed opposing populist alliances. This also marked the beginning of 'import substitution'. This 'shared power' (or 'constrained hegemony') explains the volatility of the economic situation in Peru, and the recurrence of crises.

Although the industrial bourgeoisie (and within it, the exporters) have tended to supplant the primary exporting sectors which held power before World War II, they have not yet attained permanent supremacy. The fundamental goal of the reformist governments is to 'reduce external dependency and achieve improved social justice', which is to be achieved by industrialisation and expanding the internal market by raising profit rates in the industrial sectors. In this context the 'freezing' of basic 'prices' attempts to alter the distribution of income in favour of the 'modernising' sectors of the economy, and away from agriculture and other primary-exporting sectors. Such measures are in sharp contrast to the aims of the pro-exporting and pro-oligarchy groups which generally support totally free prices. When they are in power, therefore, there is an opening up of the economy, while under reformist policies there is a selective closing of the economy to the outside world.

Let us examine why fixing basic prices is 'essential' for the political survival of reforming governments. The prices, and the means and criteria for fixing them, are as follows:

1. Prices of basic agricultural and manufactured goods: these are held below their marginal cost.
2. Interest rates: these are held constant, at levels below inflation rates or returns on capital.
3. Rates of exchange: these are over-valued.
4. Import prices: held above domestic prices by means of tariffs to protect national industry.
5. Rents, fares, electricity prices, etc.: frozen, at levels below those consistent with 'free' markets.
6. Minimum wages: above those justified by productivity.

Each sector which supports the reformist regime is helped by one or more of these fixed prices, directly or indirectly. These sectors include the industrial bourgeoisie (oriented towards the internal market), the middle classes and workers in the modern sectors of the economy. Fixed prices also tend to favour urban sectors over rural.

Fixing prices of basic (agricultural) goods directly favours all parts of the alliance. Employed workers gain cheap food, and this raises their real income and allows them to buy more manufactured products (especially durables). For the industrialists, and the secondary and tertiary sectors in general, this means low real wages and growing demand for their products.

A negative real interest rate benefits the workers (especially the middle strata), who can acquire durables on credit, and thus virtually free, while cheap credit allows investment to increase production (with rising demand assured). A high (and rising) real exchange rate eases the importation of cheap food (in response to rising internal purchasing power) during the rising phase of the cycle, and at the same time reduces the quantity of domestic primary production (already damaged by controlled domestic prices). The industrial sector, which is highly import-intensive, can obtain intermediate goods and equipment at low prices.

Thus, with regard to these three prices there is no conflict of interests among the classes supporting the internal development model. The situation is more problematic for the other three: tariffs, rents and wages.

Some industrial sectors, whose gains from low interest rates and low food prices are only indirect effects, benefit from high tariffs on competitive imports. The middle classes (and higher paid workers) are helped by fixed rents and electricity prices, as well as indirectly from the negative interest rate and from the high exchange rate (which keeps down the price of travel and some luxury imports, especially smuggled goods). Fixing a minimum wage and urban fares is designed to favour workers (especially urban ones). They also benefit indirectly from the exchange rate (cheap food).

The first potential conflict of interests is, of course, with respect to minimum wages. The industrialists do try to evade them, not so much by not paying them as by substituting capital for labour, which is encouraged by the over-valuation of the currency (and by loans for importing equipment). This increases the capital intensity of the industrial sector.

Tariffs (and controls) on imports of final goods hurt the middle and working classes. There is a latent conflict as income is transferred from the workers to the industrialists, but it is not seen as a major issue. The best organised workers themselves gain from the production of the goods (even if this is at the expense of other workers and potential workers in exporting sectors).

Finally, control of rents apparently benefits the middle classes directly but hurts the construction industry and, indirectly, other industrialists. However, if the rising rate of growth of the money supply and falling real rates of interest are taken into account, we can see that, again, the conflict is largely apparent rather than real because the interest-rate effect on demand is greater than the loss from rents.

In summary: the need on the part of 'developmental' governments to establish a 'social' equilibrium, a worker–industrialist alliance in the 'modern' sector, has inevitably required manipulation of relative prices. This also necessarily leads to economic disequilibrium and crisis. The social groups hurt by such an economic policy are exporters, suppliers of agricultural products to the internal market and some importers. The first two, those who produce foreign exchange and food, are the worst hit, so that in the end a crisis appears: partly because of the disequilibria, partly because the sectors which are hurt react, by capital flight, cuts in output, lack of investment, under-pricing of exports, etc.

The packages of economic measures thus have a socio-political rationale, even if this does not coincide with economic rationality. The economist must therefore take account of the socio-political situation if he wants his recommendations to be heard.

Relative prices and crises

In this section, we examine how this conflict has *inevitably* led to economic (and political) crises. The exceptions prove the rule: they are the result of exceptional circumstances in the external sector. A prolonged 'boom' in exports can allow the policy to continue without high inflation or balance-of-payments deficits.

The sequence in fixing prices varies. It is not part of a preconceived plan, but rather a response to the problems of the moment, to pressures from groups in the governing alliance, and from those whom the government must compensate for exclusion from it.

Fixing the *exchange rate* is probably the feature that distinguishes reformism most clearly from orthodox economic measures. Initially, it is fixed, usually without any particular thought or because international reserves are 'too high'. The 'reasoning' comes when there are pressures to devalue: then depreciation is resisted in order to avoid rises in the cost of living, whether directly, because the country imports considerable quantities of food, or indirectly, because of the high import content of industry.

In the upward phase of the cycle, internal prices rise. This leads, *ceteris paribus,* to over-valuation. The demand for foreign exchange exceeds the supply by a growing margin. The gap must be financed by borrowing and using reserves because foreign investment falls. Once the reserves run out and the limits on credit have been reached, the crisis unfolds, in this case starting from the balance of payments.

The over-valuation makes it necessary to limit imports, through prohibitions or raising tariffs. The economy thus moves away from the situation given by comparative advantage. Resources flow towards goods for the home market and away from those affected by price controls (for example, agriculture) or the high exchange rate. Use of labour and domestic inputs falls relative to imported inputs and capital. In the presence of very high effective protection and an absence of internal competition, unemployed resources, capital wastage and high prices are inevitable.

The nominal *rate of interest* tends to be fixed (or even reduced) once a crisis is over because it is not seen as a normal instrument of control by reformist governments, until a new crisis requires it to be raised as part of a stabilisation policy. When inflation increases this results in a negative real rate. Entrepreneurs therefore increase the use of capital so that unemployment rises. Imports of foreign equipment also rise. Negative interest rates reduce the propensity to save, so that personal saving covers a declining proportion of national investment; by the end of the cycle it may even be negative. This reinforces the effect of easy credit on personal consumption. Imports of consumer goods increase, along with the inputs and capital goods needed to produce durables locally.

Low interest rates may then lead to a need to ration domestic credit, which favours the sectors in the governing alliance, especially construction and industry. This further reallocates resources from the primary sector to the secondary (and tertiary). This is in line with the expansion of demand in these sectors, but it is reinforced by the growing intervention of the government itself as entrepreneur. Clearly, these tendencies can be accompanied by rapid and large rises in the money supply. Finally, given that the sectors benefiting are more import-intensive than those losing (especially than the primary), the pressures on the trade balance are intensified.

Fixing the *minimum wage* is a response to the growing political power of some groups of workers. It is accompanied by other measures (restrictions on dismissals, higher social security payments, profit-sharing), designed to favour the most privileged and the highest paid workers: civil servants, urban workers, workers in the growing sectors.

For the minimum wage to rise faster than productivity inflates the share of government spending, especially when combined with the growth in employment in the public sector. This further reduces net government saving. Financing the resulting deficit can be done initially by increasing public foreign borrowing and then by increasing domestic credit, but this comes into increasingly severe conflict with the private industrial demand for credit, which is crowded out.

The control of essential *agricultural prices* leads to an increasingly distorted relationship between food and manufactures prices, and therefore between rural and urban incomes. The result is that some people transfer their investments to other (usually non-productive) sectors, while others migrate to the city, adding to the army of those seeking work or in the tertiary sector. The reduction in agricultural production leads to higher food imports, which the government must subsidise. This puts pressure on the trade balance and on government expenditure. 'Cheap' food releases purchasing power for 'non-essential' goods, which gives an additional impetus to the growth in imports.

In summary, the policy of manipulating the basic prices of the economy leads, in accordance with the simple mechanisms of conventional economic analysis, to increased inflation rates, a serious imbalance on the current account, low absorption of labour and high urban unemployment, a worsening distribution of national income and fiscal deficit.

The severity of the crisis varies with the type of government. The two following hypotheses are suggested. First, the more authoritarian and reformist the government, the longer the period in which the elements of the crisis may remain unknown or concealed. In order to avoid losing the political support of 'the masses', the controls (and the disequilibria) will increase; the government will try to suppress the visible elements of the crisis. Second, the greater the degree of democracy and the weaker the governing coalition, the more rapidly the crisis will be perceived and criticised by the opposition; this will lead either to rapid adoption of anti-crisis measures or to a military coup.

In spite of the spectacular failures of IMF stabilisation policies in these circumstances, every time such crises have unfolded the IMF missions delivered the same diagnosis (excess of aggregate demand over supply, because of public spending), and the prescription took exactly the same form. The programme in each case included the following measures which led inevitably to economic recession: cutting public spending, drastic devaluation, economic and political restraints on wages, rises in the nominal rates of interest (on borrowing and saving) and selective reduction in tariffs.

EVOLUTION OF THE EXTERNAL SECTOR
OF THE ECONOMY, 1970–86

During this period, which includes two of the cycles identified above, a large variety of economic policies was tried, including practically all possible policies for trade and external financing. The lessons derived from this analysis help us to understand the complex and changing relationships among the economic process, the international context and the actions and reactions of various social groups in Peru.

During the last 30 years, the external constraint has been one of the most important factors in the cyclical crises and has become more serious since access to international loans has been cut off. Productive capacity to export has failed to grow sufficiently to generate the resources necessary to pay for essential imports of intermediate goods, capital equipment and consumption goods.

There are many reasons for this failure of exports, but it is worth emphasising two of them. The first is the lack of a deliberate policy to promote production for export. Export volume has grown in a series of jumps, each the result of special circumstances, such as the rise of fishmeal as a feedstuff for cattle and the discovery of oil, or the impact of direct investment, as in copper and oil. After the government took control of the principal export enterprises, including CENTROMIN (metals), HIERRO-PERU (iron), PESCAPERU (fish), PETROPERU and Tintaya, investment in production for export fell even further.

The second is that, since the end of the 1960s, production for domestic demand has been better rewarded than for export. Intense import substitution favoured the industrial sector and increased the demand for imported inputs without leading to a genuinely integrated process of industrialisation. The constant changes in policy, accelerating devaluation or postponing it, and the changes in duties, surcharges, exemptions, licences and prohibitions, have caused the Peruvian producer to take a very short-term view of exports, and therefore to treat them as a way of disposing of surpluses, especially for manufactures, and have not encouraged investment to provide a permanent stream of exports.

From expansion to disequilibrium (1970–4)

The Revolutionary Government of the Armed Forces (GRFA), starting in 1968, gave a strong impetus to the import-substitution process, and at the same time instituted major structural changes designed to modify almost all aspects of society. The consequences of this transformation persist today. The state had a central role as producer and as regulator of the economy. By 1975 it had come to control 184 enterprises, representing 31% of the country's total capital, and was responsible for three-quarters of exports and half of imports, for more than half of investment, two-thirds of borrowing, and a third of employment. At the same time, there was an increase in administrative regulation as well as in law enforcement and defence.

A second characteristic of this period was the control of basic prices. Here the GRFA instituted the classic package of measures characteristic of populist regimes, designed to encourage import substitution. It followed a policy of fixed exchange rates, control of interest rates (at a very low level), absolute protection against imports and control of essential product prices (rents, fuels, fares and other public sector prices), and introduced subsidies for a wide range of popular consumption items.

The disequilibrium caused by the growth of the state's role and the management of relative prices, as well as the collapse of the external balance, brought about an economic crisis. The period of expansion was between 1970 and 1972; in 1973–4, external disequilibrium and domestic inflationary pressures appeared.

In 1970 the GRFA began its development strategy in earnest, following a reduction in the rate of inflation from 19% to 6.2% through very restrictive fiscal and monetary policies and at the same time, an acceleration in growth to 4.3%, with the recovery of the primary sector and of construction. Nationalisation of the International Petroleum Company was followed by agrarian reform, and then by reform in labour law.

The government became the principal engine of the economy. During the three years 1970–2, GDP grew at an average of 6% p.a., with strong growth in the secondary sector. Inflation rose slightly from 5% in 1970 to 7.2% by 1972, but the system of price controls restrained inflationary pressures. The expansion of internal demand put pressure on the external balance in two ways. First, through imports of consumer goods, principally food; and second, through the import-intensive industry. Nevertheless, it was possible to maintain a precarious surplus on the trade balance.

But the rapid growth in imports and the slower growth in exports of goods, and a growing deficit on services (because of debt-servicing and profit remittances) caused the current account to move from a surplus of US$184.9 m. in 1970 to a small deficit of $31.7 m. in 1972. At the same time, the fiscal balance worsened as public sector income was insufficient to finance the expansion in public investment. The current deficit and a significant proportion of the fiscal deficit were financed by foreign borrowing, increasing the public external debt by 14.4% between 1970 and 1972 (Tables 7.2 and 7.5).

The fundamental fact about the crisis was that it was the consequence of the failure of indiscriminate import substitution (Schydlowsky and Wicht, 1979). From 1973 the inherent contradictions of the GRFA programme became apparent. GDP continued to expand rapidly, still mainly in the secondary sectors, but the economy could no longer respond adequately so that the external deficit rose and inflationary pressures appeared. The rate of inflation rose to 9.5% in 1973 and to 16.9% in 1974, although many prices were still controlled.

The savings–investment gap grew as a result of the decline in the rate of domestic saving, from 16% of GDP in 1970 to 8.5% in 1975; investment rose from 12% to 18%. The main demand for saving came from the state.

The total public sector deficit rocketed to almost 7% of GDP in 1974. Tax reform was introduced in 1972, but total tax revenue did not increase because of the proliferation of exemptions and privileges to promote different sectors. Revenue remained at about 13% of GDP.

The trade surplus finally moved into deficit by 1974 because of increased imports, driven by the overvaluation of the currency (which reached 43% in 1974), the high import content of public investment, and the rise in the oil price (Peru was still an importer in 1974). Payments for services, interest payments and repatriated profits raised the current deficit to 7% of GDP.

Political factors also contributed. The change in the political situation in the Southern Cone countries, and the international isolation in which the GRFA found itself after 1973, led to a need for a significant increase in spending to maintain military equipment. The excess of liquidity in the international banking system allowed easy access to credit.

The military reformist experiment hit a bottleneck in the external sector relatively early because of two fundamental factors. First, the stagnation of the export sector: by 1974, the economy was exporting 30% less than in 1970. During 1971 and 1972, exports fell in price as well as in volume, and the fall in volume offset the effect of the rise` in prices in 1973–4. Second, the reformist experiment inherited a high rate of debt-service. Even in 1970, the GRFA had to devote more than 25% of total export revenue to service the debt, a much higher level than that of the rest of the region at the time.

The radical programme had divided the GRFA. By 1974, clear factions in the armed forces had appeared. The revolutionary leadership was pre-occupied with institutional questions, and the state bureaucracy with conflicts among ministries, agencies and outside bodies. The regime could not undertake coherent policies or retain control of the economy. It was in this context that the first programmes to tackle the economic crisis were introduced (in October 1974, June 1975 and November 1975); these found no consensus among the different factions and therefore failed to treat the problem decisively. The political situation in the rural areas, the tensions with neighbouring countries and dissension within the government itself made any programme to correct the disequilibria impossible.

From the crisis to the unexpected boom in exports, 1975–9

In August 1975, a coup within the leadership replaced General Velasco Alvarado by General Morales Bermúdez, but conflict on the management of the economy increased, reflected in policy inconsistencies. Following a military revolt from the right, in July 1976, progressive officers were removed from the government and a military junta was imposed over the Cabinet. In mid-1976 the GRFA was finally able to adopt more coherent measures.

The June 1975 programme had merely altered the prices of certain basic goods, in order to reduce the fiscal deficit. In November 1975, a single exchange rate, of 45 soles to the dollar, was established, a devaluation from the official rate, which had been held at 38.7 since 1969.

In January 1976, taxes were raised and public sector current spending was cut. The government acted directly on the external position by restricting travel abroad and imposing import licensing. The prices of some essential goods were increased – fuels by 43%, fares by 28.6% and some foods by 12%.

The measures taken were too little too late, so that during 1975 and the first half of 1976 the economic situation had continued to deteriorate rapidly. The deficit on external trade reached $1,097 m., 8.9% of GDP. Both prices and volume of exports fell and imports rose sharply, both public and private. Including invisibles, the current deficit in 1975 reached 11.3% of GDP.

Servicing the external debt took 36.7% of export revenue. Increased borrowing by the GRFA had raised external debt to more than $1bn, 22.5% of GDP. But even this inflow of foreign capital was not sufficient to finance the deficit so that reserves fell from $692m. in 1974 to −$553m. by June 1976 (Table 7.2). (Traditionally Peru has used the concept of net reserves. Since July 1985, it has added to this holdings of gold and silver and included liabilities to the IMF.)

The central government deficit reached 5.5% of GDP and for the first time since 1970 there was a negative balance even excluding capital spending. The high cost of subsidies contributed significantly to this. The total public sector deficit grew even more because of investment by public sector enterprises.

During this period, Peru did not sign an agreement with the IMF. In 1976, it did use IMF low conditionality loans.

The package of economic measures taken in June 1976 was intended to be an orthodox one, combining strongly contractionary monetary and fiscal policies with periodic adjustments of the exchange rate, and a return to market prices. This reversal of economic policy, however, helped to bring about the political crisis in July. The currency was devalued by 44%. After a long period of stability, interest rates were raised from 12% to 13.5% on borrowing, while the rate on savings was increased from 9% to 10%. Price controls were eased.

To reduce the fiscal deficit, a tax of 15% was imposed on traditional exports, taxes on value-added, cars and fuels were increased and tax exemptions on imports were significantly reduced. Tariffs were also unified into a single ad-valorem scale. On the spending side, wages and salaries in the public sector were frozen, subsidies reduced, purchases of goods and services frozen and investment reduced. The CERTEX, a subsidy to non-traditional exports, was reduced from 40% of the export value to 30%.

The June measures had a sharp effect on real incomes. Together with freezing of collective bargaining (imposed for six months), this led to a general strike. As a result, there was a tightening of political controls. The government eliminated what was left of the free press, imposed a curfew in Lima and decreed a state of emergency. Dismissals of striking workers were authorised, seriously weakening the labour movement. In this context of repression, in January 1977, a new package of price rises was introduced and interest rates were raised to a maximum of 17% on loans and 11.5% on savings.

This brought a strong reaction from industry and from factions within the government. Faced with the impossible task of imposing fiscal discipline, the Minister resigned in May 1977. A businessman, Walter Piazza, replaced him. He tried to continue with the basic elements of his predecessor's policy, freezing spending in all public sector bodies for 12 months, and imposing large rises in controlled prices, significantly greater than the rise in wages and salaries. For the second time, a Minister for the Economy was unable to survive the imposition of a deflationary programme and Piazza was forced to resign on 6 July, only 52 days after his appointment.

Faced with the growing discontent, the government took a step back on its stabilisation policy. The Ministry for the Economy was put back under military control. The series of mini-devaluations ended and some food prices were cut. This increased current spending, thus damaging the fiscal position.

The accelerating deterioration on external account forced the government to negotiate a stand-by agreement with the IMF in 1977, the first since 1971. The Letter of Intent required an increase of 25% on petroleum prices (except petrol) and some personal tax rises. The exchange rate was freed, after being frozen for three months, leading to an immediate devaluation of 7%. A single foreign-exchange market was established, but import licensing was retained. The private sector was permitted to hold foreign exchange.

The 1977 programme collapsed quickly, with none of its goals achieved. A new package in January 1978 brought large rises in prices and higher taxes (including a broader tax base). After a devaluation in the last quarter of 1977 of approximately 50%, the government, through a 'gentleman's agreement' with bankers in the region, again fixed the rate of exchange.

In spite of the January 1978 measures, the IMF did not pay the second tranche of the stand-by, thus also blocking a credit of $260m. from a consortium of private banks. In order to achieve a new agreement with the IMF, the government imposed a collection of measures to reduce the fiscal deficit. This increased taxes and cut spending by raising some controlled prices by 50% on average. The exchange rate was freed again, breaking the 'gentleman's agreement' and leading to a devaluation of 13%.

This marked the end of the second stage of stabilisation. From 1976 to 1978, the economic situation had deteriorated dramatically: GDP fell by 1.2% in 1977 and 1.8% in 1978; inflation increased to 33.5% in 1977 and 57.8% in 1978.

Because the devaluations and the fall in demand brought higher prices for traditional exports and lower imports, the trade deficit was reduced from $1,097m. in 1975 to $422m. in 1977, 3.4% of GDP. Debt-servicing still absorbed 36% of export revenue, and the current deficit was 7% of GDP. The inflow of capital from abroad was not sufficient to finance this, leading to a serious fall in net foreign exchange reserves, which remained negative until 1978.

In spite of the tax rises the fiscal deficit grew, reaching 7.5% of GDP. This was mainly because of a rise in current spending. The level of investment by public enterprises kept the public sector deficit at about 10% of GDP. The low response of the fiscal deficit to the stabilisation programme can be explained in part by the effects of the measures themselves. The attempts to reduce spending and increase income were neutralised by increases in wages and salaries to compensate for the rise in the cost of living, by the increase in the cost of goods and services bought by the state, and by the devaluations, which increased the local currency cost of servicing the debt. And it was not possible to impose fiscal discipline on military spending. The tax measures did not succeed in raising the tax take, which remained at its historic level of about 13% of GDP. The reduction in economic activity, the proliferation of exemptions, the general tax evasion and an inefficient tax system all help to explain this.

The only consistently orthodox measures taken during this period were those on wages and salaries. By means of state intervention in collective bargaining and delayed adjustments to price rises, real wages and salaries were significantly reduced. The share of labour earnings in national income fell from 42% in 1975 to 37% in 1978. Real wages fell by 12% and salaries by 15% between 1975 and 1978. This reduction in real personal income affected production in the secondary sector.

Export boom and recovery, 1978–80
Starting in the second half of 1978, there was a spectacular growth in exports. Revenue increased from $1,954m. in 1977 to $3,916m. in 1980, resulting from a large rise in international prices for traditional exports; the 'second oil shock', which raised the value of petroleum exports from $50m. to $845m. in 1980; and the spectacular take-off of manufactured exports which reached 22% of the total in 1980.

The recovery of the external sector, helped by the more co-ordinated management of economic policy by the team led by Silva Ruete and Moreyra after May 1978, and the financial relief of a new agreement with the IMF, allowed the country to reduce the external and fiscal deficits and revive productive activity. It is important to note that, in contrast to their predecessors, the economic team was actively supported by the military government.

Economic policy was still directed towards curing the disequilibria through a combination of strongly deflationary monetary and fiscal policies and mini-devaluations. The programme was similar to those tried in the past, differing only in the time allowed and in degree. The team decided on a 'gradualist' approach, planning to cure the imbalances over a period of 30 months. The measures went beyond a simple programme of stabilisation and were directed at restructuring the entire economy. The economic team tried to change Peru's trade pattern by specific measures favouring exports of manufactures. From the second half of 1978 there was a timid opening of the economy. The National Register of Manufactures was abolished, and instead a temporary list of prohibited imports was drawn up to remain in force until 1980. The market for foreign exchange was freed, permitting current accounts in dollars, and restrictions on financing imports were reduced.

Given the critical situation of the reserves, urgent measures were taken to avoid the suspension of debt payments; these included arranging a 'roll-over' of $185m. with the commercial banks, 'swaps' with Latin American Central Banks and other short-term measures. In September, an agreement with the

IMF was finally signed, which permitted a restructuring and refinancing of the debts repayable in 1979 and 1980. The conditions of this second agreement, unlike the first, were more than achieved because of the external recovery.

The economic team faced the fiscal problem by increasing taxes on exports, imports, income (and evasion was also attacked) and companies. These measures were accompanied by attempts to reduce public spending: public sector employees were 'invited' to take early retirement in exchange for compensation, and subsidies were reduced. There were sharp increases in prices of controlled products.

From 1979, economic policy had a clear anti-inflationary bias, and was directed to offsetting the expansionary effect of the export boom on money supply. The rate of devaluation was reduced, and from February, the government introduced prior warning of exchange-rate changes. Imports were liberalised; the average tariff fell from 66% to 40%, and the items subject to prohibition from more than 1,000 to only 9. Financing requirements were eliminated. To reduce the inflow of foreign exchange, short-term credits were cancelled and the refinancing loans were pre-paid in January 1980. The debt restructuring arranged with the Paris Club was also cancelled. Credit controls were adopted to contain the growth of the money supply.

The economy recovered to a rate of growth of 4.3% in 1979, and inflation fell to 67%, from 74% in 1978. In 1978, there was a small trade surplus and the current deficit was reduced to 1.5% of GDP. During 1979, in spite of an increase in imports, the trade surplus rose to the record figure of $1,722m., 12.4% of GDP. Because debt service fell to only 22% of exports, there was a surplus on current account of 6.9% of GDP.

By 1979, the central government had a surplus on current spending of 3.5% of GDP, and the total public deficit including state enterprises was 1.1%. Tax revenue rose to 17.1% of GDP in 1979 and to 20.6% in 1980 – mainly the result of increased revenue from export taxes which reached 2.8% of GDP in 1979, but income and corporation taxes also rose. Current spending by the central government fell. Capital spending by both the central government and state enterprises continued to increase, however.

The first half of 1980 saw preparations for elections and a return to civilian government. Therefore, although the basic elements of the anti-inflationary policy were retained during the first quarter, in the second quarter prices were controlled and subsidies introduced, significantly increasing the deficit. The military government transferred power to Acción Popular (AP) in July 1980, leaving behind an economy which was apparently healthy and growing.

The attempted return to orthodoxy, 1980–4

Once Acción Popular was restored to power, it is possible to identify three periods of very different economic policy: the first, until mid-1982, in which the anti-inflation bias of policy was continued, and the government tried to follow a neo-liberal programme directed at restructuring the economy; the second, from mid-1982 to 1984, during which, because of the collapse of the external sector, economic policy was principally directed to closing the external gap, and therefore followed an adjustment programme which put inflation control at a lower priority and progressively abandoned the plans to restructure the economy; and the last year of Belaúnde's administration, July 1984 to July 1985, in which the government tried to put into practice the slogan of 'austerity without recession' as a response to the political and electoral collapse of the government party.

The AP government's economic policy surprised voters and professional observers alike. Given the basis of support for the two parties in alliance in the government, two alternative directions might have been expected: promotion of exports, consolidating the alliance between the state and that part of local industry oriented to the external market, encouraged under the previous regime; or a modernised version of import substitution. The economic team had a good margin for manoeuvre because the external and fiscal gaps had been 'cured' and the AP in alliance with a smaller party had achieved majorities in both Chambers of the legislature. As Daniel Schydlowsky noted: 'This government could do anything.'

In spite of all this, the government, while continuing with a stabilisation policy similar to that introduced by the previous regime, introduced a plan of orthodox liberalism, directed to transforming the productive base of the country back towards primary production. This followed the tendency of the decade in the Southern Cone. But in Peru it was tried, not under an authoritarian political regime, but under a return to democracy; this rapidly constrained it.

The general orientation of economic policy was directed towards opening the economy to trade and capital flows, easing controls on foreign investment, and freeing internal markets; it accepted the concept of a 'subsidiary' role for the state. The medium-term restructuring of the productive base of the economy was closely meshed with stabilisation policy. The programme was introduced in full only from January 1981 because of the November 1980 municipal elections. The boom in the export sector reached its peak during 1981. Nevertheless, because of the opening of the economy and the exchange-rate policy, there was a rapid increase in imports, which led to a reduction in the trade surplus to 4.8% of GDP. Interest payments turned this into a current deficit of 0.6% of GDP but, because of an inflow of capital, reserves increased.

On the fiscal side, there was a clear deterioration: the public sector deficit increased to 4.7% of GDP, in spite of record tax revenues. The central government and the rest of the non-financial public sector had large surpluses on current spending; the deficit came from continued high investment, financed by external and internal borrowing.

During 1981 and the first months of 1982, trade and exchange-rate policies were directed towards neutralising the monetary impact of the accumulation of reserves. The AP government extended the trade liberalisation begun in 1979, further reducing tariffs, eliminating non-tariff barriers to imports and simplifying customs procedures. The maximum tariff was fixed at 60% and the average was reduced to 32% by 1981, the intention being to reduce it gradually to an average of 10% by 1985. By December 1981, 98% of import lines were free of controls. The policy of mini-devaluations without warning continued. The devaluations lagged behind the differential between internal and external inflation, thus reducing competitiveness, a policy which was made possible because of the high level of reserves, and which reinforced the opening of the economy and the sterilisation of reserves.

The tax reform of June 1981 was intended to simplify and modernise the system rather than to increase revenue, which was still high because of the good performance of the external sector. Trade taxes, direct and indirect, accounted for 10.5% of GDP in 1980 and 7.9% in 1981. The tax on fuels was gradually becoming the pillar of tax revenue.

Interest rates were raised three times during 1981 and 1982 to encourage savings, and the market was freed to encourage competition and to offer higher real rates for deposits in local currency. Since 1978, with the liberalisation of exchange controls, there had been a rapid 'dollarisation' of the economy because of the preference for balances in foreign currency. In 1981 45% of savings in the financial system was in dollars.

The treatment of foreign capital was liberalised. The most important change was for the petroleum companies, which were given better incentives for exploration and production. Their investment and reinvestment accounted for 87% of foreign investment during 1981–5. As Decision 24 of the Andean Pact (severely regulating and limiting the role of foreign investment) remained, in principle, in force, there was not a significant inflow of direct investment. Similarly, opening the financial system to foreign banks did not lead to a significant response.

The short-lived export boom came to an end in 1981, gradually revealing the underlying economic problems, which had remained unresolved since 1976. Because it did not adapt to the change in external conditions, the AP's economic policy contributed to the worsening of the external and fiscal balances. By the middle of 1982 a return to strict adjustment measures, which aggravated the recession and fuelled inflationary pressures, was necessary.

Growth had continued during 1981 at 3%, mainly because of an exceptional harvest and the good performance of the construction sector as a result of public investment. Because of the freeing of internal prices, the rate of inflation rose to 72.3%.

The external situation, however, had worsened rapidly, with a trade deficit of 2.7% of GDP. Imports were encouraged by the trade liberalisation and the exchange-rate policy, but in addition exports fell because of a sudden fall of almost 20% in the international prices of traditional exports and because of the reduced incentives for manufactured exports, which fell by 18%. In 1981, the CERTEX subsidy had been eliminated for some sectors, and reduced and made uniform for the rest. The international recession reduced demand for all exports, and the slowing of the devaluation reduced the competitiveness of manufactured exports.

The external gap was increased by the rise in international interest rates; this had begun in 1978 but its effect had been blunted by the export boom. Debt service amounted to 54% of exports in 1981, including the advance repayments of debts, as part of the government's programme of sterilising reserves. The deficit on current account was 8.6% of GDP. Reserves also fell.

The public sector maintained the same level of spending, but tax revenue fell from 20.6% of GDP to 17.4% because of the fall in export taxes from 5.5% of GDP to 1.9%. Taxes on imports and fuels, however, kept tax revenue above pre-1978 levels. The public sector was thus able to keep its current spending in balance, but the total deficit worsened because of investment and debt repayment, to 8.9% of GDP. This was financed by increasing domestic credit.

The serious external situation meant a return to negotiations with the IMF after three years without it. This produced an Extended Credit Facility of $734m. for three years, and compensatory financing of $226m. The agreement implied strong conditionality. During 1982 the public sector deficit had to be cut to 4.3% of GDP; there was a limit of $1bn on new long-term borrowing, and a maximum use of reserves of $100m.

The regime found itself isolated from the business sectors, because of trade liberalisation and the reduction in CERTEX, and from its popular support, because of the fall in living standards as a result of the wage policy. There were also strong divisions within the governing party between the economic team and those more inclined to take account of political considerations.

The seriousness of the external situation and the commitments made to the IMF required drastic adjustment to restrain domestic demand and to alter the relation between trade prices and domestic prices, by means of deflationary monetary and fiscal policy and a new exchange-rate policy. But the economic team proved to be incapable of imposing the necessary fiscal discipline. Further, because of the 'dollarisation' of the economy, it lost control of monetary policy. The principal measures taken were in exchange-rate and price policy, with some attempts to increase tax revenue to restructure and refinance external debt.

After April 1982, mini-devaluations greater than required to maintain competitiveness, became a basic instrument for managing the balance of payments. The intention was to cut imports and encourage exports, especially the non-traditional. Nevertheless, during 1982, imports remained almost as high as in the preceding year, showing little sensitivity to either devaluation or the reduction in domestic demand. This is the more surprising as tariffs were increased to an average of 36% with a surcharge of 15% introduced to raise revenue. The strong increase in imports was in durable consumer goods and foodstuffs, accounted for in part by still unsatisfied demand from high income earners.

Traditional exports rose, but this was offset by a fall in manufactured exports. This occurred for two reasons: the revaluation of the dollar, which reduced the Peruvian gain in competitiveness, and growing protection in industrialised countries, which affected important sectors of Peruvian exports. The trade deficit reached 2.1% of GDP.

The current deficit was $1,600m. with debt service at 45% of exports. Commercial banks continued to provide finance, in spite of the impact of the 'Mexican crisis' on international financial markets, in contrast to the situation in other Latin American countries. The public deficit worsened to 9.3% of GDP during 1982, despite a fall in capital spending by the central government; this was caused by continued investment by state enterprises. GDP grew by only 0.9%, with clear signs of recession in the secondary sector, because of external competition and the fall in domestic purchasing power.

At the end of April 1983, the renewal of the agreement with the IMF was approved with some corrective measures as a prior condition (mainly increases in some prices to reduce the public deficit). The government designed a new policy with a more radical adjustment programme. As it was not possible to pay the debt service, which had reached 57% of exports, it sought to refinance and restructure the debt. It notified its creditors that it was suspending debt-servicing, and that it intended to renegotiate with the Paris Club. In July 1983, agreement was reached, giving 90% relief for two years, equivalent to approximately $440m. with restructuring over a period of eight years, including three grace years. This relief was worth $670m.

The mini-devaluations continued; interest rates were raised again; and the level of protection was increased, to reduce the large differences in tariff protection as well as to increase revenue. Imports by the state sector were exempted. Although there was no change in declared policy, these measures began the reversal of the trade liberalisation.

In August 1983, important changes were made in the management of economic policy, probably related to the November municipal elections. There was a return to 'pre-announced' devaluations in order to reduce inflationary expectations, and the rate of devaluation was reduced. Price controls on fuels, basic products and public services were used to reduce inflation.

GDP fell by 11.8% in 1983 and inflation rose to 125%. Natural disasters and the deflationary impact of economic policy explain the contraction in production that affected all sectors. There was relative success, however, in improving the external sector. In spite of a fall in exports, there was a surplus in the trade balance of 1.9% of GDP: imports fell by 30%, because of recession, the increased rate of devaluation, the tariff surcharges and the saturation of the domestic market for imported consumer goods. Thanks to the relief on debt, this took only 24.7% of exports, reducing the current deficit to 5.4% of GDP.

The economic team was not able to reduce the government deficit. Current spending rose, and tax revenue fell, because of the fall in income, to 13.9% of GDP. As public sector investment was not restrained, the total public deficit reached 12.1% of GDP.

The Economic Minister's term of office ended with the electoral collapse of the AP in the November municipal elections. Its loss of support had led to strong internal dissent, starting at the beginning of 1983. The opposition group advocated a middle-of-the-road policy, not as market-oriented as that of the government but not as ultra-populist as that of its party officials. The electoral disaster strengthened this group.

Simultaneously with this conflict within the government, there were problems in complying with the IMF agreement. The mission which visited the country at the end of 1983 did not approve the policy of 'pre-announcement' or the price restraints introduced in August; the 'pre-announcement' system was therefore ended and large price rises were decreed. The budget for 1984 included a large rise in taxes. In spite of these measures, the IMF agreement was not approved, and the resignation of the Economics Minister and then of the Prime Minister ended any hope of continuing the stand-by.

In May 1984 the new Prime Minister, Sandro Mariategui, announced a policy of austerity without recession. This reflected a temporary triumph for the centre sector of the party, and the party's intention to recover its support in the general election of April 1985. Mariategui tried to win support from the industrial sector.

The government's actions disappointed expectations, however. The only measures with immediate impact were tax reforms, including a restructuring of income tax; an immediate reduction of value added tax from 18% to 8%; and the explicit reversal of trade liberalisation. Some major categories of imports were added to those requiring prior licences and all imports of these, including textiles, clothing and shoes, were prohibited until December. Later, in 1985, more products were added to the temporary prohibition list. The surcharge on imports was raised and to this was added a new set of increases in individual tariffs, thus increasing differentials among goods. The explicit aim of these measures was no longer greater tax revenue but the provision of adequate protection to domestic output. Finally, there were various tax and other incentives to individual sectors.

The government's initial support from the business sectors dissipated rapidly. First, there was confusion in economic management, characterised by repeated advances and retreats and contradictory policies, such as a tax on interest payments and a third change in the value added tax. Second, some elements of the deflationary policy continued, such as the increase in interest rates which meant a positive real rate on borrowing, while rates on savings continued to be negative, discouraging saving in national currency. The rate of devaluation increased; credit to the private sector was reduced.

When it found itself unable to obtain the continuation of the Extended Credit Facility, the government signed, in April 1984, a Stand-by agreement with the IMF which included targets that were impossible to achieve. Thereafter, it was impossible to refinance the external debt, and Peru entered upon a unilateral suspension of payments from the second half of 1984.

There was a slow economic recovery during 1984, and the suspension of debt-servicing reduced the current deficit to 1.5% of GDP. But, as the Central Bank pointed out (BCR, 1984b),

> we have still not recovered the level of output of the past; three-digit inflation has become endemic; the problem of the debt is still there; the public sector deficit is too high; and the saving in domestic currency has fallen, aggravating the problem of dollarisation.

To which we must add that the population was becoming poorer and the social situation was explosive. This was the situation which the new democratic government inherited in July 1985.

RECENT TRENDS AND FORECASTS FOR THE EXTERNAL SECTOR TO 1990

Our central conclusion about external policy, based on the previous analysis and the economic policy and development strategy of the present government outlined here, is as follows: domestic capital formation and creating a national market must have priority in a country like Peru; policy on trade and external finance must be treated as the 'residual', in contrast to both the primary producing-exporting and the import-substitution models. (Although the latter appears to be a strategy for development 'from within', in the end it leads to an even more fundamental dependency than the former.) What is interesting in the way the present Aprista government has developed is its movement away from an initially overt, irreconcilable conflict with the commercial banks and the international institutions; it returned, little by little, to the fold as the fall in reserves forced a return to negotiations.

The change to 'heterodoxy', 1985–7

The coming to power of Alan Garcia brought a radical change in economic policy, rejecting the orthodoxy which had led to stagnation with inflation. For the first time Peru attempted, partly because of the influence of the Argentine 'Plan Austral', an economically 'heterodox' programme with some theoretical coherence. This showed a spectacular success in its first 18 months (to December 1986). The attempt is interesting because it tried to achieve changes in economic structure by means of short-term policy, embodying long-term aims in the adjustment plan. From 1987, there was a failure of nerve on the part of the economic team, and in spite of rapid growth of 6.5% during that year, constraints appeared, accompanied by the problem of erratic political management by President Garcia.

Garcia argued (1985) that the crisis affecting Peru could be attributed basically to *three factors*. The first, linked to the *international crisis*, is that the countries at the centre 'reserve high technology for themselves, and close their frontiers' to our exports, at the same time as they 'demand implacably that we repay our external debt, which was the result of the unequal exchange between our primary materials and their manufactured products.' The second is that the application of *neo-liberal economic policies* from the end of the 1970s has aggravated Peru's economic and social problems. And third, the crisis is fundamentally the result of the persistence of a *deformed and unjust economic (and social) structure*, the result of

> our history of dependency on external forces which, allied to powerful domestic interests, has brought the country to the present crisis. Lacking a national plan, lacking an established and popular leadership, we have lived by adapting our economy to the interests of international capitalism. For this reason, we have been successively an exporter of primary materials, then an importer of equipment for an industry based only in Lima, and alien to the country, and today we are merely a debtor country.

This 'external dependency' has led, through a process dating from the sixteenth century, to profound *injustices*. These are as follows:

1. *Regional* injustice, beginning with the Conquest which 'shifted the historic orientation of Peru from the Andes to Lima', where 80% of national industry is now located.
2. The *separation into economic sectors*, grossly differentiated.
3. *Social injustice*, which is reflected in the unequal distribution of national income: 2% receive high income, 'But below them there is a marginalised 70%, the rural and the unemployed, migrants, some outside the capital and some in the shanty towns.'

In order to end these severe social and economic inequalities, the President proposed 'opening the way to social democracy' within the context of an 'egalitarian society'. To achieve this, the first Presidential Message proposed a social and economic recovery, not concentrated, as has been the case for most recoveries, solely on the modern urban sector; the aim is to establish a national integrated market. Although the first target would be the rural Andean and informal urban sectors, the strategy would also lead to industrial recovery, thanks to redistribution to the 70% who are the poorest sectors.

Garcia's analysis was based on the 'four technological sectors' of Daniel Carbonetto (1985): the *modern urban sector* (MUS), the *informal urban sector*

(IUS), the *Andean rural sector* (ARS) and the *modern rural sector* (MRS) (Table 7.1). The table shows the large differences between, and within, the sectors.

The change in economic structure proposed by Garcia demands a radical change in economic policy and in the role of the state, as well as in relations with other countries. The kernel of the programme involves changing the relative productivity of the four economic sectors specified above.

The way to this rests on an 'intersectoral redistribution of capital'. Even if this reduces investment in the modern sector, the increased investment in the backward sectors has a high productive potential because low labour productivity there is combined with a high marginal productivity of capital. The mechanism to achieve this was not made clear at the beginning, but during the government's first two years it was done through public spending (which generated programmes of massive employment at the minimum wage) and by the spectacular rise in agricultural prices (relative to industrial) although this was more unintentional than planned.

In spite of assertions to the contrary, the economic team took only short-term measures, although they have important long-term implications They were operating only with a short-term model which, it must be emphasised, applies only to the modern urban sector. It is assumed that this has unused capacity, that it buys imported, non-competitive, inputs, and that it is characterised by oligopoly. The components of the model can be summarised as follows:

1. $P = (1 + m)\ (CD)\ (1 + t)$. The price equation ($P$) tells us that these are a function of the unit costs (CD), to which capitalists add a profit margin (m) and the government, its indirect taxes (t). The policy was based on manipulating the various cost components (raising wages and the cost of foreign exchange, but offsetting these by a reduction in the cost of borrowing), and thereby reducing inflationary expectations while maintaining the profit margin. This was expected to produce 'zero inflation' in the MUS. The recorded rise in these prices was scarcely 10% in the first year (although this underestimates the real rise as many businesses moved into the informal sector, lowered the quality of their products or modified their products to escape the price freeze), and the dollarisation was almost entirely reversed during the government's first 18 months (65% of the total liquidity had been in foreign currency when Garcia came to power).

2. Effective internal demand is determined by consumption (by agricultural labourers, industrial workers, the government and capitalists) and investment (public and private). Given the level of prices and the component costs, this determines the equilibrium level of output. Rises in wages should be, according to the government, the driving force of spending, rather than public spending (the usual source of stimulus in the past) or private investment (as there was unemployed capacity). And, in fact,

during the government's first two years, private consumption explained the tremendous economic revival.

The growth of demand for the output of the modern sector, however, has fairly well-determined limits, as follows:

3. In theory, potential output was a constraint, but (because of the long recession) it was estimated that, at mid-1985, there was 60% unused capacity, so this was not binding. (By end-1987, the government estimated that excess capacity was 10%.)

4. The external balance was the most worrying constraint at the beginning of the administration. The current balance in 1986 had a large deficit ($1,055m.), equivalent to 5% of GDP. Imports grew vigorously in 1986 with the economic revival, but exports fell by approximately 16% because of the continued fall in international prices for Peru's primary materials, and a fall of $70m. in exports of non-traditional products. The average purchasing power of Peruvian exports in 1986 was less than half what it had been at the beginning of the decade. Metals, especially copper, were particularly depressed. The fall in the oil price alone reduced income by about $300m.

In non-traditional exports, there were problems in selling some products, lower supply in some sectors and falls in prices notably in the agricultural sector and chemicals. There has been a clear fall in intra-regional trade following the adjustment policies undertaken by the majority of other Latin American countries because of their debts. Payment of debt with exports, arranged with the Soviet Union and some other socialist countries as part of the debt renegotiation, has been one means of avoiding these problems, permitting the export of some difficult-to-sell products.

It had been impossible since 1984 to make new refinancing agreements under acceptable terms, because of the size of the debts falling due and the conditions demanded by creditors. Therefore, in 1986, for the third consecutive year, Peru was obliged to postpone repayment of most of its public debt. Net borrowing by the public sector during 1986 was close to $600m. of which more than 80% represented unpaid interest. This was an increase of 5.6% in medium- and long-term external debt. Up to 1982, most debt was new loans, while in 1983–4 most was from renegotiation, and since 1984 most was unpaid interest. Private medium- and long-term capital, and short-term credit lines, had seen an outflow of on average $500m. a year in 1983–5, but in 1986 there was an inflow of about $220m., mainly as a result of higher commercial credits because of higher imports and the restriction of remittances.

The economic team was well aware that the renewed growth of demand would quickly lead to a loss of reserves, and for this reason proposed cutting debt service to 10% of exports of goods and services (see appendix, pp. 154–5).

Later, in August 1986, the same aim of reducing the drain on reserves was pursued further with the prohibition of the remittance of profits of foreign subsidiaries. (This measure was taken at the time when the IMF declared Peru 'ineligible'.) The regulations have thus reduced remittances from an average of $677m. in 1980–5 to $150m. in 1986 and about $30m. in 1987. From October 1986, however, Peru once again began to lose reserves steadily. Although it still had reserves worth six months of imports, the government was aware that it had to re-establish links with the international community.

The external constraint remains the most critical point of its programme. In the second half of 1987, it tried to meet it by increasing devaluations and special assistance to exports, especially of non-traditional goods, and particularly of manufactures.

5. Finally, we have the constraint of inelastic agricultural supply, which was probably the principal short-term constraint. The increase in demand from the MUS drastically raised agricultural prices, as it increased demand both for agricultural inputs to industrial production and for food (because of an increase in wages in the MUS and in employment in the IUS). There was also an increase in imports in 1986–7, which gave a further twist to the external constraint.

The system of daily mini-devaluations was abandoned, and after a large reduction in the exchange rate (12%) at the beginning of August 1985, the central rate was fixed until December 1986, in order to reduce inflation and reverse the dollarisation. It should be noted, however, that an increasing number of transactions were done under the financial rate, in which (from August 1986) there were two quotations: the rate for certificates, fixed at 25% above the central rate, and the free rate, fixed in the market. From January 1987, both the central and financial rates were devalued by 2.2% a month (an annual rate of 39%, compared with inflation which was close to 100%).

Imports of non-essential goods were restricted temporarily, followed by strict control (through the Central Bank).

The model worked well enough during the first 20 months of the administration, and for the short-term objectives. There were indeed two points which did not appear in the model, because it only considered 'one good', but which proved to be beneficial. First, it did not foresee the effects which the internal expansion would have on the demand for food. Thanks to this, prices of agricultural products rose explosively, redistributing income to peasants. Secondly, the programme to help temporary labour and the rigid control of prices in the MUS brought an unprecedented revival in informal urban activity (and income), which redistributed income to this 'marginal' group. Richard Webb (1987) has estimated that in 1986 the real income of the IUS rose by 20% and of the peasant, by 24%.

Results and forecasts to 1990

In mid-1985, the economy had had a high level of unemployment and underemployment and stagnation of output, with GDP per capita in real terms at the level of 20 years before. At the same time, inflation was high and increasing (approaching 250%), which led to speculation and dollarisation of the economy, and discouraged productive investment. Linked to these problems, there was a climate of lack of confidence and interest by economic groups in exploring development opportunities, which was translated into transfers abroad (the total of exported capital is estimated, conservatively, at US$7bn).

This situation had damaging effects on the allocation of resources, stability of costs and income distribution, with a consequent explosion of severe social tensions. Terrorism increased, endangering the democratic system. Peru faced serious difficulties in access to international financing and in debt-servicing. All these problems had been changed for the better during the first two years of the government, with increasing growth, the end of dollarisation, income redistribution and lower rates of inflation. These successes, however, were precarious.

By the middle of its term of office, December 1987, the economic situation could be summarised as follows:

1. Economic growth, after exceeding expectations in 1986 and 1987 (5% p.a. expected, and 7.6% achieved), had fallen as the constraints started to appear:
   (a) Practically all the excess capacity had been brought into use in the strategic sectors of the economy, such as cement, steel, paper, even though there was still 10% excess on average.
   (b) International reserves had fallen to very low levels, because of the high demand for foreign exchange, increased by speculation in 1987.
   (c) Investors were worried by government policy.
2. Inflation had increased (from the end of 1986) because:
   (a) It had been necessary to increase tariffs and control prices.
   (b) There was growing uncertainty about future changes, fuelled by the rapid fall in international reserves.
   (c) There was speculative stock-building by businesses, aware that the negative interest rates and the cost of foreign exchange would have to rise.

In addition, dollarisation of the economy was returning, the terms of trade had turned back against agriculture and, above all, there was a growing threat from the guerrillas in an atmosphere of increasing social unrest. It was clear that, in 1988, it would be necessary to raise basic prices and that both inflation and growth would deteriorate; in other words stagflation.

We would argue that this failure of the heterodox economic policy is attributable to three central factors:

1. The absence of structural changes during its application, specifically the fact that there was no change in patterns of production or of consumption to reduce the marginal propensity to import.
2. Growth in the economy had been general, instead of directed selectively towards popular consumption goods and the inputs needed to make them.
3. There had been inadequate stimulus for non-traditional exports.

These conclusions lead us to the forecasts presented in Table 7.2 for the balance of payments to 1990. (These are based on reworking and updating those presented in BCR, 1984a.)

Before presenting the basic scenario, it is necessary to consider what the goal should be for economic growth during the period under consideration. GDP in Peru grew in real terms at an annual rate of 5.3% between 1961 and 1976. Since 1977, output has suffered a long period of stagnation and crisis, which, in combination with the increase in population, has meant that in 1984 real GDP per capita was 20% below that in 1976. Taking this as a reasonable measure of personal income, it is a priority that the economy should at least recover the 1976 level of GDP per capita. This relatively modest and unambitious goal implies that the economy should grow by 7% p.a. between 1985 and 1989. This rate is high, but similar to that recorded in 1961–6 and 1970–4, and starts from a point with a large quantity of resources underemployed. The urgency of achieving this goal can be better appreciated if we note that, if growth were 4%, the 1976 level would be reached only in 1999.

For exports (Table 7.3), *traditional exports* behave differently from non-traditional. Their prices fluctuate in world markets and their volumes are not very sensitive in the short term to internal policies, as most require investment with long maturity periods, much of which is foreign or financed by foreign borrowing. In the past, some resources have been exhausted, and there have been crises in some sectors. Total export capacity has remained practically unchanged for the last 15 years. Given that primary export prices were extremely depressed at end-1987, for the forecast for 1988–90 we assume a gradual recovery (5% p.a.).

For volume, we expect growth to be 2–3% p.a., taking account of some mining operations which will come into production in the period, the gradual recovery of the agricultural sector and of marine resources, but also the gradual fall in output of oil. No change was assumed in incentives to direct investment which might stimulate new mining investments, in particular in petroleum. This would probably only have effects over a longer period as such projects require long periods of investment, and are high-risk. On the other hand, some metal products could be seriously affected by technological change.

Traditional agricultural and marine products would be difficult to increase, given the growing use of substitutes for cotton and fishmeal and the presence of quotas in some markets, for example for sugar and coffee. These may hold prices above a free market level, but they restrict the volume. It seems unlikely that traditional products could be increased more than in the base scenario. A change of 10% in prices would make a difference of $300–400m.

Non-traditional products are mainly manufactures, whose prices vary less than for primary goods. Their volumes depend partly on external factors, such as protectionism in the markets, but also on internal factors, including local demand, production capacity and policy.

Peru can create industries which would be internationally competitive. But these must be based on the natural resources and the type of labour available, and possibly on the relatively low energy costs (especially if it is possible to complete the hydro-power programme). In certain sectors, especially mining and fishing, it would also be possible to compete in providing technology, especially in countries at similar or lower levels of development in Africa, Oceania and Asia.

Processing of agricultural, fish, mining, forestry and tropical products, as well as Andean specialities, could be the basis for an industry including a combination of semi-processed and finished manufactures, mass production goods and speciality products, mass and luxury consumption products, and capital goods using intermediate technology.

Non-traditional exports are more sensitive in the short term than traditional to internal policy because of the considerable excess capacity and because sales can be increased by means of quickly maturing investments and by shifting production from the national market to exports. The forecast is that these could average US$1bn p.a. with traditional at $2–2.5bn.

In the medium and longer term, Peru has many potential products which could compete internationally, but to export them it will need to overcome particular problems. It is highly competitive in cotton because of its quality, but the policy has been to promote substitute crops like maize and rice. These not only restrict cotton exports but also hinder the development of exports of textiles and clothing. It is obvious that Peru's capacity to increase sugar exports, when faced with the subsidies in the United States and the European Community, is marginal. Replacing this product could lead to a substantial increase in relatively high-value agro-industrial production and exports. In the case of alpaca wool, genetic research and new systems of cattle management could substantially increase production; this would also support development of the textile industry.

To these, we can add some new products where Peru has particular export advantages. It may be possible to 'cultivate' intensively some sea resources, including fish and shellfish. World demand for these products is one of the most dynamic growth areas, and there are opportunities not only for those already exported like shrimp and scallops, but a broad range of products which could supply protein for poorer countries, as well as frozen fish for intermediate markets and luxury products for the Asian and industrial markets. Among tropical products, both woods and tropical foods have been underdeveloped.

It is necessary to ensure in advance that the product is suitable to its market. This is a substantial change from past practice; exports of surpluses meant the products were suitable for the internal market. It implies more resources for design, research and marketing, on a continuing basis. A second requirement is selectivity in choosing exports, to establish which branches have the greatest potential over a reasonable time horizon. Third, initiative and an aggressive export mentality are necessary in both the private and public sectors. This requires the country to have a permanent export policy and not to alternate between rewards and disincentives to exports.

Latin America is an area to which Peru has given little attention in the past. If it wants to reduce its present linkages with the US and the EC, more trade here, especially with the other Andean countries and Brazil, could be an appropriate strategy. In the early 1970s, the Andean Group planned a system of general integration which would start from measures to free trade, then move to a common external tariff, and eventually form a true wider market to promote intra-trade and rationalise production. The hard realities of negotiations meant that exceptions to the rules left a high proportion of production outside the scheme.

Nevertheless some initial success was achieved in increasing trade among its member countries. For certain countries, especially Peru, the Andean market was a promising one for some products with marginal capacity to compete in other markets, including metal products, steel and chemicals. When the region's balance-of-payments problems increased, adjustment programmes by some countries not only changed relative exchange rates but also led to a gradual closing of national markets, which brought a dramatic fall in regional trade and growing disenchantment. Many of the reasons which stimulated integration in the 1960s, however, remain valid. There are still economies of scale to be gained from the sub-regional market, although new technologies in many cases reduce these. The idea of a wider market which could have the same weight as those of the large countries of Latin America like Argentina, Brazil and Mexico also remains a possible goal.

At present, the future of Andean integration is unclear because of countries' internal difficulties and, in some countries, a reduced role for government. In order to re-establish the original enthusiasm an alternative of partial integration is needed which would allow countries the freedom to use the principal tools of economic policy, with more complete integration as an ultimate objective. First, the Andean Group could cut the cost for individual countries of new technological innovations, especially in microelectronics and genetic applications. This could begin with basic research and training, and extend to experimental production; the Andean market could be a step towards international competitiveness. Secondly, some industrial products need to be adapted to compete at world level. Joint programmes could reduce the cost to each country of this restructuring. The companies affected would need to be involved in the planning process. Thirdly, there are opportunities for regional co-operation which would strengthen the links among the Andean Group and increase its international standing in negotiations with other areas. These include, on the financial side, strengthening the role of the Andean Reserve Fund (FAR) and the Andean Development Corporation (CAF); research on social programmes; co-operation on agriculture, cattle-raising and fishing; joint commercial negotiations, both bilateral and multi-lateral.

There are three other large markets which could be relevant to Peru, individually or as part of a process of Latin American integration. The most important of these is Brazil, which will be one of the most important economies in the world by the beginning of the twenty-first century, with a large internal market and a financial and technological superiority to the rest of Latin America. The design of a strategy for relations with Brazil, and for Peru to act as an 'economic link' between it and the other area of high economic growth, the Pacific Basin, is a subject which deserves serious analysis.

Among the countries of the Basin, Japan, Singapore and Hong Kong are particularly important as suppliers of finance and consumers of luxury products: Malaysia, Indonesia and Thailand would be countries with similar levels of development with which trade in technology is possible; South Korea and Taiwan are producers of advanced manufactures; and Australia and New Zealand have many similarities in natural resources, such as mining and fishing. All offer large potential for trade (and, probably, financing) for Peru and Latin America as a whole. Peru has an exceptionally favourable location to take advantage of this; it would require more contacts between the business sectors.

For Mexico, the third opportunity, transport difficulties and the natural linkage of Mexico with the US impede closer relationships with Latin America.

Sales of services (excluding tourism, which was treated as a non-traditional export) were expected to grow only in line with world inflation. They consist mainly of income from diplomatic missions in Peru, insurance and tele-communications

Imports are mainly of intermediate and capital goods, and in recent years have amounted, on average, to about 11% of GNP. But a rapid expansion of production usually leads to a greater increase in imports because of higher investment and stock-building. The manufacturing sector has been developed in conditions which favour intensive use of capital and imported inputs. The traditional mining sectors also have a high share of imported capital goods to meet the need for infrastructure and sophisticated machinery. Given that technology and industrial structure are difficult to change in the short run, these imports are essential for economic growth. Estimating from the structure and sectoral composition of imports over the last 25 years, an elasticity of 1.2 relative to GDP has been found, implying total imports in the forecast period of $10 billion (see Table 7.4).

There are natural and structural limits to the domestic production of some agricultural and capital goods, but there are opportunities for substitution for other imports. In the medium term, it is not possible to achieve significant changes in consumption habits or in the use and development of technology. Nor is it possible to achieve an increase in arable land. But this does not mean that it is not essential to make efforts in these directions for the future.

In 1984 food products were 10% of the total, principally meat, dairy products, wheat and soya oil. A substantial reduction would only be possible through rationing. To increase pastures without displacing existing cultivated land could be done in the 3,000 hectares from the Majes project, but it would still be necessary to import new cattle. It is not really possible to reduce wheat imports significantly. Local production is almost entirely of soft grains; to increase production of hard bread grains would require increasing productivity or cultivated land, changes which could only be achieved over the long term. Imports of soya oil are worth approximately $50m. The quality of the land does not permit profitable cultivation of soya. An increase in palm oil output to replace some imports of soya oil (in combination with fish oil) could only be achieved over six or seven years, as advances are made at the edge of the forest.

Foreign spending which could be restrained without adversely affecting growth would be tourist spending abroad and imports of luxury consumption goods. Luxuries represent 4% of total imports, and tourism 3%.

Analysis of *external financing* must consider two components: direct investment and borrowing. Foreign investment has an important role in a country like Peru with mineral and oil resources and without a high level of internal saving, and has advantages in taking on high risks. It was assumed that net direct investment would be nil during the three year period. Some new investment is expected, although this may prove optimistic, but high mining and oil investments in the past decade will lead to a substantial outflow.

Foreign borrowing depends partly on internal decisions (how much does a country want to increase its debts?), and partly on the supply of international finance. Past evidence suggests that, for Peru, if such borrowing is not to be an unsustainable burden on the economy, the ratio of debt to output should not exceed approximately two-thirds. A higher ratio might permit an artificial growth of the economy in the short term, but would lead to later crises in which this extra growth would be lost. In the past 15 years, the ratio was greater only in periods of great difficulty (1977–8 and 1983–4).

This analysis of the individual variables leads to a cumulative deficit on current account of almost $1.7bn (see Table 7.2) for the three years 1988–90. Probably it will be much greater as our forecasts for non-financial services exports are very optimistic. This implies that, in order to remove the external constraint, it is essential to make efforts on both the international and the national level. Relations must be re-established with the commercial banks, given the large inflows needed by the public sector ($900m. p.a. on average). A large increase in non-traditional exports must also be achieved and international agreement obtained on reducing financing costs.

The greater part of the foreign exchange gap must be covered by improving the balance of trade, through energetic policies to reduce 'inessential' imports and increase exports.

Non-traditional exports should have priority as they increase output and utilisation of resources. In the medium term, traditional exports should be stimulated with equal vigour, thus encouraging a significantly higher inflow of foreign investment. Both types of exports require new permanent measures, which should be an integral part of macroeconomic policy and a coherent development strategy. Foreign borrowing should be complementary to these efforts, especially from sources of soft credits, such as the international organisations, given the high cost and poor prospects for borrowing from the commercial banks. If these efforts are insufficient, the only alternative is to reduce imports still further, which would require acceptance of a lower rate of growth, and a slower recovery to the 1976 income level.

APPENDIX

The 10% limit on debt-service is justified by the following arguments:

1. In relation to the short- and long-term government objectives, to improve immediately the living conditions of the majority of the population and to establish a new pattern of development, that is, to satisfy the 'internal social debt', it was essential to cut the payments.
2. The duration of the moratorium was initially fixed at six months. The government then extended it to 'until conditions change', that is, until the terms of trade improve, interest rates fall and the industrial countries reduce their protection.
3. Concerning different types of debt: in the government's first two years, the limit was restricted to specified official external debt, according to criteria of borrower, maturity and the nature of the credit.

The government had no idea of 'capacity to pay' of the sort which economists use; the figure of 10% was not based on calculation. Nor was it a question of limiting the payment to some specified maximum percentage of exports, derived from future import needs or from some criterion of equilibrium in the balance of payments, or some target level for international reserves. There were various reasons given for this informal procedure, suggesting a confused combination of all of them (a reflection of the 'mental state' and the knowledge which the government possessed when it took power).

The first was that a set of economic criteria would have been too complex for the layman (and the 'limit' was intended to impress him); it would have been necessary to recalculate the payments at least every quarter as the terms of trade, GDP, imports, the global deficit on the balance of payments or reserves changed. It would appear that a precise and (apparently) simple limit of 10% was adopted as a means of forcing on the government itself a drastic reduction of debt servicing.

The second explanation is that, in terms of the government's goals, it was not possible to calculate a capacity to pay. It was proposing a radical change in the pattern of production and consumption, such that in the long term – once economic and social equilibrium had been attained – there would be no need for reserves as a support for the balance of payments. But, until this final equilibrium is attained, the country needs a cushion of reserves.

In the third place, the idea of the partial moratorium on the external debt is an idea which emerged only a few weeks before the first Presidential Message. Until then neither Alva Castro (1984) nor Alan Garcia (1985) had considered such a limit.

Table 7.1 Characteristics of the 'technological sectors' of Peru: 1981 and projections for 1991

Economic sectors:		Modern urban	Informal urban	Modern rural	Andean rural	Total
1. Economically active population '000 people	1981	2,566.0	1,271.6	756.0	1,134.1	5,227.6
	1991 A	3,409.1	1,904.4	983.1	1,252.1	7,549.3
	1991 B	2,969.7	2,363.8	963.1	1,252.7	7.549.3
% of total	1981	44.8	22.2	13.2	19.8	100.0
	1991 A	45.5	25.2	12.7	16.6	100.0
	1991 B	39.3	31.3	12.7	16.6	100.0
Annual growth rate	1991 A	2.9	4.1	2.4	1.0	2.8
	1991 B	1.5	4.0	2.4	1.0	2.8
2. Value of output $m	1981	11,085.0	990.8	1,360.9	680.4	14.117.1
	1991 A	18,056.3	1,037.6	2,113.4	680.4	21,887.7
	1991 B	15,656.5	5,381.0	2,113.4	2,254.9	25,385.8
% of total	1981	78.7	7.0	9.6	4.0	100.0
	1991 A	82.5	4.7	9.7	3.1	100.0
	1991 B	61.6	21.6	8.3	8.9	100.0
Annual growth rate	1991 A	5.0	0.8	4.5	0	4.5
	1991 B	3.5	17.8	4.5	12.7	6.0
3. Value of capital $m	1981	33,357.6	546.4	3,024.2	249.5	37,177.7
	1991 A	54,160.8	572.2	4,692.0	245.0	59,678.0
	1991 B	46,909.4	2,978.6	4,692.0	2,163.4	57,243.4
% of total	1981	89.7	1.5	8.1	0.7	100.0
	1991 A	90.8	1.0	7.8	0.4	100.0
	1991 B	81.9	5.2	8.2	4.7	100.0
Annual growth rate	1991 A	5.0	0	4.5	0	4.5
	1991 B	3.5	17.9	0	26	4.0

Table 7.1 (continued)

Economic sectors:		Modern urban	Informal urban	Modern rural	Andean rural	Total
4. Average monthly income						
$m	1981	180	63	90	48	116
	1991 A	220	47	100	43	126
	1991 B	219	157	100	110	168
5. Average productivity						
$m	1981	4,320	816	1,800	600	2,464
per year	1991 A	2.0	4.0	1.9	1.0	n.d.
Rate of growth	1991 B	2.0	9.5	2.0	8.6	n.d.
6. Capital per worker						
$m	1981	13,000	450	4,000	220	3,490
	1991 A	14,795	300	4,871	195	7,905
	1991 B	15,796	1,260	4,871	2,126	7,582
Rate of growth	1991 A	2.0	24.0	2.0	1.0	2.0
	1991 B	2.0	10.8	2.0	25.6	1.5

Note: Values are in 1981 US$.
Source: Calculated from Carbonetto (in Alarco 1985, Tables 16–18).

Table 7.2 Balance of payments 1970–86 ($m) and projections to 1990

	1970	1971	1972	1973	1974	1975	1976	1977	1978	1979	1980
I Current account	185	-34	-32	-192	-807	-1,535	-1,072	-783	-164	953	-102
A Trade balance	334	159	133	79	-405	-1,097	-675	-422	304	1,772	826
1. Exports	1,034	889	945	1,112	1,503	1,330	1,341	1,726	1,972	3,676	3,916
2. Imports	-700	-730	-812	-1,033	-1,908	-2,427	-2,016	-2,148	-1,668	-1,954	-3,090
B Financial services[a]	-149	-125	-121	-181	-219	-284	-375	-439	-646	-931	-909
3. Public sector	-34	-51	-53	-70	-101	-177	-216	-262	-344	-435	-437
4. Private sector	-115	-74	-68	-111	-118	-107	-159	-177	-302	-496	-472
C Non-financial services	-82	-107	-83	-132	-228	-231	-104	-26	48	10	-166
D Transfers	82	39	39	42	45	77	82	104	130	152	147
II Long-term capital	24	-28	115	383	895	1,135	642	728	444	656	463
E Public sector	101	15	120	314	693	793	446	659	405	617	371
5. Receipts	164	158	210	418	820	917	781	1,067	849	1,084	1,208
6. Refinancing	26	26	76	254	215	160	15		227	539	372
7. Amortisation	-121	-156	-164	-352	-338	-284	-282	-402	-659	-980	-1,203
8. Other[b]	32	-13	-2	-6	-4		-68	-6	-11	-26	-6
F Private sector	-77	-43	-5	69	202	342	196	69	39	39	92
III Basic balance	209	-62	83	191	88	-400	-430	-55	280	1,609	361
G. Short-term capital and errors and omissions	48	-14	-32	-178	194	-177	-438	-294	-204	-30	361
IV Balance of payments	257	-76	51	13	282	-577	-868	-349	76	1,579	722
Memorandum items											
Net reserves	423	347	398	411	693	116	-752	-1,101	-1,025	554	1,276
Current ac./GDP (%)	2.9	-0.5	-0.4	-1.8	-6.0	-9.3	-6.8	-5.5	-1.3	6.1	-0.4
Current ac./exports (%)	17.9	-3.8	-3.4	-17.3	-53.7	-115.4	-79.9	-45.4	-8.3	25.9	-2.6
Terms of trade (1978=100)	n.d	n.d	n.d	n.d	n.d	120.0	111.9	116.9	100.0	134.5	152.7
Debt service/exports (%)	n.a	n.a	n.a	n.a	n.a	n.a	n.a	29.6	29.2	19.7	28.6
Exchange rate (Intis/$)	0.04	0.04	0.04	0.04	0.04	0.04	0.04	0.06	0.08	0.16	0.22

Table 7.2 (continued)

	1981	1982	1983	1984	1985	1986	1987	1988	1989	1990
I Current account	−1,729	−1,609	−871	−221	125	−1,055	820	486	−581	−524
A Trade balance	−553	−429	293	1,007	1,172	−16	−178	−132	−224	−153
1. Exports	3,249	3,293	3,015	3,147	2,978	2,509	2,586	2,806	3,154	3,563
2. Imports	−3,802	−3,722	−2,722	−2,140	−1,806	−2,525	−2,766	−2,938	−3,378	−3,716
B Financial services[a]	−1,019	−1,033	−1,130	−1,165	−1,011	−831	−352	−268	−308	−351
3. Public sector	−453	−548	−636	−806	−707	−605	−210	−118	−143	−176
4. Private sector	−563	−485	−494	−359	−304	−226	−142	−150	−165	−175
C Non-financial services	−318	−314	−253	−221	−170	−304	−391	−225	−199	−190
D Transfers	161	167	219	158	134	96	102	140	150	170
II Long-term capital	565	1,194	1,384	1,189	691	603	285	636	846	670
E Public sector	305	989	1,431	1,392	814	586	157	536	736	550
5. Receipts	1,620	1,934	1,530	1,026	693	475	425	801	1,016	850
6. Refinancing	80	109	1,024	499	201					
7. Amortisation	−1,394	−1,054	−1,145	−1,441	−1,329	−1,453				
8. Other[b]	−1	—	22	1,308	1,249	1,564				
F Private sector	260	205	−47	−203	−123	17	128	100	110	120
III Basic balance	−1,164	−415	513	968	816	−452	−535	150	265	146
G. Short-term capital and errors and omissions	660	539	−553	−721	−536	−7	−121	−50	−70	−85
IV Balance of payments	−504	124	−40	247	280	−459	−656	100	195	61
Memorandum items										
Net reserves	772	896	856	1,103	1,383	924	268	368	563	624
Current ac./GDP (%)	−6.8	−6.3	−4.4	−1.1	0.7	−4.0				
Current ac./exports (%)	−53.2	−48.9	−28.9	−7.0	4.2	−42.0				
Terms of trade (1978=100)	125.0	102.9	110.3	101.1	86.8	64.3				
Debt service/exports (%)	46.8	36.7	20.1	17.4	16.3	15.0				
Exchange rate (Intis/$)	0.29	0.42	0.70	1.63	5.20	13.99	13.95			

a. Excluding cost of unpaid debt servicing.
b. Includes other public sector borrowing and, from 1983, equivalent to net movement of arrears on external debt.
Source: Banco Central de Reserva del Peru.

Table 7.3 Principal exports 1970–86 ($m) and projections to 1990

	1970	1975	1980	1981	1982	1983	1984	1985	1986	Projections			
										1987	1988	1989	1990
I Traditional products	1,000	1,234	3,071	2,548	2,531	2,460	2,421	2,264	1,861	1,896.2	1,955.9	2,154.3	2,353.2
Fishmeal	303	168	195	141	202	80	137	118	204	238.9	285.1	312.1	347.2
Volume ('000 tonnes)	1,873	781	417	315	616	205	401	508	716	784.3	862.7	931.7	1,006.3
Price ($/tonne)	162	215.8	469.4	448	328.5	386.7	342.4	232.6	285.5	304.1	330.5	335.0	345.0
Cotton	52	53	72	63	85	44	23	51	39	21.3	25.0	26.3	28.7
Volume (00,000 lb)	1,456	737	702	685	1,287	670	246	624	473	212.8	250.0	260.0	273.0
Price (cents/lb)	35.8	71.9	101.8	92.8	66.1	66.4	92.5	82.6	82	100.1	100.1	101.0	105.0
Sugar	61	269	13		20	35	49	23	22	15.0	13.4	18.4	22.6
Volume ('000 tonnes)	403	422	53		59	89	116	64	55	33.0	30.0	33.0	35.0
Price (cents/lb)	6.9	29.3	11.4		15.2	17.9	19.4	16.8	18.5	20.5	20.5	25.6	29.7
Coffee	44	49	140	107	114	116	126	151	272	153.4	151.9	157.1	172.9
Volume ('000 tonnes)	44	42	44	46	43	55	52	60	74	75.0	78.2	80.9	83.0
Price (cents/lb)	45.8	53.8	146.9	107.4	119.4	96.8	112.7	115.9	169	94.0	89.3	89.3	95.8
Copper	252	183	750	529	460	442	442	476	437	488.3	541.3	564.7	626.0
Volume ('000 tonnes)	213	156	350	324	335	292	337	363	341	351.6	361.6	368.0	372.0
Price (cents/lb)	53.6	53.2	97.4	74.1	62.3	68.8	59.5	59.3	58	63.0	67.9	69.6	76.4
Iron	72	52	95	93	108	75	58	76	58	64.7	63.0	62.7	68.3
Volume (m. tonnes)	9.9	5	5.8	5.3	5.7	4.3	4.2	5.2	4.2	4.5	4.7	4.9	5.1
Price ($/tonne)	7.3	10.4	16.5	17.7	19.1	17.5	13.9	14.6	13.8	14.4	13.4	12.8	13.4
Gold	0	0	40	74	56	69	67	43	8				
Volume ('000 troy oz)	0	0	65	157	149	164	183	135	21				
Price ($/troy oz)	0	0	616.5	472.7	375.6	420.8	366.7	320.6	354.2				
Silver	29	92	315	312	205	391	227	140	110	91.4	0.0	142.2	168.3
Volume (m.troy oz)	16.8	20.7	16	28	26	32.7	26.8	22.3	19.5	12.0	0.0	18.0	19.8
Price ($/troy oz)	1.8	4.5	19.7	11.1	7.9	11.9	8.5	6.3	5.6	7.6	7.8	7.9	8.5
Lead[a]	63	99	384	218	215	294	234	202	164	219.7	223.3	225.9	249.2
Volume ('000 tonnes)	163	142	152	146	177	191	181	174	130	136.7	139.9	143.3	147.0
Price (cents/lb)	17.5	31.6	114.4	68	55.2	69.6	58.7	52.7	57.4	72.9	72.4	71.5	76.9

Table 7.3 (continued)

	1970	1975	1980	1981	1982	1983	1984	1985	1986	1987	Projections		
											1988	1989	1990
Zinc	49	163	211	267	268	307	300	268	246	242.9	245.6	258.0	281.4
Volume ('000 tonnes)	334	358	468	472	491	522	511	459	491	453.4	458.4	469.9	481.6
Price (cents/lb)	6.6	20.6	20.4	25.4	24.8	26.7	30.2	26.4	22.7	24.3	24.3	24.9	26.5
Petroleum, crude and refined	7	41	792	690	719	514	618	645	236	305.6	342.3	321.9	323.0
Volume (m. barrels)	2.4	4	22.4	19.9	22.8	20.5	23.5	27.1	22	19.2	18.5	17.4	17.0
Price ($/barrel)	2.8	10.1	35.2	34.6	31.6	26.6	26.3	23.9	10.7	15.9	18.5	18.5	19.0
Others[b]	68	65	64	54	79	63	100	71	65	55.0	65.0	65.0	65.0
II Non-traditional products	34	96	845	701	762	555	726	714	648	690.0	850.0	1,000.0	1,210.0
III Total value	1,034	1,330	3,916	3,249	3,293	3,015	3,147	2,978	2,509	2,586.2	2,805.9	3,154.3	3,563.2

a. Includes silver content.
b. Principally minor metals.
Source: Banco Central de Reserva del Peru, Department for the External Sector.

Table 7.4 Imports 1970–86 ($m) and projections to 1990

	1970	1975	1980	1981	1982	1983	1984	1985	1986	Projections 1987	1988	1989	1990
I Consumption goods	75	216	372	558	445	335	240	112	351	332	290	270	250
Public sector	28	42	108	169	28	82	23	11	116	112	113	110	109
Private sector	47	174	264	389	417	253	217	101	235	220	177	160	145
II Intermediate goods	257	1,173	1,172	1,401	1,321	1,025	949	841	1,279	1,475	1,629	1,779	1,980
Public sector	74	596	420	442	395	441	325	296	372	471	451	500	529
Private sector	183	577	752	953	926	584	624	545	907	1,004	1,178	1,279	1,451
III Capital goods	187	796	1,087	1,454	1,411	900	771	558	691	753	849	1,157	1,311
Public sector	99	425	426	511	518	457	400	169	158	146	161	181	210
Private sector	88	371	661	943	893	443	371	389	533	607	688	976	1,101
IV Others	181	242	459	389	545	462	180	295	204	195	170	172	175
Public sector	137	208	398	324	480	362	110	227	159	150	130	132	135
Private sector	44	34	61	65	65	100	70	68	45	45	40	40	40
V Total	700	2,427	3,090	3,802	3,722	2,722	2,140	1,806	2,525	2,755	2,938	3,378	3,716
Public sector	338	1,271	1,352	1,412	1,421	1,342	858	703	805	879	855	923	979
Private sector	362	1,156	1,738	2,350	2,301	1,380	1,282	1,103	1,720	1,876	2,083	2,455	2,737
Memorandum items													
Principal foods	69	313	423	503	371	431	295	204	386				
Wheat	32	137	141	167	156	151	143	104	114				
Maize and sorghum			65	50		61	18	32	33				
Rice	2	57	93	60	55	40	11		31				
Sugar		33	32	99	17	63	34		46				
Dairy products	5	39	44	55	60	39	29	22	50				
Soya	5	40	35	44	39	55	39	33	40				
Meats	25	7	13	28	44	22	21	13	72				

Source. Banco Central de Reserva del Peru, Department for the External Sector.

Table 7.5 External public borrowing and debt, 1970–86 (US$m)

	1970	1971	1972	1973	1974	1975	1976
Loans by purpose							
Investments	91	67	91	305	668	634	467
Food imports	15	25	76	71	41	64	65
Refinancing	26	26	76	254	215	160	15
Other	58	65	43	42	111	219	249
Total	190	183	286	672	1,035	1,077	796
Loans by source of finance							
Official agencies	39	50	89	139	270	359	236
Commercial banks	15	22	87	397	541	417	260
International orgns	26	32	34	24	41	35	38
Socialist countries			14	28	100	143	113
Supplier credits	110	80	62	84	83	123	149
Total	190	184	286	672	1,035	1,077	796
Credits agreed by duration							
1–5 years	43	61	126	100	110	421	336
5–10 years	96	27	174	555	446	292	313
10–15 years	13	67	92	228	662	212	457
more than 15 years	74	66	108	142	76	59	277
Total	226	221	500	1,025	1,294	984	1,383
Total external debt							
Long-term	2,190	2,242	2,370	2,709	3,441	4,352	5,250
Public[a]	945	997	1,121	1,491	2,182	3,066	3,554
Central Bank[b,c]	41	34	67	17	0	0	385
Private	1,204	1,211	1,182	1,201	1,259	1,286	1,311
Short-term[b]	1,491	1,450	1,462	1,423	1,796	1,905	2,134
Total	3,681	3,692	3,832	4,132	5,237	6,257	7,384

a. Until 1982, includes effect of revaluation.
b. Includes revaluation effects.
c. Includes IMF gold tranche.
Source: Ministry of Economy and Finance, Credit Department; Banco Central de Reserva del Peru, Department for the External Sector.

1977	1978	1979	1980	1981	1982	1983	1984	1985	1986
434	347	369	625	1,085	1,358	993	820	408	
85	98	109	171	132	92	172	106	65	
	291	928	380	163	109	1,024	499	201	
548	339	217	403	320	484	365	100	185	
1,067	1,075	1,623	1,580	1,700	2,043	2,554	1,525	859	
260	306	384	257	149	138	315	193	208	
32	240	683	648	895	838	745	272	5	
79	56	96	177	186	237	200	260	198	
417	207	65	191	156	180	364	218	241	
279	266	395	307	314	650	930	582	207	
1,067	1,075	1,623	1,580	1,700	2,043	2,554	1,525	859	
396	169	547	149	299	140	163	102	1	
155	91	169	201	343	1,168	692	116	74	
311	92	735	935	957	738	446	217	270	
146	113	305	354	440	540	624	310	97	
1,008	465	1,757	1,539	2,039	2,586	1,925	745	442	
6,263	7,226	7,941	8,126	8,090	9,197	10,925	11,976	12,629	13,173
4,311	5,135	5,764	6,043	6,127	6,825	8,256	9,648	10,462	11,048
626	751	869	710	455	707	1,089	862	825	788
1,326	1,340	1,308	1,373	1,508	1,665	1,580	1,466	1,342	1,337
2,304	2,098	1,393	1,469	1,516	2,268	1,520	1,362	1,124	1,323
8,567	9,324	9,334	9,595	9,606	11,465	12,445	13,338	13,753	14,496

Table 7.6 Real GDP by productive sectors, 1974–86 ('000 Intis, 1970 prices)

	1974	1975	1976	1977	1978	1979	1980	1981	1982	1983	1984	1985	1986
Agriculture	39,422	39,106	40,241	40,684	38,934	40,219	38,530	43,269	44,740	41,222	44,856	45,905	47,623
Fishing	3,093	2,623	3,189	3,013	3,920	4,292	4,073	3,572	3,500	2,099	4,028	4,332	4,461
Mining	21,026	18,251	19,638	26,023	29,976	32,807	31,330	29,822	32,303	29,910	31,838	33,773	32,930
Manufacturing	76,965	80,582	83,966	78,508	75,682	78,634	82,802	82,719	80,496	66,601	68,474	71,257	83,969
Construction	15,927	18,603	18,082	16,671	13,986	14,503	17,230	19,126	19,566	15,368	15,603	13,560	16,438
Government	23,076	24,114	24,596	25,285	25,159	25,033	25,420	26,015	26,535	27,066	27,066	26,931	27,519
Others	124,370	127,852	131,771	130,456	127,312	133,039	138,594	143,796	144,292	127,051	132,063	134,514	145,524
GDP	303,879	311,131	321,483	320,640	314,969	328,527	337,979	348,319	351,422	309,317	323,823	330,860	358,464
GDP per capita (Intis)	20.5	20.6	20.0	19.2	19.5	19.5	19.6	19.3	16.5	16.9	16.8	17.7	

Source: Banco Central de la Republica del Peru, Income and Output Department.

8

ZIMBABWE

PETER ROBINSON

INTRODUCTION

The recently released First Five Year National Development Plan (1986–90) provides a basic point of reference for this chapter. Although articulating the government's objectives and laying out its strategy for contending with a slow-growing world economy, the Plan is not a sufficient statement of national intent and economic options, for the following reasons: it glosses over tensions and contradictions in Zimbabwe's political economy which require to be analysed if operational conclusions are to be reached about what is politically as well as technically feasible. Secondly, it assumes that development will not be impeded by drought, interruptions to transport routes or a downturn in the world economy, while acknowledging that these assumptions 'can be easily violated by circumstances beyond Zimbabwe's control' (Plan, p. 14). With certain internal adjustments, the Plan's figures can be taken to be consistent with the High scenario.[1]

Economic and political environment

The most visible change at Independence was the redirection of policy towards attacking the extreme inequality in income distribution. The conventional objective of GDP growth was not, however, neglected. The Transitional National Development Plan (1982/3–1984/5) was based on an annual real GDP growth rate of 8%, significantly higher than the best sustained annual average achieved under the UDI government (6.3% between 1970 and 1974). The escalating social polarisation and intensification of the liberation struggle meant that growth in the succeeding five years (1975–9) fell to an average of −2.4% p.a. While the whites were to a large extent shielded, the black majority suffered the full negative consequences of this, and its redress became an urgent priority for the new government. The immediate post-Independence boom (real GDP growth of 11% in 1980 and 13% in 1981) was reversed by a combination of drought, world recession and the contractionary policy measures adopted from the end of 1982, whose aim was to reverse the unsustainable negative trend in the balance of payments. GDP fell over the following three years.

Apart from expansion of health and education most of the distribution gains made in the first two years were lost. For example, by mid-1984 average real wages for all sectors apart from agriculture were back to 1979 levels, despite minimum wage legislation (Davies, 1986).

In the post-1980 redistribution of assets, the main thrust of policy was resettlement, but that was one of the first to be curtailed when budget cuts were made. By the end of 1984, only 36,000 families had been resettled, as against a target in the Transitional Plan of 162,000 (Plan, p. 28). That target is now regarded as very ambitious (the official reason for slowing resettlement is that the required planning and implementation capacity was inadequate to the task), yet population growth is such that its achievement would have only absorbed new farmers, not relieved the long-overcrowded communal areas. To the extent that land was the central issue in the liberation struggle, lack of substantial progress in its redistribution is taken as a potent indicator of the new government's failure to move towards its overall goal of socialism (Mandaza, 1986).

Whether or not the government is in fact less hostile to capitalism than some of its public pronouncements might suggest, it is certainly nationalistic in outlook, as is reflected in its attitude to foreign investment. Stated policy is that the foreign stake in the economy should not be increased by allowing dilution of local control of existing enterprises, and should rather be reduced by foreign shareholdings being taken over by local companies or (preferably) by government. The inconsistent application of this policy, however, coupled with the rescue of failing enterprises in 1983–4, suggests that the nationalistic interpretation is more relevant than the socialist.

The rationale for ruling out the sort of major structural change required for socialism may be either external (the reality of Zimbabwe's proximity to and dependence on a power which would view the implementation of a successful politico-economic transformation in the region as impermissible), or internal, the ruling party being judged to lack the ideological cohesion and determination to carry through such a programme, or more fundamentally to be developing in an anti-revolutionary, bourgeois direction which makes a mockery of the socialist rhetoric. Roughly two-thirds of the economy's capital stock is still foreign-owned. Socialism is not, however, indefinitely precluded. A neo-colonial form of capitalism might be seen as a necessary stage during which the productive forces are built up and political consciousness raised in response to emerging contradictions (Mandaza, 1986). In the case of Zimbabwe, this stage is likely to be intensified by the process of South African liberation.

In the Plan itself, the section on 'Objectives', while not explicit, does reflect some of the tensions between the immediate and the longer term. Three levels of intention are identified (goal, aim and objectives) as follows:

The development objectives of the Plan outlined below derive from Government's socio-economic goal which states that 'the fundamental goal and aspirations of the people of Zimbabwe is the establishment and development of a democratic, egalitarian and socialist society' whose main aim is the development and enhancement of the mental and cultural faculties as well as efficient production and distribution of goods and services in order to raise the living standards of all Zimbabweans. (Plan, p. 10)

The Plan goes on to admit that even the objectives fall into the long-term category. It calls, therefore, for its achievement to be judged primarily in terms of the degree to which it meets its numerical targets rather than the objectives which are listed as:

1. transformation and control of the economy and economic expansion;
2. land reform and efficient utilisation of land;
3. raising the standards of living of the entire population, in particular, the peasant population;
4. enlargement of employment opportunities and manpower development;
5. development of science and technology;
6. maintenance of a correct balance between the environment and development.

It seems to endorse the immediate task as being to maintain the momentum of growth within essentially the existing structure. Rather than treating the government's egalitarian aspirations as a constraint on growth, therefore, it may be more relevant to regard the Plan's 5% growth target as the constraint, and distribution, public control, etc., as objectives.

It remains, however, to specify indicators for the assessment of performance. GDP growth must be supplemented by distributional measures. Agricultural support policies, particularly in pricing, have had some beneficial effects for peasant farmers in the communal areas. Aggregate *private consumption* does, therefore, reflect a wider participation in the economy than previously and, added to the expanded provision of social services reflected in growth in *government consumption,* would be a more relevant indicator to adopt than GDP growth itself. Secondly, in view of the character of the present political order (as well as more mundane considerations of data availability), it would seem appropriate to adopt the level of formal *employment* as the supplementary distributional proxy required.[2]

We argue that in the present structure of the economy import capacity is the basic constraint on development. Policy must necessarily be directed at either an increase in the availability of foreign exchange, by enhancing exports and augmenting capital inflows, or a change in the structure of the economy to reduce import dependence and capital inflows; either must be consistent with the objectives. The alternative strategy envisages an integrative approach which would result in a more widespread sharing of the fruits of growth, higher employment, more equitable distribution of income and a more sustained reduction in the import requirements which currently make the economy so vulnerable to outside influences. While this strategy would have a limited life and lead into a subsequent phase of intensified industrialisation, it would significantly reduce the risks the economy will be facing in the foreseeable future in the volatile southern African region.

The regional dimension

The most significant of Zimbabwe's links to South Africa are:

Trade. Although the proportions have, on average, been declining since Independence, South Africa, in 1985, still accounted for 10.1% of Zimbabwe's exports (down from 20% in 1981) and a larger proportion of its imports (18.3%). On the export side there is a wide spread of primary commodities (such as cotton, maize) but manufactured products (intermediates such as steel and cement, as well as a range of final goods) dominate (see Table 8.2). Among imports, the most problematic to be sourced elsewhere would be the spare parts and replacement units for equipment of South African origin, e.g. certain categories of mining plant.

Transport routes. With the closure of the Rhodesia–Mozambique border in 1976, Beira and Maputo ports and their associated rail and road arteries were under-utilised and therefore not maintained. Consequently, since 1980, Zimbabwe has continued to use primarily South African ports. Even those commodities (principally steel, sugar and ferrochrome) destined for Maputo have had to travel through South Africa because of persistent bandit attacks on the rail link. In 1985, at least 80% of Zimbabwe's overseas trade was dependent on South Africa's transport routes (Zimconsult, 1986).

Investment. At Independence, approximately 38% of total foreign capital was of South African origin, giving South Africa a 26% share in Zimbabwe's total capital stock (Clarke, 1980). Purchase of some South African holdings by the government or the Zimbabwe private sector has lowered these proportions, but not by very much (Riddell, 1987). Even these figures underestimate the degree of linkage between Zimbabwean and South African firms. Ownership in Zimbabwe is still largely concentrated in the hands of either multinational companies groups or white entrepreneurs. MNCs, even those not of South African origin, tend to regard the South African branch as the regional headquarters, while the others have sociological as well as technological links and frequently take their lead from South Africa.

The dependency is not uni-directional, and while South Africa is far better placed, in terms of preparedness as well as economic power, to withstand sanctions than the Frontline States would be, it is not clear that South Africa will seek to implement its own comprehensive sanctions. The issue of transport routes has a significance that goes beyond the present confrontation in South Africa. Maputo, Beira and Nacala are the natural outlets to the sea for most of the trade of the independent states that are currently forced to use the South African routes. The attraction of a project such as the Beira Corridor development programme is that, besides being a means of coping with a sudden closure of the South African border, restoring the infrastructure and efficiency of the Mozambique routes will give rise to considerable long-run economic advantages. Zimbabwe alone may save Z$60–80m. p.a.

Zimbabwe's membership of the Southern African Development Co-ordination Conference (SADCC) and the Preferential Trading Area (PTA) could be a positive factor. Its exports to the region are dominated by a small number of products (sugar, yarn, asbestos, coke, rail equipment, metals and soap), with growth severely limited by the import capacity of the countries concerned. A recent study (Michelsen Institute, 1987: 28) attempted, without success, to identify sectors and products where significant expansion of trade within the region could take place.

Without mentioning South Africa, the Plan emphasises transport routes as a vulnerable point. A considerable amount of work has already been done in pursuance of the objective of making the SADCC states independent of the South African transport system. With the benefit of hindsight, SADCC should have oriented this to providing alternative routes on a contingency basis rather than concentrating on economically sound but essentially medium- to long-term projects. Despite recent efforts to remedy the situation, particularly with respect to accelerating the upgrading of the Beira Corridor, from an economic viewpoint the immediate termination of trade with South Africa would be far more injurious than simply being forced to use Beira as a transport route for overseas exports and imports.

THE EXTERNAL SECTOR

Trade in historical perspective

Trade, together with domination of the economy by foreign interests, have been central elements in the socioeconomic development of Zimbabwe at least since 1890, when the British government authorised the chartered British South Africa Company to occupy Rhodesia. This situation prevailed until the status of a self-governing colony was conferred in 1923. Following the declaration of UDI in 1965, the role of trade and finance was once again highlighted by the international imposition of sanctions, which officially remained in force until the transition to Independence in 1980.

The ratio of exports plus imports to national income reached a peak of 125% in 1929, just prior to the international economic collapse (Girdlestone,

1982). At UDI the total still exceeded 100%. The impact of sanctions is seen in the very sharp decline (to 71%) between 1965 and 1966.

Over the period to Independence, tight control over the import-allocation system, coupled initially with rather rapid import substitution, resulted in the share of imports being further reduced up to 1972, rising slightly thereafter to reach 32% by 1975, marking the end of the early 1970s boom. Throughout the UDI period the share of exports tended to decline so that, with falling real income and a rising share of imports towards the end of the period, a negative balance of trade was inherited by the new government.

After Independence, import allocations were initially increased but, with exports failing to keep pace and other liabilities in the balance of payments growing, an IMF-type contractionary policy was initiated in 1982–3, reducing the import share of a declining national income to about 30%, while exports increased to a more satisfactory level matching that of imports. At the end of the initial post-sanctions adjustments, therefore, trade is still about 60% of GDP.

For the period 1981–3, Kadhani and Green (1985) analyse the current account deficit, using 12 factors to explain its growth relative to potential output. The exchange rate has a marginal impact compared with other influences. In all, external shocks (conditions in the world economy, the influence of the weather on agriculture and the effects of South African destabilisation tactics as regards transport of exports and imports), together with the particular situation after Independence (requiring a significant inflow of machinery and spare parts for replacement and maintenance), were found to account for 46%, 65% and 75% of the total deterioration to be explained in each year, with the remainder being assigned to expansion of output and investment, import and exchange-rate policy, remittance of profits and increasing payments on foreign debt. It is salutary in the context of this study to note that in 1983 external market factors (deterioration in the terms of trade, interest rate increases and the declining world economy) accounted for nearly 60% of the deterioration.

Table 8.3 gives the conventional breakdown of the balance of payments. Table 8.4 attempts to present the data on the basis of a division between the productive sector (domestic and foreign private companies and parastatals) and the household sector (flows relating to individuals or families), with the remaining sector being government. Imports are cif as this is more relevant as an indicator of the cost of importing. Dividend credits are overwhelmingly the profits of the National Railways of Zimbabwe operations in Botswana. Those assets, however, are in the process of being transferred to the Botswana authorities so that this positive item will decline sharply. Service imports include the foreign-exchange costs of expatriate workers.

Between 1978 and 1981 only the government sector registered an improvement, most of the overall deterioration in the current account being due to the very rapid increase in imports under the productive sector. Between 1981 and 1984, these trends in the three sectors were reversed, with the current account deficit being considerably reduced but not yet eliminated.

The main policy measures responsible for this were the changes in import allocation, devaluation (20% in December 1982) and the measures announced in March 1984 (temporarily stopping the repatriation of dividends and branch profits, resolving the outstanding issues of the external securities pool and the backlog of blocked funds through government 4% bonds, and permanently reducing emigrants' costs by the same means). The effect was to produce substantial immediate savings on the invisibles account, while (short of measures contrary to the Lancaster House agreements such as reneging on pension payments) effectively plugging the leakage points in the balance of payments. In future, therefore, policy to change the overall balance has to be directed almost exclusively to trade in goods and services, transport and the level of foreign debt. From a small base, there would appear to be considerable scope to increase receipts from tourism and from service exports of all kinds. On the transport side, cost savings should arise from the development of the Mozambique routes.

Table 8.5 shows the composition of exports and imports by principal commodity groups over the period 1978–84. The most marked changes on the export side are in beverages and tobacco (tobacco, one of the commodities most affected by sanctions against Rhodesia, rapidly regained its world market position after Independence), and on the import side an increase in the share of machinery and transport equipment (the ending of sanctions resulting in many firms attempting to upgrade or replace old equipment). The details of these changes are given in the disaggregated Tables 8.6 and 8.7.

The volatility of agricultural exports is illustrated by the changes in a commodity such as maize (around 500,000 tonnes in 1978 and 1983 as against 62,000 tonnes in 1980 and zero in 1984), coupled with rapidly changing prices even in nominal terms ($50 per tonne in 1978 followed by $78, $118, $146, $115, to $82 per tonne in 1983). Tea, coffee and beef have shown significant growth since Independence in both quantity and value terms. Among minerals, the most marked trend is in asbestos, which has been declining from a peak of 285,000 tonnes in 1979 to 155,000 tonnes in 1984. Manufactured exports showing a significant improvement include paper, yarns and threads, fabrics, cement and the 'other' category of machinery and transport equipment.

On the import side, the 1979 rise in the price of petroleum products increased their import cost from $73m. to $139m. in one year, despite a volume cut of about 12%. By 1984, the cost had increased to $221m., 18% of imports by value. Other major imports in recent years have been resins (plastics), textile piece goods, iron and steel plates and sheets, power machinery and switch gear, telecommunications equipment, excavating and road construction machinery, vehicle kits, and productive machinery and spare parts for, in particular, agriculture and the textile and leather industries.

South Africa has been the single most important trading partner, particularly with respect to manufactured exports, and chemicals and machinery and equipment imports. While South Africa accounted for 18–19% of exports and imports in 1984, Europe (particularly the United Kingdom) made up a further 30%. Other overseas countries with a significant share are the United States (6–9%) and Japan (5%). The most significant change in recent years has been the increase in the share of exports to the UK, from 6.9% in 1981 to 12.8% in 1984, with marked increases in the categories of food, tobacco and manufactured goods (see Table 8.2).

Role of exports in the Five Year Plan

Given the structure of the economy, and the lack of alternative means of finding foreign exchange within the balance of payments, it is now widely accepted that priority has to be given to export promotion. This perception does not derive from a rejection of import substitution or support for general trade liberalisation. Rather, it arises as a necessary condition of an industrialisation that has significant self-reliant features, but which is still immature. Quite apart from considerations of market access, transport costs, etc., Zimbabwe's political economy would not countenance the sort of labour-repressive measures needed to compete seriously in the range of products and markets which formed the basis of the export expansion strategies of the first generation of NICs.

The Plan's GDP growth target of 5.1% p.a. is critically based on the assumption that investment will be targeted to export industries and that this approach will ensure an export growth averaging 7% p.a. over the period.[3] The importance of this assumption is underscored as follows:

> Unless an aggressive export policy is pursued, exports would grow at about 4% per year and this rate is not sufficient to meet the country's international obligations and to support the projected growth in GDP. The balance of payments position could deteriorate seriously in the middle of the Plan period when repayments of foreign loans will reach their peak. (Plan, p.17)

Four per cent is the rate which the World Bank uses in its medium-term growth scenario. The Bank is, however, far less sanguine about the conditions for achieving it:

> The resultant overall growth rates of three to four percent per annum are not high. But this achievement will require significant policy support, both in maintaining a supportive environment for traditional exports and in encouraging rapid growth of new exports. (World Bank Memorandum, p. 64)

The Bank Memorandum (pp. 30–3), in common with several recent treatises on Zimbabwe's macroeconomic prospects, has dealt in detail with the potential for increasing exports (UNIDO, 1985, Chapter 10). Although differing in detail, the broad qualitative conclusions are as follows:

1. For Zimbabwe's present major exports (tobacco, gold, ferro-alloys, cotton lint, asbestos, nickel, iron and steel, sugar and coffee/tea), each over 3.5% and together accounting for 72.6% of the total, prospects are poor.
2. While whatever possible increases in these traditional areas should be made, rapid growth requires emphasis also to be placed on new products and markets; while there are some special cases (e.g. Lomé Convention beef exports to the EC), the most promising new areas are the export of manufactured intermediate, capital and consumer goods, particularly to countries in the region.

In view of these conclusions, it is worth looking more carefully at the differences between the Bank and the Plan scenarios. Table 8.1 summarised certain key growth rates and showed that with a higher growth rate of investment and hence imports, particularly of capital goods (the World Bank Memorandum, Table 3.4, has growth of machinery and transport equipment at 11.3% p.a. while the Plan, Table 10, has capital goods growing at 5.2% p.a.), but a lower growth of exports, a lower real GDP growth can be expected. The scenario given in the Plan may well be more consistent, but whether it is also more realistic is a separate issue.

Table 8.1 attempts to compare the two scenarios, but the aggregation schemes are different. For manufactured exports, the Plan figures are somewhat above those of the Bank. The rate of growth of agricultural exports is high in both, with the Plan's 6.6% p.a. again exceeding that of the Bank's 5.1% p.a. The real difference between the two, however, lies in the assumed rate of growth of exports of the mining sector (Bank = 1.7% and 3% for gold), both as minerals (Plan = 7.4%) and in semi-processed form (Plan = 7.9% for intermediate goods).

In the Bank's view, the most promising mineral prospects are in gold, so gold might conveniently be taken as a benchmark for analysing the Plan figures for the mining sector (without state subsidies, items such as asbestos and copper may even decline). Since Independence, the only major new mining project has, in fact, been a gold mine (Renco); at 1985 prices, the investment cost of a similar operation would be of the order of Z$45m., yielding an annual foreign-exchange return of about Z$35m. (at a gold price of Z$540 per ounce).

Now the Plan makes provision for an average of Z$192m. p.a. to be invested in the mining sector (27% by government) and expects an annual average increment of Z$115m. to export earnings. The latter figure is equivalent to three Rencos p.a. plus a small expansion elsewhere in the sector. There is not anything like that number of new mining projects waiting in the wings to be implemented, whether in gold or in other minerals, and even under the most favourable technical conditions, the lead time on mining ventures would preclude the rate of growth anticipated in the Plan for the 1986–90 period.

Accepting that the export targets in the other sectors will be difficult enough to achieve, this discussion on mineral exports strongly suggests that the Plan's rate of growth of exports was derived from matching the import constraint to a preconceived idea of the GDP target, rather than the other way round, i.e. of relaxing the foreign-exchange constraint sufficiently for the Plan's other targets to remain consistent with one another at levels which are politically acceptable.

Table 8.1 indicates that if only 4% export growth is achieved, while debt and investment are kept to planned levels (the Principal scenario), the consequences would be GDP growth of 2.4% p.a. with private consumption at 1.2% p.a. With the 'alternative' strategy (see below) considerably better growth performance can be achieved with 4% export growth, but the results still fall far short of the Plan's 5.1% GDP and 4.9% consumption growth targets. Without a commitment to the structural change implicit in the alternative scenario, if GDP, consumption, employment and investment growth are to be sustained in the face of external economic conditions which may well turn out to be more adverse than is assumed in the Plan, the necessity for a rapid expansion of exports becomes critical. The following section examines the potential role of government policy in bringing this about.

Export policies

Apart from the adoption of a floating exchange rate, the two principal export-oriented policies already in place are the Export Incentive Scheme and the Export Revolving Fund.

'The Export Incentive Scheme is a mechanism through which a tax-free cash payment may be made to registered Zimbabwe exporters on the basis of actual export performance under the list of qualifying export commodities' (CZI Export Directory, 1986: 17). The rate that has applied since 1 August 1984 is 9% tax-free, equivalent on a taxed basis to 18% on the fob price. The approved list covers a wide range of agricultural and manufactured goods, excluding raw materials used by Zimbabwe industries, steel and ferrochrome. Goods with less than a 25% local content are also excluded.

Under a World Bank loan of $70.6m., the Export Revolving Fund was initiated on 1 April 1983. The object is to provide the foreign exchange needed for imported raw materials, spare parts, etc., to manufacture goods for export. Industrialists are able to accept export orders knowing that any imported raw materials will automatically be covered.[4]

One lesson from the experience of the first-round NICs is that institutional. support for exports may be of critical importance. State trading corporations which allow firms to concentrate on manufacturing while the marketing side is handled by specialised expertise are particularly significant in this regard. The Plan envisages 'a State Trading Corporation (STC)', while the Governor of the Reserve Bank recommended that 'Japanese-style exporting houses' be established either by groups of companies or in joint ventures (*Herald*, 3 April 1986: 9).

In view of the need to increase export growth rapidly, additional incentive schemes are under discussion. The UNIDO report (1985: 265) argues for providing a proportion of export earnings in 'free' foreign exchange which the exporter can use as he wishes. A critique of this proposal, based on the 1974–7 Export Bonus Scheme, concludes that the allocation should be tied to capital or intermediate goods imports (Gray, 1985: 5).

There is a high degree of inertia preventing Zimbabwean enterprise from moving from a domestic focus into export markets; export promotion policies are therefore critical. The inward-looking legacy of the sanctions era has to be replaced by an outward orientation, by the government initiating a process of exhortation and incentive enhancement to create an 'export culture' within both the private business and parastatal sectors (Girdlestone, 1982).

Import dependence

During the UDI period, sanctions dramatically reduced imports. Import-substitution policies (coupled with demand and relative price changes) simultaneously altered the import composition away from food, other primary commodities and manufactured consumer goods, with the result that fuels and manufactured intermediate and capital goods became dominant. Although they are not limited to consumer goods production, the import-substitution industries that emerged remain heavily dependent on imported capital and intermediate goods.

Although agriculture and mining are less import-dependent than manufacturing, import capacity determines to a significant extent the overall level of activity. Investment, and hence growth, are heavily import-dependent because profitability depends on imported inputs, and because the very high import content of investment may lead to intentions having to be frustrated when foreign exchange is in particularly short supply. These points warrant spelling out in considerably more detail.

1. *Import content of production.* Given the relatively high degree of linkage within the manufacturing sector, it is important when analysing the import content of production to look at total import utilisation (direct plus indirect). The results for the six-sector input–output model that was elaborated in connection with the Five Year Plan are shown in Table 8.8.

Although data limitations caution against too much reliance being put on these figures, the indications are that, of the productive sectors, agriculture has by far the lowest import content per unit of output (16%), followed by mining (20%) and industry (at an overall level of 26%). Within industry, which in the model embraces the GDP sectors Electricity and Water and Construction as well as Manufacturing, the final goods sub-sector is at the same level as mining (20%), with intermediate goods (35%) lying in between and capital goods by far the most import-intensive (40%).

Superficially, these figures support the notion that further import substitution should be concentrated on capital goods. In the short run, however, intermediates are more important. For total imports the capital goods share is 27.9% due to the influence of the direct imports required for investment, but the corresponding figure for intermediates is still 47.9%. In terms of absolute savings it is import substitution in intermediates that is indicated.

2. *Import content of demand.* Among final demand categories, while consumption has a very low direct import content for a developing country of Zimbabwe's size (4%), the import dependence of the domestic production structure raises the total to 17–20%. Even though about two-thirds of exports originate from agriculture and mining, overall exports have a similar level of import content (20%).

The significance of Zimbabwe's high import content of investment in relation to other demand categories was first highlighted by Kadhani and Green (1985). In the short run, attempts to increase investment will increase imports. If a rapid increase in foreign debt is impossible or undesirable, expansionary policies may simply force a policy reversal. Export promotion makes sense not as an end in itself, but as a means to relaxing these constraints on short and medium-term growth.

The value of imports in absolute terms for the main categories of final demand brings out an analogous point to the one made about import substitution in relation to production, namely, that the actual volume of foreign-exchange expenditure must be considered. Private consumption accounts for 36% of total imports, while investment accounts for 29%.

3. *Import volume, capacity utilisation and growth.* While there is a strong relationship between the growth of imports and of GDP, it is not as straightforward as has been implied thus far. Growth requires disproportionately high growth in imports, but when import allocations are reduced, GDP does not fall as fast as imports because investment is the most volatile component of final demand. The implication is that import capacity has to be maintained by finding other elements of the balance of payments to be squeezed. 'With debt service approaching 30% of export earnings in 1983, reversion to the unselective 1980–2 borrowing policy is also patently untenable' (Kadhani and Green, 1985). The stage was thus set for the March 1984 measures.

Changing the structure of demand to reduce import content can be done either by changing the balance between the final demand categories (more low import-content exports or consumption at the expense of investment) or by changing the sectoral composition within a particular category (such as increasing demand for agricultural and mining goods at the expense of manufactures within private consumption). The balance between investment and other elements of final demand should be determined directly by considerations of growth strategy, with the import-content problem arising when the implications of the strategy are analysed and the foreign-exchange constraint is encountered. In the Plan, it is only changes of this kind that are considered; the option of trying to change import content within demand categories forms an important part of the alternative strategy.

The import allocation system

The system of foreign-exchange allocation is a legacy which remains unaltered in its essentials from the UDI era. The overall level of allocations is set as a result of a balance-of-payments forecast carried out twice a year by the Treasury in consultation with the Reserve Bank, using information on export prospects and import requirements from a number of government and private sector sources. The allocations themselves are issued on a quarterly basis, responsibility for this ultimately being assumed by the Ministry of Trade and Commerce. For the importation of capital goods, the Ministry of Industry and Technology is also involved.

While the global allocation is divided according to priority categories and scrutinised from a national viewpoint, the individual allocations within each item are made principally in favour of established importers. Allocations cannot be sold or carried forward, so that the system appears very rigid. Without some guarantee of continuity in allocations, however, new investment would be discouraged and existing companies, not necessarily the most inefficient ones, might consider closure.

There is some scope for 'newcomers', although the criteria are fairly demanding: 'In essence the newcomer must establish that a continuing foreign exchange saving will result from his or her addition to the system or expansion within it' (Zimbabwe, 1981: 71). When investment projects are submitted to the Industrial Projects Committee, the principal criterion on which they are accepted and currency allocated for the imported component of the capital cost is that a net foreign-exchange saving should be demonstrated within 12 months.

Some features of the system which give potential importers alternative forms of access to foreign currency are the powers to issue one-off allocations for special purposes, and the existence of the Export Revolving Fund, commodity import programmes (CIPs) and barter trade.[5] Both barter trade and CIPs represent highly tied forms of expanding imports and, although welcome in the short run, to the extent that these are used for capital goods, the longer-term economic cost of mismatched equipment, lack of spare parts, etc., may be quite high.

Overall the system is not as non-market-oriented as some critics maintain because the six-monthly bids are essentially demand-driven. Although it is relatively smooth working, there is considerable scope for improving its administration (Green, 1985, note 34). A more fundamental concern is with the fixation on short-run balance-of-payments performance in determining allocations. This may be appropriate for commercial applications, but in the case of projects it introduces a significant bias against those with a start-up period longer than a few months, while also subordinating other national objectives such as employment, acquisition of skills, regional development, etc.

There is an urgent need for the government to develop a consistent and comprehensive methodoloy for translating broad objectives into specific operational decisions about pricing, subsidies, projects and indeed foreign-exchange allocations. Social cost-benefit techniques have a role to play here, although for large projects (e.g. in power and petrochemicals) more sophisticated tools may be needed (MacDonald and Robinson, 1986).

While in the case of projects the destination of the foreign-exchange allocation is known, this is not true of allocations made for raw materials and spare parts. The data do not even permit sectoral totals to be compiled, e.g. for the manufacturing sector. The basis for making new allocations or changing existing ones would be immensely improved by creating a detailed data base on the destinations of imports.

Finance in historical perspective

On the finance side, although foreign portfolio and loan capital have played an important role (Table 8.4), at Independence it was the legacy of foreign equity capital which was most significant. In 1982, the overall foreign share was between 43% and 59%; earlier estimates were higher at between 66% and 72% (Riddell, 1987: 282).

During the sanctions period, the lack of access to foreign financial flows was at least as significant as the trade restrictions, but there was no massive withdrawal of foreign capital. In fact, restrictions on external factor payments, which would certainly not have been tolerated by foreign capital except in the exceptional circumstances of the time, provided a substantial source of foreign funds for investment purposes. The reinvestment of dividends has been identified as having been 'critical' to the import-substitution programme, not simply from a balance-of-payments viewpoint, but as a supplement to domestic savings for capital accumulation (Green, 1985: 24). Since Independence, new foreign equity inflows have been small and more than counterbalanced by outflows as foreign shareholdings have been acquired by the government in a number of previously foreign-dominated companies.

With only the South African capital market to any degree accessible, foreign debt at Independence was rather modest at about 16% of GDP. Including the funds blocked during the sanctions period, by 1984 total foreign debt had risen to 53% of GDP, an annual average increase of 50%. In consequence, by 1985 debt-service amounted to over 28% of exports (Plan, p. 44). The use of foreign loans, therefore, represents a marked departure from past practice; the government has expressed concern over the current level of debt and the Plan target is to reduce the debt-service ratio to 20% by 1990.

Foreign aid

With the ending of sanctions against Rhodesia, and as a new country taking its place in the international community, there was a wave of support for Zimbabwe. External assistance disbursement (soft loans as well as grants) amounted to US$121m. in 1980 and US$266m. in 1981. In March 1981 donors pledged nearly US$2.2bn towards the development programme presented by the government. These pledges were slow to materialise, however, with disbursements in 1982 and 1983 being of the same order of magnitude as 1981 (US$297m. and US$276m. respectively).

With a rapidly increasing deficit on the current account, the government held a meeting of donor representatives in Harare in December 1983 to identify reasons for the slow rate of disbursement. The figures indicate some improvement in succeeding years: 1984, US$372m., 1985, US$347m. Of the total disbursed ($1.7bn), the largest single donor was the USA (US$271m.), followed by the World Bank (US$267m.), the UK (US$167m.) and Sweden (US$104m.). About three-quarters was from bilateral donors. The World Bank, the EC and the UN High Commission for Refugees together accounted for over 80% of the multilateral total.

The Five Year Plan is counting on an annual average of Z$100m. in grants. Loans to the parastatals and the government, presumably intended to be largely concessionary, are expected to average Z$158m. amd Z$212m. p.a. respectively (Plan, Table 14, p.52). This gives an annual total of Z$470m., equivalent, at the exchange rate used, to under US$300m. In view of recent performance, this would seem by no means over-ambitious (it would be nearly covered by the existing undisbursed commitments). Much will depend, however, on political factors.

Developments in the region will also play a crucial role in the next five years. The independence of Namibia, for example, will direct donors' energies to that country. On the other hand, an escalation of the struggle might catch donors out in their anti-apartheid rhetoric and obtain increased assistance for Zimbabwe. Much of such aid is expected to go into regional

projects. While these are crucial for Zimbabwe, the benefits will not materialise directly through the balance of payments.

Foreign debt

After Independence major projects that had been waiting for a stabilisation
of political conditions were commissioned, committing the country to substantial new debts on very unfavourable conditions. The principal example of
this is the Z$800m. Hwange power project, which is also an example of the
tensions which exist in Zimbabwe's external sector policies, particularly
between commitment to a regional development approach through SADCC
and self-sufficiency. In taking up a project framed by the former government
specifically,to make Rhodesia more independent of its neighbours in electrical power, an opportunity to make a clear commitment to SADCC was lost,
with a substantial opportunity cost in economic growth to Zimbabwe and the
region. According to the World Bank, debt service for 'water and electricity'
rose from US$5m. in 1980/1 to US$10m. in 1982, to US$42m. in 1983 and
US$82m. in 1984 and will have peaked at US$112m. in 1987.

It appears that repayments began before any power became available from
the plant. It would perhaps be going too far to blame the Hwange project
alone, but if Zimbabwe had taken full advantage of the possibilities for
exploiting regional complementarities in energy and other sectors, it might
well have been able to avoid resorting to the IMF policy package as balance-
of-payments pressures rose.

Finding itself unable to increase concessional financing from donor pled-
ges, the government had to resort to increased short-term borrowing from
commercial banks and to the use of IMF facilities (SDR 175m. under a
stand-by arrangement, SDR56m. under the compensatory financing facility,
and SDR2m. from the buffer stock financing facility).

In the Plan the figure quoted as the debt-service ratio in 1985 is 28.4%,
falling to 18% in 1990, on unspecified assumptions about export prices and
currency movements. Even if the 1990 debt-servicing figure is consistent with
the Plan's scenario, export growth (as was argued above) is very ambitious.
Ignoring the fact that the level of debt would then also be different, 4%
export growth would give a debt-service ratio of 21%, still representing a
seven-point improvement over the 1983 figure. Whether Zimbabwe's stage of
development and chronic structural dependence on imports would not justify
more rapid accumulation of debt and a concomitant rise in the debt-service
ratio is a fundamental question, especially in the event of a shortfall in
planned exports. The answer is not a straightforward one because export
activity is not simply a question of earning foreign exchange but of employment and the utilisation of imports. With lower exports, the same employment and consumption growth over the period (though a lower GDP
growth) could be achieved through increasing investment demand and
changing the import pattern accordingly. The level of import growth con-

sistent with these assumptions is calculated to be less (5.1% p.a.) than the level given in the Plan scenario (6% p.a.).

The implications for debt would be an increase in the order of $1bn over the five years. In principle, this would probably not raise the 1990 debt-service ratio above the 1985 level of 28%, suggesting that the government should perhaps shed some of the caution engendered by the early experience of trying to manage the national foreign debt, and be more willing to borrow to maintain growth. It is not simply a question of willingness on the Zimbabwe side, however. As will be discussed in more detail, conditions in the world economy raise considerable doubts as to whether it would be possible to achieve an increase in borrowing of this magnitude. For medium- or long-term loans, international financial institutions, whether developmental or commercial, must lend against future export earnings and a country trying to increase its borrowing to make up for missed export targets might find it hard to make a case. While they are reasonably satisfied with much of Zimbabwe's policy stance (e.g. on the exchange rate), the level of the government budget deficit and the stand-off with the IMF are factors which, over and above the current general disinclination to lend to the Third World, would influence the banks against increasing commitments to Zimbabwe in particular. Short-term loans have typically been backed by gold, and a massive increase of debt cannot be counted upon without providing some form of security.

The option of rescheduling should, however, be given serious consideration. Indeed, from the viewpoint of the first quarter of 1987, with import allocations for productive sectors cut by up to 40%, the ramifications of a poor agricultural season becoming evident, and the likelihood of further disruptions occurring during the year as sanctions come to be implemented, the case for reversing Zimbabwe's role as a net exporter of capital by rescheduling a major part of the country's foreign debt would seem to be overwhelming. Despite the unfavourable climate just outlined, it is widely recognised that Zimbabwe has an uneven repayment schedule with a sharp peak in 1987-8. The reluctance of the authorities to pursue rescheduling would seem to be based on the view that it would thereby lose its international standing and hence access to future foreign loans. The fallacy of this view is evident from the experience of many other countries which have survived debt reschedulings in the past, such as Peru, Turkey, Mexico and Argentina. A sense of 'national pride' in perpetuating an unblemished record is destined to have very costly implications for Zimbabwe over the next few years.

Foreign investment

The sectors where foreign capital is dominant are mining (90%) and manufacturing (70%). The government's attitude to foreign investment is perhaps best described as ambivalent. According to a 1984 paper by Riddell, this results in an attitude amongst existing investors of making the best use of existing resources but not bringing in new funds (nor, at the other extreme, withdrawing funds) and little enthusiasm among potential new investors to start operating in Zimbabwe. The outflow arising from purchases by the government, or by Zimbabwean companies, of foreign-owned shares has been particularly of South African capital.[6] For the period 1981–4, total credits of $33m. were offset by debits of $53.1m. In view of this, the Plan's statement that the Z$200m. of new foreign investment that has been included in the financing of the development programme 'surpasses the current inflow of foreign capital to a considerable degree' reads as quite an understatement. From a comparative viewpoint Zimbabwe can hardly be said to be heading the league tables: whether by the economic criteria which, surveys suggest, most investors look at (rapid growth, high income, existing investments, large low-cost labour force, historical ties), or the policy ones the World Bank and others argue are important (friendly political climate, low political risks, favourable regulations), Zimbabwe is not an obvious candidate.

The Plan argues that economic recovery 'aided and influenced by the economic programme of this Plan, will motivate the private sector to increase investment and cooperate with the public sector in the implementation of priority development projects'. Government policies will favour growth. 'Incentives will be introduced in order to encourage development in general as well as export-oriented projects and projects which aim at substituting imports for local products' (Plan, p. 44).

While there could be some truth in these arguments if the Plan were destined to achieve very high levels of growth, doubts about reaching even its own rather modest targets make this seem a bit thin. The local private sector is looking to signs of investment from abroad before committing its own resources in greater measure, while the reverse is undoubtedly the case for potential foreign investors. The government may consequently feel that it has to try to encourage both local and foreign private investors to overcome the current general investment malaise, without necessarily believing foreign investment will be forthcoming in the quantity needed to fill the gap in the Plan's financing.

Given the present agenda of pursuit of a rather conventional growth strategy with something of a distributional bias, rather than one of building socialism, the government should present a more consistent image to existing and potential new investors. At the same time, it should equip itself with the technical skills to make informed judgements on which foreign investors to go for and which to reject. Provision of technology and access to world markets are two areas where private foreign investment could be useful. Projects which simply replicate Zimbabwean enterprise may have very short-run employment and balance-of-payments advantages, but these have to be weighed against costs in the longer term.

Alternative forms of foreign participation, which may well prove 'more flexible and advantageous' (UNIDO, 1985: 135), should also be considered. These would be more in line with the government's ownership objectives, while bringing specific benefits where applicable. The government's in-sistence on the question of ownership is clearly unpalatable to private sector interests. The important mining industry, dominated by foreign capital but relatively skill-intensive, and where the government does not currently have the capacity to take it over without prejudicing output, employment and future expansion, is a case where regulation would be sufficient. In addition to the control exercised through foreign-exchange allocation, labour legis-lation, etc., the requirement that all marketing be channelled through the Minerals Marketing Corporation has institutionalised a way of regulating multinationals at exactly the point where the country's interests have been judged to be most at risk.[7]

The irony in the parastatal sector is that the attempt to keep salaries within bounds (consistent with the official goal of reducing income disparities) in an environment dominated by the private sector is leading to a situation where control is being lost to a new species of foreigner: the expatriate, employed by a bilateral or multilateral donor agency. Attempts to train more Zimbab-weans to obviate the need to employ expatriates are turned into the provision of training for the private sector when skilled workers are continually being attracted away by better pay and conditions. Another perverse feature of recent experience is the government's failure to insist on local procurement, particularly again where projects are foreign-funded.

Implications for the balance of payments

Even without taking more pessimistic scenarios of world economic condi-tions into account, the financing part of the Plan would appear problematic, particularly with respect to foreign investment. If the foreign financing total is to be reached, greater reliance will have to be placed on aid and debt flows. The problems identified at the 1983 donor conference of poor co-ordination between ministries and lack of knowledge of how best to operate in the donor environment and of project management skills have, however, yet to be adequately addressed.

In the wake of the March 1984 measures, there are few loopholes in the balance of payments which remain to be stopped up to improve the avail-ability of foreign exchange for imports. Indeed, the temporary freeze on dividend remittances has now to be reversed. In view of the above pessimistic analysis of the prospects for foreign inflows on the capital account, the burden of maintaining adequate levels of imports to sustain and expand the economy has therefore to fall on maintaining, and increasing, levels of exports and on very careful management of import allocations.

Exchange rate: effect on overall balance

In Zimbabwe's conditions, devaluation is not intended to reduce the volume of imports, which is anyway under administrative control, but to increase export revenues, through volume increases, in order to make an increase in imports possible. In practice, the volume of imports was reduced quite dramatically at the time of the December 1982 devaluation, while export volumes showed only limited growth between 1982 and 1983 and actually declined by 1984. The improvement in the balance of trade between 1982 and the end of 1984 was due mainly to lower import prices and reduced import volumes, although towards the end of the period improved export prices did play a role.

Since the devaluation, the exchange rate has been linked to a trade-weighted basket of other currencies, the exact composition of which is not revealed by the Reserve Bank (Manungo, 1986: 101). In nominal terms, further depreciation of the Zimbabwe dollar has taken place against all major currencies except the Rand. It would appear, however, that this decline has not fully compensated for relatively rapid domestic inflation.

The criterion in controlling the exchange-rate decline seems to be to maintain the viability of the primary exporting sectors, which would otherwise have to be explicitly subsidised, while not devaluing so far as to give windfall profits, which might be remitted, or increase the local currency costs of imports and foreign debt service to unsustainable levels. It is a delicate balance. A reasonably competitive exchange rate is also essential for the expansion of manufactured exports, although they have a high foreign content. This is partly overcome by the export promotion scheme, which in effect creates a selective two-tier exchange-rate structure. This is more satisfactory than a general devaluation for increasing the attractiveness of the export market in relation to the domestic

GROWTH STRATEGY

Evaluation of the Plan

It was argued above (page 167) that consumption and employment growth provide simple, but operationally defensible, goals. In the Plan itself, aggregate consumption is downplayed, being mentioned only in the Statistical Annex which gives annual average growth rates of 4.9% for private and 4.2% for public consumption. In relation to the population growth rate assumed in the Plan of 2.76% p.a., this gives a per capita increase of less than 2%; at the more often quoted figure of 3.5% p.a. for population, the per capita increase would be only 1.2%.

This, of course, says nothing about the distribution of increased aggregate consumption and here the proxy of employment becomes relevant. The Plan estimates that the development path defined by the chosen investment strategy will result in an increase in formal wage employment of 144,000 jobs over the five years, equivalent to an annual average of 2.7%. In addition,

> during the Plan period, 15,000 families with about 100,000 dependants will be resettled each year. Establishment and development of small-scale industries in growth points and rural areas, as well as general encouragement of co-operatives and self-employment schemes will provide additional gainful employment. (p.3)

This is to be compared to the annual growth in working-age population over 1985–90 of 4% p.a. In the face of this, plus the accumulated backlog (255,000 from the last three years alone), the Plan frankly admits that 'the problem of unemployment is a major national issue and it looms as one of the most socially destabilising problems throughout the Plan period' (p.2). In the Plan's defence, it can at least be said that a credible attempt is being made to work within the existing stringent structural constraints; without the key orientation to 'distribute investment in favour of material production sectors' performance on all criteria would be lower, with annual average growth rates for private consumption of 3.3%, government consumption of 3.6%, and employment of 1.5%.

The Plan lays considerable stress on rural development and decentralisation. An attempt has been made to piece together information from the 1982 Census and from the Plan to arrive at a picture of the changing composition of the labour force and the spatial distribution of the population between urban and rural. The following results emerged. Unemployment was likely to increase from 200,000 in 1982 (10.8%) to 400,000 in 1990 (11.8% of the labour force). If the CSO figures for formal employment in 1982 (1 million) were combined with the Census total of 1.2 million, there would appear to be 200,000 self-employed or informal-sector income earners; on the same basis, this figure might rise to 300,000 by 1990. Taking this into account and removing the resettled peasant farmers from the communal total (75,000 families with an average of 1.4 farmers per family, giving 100,000) would give a wage or self-employed (outside of communal farming) total of 1.6 million (47% of the 1990 labour force). The number of communal farmers in 1990 would then become a residual figure of 1.5 million, an increase of 400,000 since the Census. With the Plan's assumptions about total population (9.4 million) and urbanisation (40% in settlements of over 2,500 people), by 1990 the urban population would be 3.75 million, which would correspond to an annual average urban growth rate of over 10%, a high but not inconceivable figure, given the experience of other countries (the implications for housing are discussed below). Relating an estimate of the number employed in rural areas outside of communal areas in 1982 (450,000) to the total population in those areas (1.5 million) and using the same dependency ratio for 1990 would give a population of 1.65 million at the end of the Plan period. The population of the communal areas would then emerge as a residual at 4 million, a *decrease* of 300,000 from the 1982 Census figure. When combined with the increased number of farmers, this would imply a rapid decline in the dependency ratio in communal areas.

Although in danger of reading too much into the figures given in the Plan, these results would certainly be consistent with the simultaneous achievement of raising the standard of living of the peasant population and of relieving environmental pressure in the communal areas. Higher per capita income would accrue from more intensive use of labour and a lower dependency ratio. With only 75,000 families being resettled, however, the other specific objective of land reform can hardly be said to be playing a key role in the Plan scenario.

Is it realistic to assume that a decline in the population in the communal areas can be achieved during the Plan period? The implications of such a strategy for urban growth can best be seen by examining the housing problem. The Plan itself states that the urban housing backlog was 240,000 units in 1985 (p.33). With the demographic assumptions given here there would be a requirement for an additional 310,000 units during the Plan period, or a total of 550,000 urban houses in all. The best the Plan can do, however, is to allocate resources for building only 75,000–100,000 houses over the period. Not all of these will be urban, but even if this were the case, there would still be a backlog of at least 450,000 units by 1990 – a level of backlog which, even under the favourable assumptions of all targets of the Plan being met, is likely to be socially unsustainable. The communal areas are likely to be left with their familiar problems, overcrowded, environmentally threatened and offering very low levels of per capita income.

In short, the Plan is not destined to redress to any significant extent the existing structure of poverty and inequality. The pressure on incomes, jobs, housing, social infrastructure and the land is immense, making it difficult to find a strategy which ameliorates more than a subset of these problems. With the very real possibility of the Plan's scenario being disrupted and even poorer performance eventuating, it would appear vital for the government to be exploring the possibility of more radical strategies which, over a longer time-horizon perhaps than the Five Year Plan, would make the economy less vulnerable to the pressures it now faces and better able to fulfil the needs of the population.

Three risks to the Plan

The world economy. The key aspects to be examined are export prospects and financing the balance of payments. For exports, it is convenient to focus on three major markets, which are roughly correlated with particular commodities: *South Africa* (11% of exports in 1984), cotton, beverages and tobacco, some steel, cement and chemicals, metal products and a major proportion of manufactured 'final' goods such as clothing, footwear, furniture;

the *regional market* (12% of exports in 1984), sugar, barley, oil cake, cement, asbestos, coke, a major proportion of capital goods exports, yarns and fibres, soap, coal; and *industrial countries/other markets* (77% of exports in 1984), major primary commodities (tobacco, cotton, sugar, tea, coffee, meat, gold, asbestos, nickel, copper) and manufactured intermediates (ferro-alloys, iron and steel).

It has previously been argued that the mining export projections in the Plan are far too ambitious. Allowing, however, for a different sectoral distribution of export growth than is given in the Plan in relation to the above market segments, the three scenarios may be applied as follows: *High*, with relatively slow growth in the southern African market (3.4%) with volumes almost constant, counterbalanced by rapid growth (9.9% p.a.) in PTA/SADCC exports with 7% in the remaining segment, 6% overall; *Principal*, with 4% in the regional market, only 1.8% in South African exports, and 4.3% in the remainder, giving 4% overall; and *Low*, with the regional market severely affected by world economic depression and South Africa's position compounded by escalating labour unrest etc., with zero growth in southern African exports and exports to the rest of the world growing at 3%, with overall growth (2.5% p.a.) falling short of the world trade average (3% p.a.).

With exports the driving force of the model, the implications for other macroeconomic aggregates over the period 1986–90 are summarised in Table 8.1. Reduction from 6% to 4% p.a., High to Principal, with imports adjusted so that debt overall is no higher, leads to a reduction in GDP growth from 5.1% to 2.5%, private consumption from 4.9% to 1.4% and the employment level at the end of the period from 1,180,000 to 1,038,000. With the same growth in investment over the period (5.3%), the same sized capital stock would be available for the period following 1990 but with slightly more capacity available in the Principal scenario. For the Low scenario, it is presumed that post-1990 considerations are sacrificed (with zero growth in investment) in an attempt to sustain consumption and employment in the face of very adverse external conditions. Setting the low levels of consumption growth projected for the Principal scenario as targets (1.4% and 1.0% p.a. respectively for private and government consumption) leads to a result in which debt is only slightly lower, while the level of employment in 1990 falls below 1 million. Despite zero investment growth over the period, there would be considerable excess capacity in 1990.

In its financing projections the Plan assumed a rapid increase of annual net medium-term loans followed by a reduction. When account is taken of the oil import savings to be made on the High scenario assumptions, amounting by 1990 to about $124m., the loan increase required, with a lower foreign investment contribution but the same level of financing overall, is more modest and may reasonably be taken as consistent with the other High scenario assumptions. On the other hand, the assumption of the same debt level for High and Principal may be stretching credibility a bit on the financing side, particularly in view of the fact that the Principal scenario also involves higher interest payments on existing debt, a large proportion of the non-concessional debt (itself amounting to two-thirds of the total) being affected by variations in interest rates. From the debt figures above, this fact alone would tend to increase the deficit by around $10m. for each 1% increase in LIBOR. Financing becomes even more problematic in the Low scenario, where debt accumulation up to 95% of the level to be attained in the High and Principal scenarios has been assumed so that the other aggregates correspond. It is not unlikely that if the assumptions of the Low scenario were to materialise in the world economy, not even the 1.4% GDP growth calculated would be achieved, owing to further cuts having to be made to meet creditor requirements.

The Principal and Low figures would correspond to significantly declining real per capita incomes, while the corresponding employment figures would be a cause for considerable concern. This gives rise to the imperative to seek an alternative development strategy.

Effect of South African instability. Results from the input–output model suggest that the impact effect of a closure of the South African border might be a reduction in investment of 25%, consumption of 22%, national income of 16%, with 160,000–180,000 jobs being put at risk. How quickly the economy might recover would depend on many factors, not least the state of preparedness. In Table 8.1, two sets of five-year averages are given for comparison with the Plan and other scenarios. Case (a) assumes that the Principal growth rates of exports, imports, government consumption, investment and stock accumulation apply in all years except the impact year (1987). This leads to negative growth rates on average over the five years for private consumption, investment, employment and GDP, but lower 1990 debt than the Principal scenario. As sanctions against South Africa become more widespread, if Zimbabwe proves able to capture regional and overseas markets previously supplied by South Africa, the 4% p.a. export growth figure could prove a serious underestimate for 1988–90. The scenario presented may, therefore, be unduly pessimistic, but it does at least provide a benchmark against which the importance of an aggressive drive to capture South Africa's markets can be seen.

Case (b), while retaining the assumption of 4% export growth in all years except 1987, allows for increased imports, this being reflected in debt accumulation up to a level comparable with the High and Principal scenarios. Increased imports make it possible to retain the target capital formation growth of 5.3% p.a., while at the same time ameliorating the reduction of growth in private consumption. With these assumptions, employment in 1990 is still calculated to lie below the 1 million mark, with an apparent loss of 100,000 jobs in relation to the 1985 base-year figure. Far-reaching measures would have to be implemented to overcome a potential job shrinkage of this magnitude. An acceleration of export growth over the 4% p.a. level assumed would expand employment both directly and indirectly, by relieving the foreign-exchange constraint. From a comparison of the figures it would appear that, under sanctions, export promotion should be treated as even more of an imperative than under the most adverse scenario of world economic conditions.

In 1984 Zimbabwe's trade volumes amounted to over 3.8m. tonnes, of which overseas trade was about 2m., the remainder being split between South Africa and the rest of the region, of which 0.8m. was petroleum products. At present, it is thought that overseas trade amounts to 3m. tonnes, South African trade adding a further 0.8m. It is the road and rail links to Beira rather than aspects of the port itself which have been the bottlenecks, but with the completion of emergency repairs the system should be capable of handling 2.5m. tonnes (plus petroleum requirements via the pipeline) on a routine basis and could probably cater for a higher volume if absolutely necessary. Admittedly, special arrangements would have to be made for the commodities which Beira is not currently equipped to handle, for example grain, would have to be bagged. The main part of the Corridor rehabilitation and expansion programme is scheduled to be completed by mid-1989, by which time Beira should have adequate capacity for all the overseas trade of the sub-region.

Apart from the question of transport routes, other areas which are receiving attention are the identification and stockpiling of strategic raw materials and spare parts, the provision of appropriate financial facilities such as export credit guarantees, trade credits, etc., and the identification of new sources for imports and exports. It is important to try to assess the likelihood of a border closure over different time horizons. The border can be closed by either side, but in the short run, the question is whether South Africa will pre-empt matters.

South Africa has not shown unwillingness in recent years to implement measures against neighbouring countries. With the exception of military operations in Angola, however, the cost has been minuscule. The closure of the Zimbabwe border would have substantial costs for South Africa in terms of lost transport revenues and lost trade. It is not, therefore, a decision which South Africa would take lightly. However, consistency in policy-making cannot be assured from the South African government.

The escalating conflict within South Africa itself is already having a significant impact on the Zimbabwe economy. Consumer boycotts within the black townships, compounded by the sharp fall in the Rand, were already a cause of concern by January 1986. The Plan's tacit assumption of 'business as usual' looks increasingly untenable.

Drought. Other than making reference to normal rainfall amongst the Plan's underlying assumptions, no analysis of the impact of climatic variations is carried out. The FAO has argued that African countries should stop looking at droughts as 'extraordinary events. They should rather recognise that droughts are part of the normal African environment and should therefore prepare themselves to cope with drought' (*Herald*, 13 August 1984).

In the case of Zimbabwe, Masaya (1985) has examined the effect of rainfall on crop cycles and suggests that three- and five-year cycles should be incorporated into national planning. The implication is that at least one year of poor rainfall is likely to occur during the Plan period, although the country may not be subjected to a recurrence of the exceptional drought of 1982–5.

The economic cost of a drought, to say nothing of its human dimensions, is considerable. In 1983, the government quantified the one-year consequences of the drought for the national economy under three headings:

1. a balance-of-payments impact arising from the loss of export earnings and imports of food and equipment for relief and drilling programmes of $131m.;
2. direct loss of crop and livestock output of $300m.; and
3. an increased burden on the government budget, mainly to finance relief programmes in the worst hit areas, of $250m.

A more detailed analysis that included secondary effects would certainly reveal a substantially larger cost in terms of immediate consumption forgone and negative consequences for growth.[8]

Industrial structure

Those who were expecting that the Independence government would effect sweeping changes in the structure and operation of the economy have been disappointed. It is salutary to reflect, however, on the experience of neighbouring Mozambique, which pursued a socialist order far more aggressively after 1975 but soon found itself impoverished by the flight of capital and skills, with a legacy of almost no education of its people during the colonial period, and retaliation by the forces of imperialism for having attempted to move out of line. Subsequently, a series of natural disasters and an escalating level of bandit activity have totally debilitated the economy. Although Zimbabwe has a much stronger and more diversified economy and a population with a much higher level of education, a more decisive policy might not have been allowed to succeed.

Gradualist policy is not just a question of political economy. The structure of production itself and the existing inter-sectoral linkages make for a system which in many respects is quite fragile, and policies which did not take account of this and led to significant disruption to output and employment would be hard to justify. On the other hand, the Plan's attempt to work with and through the existing structure essentially fails to fulfil the primary articulated goals of the government to any significant extent.

The question which then obviously arises is whether the structure can be changed so as to create more room for manoeuvre and open up the possibility of widespread development in terms of a high level of employment, high and evenly distributed incomes and widespread and equitable access to social services. At the level of theory and policy debate, two conflicting approaches to structural change to achieve these goals can be identified.

1. *Full integration into the world capitalist system:* this would involve making comparative advantage the cardinal principle of trade policy, faster growth being claimed to arise from the multiplier effects of increased export activity, aided by the financing that an export orientation would attract.
2. *Semi-autarky:* in this approach, redistribution of assets and income would alter the pattern of demand and subsequently production to a more indigenous resource-based structure, less dependent on imports and thus less subject to the vagaries of the world economy. GDP growth might be slower (although the Zimbabwe model indicates otherwise), but the rate at which primary objectives would be fulfilled would be faster.

The iron and steel plant provides an interesting focus for comparing the two strategies, as the one recommends its closure while the other would support the government's actual policy of a Z$400m. investment programme to modernise and diversify the plant. Although 80–85% of Zisco's output is exported, closure of the plant would certainly have a very significant negative impact on the engineering industries, in the Midlands in particular, as these have been established to process its output, and would probably not make sense with imported raw materials. Under current market conditions, Zisco requires a significant government subsidy to remain in production. The justification is not just the short-run adjustment problems that would arise from closure, but the perception that the engineering and capital goods industries that Zisco has spawned have a significance in terms of the acquisition of skills and the furtherance of creativity and indigenous technological development that is not reflected in the financial figures.

The first strategy, placing exports at central stage, has to contend with the assumed poor market conditions. In addition, in order to get significant export growth rates overall, manufactured exports have to be projected at very high levels, but there are significant constraints to export expansion from the existing productive structure. The UNIDO study of the manufacturing sector in Zimbabwe analyses the inadequacy of present plant with respect to exports. The proportion of exporters with adequate capacity is highest (88%) for the regional, PTA, market, but this is severely constrained in terms of foreign exchange. The proportion is reasonably high for the South African market (54%), but that market is fraught with difficulties. The proportion is only 30% for the overseas market which must be the major target under an export promotion strategy.

The other major point on which attention is focused by the study is the domestic orientation of the vast majority of manufacturing firms involved in exporting. 'Most are reluctant to increase substantially their exposure to export markets without a firm domestic base' (UNIDO, 1985: 263). In part, this reflects a natural reluctance to be involved in a market prone to greater uncertainty and volatility and in which there is more competition than is the case with the domestic market. Equally important is the typical situation that domestic prices far exceed those to be obtained from exports, in part because of the high degree of monopoly. Manufacturers therefore only 'look for export markets when additional plant capacity exists and marginal costs are covered. This arises especially when domestic demand falls' (ibid.: 260). The study shows that exports rise when output falls, and anecdotal information suggests that manufacturers' behaviour is even more perverse in the very short run. As the domestic market declines, rather than immediately trying to replace domestic sales by exports, manufacturers attempt first to retain their own domestic market share at the expense of their competitors (if any). Only when the decline persists do they explore possibilities and begin to reverse the trend.

From a planning perspective, the relatively high export ratios that are observed in times of recession should not be used to project export levels at higher utilisation of capacity, unless export incentive schemes offset this tendency. To make the export promotion strategy work, therefore, it seems that domestic demand has to be kept in check, with negative consequences for consumption.

The export promotion strategy would entail wage control, in order to guarantee price competitiveness, but this would not necessarily increase employment, again for structural reasons: in Zimbabwe labour–capital sub-stitutability would appear to be low. The choice of technology is often made from a very restricted list of options owing to lack of access to information, ties to suppliers in high labour-cost countries, financing through commodity import programmes or other forms of tied aid or, significantly, the require-ment that the product meet some internationally defined standards in order to be suitable for export.

In contrast, in a domestically-oriented strategy increased labour costs, while squeezing margins in the short run, in aggregate do mean higher domestic demand. Raising wages in this context can therefore result, through multiplier effects, in higher employment overall.

It will also be necessary to change the structure of demand, particularly its import content. As regards direct import content, the scope is rather limited with direct imports for private consumption, for example, being only 4%. This could be reduced somewhat further by eliminating luxury goods altogether, but it already largely comprises necessities such as medical supplies. The indirect import contribution appears to be rather insensitive to changes in the sectoral shares of consumption, exports or even investment. It is only when the changed composition of demand leads to the adoption of new technologies and productive processes that a significant change may take place.

What is not always obvious in traditional import substitution or efficiency improvements in the modern sector is the high level of investment, predominantly in foreign exchange, frequently needed to bring these changes about. To use income redistribution to effect a pattern of domestic demand with a much lower import content, and one which typically would not require sophisticated machinery for its production, requires a profound reorientation of the demand-productive system. An attempt is made in the next two sections to flesh out this approach into a more detailed strategy that can be compared and contrasted with the Plan's scenario.

An alternative strategy

An alternative style of development has to be found which involves the mass of the people in a much more meaningful way and addresses directly questions of employment, basic needs etc. (Streeten, 1975). What is laid out here is not a profound departure from current economic policy in Zimbabwe, but rather a shift of emphasis, which is feasible and potentially extremely rewarding within a reasonable time period. It is a strategy with a limited life, a period of bringing the benefits of the exchange economy to the mass of the population, while consolidating and refining the existing modern sector and at the same time minimising the effects of economic destabilisation against the Frontline states by South Africa that are likely to occur simultaneously. It provides a constructive breathing space in which to prepare, by means of political mobilisation, the acquisition of technical skills and experience and a thoroughgoing national planning effort, for a phase of much more profound structural change in the economy. At that time the emphasis will switch to both heavy and light industry for the greatly expanded domestic market and carefully investigated export markets.

The strategy is labelled 'semi-autarkic' to emphasise that the key element is the management of the economy's links with the outside world. Policies for trade and financing cannot themselves constitute a strategy to achieve overall socioeconomic development goals; policies in other areas must be formulated to complement the external sector orientation.

Starting from the binding constraint of the structural import-dependence of the economy, and rejecting export promotion as a solution (on political and philosophical grounds as well as economic infeasibility in the particular circumstances of Zimbabwe), the remaining option is to attack the import-dependence directly. In practice, this means the following measures, both of which imply strong backward linkages within the economy: a redistribution of income so that demand expansion will be predominantly in favour of relatively unsophisticated mass consumption goods, entailing a very high proportion of domestic content in their manufacture; and a redistribution of basic productive assets (principally land) so that the mass of the population which cannot be absorbed into the employment structure of the formal economy can be given a means of livelihood, the investment requirements of which would in turn be served by domestic industry.

This strategy does not eschew links with the outside world and would continue to require considerable efforts to be made to maintain and increase exports, but it does expand the domestic market in such a way as to minimise imports. It requires a reorientation from the implicit race to 'catch up' in industrialisation, a race in which, with the gap ever-widening particularly in the crucial area of technology, Zimbabwe can hardly be given even an outsider's chance in present circumstances. The strategy has to lay emphasis on agriculture and rural development in order to reach the mass of the population which has hitherto been subjected to the ravages of uneven development, being permitted access to the high productivity sectors of the economy only as workers with scant political rights. This implies not only increasing the income-generation potential of communal households, but dramatically improving their access to goods and services (from both the public sector and the private).

To make a real impact on the inherited structure of inequality, resources have to be consistently channelled into the communal areas, away from prestige projects, maintenance of excessively high standards in facilities used by the middle classes, and unquestioning across-the-board acceptance of technological choice and product definition made by the multinational corporations operating in the modern sector. Raising industrial demand for mass consumption goods and capital and intermediate goods inputs needed for rural development would have a beneficial effect on employment and economic activity in the industrial sector. The required shift of emphasis within that sector would also lower the average import-dependence of production and create stronger linkage effects on the input side.

While commercial expansion in the rural areas would bring direct benefits to urban industry, this pattern of consumption growth could only be sustained by significant development of peasant agriculture and of small-scale rural industry (mainly, but not exclusively, linked to agriculture either on the input side or in the processing of agricultural products). It is important to stress that the emphasis in the alternative strategy on agriculture and rural development rather than on industry should not be taken as a

denial that, in the broad sweep of economic history, it is the exploitation of
new technologies through industrialisation that has provided the engine of
growth. Relatively speaking, Zimbabwe already has a very significant industrial base, ranging from an integrated iron and steel plant to a wide range
of intermediate and final goods industries. It should not isolate itself from
further exploitation of the benefits of industrialisation, but at this particular
juncture it should not overexpose itself by an emphasis on industrialisation
to the exclusion of other sectors, which would then necessarily imply a strong
export-orientation, given that in the next 5–10 years at least, the southern
African situation threatens disruption to trade in particular, world economic
prospects are bleak, and domestic technological and organisational capacity
are relatively weak and under-developed.

Improvement of economic conditions at the grassroots would lay the basis
for mass politics to become a reality, but its expression would depend on the
reaction of the leadership and on outside political and military events. At the
end of Japanese colonialism, land redistribution, widespread education and a
widening of economic opportunities took place in both North and South
Korea, but these phases of development became the precursor to the quite
different social and political systems that finally emerged. One common
feature that can be pointed to, however, is that the significant industrialisation that has taken place on both sides of the 38th parallel, associated with
very rapid average rates of growth, was firmly based on earlier phases when
the economy was opened to the mass of the people and technical organisational skills developed.

Quantification of the alternative strategy

A quantitative elaboration is desirable so that it can be compared directly
with the Plan. Unfortunately, there are serious difficulties in attempting this.
Despite its shortcomings, it was possible to justify using the six-sector
Zimconsult model to examine the consistency of the Five-Year Plan as it was
a case largely of continuing trends. In quantifying a scenario where structural
change is taking place, the shortcomings of the model become more critical.
Data on the communal areas are scant. As the model stands at present, it has
a single sector for communal as well as large-scale state and commercial
farming.

None the less, the figures for the cost per job and value-added per unit of
material input and more importantly of imported inputs, give a clear *a priori*
rationale for emphasising agriculture in a strategy aimed at spreading
development across the population as fast as possible (see Table 8.9). The
cost of making employment more viable in the communal areas will be lower,
as will be the use of material inputs, particularly imports. The low import
content of investment in agriculture will reduce overall import content in

investment. The results for a rural strategy could therefore be expected to be considerably better than for the model runs which emphasise 'agriculture' (described below).

The basis for the low ratios in the table is that agriculture is based on a natural resource which has a zero import content and a relatively modest initial cost. At a higher level of sophistication such as the installation of irrigation, the picture changes. The choice of technology should be guided by the principle of maximising linkages to the existing capital goods sector.[9] Costs would also depend on the political means by which change is effected: bringing un- and under-utilised commercial farm land into productive use (Kadhani and Green, 1985) is a promising one because such a 'market-oriented' approach to land reform would be less likely to provoke an economically destructive reaction from the existing commercial farmers in particular and the established bourgeoisie in general, but it would not be a cheap one to implement.[10]

The results in Table 8.1 use constant technological coefficients, for import content of final demand and growth rate of fixed investment and stocks. This means that each set of options has the same overall level of capital stock in 1990, this being used as a crude way of ensuring that performance over the 1985–90 period is not improved at the expense of post-Plan prospects. (This is only a proxy as the composition of the final capital stock, the capacity to export in the period after 1990, etc., would be crucial factors to consider in a more detailed analysis of strategic options.) Immediate post-Plan growth would be determined by the degree of surplus capacity and it is for this reason that a capacity utilisation indicator is included in the penultimate column of the table.

With the above assumptions, the alternative strategy emphasising agriculture, final goods and services in consumption with investment priorities following from this, performs better than the Plan for each of the three scenarios of the study: High, Principal and Low. In all three cases, the more productive use of imports made possible by the reorientation of consumption and investment results in higher growth of private and public consumption and of employment than is the case in the conventional scenarios based on the strategy encapsulated in the Plan.

How realistic is it to make the crucial assumption that the composition of consumption and, with a lag, investment can be changed? Again, it is difficult to give a precise and definitive answer to this question, but Table 8.10 reveals that the demographic pattern of development will be a significant determinant of the overall growth of imports for consumption. The first section of the table gives 1985 estimates for the three main demographic groups: the urban, high and low density areas and the rural areas. The remaining sections give three spatial-cum-income distribution scenarios for 1990, based on the common Plan figures of 2.76% p.a. growth in total population and 4.84% p.a. growth in total private consumption. For ease of comparison, it is further assumed that the two urban per capita expenditure figures are the same in 1990 as they were in 1985 ($675 and $4,934 p.a., respectively); the average rural per capita income then reflects the differing demographic assumptions. Imports for consumption of the three groups (direct and indirect) are calculated on the basis of the assumed import content figures given in each case.

Plan scenario. Rapid urbanisation takes place, reaching 40% in 1990; it was concluded previously that this assumption is highly unrealistic, but it provides an interesting reference point for comparative purposes. Required growth of imports for private consumption: 5.4% p.a.

More likely Plan outcome. If the macroeconomic aspects of the Plan remain accurate, a more likely outcome in spatial development terms is an urbanisation proportion of 30%. Required growth of imports for private consumption is then reduced to 4.6% p.a.

Rural-focused strategy. Here it is assumed, for the sake of discussion, that the urban–rural proportions remain the same as they were in 1985, while the import content of per capita consumption declines by 3.3% p.a. in the urban areas and increases by 6.2% p.a. in the rural areas. The import content figures are a proxy for the changed style and rural orientation of development, implying somewhat less sophisticated goods in the urban areas than the other scenarios, but a greater range and higher quality of goods in the rural areas. Required growth of imports for private consumption is then only 2.04% p.a., the same rate as the national average increase in per capita consumption.

Apart from illustrating the point that changes in import content of consumption may not be as infeasible as the aggregate figures might have suggested, the income distribution profile in the table quantifies the basic argument in favour of a rural income redistributive strategy. Per capita expenditure differs by a factor of 2.57 between rural and HDA, 18.76 between rural and LDA, and 7.31 between HDA and LDA. A relatively rapid growth of per capita income affecting 74% of the total population would appear to be possible without reducing urban per capita income or introducing substantial policy changes which would have to discounted on the grounds of political feasibility. The development spin-offs of a substantial widening of economic involvement would go far beyond the gains reflected in an improvement in income distribution statistics.[11]

With respect to the figures derived from the input–output model, it has to be emphasised that the fact that no change in the shares in final demand (to increase domestic to import ratios) or the technology of production (in favour of domestically-oriented production over imports) has been included, has omitted precisely the sources from which the major gains are expected to arise from the alternative strategy. If the data permitted informed judge-ments to be made about these, the superiority of the alternative strategy would be far more marked, at least in the longer term. The gains from a shift in the structure of production to accommodate the changed pattern of demand and from employing a level of technology with a lower investment and recurrent import content, would anyway take some time to materialise.

How long the phase of rural development-oriented 'semi-autarkic' strategy should last is an empirical question, warranting detailed investigation. For a start, the success of such a strategy would depend critically on being able to mobilise suitable people in sufficient numbers to execute it. While organisa-tion and training can assist to an important degree, effectiveness at the grass roots in a rural development programme seems to depend on personal temperament and sensitivity to the subtleties of the situations encountered. Inevitably, these aspects make it difficult to plan for a rigid time-table of implementation in the way one might for the opening-up of a new series of mineral deposits, for example. While in terms of time this might be a disadvantage, there would be substantial learning and political involvement advantages in the nature of the programme, one objective being that the mass of the people gradually come to make for themselves key decisions affecting the structure of their lives. The strategy not only seeks to spread economic resources more evenly, but political resources too. Zimbabwe is a society in which democratic forms were systematically denied during the colonial period and the opportunity for people to gain the experience required to take command at local levels and to participate meaningfully at the national level, needs to be given.

The direct financial costs of implementing an integrated rural develop-ment strategy throughout the communal areas would undoubtedly be very high. It is not being proposed that all other activities should be totally subordinated to that objective as, apart from very real absorptive capacity constraints, other targets already identified, such as export promotion, have to be supported simultaneously for the overall strategy to make sense. It is unlikely that the broad objectives will be obtained in less than ten years. In the second half of that period, the next phase of economic development, aimed at significant widening and deepening of the industrial sector, should be initiated on a planned basis, while the political thrust towards a thoroughgoing democratisation of the society should be continued, but concentrated in this phase on the urban workers.

The inertia of socio-political systems can be overcome in times of crisis with significant results in terms of changed economic structures. The impor-tant phase of import-substituting industrialisation which took place in a Rhodesia subjected to international sanctions was the product of the sense of purpose and determination arising from the cohesiveness of those with political and economic power at that time. With the emerging confrontation with South Africa, another historical moment may be approaching when the country could be unified and galvanised into making a proper start on the building of socialism. 'This is economic war – prepare for it', Prime Minister Mugabe said at a press conference on 8 August 1986: is that the start of a new epoch for Zimbabwe?

NOTES

1. A variant of the Chapter 2 scenario, which assumes 3.5% growth in industrial countries, 7% trade and 3% real interest rates, with 3% inflation and $15 for oil (Table 2.1).
2. It would be desirable to include health, schooling and other social indicators, but the use of these as measures poses rather tricky problems. For the purposes of this chapter, crude proxies will suffice.
3. The Plan's figures assume a continuation of the oil price at 1985 levels. Taking account of lower oil prices, as well as some other updates to the data used in the model, allows the High scenario figures given in Table 8.1 to attain the same levels of consumption, employment, investment and debt as the Plan, but with a lower export growth of 6%.
4. Discussions over a new loan for expanding the Export Revolving Fund are apparently stalled over the Bank's insistence that it be coupled with some liberalisation of imports.
5. In April 1986, there were eight CIPs in operation, involving Canada, West Germany, Finland, France, Netherlands, Norway, Sweden and the USA. Details of barter deals are not released, nor are aggregate figures published.
6. While South African capital is a special case, an interesting general feature of the UDI period was the 'pseudo-localisation' that took place through enforced Rhodesianisation of management of the branches of multinationals and the reinvestment of profits which would otherwise have been repatriated. In the absence of the resources needed to take direct control of these enterprises, the independence government could do worse than to foster this pseudo-localisation.
7. In practice, much of the marketing continues to be done through established channels, throwing doubt on whether the purpose for which the Corporation was set up is currently being fulfilled. The mechanism is at least in place, and as the Corporation gains in experience it is to be hoped that it will increasingly take the lead.
8. Although not bearing directly on the question of the choice of long-run strategy, the effects of periodic drought would possibly be more adverse under the semi-autarkic strategy discussed below (pages 193–9) where a higher proportion of the population would be living in the rural areas and directly dependent on agriculture. If, however, sufficient water is assured for households to have a vegetable garden, food security might be less of a problem than with a more urbanised population.
9. The capital goods sector would have to grow, but this growth would be concentrated in familiar sub-sectors, e.g. agricultural implements and transport equipment, so that the concomitant export focus would be regional rather than international. The political economy aspects of this, ownership patterns, interests of the multinationals, competition from aggressive exporters such as Brazil, warrant further analysis. Detailed consideration of which technologies are 'appropriate' would also be required, particularly in relation to the decentralisation of agro-based industries on a smaller scale to their urban counterparts.

10. Land tenure is another crucial area which lies beyond the scope of this chapter. Different forms have implications for financing requirements, fulfilment of social objectives and contribution to economic growth. The government's approach to date, of having four different 'models', has merit in that no one tenure system could be uniformly successful throughout the country.

11. This point is obvious in a Marxist framework, but is also one that has gained a certain currency in orthodox circles, following analysis of the main problems identified from the immediate post-World War II phase of development in countries which had already achieved nominal political independence. For example, an ILO mission reported of the Philippines (Ranis, 1974) that 'it is essentially the non-participation of more than four-fifths of the population in productive and innovative activity which lies at the root of the problems to which the Mission was asked to address itself ' and proposed a policy package aimed at 'releasing the energies of large numbers of persons who are at present economically disenfranchised'.

Table 8.1 Scenarios for the Zimbabwe economy, 1985–90

Scenario	Exports % p.a.	Imports % p.a.	Debt index	GDP % p.a.	PrCons % p.a.	GovCons % p.a.	1990 Emp't (ths)	1990 Cap Util	GFCF % p.a.
Reference scenarios									
Five Year National Dev Plan	7.0	6.0	n.s.	5.1	4.9	4.2	1,173	n.s.	5.3
World Bank Memorandum	3.9	6.3	n.s.	4.2	3.0	n.s.	n.s.	n.s.	8.4
Main and alternative strategies – world economy scenarios									
High	6.0	5.2	100	5.1	4.9	4.2	1,180	93	5.3
Alt high	6.0	5.2	100	5.6	5.5	5.0	1,256	93	5.3
Principal	4.0	3.25	100	2.5	1.4	1.0	1,038	82	5.3
Alt prin	4.0	3.25	100	2.9	2.0	1.5	1,102	82	5.3
Low	2.5	1.29	95	1.5	1.4	1.0	994	79	0.0
Alt low	2.5	1.29	95	2.0	2.0	1.4	1,057	79	0.0
SA border closure in 1987 – Impact and five-year average effects									
Impact (1987)	−10.9	−18.2	73	−15.7	−21.7	0.0	853	68	−25.0
5-Yr Av. (a)	0.8	−1.6	79	−1.4	−3.6	0.8	859	69	−1.6
5-Yr Av. (b)	0.8	1.5	100	0.2	−1.5	0.0	923	75	5.3

Table 8.1 (continued)

Scenario	Exports % p.a. 1984 share	Imports % p.a. 1986–90 growth p.a.	Debt index 1990 share	GDP % p.a.	PrCons % p.a.	GovCons % p.a.	1990 Emp't (ths) 1985 share	1990 Cap Util 1986–90 growth p.a.	GFCF % p.a. 1990 share
				Imports					
Plan									
Agriculture	7.9	3.1	3.6						
Intermediate	48.8	6.9	56.5						
Mining	1.5	2.9	1.2						
Capital goods	33.7	5.2	31.1						
Consumer goods	8.1	4.0	7.3						
WB									
Food							1.0	0.0	0.7
Petroleum							19.0	4.5	16.2
Intermediate							37.0	7.0	35.3
Machinery & transport equip.							35.0	11.3	40.9
Misc Manuf.							7.0	7.1	6.7
				Exports					
Plan									
Agriculture	41.0	6.6	39.6						
Mining	26.9	7.4	26.9						
Intermediate	20.1	7.9	20.8						
Capital	1.5	13.5	1.9						
Consumer goods	10.5	7.9	10.7						
WB									
Agriculture							41.0	5.1	44.0
Metals & minerals							38.0	1.7	30.0
Gold							10.0	3.0	9.0
Gen. manuf.							8.0	13.0	16.0
Other							4.0	-4.4	2.0

Sources: Plan, World Bank Memorandum and runs of Knox/Robinson/Stoneman input–output model.

Table 8.2 Exports, manufactured exports and imports by country or area of destination, 1983 (percentages)

Country/area of destination	% of total exports	% of total mfd exports incl. metals	Mfd export as % all exports	% of total imports
EEC[a]	36.2	30.5	42.1	31.7
South Africa	16.6	21.9	65.7	24.5
Far East/Australasia	10.1	11.2	55.6	6.3
North Africa/Middle East/Indian sub cont.	6.9	3.5	25.7	1.0
USA	6.9	10.4	75.3	9.5
Scandinavia	0.8	0.7	39.7	1.1
Other Europe	5.6	6.3	57.0	2.7
SADCC States[a] of which	11.2	12.8	56.8	8.2
Zambia	(3.3)	(1.5)	(23.0)	
Botswana	(4.2)	(6.8)	(81.9)	
Other African	2.7	0.8	15.2	
Other countries	3.0	2.0	32.4	
Total	100.0	100.0	50.0	100.0

a. Portugal and Spain are included in statistics for the EEC and Namibia in statistics for SADCC, although the countries were not at the time members of these respective official groupings.

Source: UNIDO (1985), Table 10.4.

Table 8.3 Balance of payments (Zimbabwe $m.)

Item	1979 Cr	1979 Dr	1980 Cr	1980 Dr	1981 Cr	1981 Dr	1982 Cr	1982 Dr	1983 Cr	1983 Dr	1984 Cr	1984 Dr
A. Goods, services and income												
Merchandise	734.0	594.9	928.9	860.5	1,001.9	1,059.4	998.2	1,114.3	1,173.9	1,086.6	1,483.7	1,237.1
Exports/Imports	654.4	549.3	787.5	809.4	894.6	1,017.5	817.6	1,081.8	1,027.3	1,056.2	1,277.0	1,199.4
Re-exports	3.7		6.5		7.3		20.7		20.2		22.0	
Gold	66.6		115.2		76.3		140.5		98.9		159.6	
Internal freight	18.3	45.6	19.7	51.1	23.7	41.9	19.4	32.5	27.5	30.4	24.8	37.7
Shipment services	18.8	46.4	25.9	65.1	16.8	128.6	14.8	122.0	18.0	185.3	22.3	163.9
Port dues		21.7		21.0		30.3		33.5		35.5		40.1
External freight	18.8	24.7	25.9	44.1	16.8	98.3	14.8	88.5	18.0	149.8	22.3	123.8
Other transport services	24.9	39.3	38.7	51.4	31.2	52.1	54.5	40.3	60.8	56.5	71.2	62.3
Passenger fares	4.3	21.4	11.0	21.5	16.5	22.2	20.9	16.0	30.2	16.6	36.1	11.3
Port services	20.6	17.9	27.7	29.9	14.7	29.9	33.6	24.3	30.6	39.9	35.1	51.0
Travel	5.6	71.8	15.9	102.4	16.8	103.4	20.4	78.9	25.8	73.4	31.2	83.0
Business and holiday allowances		63.7		92.3		89.5		64.4	8.2	56.2	9.4	58.5
Tourism	5.5		15.7		16.6		2.0		3.0	0.2	6.1	
Other	0.1	8.1	0.2	10.1	0.2	13.9	5.9	14.5	14.6	17.0	15.7	24.5
Direct investment income	23.4	42.0	26.7	50.0	33.6	79.2	35.5	95.3	39.1	92.2	39.7	14.9
National railways	22.9		26.0		32.2		34.6		37.9		38.4	
Dividends and profits of companies and persons	0.5	42.0	0.7	50.0	1.4	79.2	0.9	95.3	1.2	92.2	1.3	14.9
Other investment income	18.4	24.3	37.8	32.9	31.0	64.5	25.1	122.9	30.4	184.6	28.8	205.6
Interest: public sector	10.3	4.1	22.7	5.9	16.7	27.5	14.4	75.2	12.1	127.7	12.3	166.9
private sector	1.0	5.5	1.5	8.9	1.5	15.9	1.5	24.4	3.9	33.6	2.8	25.9
Dividends – persons	6.5		9.0		12.3		8.9		14.2		13.7	
Former residents' remittances	0.6	14.7	0.6	18.1	0.5	21.1	0.3	23.3	0.2	23.3		13.1
Other	4.0		4.0						50.0	116.3		

Other goods, services and income												
Official	0.7	2.1	15.8	3.6	8.3	14.3	20.9	11.4	21.6	22.5	30.8	24.8
Private	10.8	51.7	15.2	55.3	19.9	74.3	27.4	82.2	28.4	93.8	33.5	103.3
Labour income	0.8	23.4	2.5	23.5	0.2	3.5	0.4	2.8	0.7	2.2	0.6	3.0
Property income	0.7	7.0	1.8	8.8	1.4	9.5	1.1	12.9	1.0	14.1	0.8	9.0
Other	9.3	21.3	10.9	23.0	18.3	61.3	25.9	66.5	26.7	77.5	32.1	91.3
B. Unrequited transfers												
Private	29.7	67.7	33.0	110.5	47.7	133.2	50.7	147.4	66.3	188.4	125.3	183.3
Migrants' funds	0.7	13.7	0.3	23.9	0.4	26.6	0.7	30.1	0.1	30.8	0.6	23.0
Non-commercial transactions	4.5	27.0	2.1	38.9	18.4	53.9	22.3	50.9	4.0	50.1	21.3	50.3
Workers' remittances	7.2	0.4	6.0	0.8	0.5	1.7						
Pensions	5.1	13.5	3.5	29.7	2.6	37.3	2.5	54.4	2.7	64.9	3.2	71.3
Other	12.2	13.1	21.1	17.2	25.3	15.4	23.5	12.0	59.5	42.6	100.2	38.7
Official	37.1	68.9		6.3	38.6	4.2	71.7	9.7	117.8	117.8		8.0
Government	33.5	59.2			32.3	4.0	64.0	7.2				
Non-commercial transactions	3.6	9.2		0.2			7.7				2.5	
Other		0.5	6.3	6.4					9.7		8.0	8.0
Net balance on current account	73.9		156.7		439.3		532.8		457.0		101.9	
C. Capital account												
Government	128.6	10.6	33.0	54.6	150.7	46.3	257.6	99.1	267.5	77.9	302.5	150.9
Other public authorities	0.5	6.9	0.7	3.7	57.9	2.2	192.2	2.8	317.1	225.3	171.3	80.0
Private transactions including statistical discrepancy	81.5	19.4	126.5	26.1	220.4	70.3	339.5	169.0	98.2	80.9	99.0	75.7
Net balance on capital account	173.7		75.8		310.2		518.4		292.7		266.2	
Net balance on current and capital account	98.8		80.9		129.1		14.4		158.3		164.3	

Source: CSO, *Quarterly Digest of Statistics*, September 1985.

Table 8.4 An alternative disaggregation of the balance of payments (Zimbabwe $m.) (various years, current prices)

Line	Cr item	Dr item	1978 Cr	1978 Dr	1978 Bal	1981 Cr	1981 Dr	1981 Bal	1984 Cr	1984 Dr	1984 Bal
1	Exports	Imports	638.7	483.3	155.4	964.8	1169.6	-204.8	1455.7	1379.7	76.0
2	Pr. and dividends	Pr. and dividends	16.5	26.4	-9.9	33.6	79.2	-45.6	39.7	14.9	24.8
3		Interest – private loans	0.6	7.2	-6.6	1.5	15.9	-14.4	2.8	25.6	-22.8
4		Interest – parastatals					2.8	-2.8	—	38.7	-38.7
5	Service exports	Service imports	24.6	45.3	-20.7	34.6	104.2	-69.6	68.6	154.3	-85.7
6	Productive sector total		680.4	562.2	118.2	1034.5	1371.7	-337.2	1566.8	1613.2	-46.4
7	Other unrequited transfers	Other unrequited transfers	9.6	10.3	-0.7	25.8	15.4	10.4	100.2	38.7	61.5
8	Travel	Travel	9.8	74.1	-64.3	33.2	113.9	-80.7	67.2	73.6	-6.4
9		Education	0.1	5.3	-5.2	0.1	11.7	-11.6	0.1	20.7	-20.6
10	Pensions and dividends – persons	Pensions	9.2	7.7	1.5	14.9	37.3	-22.4	16.9	71.3	-54.4
11	Workers remittances	Emigrants' costs	3.7	26.1	-22.4	1.4	47.7	-46.3	0.6	36.1	-35.5
12	Household total		32.4	123.5	-91.1	75.4	226.0	-150.6	185.0	240.4	-55.4
13	Foreign aid	Interest on debt	1.3	3.2	-1.9	75.9	24.7	51.2	117.8	128.2	-10.4
14	Embassies and other		0.5	0.5	—	18.0	20.7	-2.7	43.1	32.8	10.3
15	Government total		1.8	3.7	-1.9	93.9	45.4	48.5	160.9	161.0	-0.1
16	Current account		714.6	689.4	25.2	1203.8	1643.1	-439.3	1912.7	2014.6	-101.9

Direct equity investment	4.0	2.3	1.7	5.9	3.3	2.6	10.0	13.0	−3.0
Private long-term	3.4	23.7	−20.3	94.0	43.8	50.2	3.4	21.2	−17.8
Blocked funds					8.7	−8.7		0.1	−0.1
Banks – short-term		4.1	−4.1	8.6	4.9	3.7	52.0	41.4	10.6
Parastatals – long-term	3.0	7.2	−4.2				143.7	60.3	83.4
Other – short-term				87.0	19.1	67.9	27.6	19.7	7.9
Productive sector total	10.4	37.3	−26.9	195.5	79.8	115.7	263.7	155.7	81.0
Portfolio investment		5.6	−5.6	1.6	22.4	−20.8	55.0	48.3	6.7
Official long-term capital	130.9	3.9	127.0	53.7	15.0	38.7	247.5	102.6	144.9
Official short-term capital		55.1	−55.1	226.5	8.2	218.3	257.4	480.4	−223.0
Government total	130.9	64.6	66.3	281.8	45.6	236.2	559.9	631.3	−71.4
Capital account[a]	141.3	101.9	39.4	477.3	125.4	351.9	796.6	787.0	9.6
Net Balance – current & capital[b]	855.9	807.3	48.6	1767.0	1768.5	−1.5	2742.9	2801.6	−58.7

a. Net balance includes errors and omissions (−16 in 1978, +85.9 in 1981 and +33.6 in 1984).
b. Balance on capital account from Reserve Bank presentation (official short term below the line) is −32.2 in 1978, +133.6 in 1981 and +232.6 in 1984.
Sources: Reserve Bank and Central Statistics Office.

Table 8.5 Exports and imports by principal commodity groups, 1978, 1981, 1984 (percentages)

Commodity groups	Exports			Imports		
	1978	1981	1984	1978	1981	1984
Food products	18	15	13	1	2	7
Beverages and tobacco	18	25	23			
Crude materials except fuels	22	19	19	3	3	3
Mineral fuels, related products and electricity	1	1	1	23	21	21
Animal and vegetable oils and fats	1				1	1
Chemical and related products	1	1	2	15	14	15
Manufactured goods classified by materials	30	27	33	17	19	15
Machinery, transport, radio/TV, electrical equipment	5	2	2	25	32	31
Miscellaneous manufactured articles – not elsewhere classified	4	10	7	15	8	7

Source: Central Statistical Office. *Statistical Yearbook* 1985, Table 11.2.

Table 8.6 Exports of principal commodities, 1978–84 (Zimbabwe $m.)

Commodity	1978	1979	1980	1981	1982	1983	1984
Food products (0)							
Meat, fresh, frozen or chilled	35	33	14	5	4	11	27
Other meats	3	5	5	4	3	7	11
Maize	25	17	7	35	40	41	
Malted barley	3	3	3	4	4	4	2
Tea	8	7	6	6	6	10	25
Coffee	12	11	7	10	15	19	30
Beverages and tobacco (1)							
Barley leaf stripped and scrap	1	0	2	4	2	1	1
Flue cured leaf	71	60	73	121	27	11	7
Flue cured stripped	24	19	43	92	161	215	275
Manufactured tobacco	6	5	5	6	2	3	3
Crude materials except fuels (2)							
Asbestos	57	71	80	76	61	69	74
Manufactured goods classified by materials (6)							
Paper, paperboards and manufactures thereof	1	1	1	1	2	5	8
Yarns and threads	3	5	6	4	3	3	14
Fabrics	5	4	5	3	2	5	9
Cement	1	1	2	2	2	4	6
Machinery, transport, radio/TV and electrical equipment (7)							
Other	2	1	0	2	2	3	8
Total	559	645	788	888	807	1,026	1,271

Source: Central Statistical Office, *Statistical Yearbook, 1985*, Table 11.3.

Table 8.7 Imports of principal commodities, 1978–84 (Zimbabwe $m.)

Commodity	1978	1979	1980	1981	1982	1983	1984
Food products (0)							
Other	3	8	23	10	6	13	74
Fuels and electricity (3)							
Electricity	13	14	19	20	21	20	22
Motor spirit	30	53	66	51	49	62	57
Aviation turbine fuel	7	13	15	18	18	26	30
Gas oil	32	67	76	93	67	92	124
Other petroleum products	6	8	9	16	12	11	9
Chemicals (5)							
Resins	9	16	21	26	19	27	33
Manufactured goods classified by materials (6)							
Textile piece goods	12	15	26	37	30	28	34
Iron, steel, plates and sheets	12	21	29	29	27	21	25
Tubes, pipes, and fittings	2	2	4	5	9	7	11
Machinery and transport equipment (7)							
Farming machinery	6	8	17	19	18	28	15
Textile and leather machinery	3	4	10	19	19	10	7
Excavating and road construction machinery	3	5	9	16	20	25	23
Power machinery and switchgear	4	4	6	14	50	36	36
Telecommunication equipment	4	5	9	10	15	27	52
Bus, lorry, chassis and parts	8	9	16	32	32	22	13
Motor-car assembly kits	6	9	14	22	19	15	11
Other	25	34	58	92	102	113	138
Total	404	549	809	1,018	1,082	1,062	1,201

Source: Central Statistical Office, *Statistical Yearbook, 1985*, Table 11.4.

Table 8.8 Direct plus indirect imports using input–output analysis (percentages)

	Agric.	Intm. G	Cap. G	Final G	Mining	Other
By sector						
Direct	6	25	30	8	7	5
Total	16	35	40	20	20	12

	Pr. cons.	Gov. cons.	Exports	Investment	Total
In final demand					
Direct	4	4	0	24	7
Total	20	17	20	50	24

Zimbabwe $m.

Sector	Direct imported inputs	Indirect imported inputs	Total imported inputs	% of $1445 m
Agriculture	47.7	89.3	137.0	9
Intermediate	129.5	53.8	183.2	13
Capital	188.2	58.3	246.5	17
Final	173.8	269.6	443.4	31
Mining	23.8	42.9	66.7	5
Other	280.7	87.4	368.1	25
	843.7	601.3	1,444.7	

Demand Category				% of $1987 m
Private consumption	142.9	569.0	711.9	36
Government consumption	49.7	164.7	214.4	11
Exports	—	391.4	391.4	20
Investment	274.8	292.9	567.7	29
Stocks	74.0	27.1	101.1	5
Totals	541.4	1,445.1	1,986.5	

Source: See text for explanation.

Table 8.9 Sectoral value-added and employment ratios

	Agric.	Int.	Capital	Final	Mining	Other	Total
Employment (th)	262	58	53	108	56	489	1026
GDP contribution (%)	14	10	7	17	6	46	100
Capacity utilisation (1984)	87	93	73	78	91	74	80
VA/unit material inputs	1.32	0.56	0.67	0.57	0.97	3.77	1.15
VA/total import usage	6.34	3.38	1.76	2.37	5.58	7.74	4.29
Cost/job (th $)	7.5	52.6	36.0	44.1	32.2	13.0	19.2

Source: Zimconsult.

Table 8.10 Income distribution scenarios and import consequences

Item		HDA	LDA	Urban	Rural	Total
1985 base assumptions						
Population	(th)	1,807 *22.1*	319 *3.9*	2,126 *26.0*	6,049 *74.0*	8,175
Pr. Consumption	($m)	1,219 *27.8*	1,574 *35.9*	2,793 *63.7*	1,591 *36.3*	4,384
Expenditure per capita	($)	675	4,934	1,314	263	536
Pr. Cons Imports	($m)	244 *27.8*	428 *48.8*	672 *76.6*	205 *23.4*	877
Import content	(%)	*20.0*	*27.2*	*24.1*	*12.9*	*20.0*
Imports/capita	($)	135	1,342	316	34	107
1990 Plan scenario						
Population	(th)	3,373 *36.0*	375 *4.0*	3,748 *40.0*	5,621 *60.0*	9,369
Pr. Consumption	($m)	2,277 *41.0*	1,850 *33.3*	4,127 *74.3*	1,427 *25.7*	5,554
Expenditure per capita	($)	675	4,934	1,101	254	593
Pr. Cons Imports	($m)	455 *39.8*	503 *44.1*	958 *83.9*	184 *16.1*	1,142
Import content	(%)	*20.0*	*27.2*	*23.2*	*12.9*	
Imports/capita	($)	135	1,342	256	33	122
1990 More likely Plan outcome						
Population	(th)	2,436 *26.0*	375 *4.0*	2,811 *30.0*	6,558 *70.0*	9,369
Pr. Consumption	($m)	1,644 *29.6*	1,850 *33.3*	3,494 *62.9*	2,060 *37.1*	5,554
Expenditure per capita	($)	675	4,934	1,243	314	593
Pr. Cons Imports	($m)	329 *30.0*	503 *45.8*	832 *75.8*	266 *24.2*	1,098
Import content	(%)	*20.0*	*27.2*	*23.8*	*12.9*	
Imports/capita	($)	135	1,342	296	41	117
1990 Rural-focused strategy						
Population	(th)	2,071 *22.1*	365 *3.9*	2,436 *26.0*	6,933 *74.0*	9,369
Pr. Consumption	($m)	1,398 *25.2*	1,801 *32.4*	3,199 *57.6*	2,355 *42.4*	5,554
Expenditure per capita	($)	675 *—*	4,934	1,313	340	593
Pr. Cons Imports	($m)	236 *24.3*	414 *42.7*	650 *67.0*	320 *33.0*	970
Import content	(%)	*16.9*	*23.0*	*20.3*	*13.6*	
Imports/capita	($)	114	1,134	267	46	104

Note: Numbers in italics are proportions.

PART THREE
TRADE AND FINANCING, PERFORMANCE AND POLICIES

9

EXPORTS

HOW TO INTERPRET PERFORMANCE

An elementary difficulty in explaining the past performance, assessing the expectations and policy prescriptions of the country studies, and applying these to other countries is the lack of agreement on how trade flows are determined. This will be discussed more fully in Chapter 16 on the role of the external sector and in Chapter 18 on the role of government and policy. Conventional modelling of aggregate trade prospects focuses on demand as the overall constraint, separating this from the choice among suppliers which may be determined by competitiveness. Changes in the structures of demand and production apparently leading to a steadily increasing share of trade in output are used to explain elasticities greater than 1 on output. The uncertainties are such that the effects of even discrete changes, for example from tariff changes, are difficult to estimate. An individual trader sees the aggregate demand movements and any general country-level constraints on competitiveness, but he will also see a range of current opportunities to make changes among products or among markets. He may perceive these choices as much more important in quantitative terms and much more within his own power to control than the movements in aggregate demand or prices. This does not necessarily mean that there is a conflict between the micro- and macroeconomic perceptions of the appropriate 'model' of export determination. But the unexplained elasticity and the uncertainties about how well an exporter can find and interpret different types of opportunity make it difficult to move from observation to policy prescription.

This chapter will concentrate on examining the aggregate performance of exports relative to demand, and the influence of the composition of exports, by commodity and market, on prospects. It is important to examine how far the countries and areas which have achieved increases in share in the past have done so on the basis of high initial shares in rapidly growing markets or in appropriate commodities, and how far they appear to have chosen to move into these or to improve their performance in their existing markets or products.

The additional objectives noted in Chapter 3 have important implications for what can be considered 'good' export performance. Only the potential objective of reducing external dependence, which is not considered immediately binding even in the Zimbabwe and Peru chapters, could eventually be in direct conflict with high exports, but the efficiency and diversification objectives of Thailand and Colombia suggest possible constraints on an objective of maximising exports. The concept of flexibility, of an economy's ability to respond to new opportunities, and the possible objective of reducing the risks from unexpected shocks do have some implications for exports. Both suggest that more diversified exporters, and in particular those with a high and growing share of manufactured exports, should have better long-term prospects. They can respond to changes in the most promising commodities and markets more easily by increasing or reducing existing flows, rather than establishing new ones. The alternative of concentrating on a single commodity (or on a set of commodities which have similar demand or supply characteristics) because either the supplying country appears to have a strong comparative advantage in it or demand seems strong can produce more rapid short-term growth (the experience of the oil-exporting countries is the extreme example), but has risks.

DESCRIPTION OF PERFORMANCE

The exports of non-oil-exporting developing countries taken together tended to lose share until the second half of the 1970s. Between 1953 and 1966 (Cutajar, 1967) the share of all developing countries fell from 27% to 20%. Between 1960 and 1968, the volume of non-oil developing countries' exports grew only $4\frac{1}{2}$% a year when world trade was growing at more than 7% (see Table 9.1), falling to a share of only 13%. It was only in the period of very rapid trade growth between 1968 and 1973, when total world trade rose at nearly 10% a year, that the volume of non-oil developing countries' exports rose by as much as 9% p.a. There were large fluctuations recorded in the mid-1970s, and only large increases in 1976 and 1978 raised the average for 1973–81 well above the world figure, and began a regular out-performance that lasted into the 1980s. Because of adverse changes in the terms of trade for primary products, however, by 1980 their share in total world trade was still only 13%, and in 1985 15%.

Data for manufactured exports are reasonably reliable only since 1970. They show the same pattern, but in a more pronounced way. Their share was only 7% in 1970, rising to $7\frac{1}{2}$% by 1975. They rose faster than the average by large, and increasing, margins in the late 1970s and early 1980s. Although recent data are always uncertain, they appear to have fallen back sharply towards the average in 1984, and possibly below it by 1985. In 1986, however, they again grew much faster than the total. While the data thus clearly support the view that developing countries can increase their share of trade, even when it is growing relatively slowly as it was in the early 1980s, they also suggest that such an increase has occurred in only a very small proportion of the last 30 years, and cannot be assumed to be an established trend. Their share in total trade in manufactures had reached 10% by 1980 and 12 $\frac{1}{2}$% by 1985. The large disparity between their shares of the total and of manufactures had therefore nearly disappeared, partly because of the rise in manufactures, but principally because of the declining prices, and their declining share of trade, of primary commodities.

If one groups the developing countries by continents, striking differences emerge. In the 1960s, all areas grew more slowly than the world average, although Asian exports were already growing fastest. Since then, the African countries,[1] except for a short period of rapid growth between 1968 and 1973 (when manufactures grew by 10% p.a.), have consistently lost share and have suffered particularly large variations. The Asian countries grew most rapidly throughout the period, except perhaps after 1980. From then until 1985, Latin America appears to have grown at least as fast. In 1986, Asian performance improved sharply, while Latin America had much poorer growth. The increase in Asia's share of trade in manufactures began earlier, in about 1970, although there was a pause in 1973–4. It continued to rise through the 1970s (see Table 9.2), but seems to have levelled in the 1980s, both relative to the world and to other developing countries. While Asia was gaining share, this appears to have been principally at the expense of the industrial countries: there was a small fall in Africa's share, but Latin America maintained its share.

The 26 countries included in this study as industrialising developing countries account for 85% of all exports of manufactures by developing countries (including OPEC) or over 90% of those by the non-oil exporting (see Table 9.3). The degree of concentration is even greater than this implies. South Korea, Hong Kong and Taiwan account for about 18% each. With the 8% from Singapore, only four countries account for over 60% of the total. Brazil and India raise the NICs' proportion to over two-thirds. Of the rest, only Malaysia, Mexico and Thailand are normally over 2%. This represents a large increase in concentration since 1970, but since 1980 the changes in the principal Asian exporters have been smaller. Hong Kong, indeed, has had little change since 1970. The main rise for Taiwan was completed by 1978. Although South Korea's changes have been more variable, it also appears to have stabilised in the late 1970s. This accounts for the ending of the rise in the share of all ldcs in total trade in manufactures.

The rise in the aggregate share was therefore effectively the change in the shares of South Korea. Taiwan, Singapore and Brazil. But a number of other countries, although starting from a smaller base, also achieved rapid rates of growth in the 1970s (Table 9.1). Malaysia was at the average for Asian countries and Thailand rather above it. Colombia and Peru were near the Latin American average (although with large fluctuations) and thus little better than the world average. Zimbabwe, like the African countries on average, was well below this, although the constraints on its trade in the 1970s make comparisons difficult. The countries that did grow particularly rapidly were the Philippines, Sri Lanka, Uruguay and, particularly by the standards of other African countries, Morocco, Tunisia and the Ivory Coast. For most of these countries, the rise in manufactures helped to secure better than average performance for exports as a whole. Thailand, Sri Lanka and Morocco have continued to perform relatively well, but the Philippines, Tunisia, the Ivory Coast and Uruguay are now growing at or below the world average. Egypt, Pakistan, Brazil and Mexico have improved their performance in the last few years.

A comparisón of manufactures with the other exports of the developing countries shows their role from a different perspective. In the mid-1970s, their share in total exports rose from about a third to an average of 40%, with a further step rise to about a half during 1982–4 (see Table 9.4). It is noteworthy that in the 1980s, the rise in their value accounted for the whole rise in the value of developing countries' exports; although the volume of other exports also rose, this was more than balanced by their falling prices. In the 1970s as well, some of their rise in share is accounted for by a more rapid rise in their prices. In the Asian countries manufactures were close to half the total by 1970, and showed a further rise in the late 1970s to just over 60% and then to 65–70% by the mid-1980s. The Latin American countries' share was only at 20% in 1970, and although it rose slightly in the mid-1970s, they saw no lasting increase until the 1980s. The rise in the volume óf manufactures was then accompanied by a sharp fall in the value of non-manufactures. The changes in Africa's share are largely accounted for by changes in the prices and values of other exports.

The countries with good export performance among the NICs, and those which account for most of the rise in the share of developing countries in world exports, are thus mainly those which were already highly dependent on exports of manufactures at the beginning of the 1970s and which remain exceptional in this respect. Only Singapore has since moved into this group (other countries with apparent high shares, like Chile and Peru, have high exports of semi-processed metals). Of the other countries with rapidly growing exports, Thailand, the Philippines and Sri Lanka all began with low shares of manufactures. The 'successful' exporters are thus small in number, particularly those which have joined the group since 1970, and geographically concentrated. Only Pakistan had a high share of manufactures in total exports and slow export growth, and recently its growth has improved.

The differences between the export performance of the developing countries and total trade in manufactures, and the wide variations among them, are warnings against attempting to derive the potential export success of any particular country directly from aggregate forecasts. The first step to identifying reasons for the differences is to look at more disaggregated indicators of demand. There appear to be advantages from starting with a composition of exports biased towards the more rapidly growing sector: manufactures, and area: Asia.

COMPOSITION OF EXPORTS

There are two important aspects to this composition: the shares of different types of exports and, for individual countries, the concentration on the principal exports. For the countries with structural targets, the type of products, that is, the choice between manufactures and among sectors within manufactures, is important.

In the past, manufactures have grown faster than other goods. One of the notable changes in world trade in the early 1980s was the decline in confidence in that differential. The income elasticity of demand for manufactures is normally expected to be higher than for primary goods; the opportunities for increased specialisation are most likely to occur in industry; at least until recently, protection and other structural constraints on trade have been strongest in primary goods. Although it appears to have become more irregular, the period averages in Table 9.1 do not suggest any large change: the differential has remained about 1.5 points. A more cautious view of the future is possible, particularly if the fall in the price of oil continues to bring a revival in energy consumption and trade, but this would not affect the advantage of manufactures over other commodities.

The most traditional developing country manufactured exports, textiles, have fallen fairly steadily in share since 1970–1, from 16–17% to below 10% (see Table 9.5) by 1984–5. This was initially balanced by a more than equal rise in the share of clothing exports, but after a peak in 1976 their share began to fall off, and even the apparent revival in 1985 only brought their combined share back to around a quarter. This coincides with the growth in protection against developing country trade in textiles and clothing under the Multi-Fibre Arrangement discussed later in this chapter, but also with the rise in total exports of manufactures: the gains in share appear therefore to have been principally in new exports. The share of textiles had been much greater for Asian exporters (about 20% in 1970, itself a fall from a quarter in the late 1960s), and has fallen much more steeply, so that it is now about 10%. The small rise in their exports of clothing has meant that these together account for only about 30%, compared with 40% in the early 1970s. For Latin

America, textiles and clothing have been of much less importance, and have remained under 10% of the total.

Steel has risen sharply in its share of Latin American exports, doubling to over 10% of the total, with most of the rise in the last few years, when Latin America was improving its relative performance. In Asia, it has kept pace with other exports, but has not increased its share. Chemicals, which have been another major export for Latin America, rose in the mid-1970s, although they have become slightly less important since then. They are of minor importance for Asia. For both the Asian and Latin American countries, the major change has been in exports of machinery and transport. In Asia, they started to rise in the early 1970s, and have continued to do so, rising from 10% to about a third of the total. Except for slower growth in the early 1970s, the pattern for Latin America has been remarkably similar. The rise was also the main change in the export composition of Hong Kong, Singapore and South Korea between 1970 and 1979 (Fields, 1985).

There is little difference between the share of intra-developing country trade in exports of manufactures and its share in all ldc trade, and the difference has in fact diminished (in 1985 it may have fallen below its share in the total) (Table 9.5). For the Asian countries, there has been little change, except for a fall in the mid-1980s. Latin America, with a rather similar proportion of intra-ldc trade in total, had a much larger share in its exports of manufactures, at well over a third (compared to around 20%) throughout the 1970s, until a sharp drop in 1983. For all developing countries, chemicals and machinery and transport were more important in intra-trade than in total exports, but the differential for machinery has fallen because of a much greater rise for other countries. The share of textiles has fallen, and that of clothing has always been much smaller than its share in their exports to all areas. The greater importance of ldc markets for chemicals is the result of greater intra-Asian trade; the negligible importance of clothing trade within Asia explains the difference for this sector. The differences for Latin America are found in the greater importance (except in recent years) of chemicals and machinery and transport, and the smaller importance of steel.

These differences suggest that the direction of exports and the choice of commodities are closely linked choices. Some commodities (clothing, particularly in the Asian countries, and steel, at least in Latin America) are too widely produced (or protected) in all developing countries to offer scope for high intra-area trade. Chemicals have been an important product in this trade. Machinery and transport equipment have also been important, but the principal increase in exports of these has come from other markets. If developing countries are more likely to have a comparative advantage in primary products relative to industrial countries and in manufactures relative to developing countries less developed than themselves, this would suggest that intra-trade should be greater in manufactures. Only Latin America shows that pattern. The greater importance of industrial country markets for Asia suggests that an advantage in some manufactures relative to industrial countries can outweigh the general presumption of a disadvantage in manufactures.

Even at this level of aggregation, it is clear that there has been a diversification of exports into manufactures, and then among manufactures, that has gone well beyond the early stages of industrialisation or exporting. This means that a choice of individual products or industries must be made in the context of a whole structure of production. The markets and product advantages to look for may thus depend on existing linkages and domestic demand as well as on international potential for new products.

Except for value variations corresponding to the rises in oil prices, the share of manufactures in the imports of non-oil developing countries has not changed: it has been approximately 60% since 1974, with the share for Asia slightly lower than that for Latin America, but the same pattern for both. What is even more striking is the small change in the composition of manufactures: except for a small fall in the share of textiles, offset about equally by the other components, this has remained almost constant for the last 15 years. Machinery and transport account for about half the total. This share has grown more for Asia, but is still only about half there, while Latin America has seen it approximately constant at 52–55% (see Table 9.6).

There has been a sharp increase in total in the coverage of imports by exports (its implications for external financing are discussed in Chapter 14), but it is particularly pronounced for manufactures. For all non-oil developing countries, exports were only about 40% of imports in the first half of the 1970s, but this rose above 50% in the second half and had reached 57% before the rise in total coverage in the 1980s. By 1985, the value of manufactured exports was about three-quarters that of imports, an important structural change in the relationship of these countries with the rest of the world. The change has been most marked for the Asian countries: not only has the general rise been characteristic of the whole period, while in Latin America it has occurred only since 1982, but manufactures have risen from approximately 50% of the level of imports to 100%. The Asian countries are no longer net importers of manufactures. In Latin America, the ratio was still below a third as late as 1982, and is only approaching a half in the mid-1980s.[2]

The developing countries have been net exporters of textiles and (by very large margins) of clothing throughout the period. The most notable changes have been the large rises in ratios for machinery and transport for Asia (from under 20% to about 70%) and for Latin America (5% to 29%), and the reversals in balance for Latin American steel and textiles. This transformation in a relatively short period (in terms of industrial investment and structural change) illustrates how misleading current trade flows can be as a measure of the potential.

At the 3-digit level of trade classification, the goods in which the developing countries had a high share of total trade in manufactures in 1982–3 (see Table 9.7) were still mainly goods requiring limited processing such as metals or the traditional sectors such as textiles, clothing and footwear, leather goods and fur, and wood. But since 1970 their share had risen sharply also in telecommunications, electrical machinery, toys, some chemicals, iron and steel and ships and rail vehicles. Among these, the first two and the last two are products in which their share had still been small in the late 1970s. Among non-manufactures, they had particularly important rises in share in fish, fertilisers, rice and gas, while losing share in more traditional exports like oil, coffee, cotton, rubber, cocoa, maize and oil seeds. They also lost share in meat. The changes in fresh fruit and vegetables, which are suggested as good potential exports in some of the country studies, were not impressive. Their rise in tobacco share took place in a declining total market. Their share remained particularly small in road motor vehicles, specialised machinery, aircraft, paper products and capital goods.

Only a few industrialising countries are even approaching the pattern of trade of the industrialised countries. Table 9.8 shows that by 1982-3, except for Argentina and India, all the NICs exported as one of their five principal exports at least one out of cars, machinery or electronics products, the products characteristic of the industrial countries, but only one of the countries identified as 'new NICs', did so, and none of the other middle-income countries. Only Hong Kong and Singapore (which are exceptional because of their small size) have two of the 'industrial country' exports among their five principal exports. Textiles and clothing were still very important to all the Asian NICs except Singapore, and to Thailand and Colombia among the next group, and to 60% of the third group. Raw and lightly processed foods and metals continue to dominate the exports of even the 'new NICs'. Of the popular non-traditional primary exports now being considered, fresh fruit, vegetables and fish are important only to India, Colombia and Thailand. The countries whose exports have grown most rapidly have not had or achieved an 'industrial country' composition of exports; Pakistan, the Philippines and Sri Lanka (and South Korea) still have high shares of textiles and clothing or primary products.

Although there are wide variations, another clear difference among the groups is in the concentration ratios of the principal exports. For the NICs, the principal export accounts on average for a quarter of exports; the top five for about a half; and the top 16 for about three-quarters. The measure for one product would be just under 20% without Mexican oil; the second highest is Hong Kong (clothing exports are a third of its total). This is much higher than the ratios characteristic of the industrial countries (except Japan which is quite close to the NICs' average), and the new NICs are higher, particularly at the 16-product level, indicating that diversification has taken place but not to the extent of giving a very wide exporting base. The other countries are in general much more concentrated on a few (under five) commodities; in none of the NICs or new NICs do the first 16 account for 90% of the total; among the next group, in none are they less than 80%, and half are above 90%. The Asian countries are on average less concentrated than the other areas (this is apparent within groups as well as for the area averages), with the concentration of Latin American countries on one or two commodities not very different from the African,[3] and differences emerging only at the level of 5–16.

These differences at the level of individual commodities are confirmed at the level of more general concentration ratios (see Table 9.9). In 1983, the same year for which the commodity ratios were used, the NICs exported most commodities, with most diversification/least concentration by the two measures chosen, and the new NICs and the other countries followed, in that order. The differences between the most advanced and the industrial countries, particularly Japan, are less obvious on these measures, with the concentration ratios of Brazil, India and South Korea in particular approaching the industrial country level. The figures for 1970, however, show a very different pattern. Although they were already the most diversified, the NICs in general exported relatively few commodities. The new NICs showed little difference from the other countries in the indices. They had the second fewest products, but the others were actually nearest to the numbers exported by the typical industrial country. There was little difference then between the diversification ratios for the new NICs and the others. The 1970s and the period of rapid growth by the NICs therefore saw a very strong increase in the number of products they export, sufficient to reverse the previous order. The new NICs shared both these trends, at lower rates, and also reduced their concentration ratios. The others reduced their concentration, but did not make as much progress on number of products (cf. UNIDO, 1988).

All the African countries included here show only a very small increase in the number of commodities, and almost no change in the other ratios. There is little difference between the changes for the Asian and Latin American countries, suggesting that the differences are associated with rapid or slower development of exports, not with different trade patterns by area. The generally higher concentration ratios for Latin America are largely the result of the inclusion of the two oil exporters (without Mexico and Venezuela the 1983 figure would be 0.30, still higher than Asia, because of the inclusion of Colombia, but clearly lower than the African).

The industrial countries all showed little change on either index, and the change in the number of products represents mainly the change in the classifications.

The spread of individual countries within the categories confirms these differences among them. All the NICs show rises in diversification, but about half the 'others' show almost no change, and a few show rises in concentration. Changes in concentration are more widespread among the new NICs and the others. Within the new NICs, the two countries with the smallest number of commodities in 1970 (Malaysia and Colombia) had the spectacular increases (like the NICs), while Peru and Thailand, which already were high, showed relatively little change (like the 'others'). They all, however, showed gains on both the diversification and concentration indices.

TRADE BY REGIONS

The distribution among regions of a country's exports can affect its export prospects through differences in the general growth in demand in different markets, but also through differences in the amount of this growth that is transmitted to trading partners. This can vary with product composition, degree of protectionism or relative prices. More structural differences in the type of product that is demanded can arise from the differences already noted between developed country and developing country markets. The number and diversification of markets are important to uncertainty and risk.

Although there was a fall in the early 1980s, the combined share of the industrial countries in developing country exports has remained fairly constant at around 60% since 1970 (see Table 9.10). Although they are clearly, therefore, the largest market, the others cannot be neglected: the share of the oil exporters rose after 1973, from about 2–3% to a peak of 7–8% in the early 1980s, before falling back to 5% by 1985. Less predictably, the share going to other non-oil developing countries also rose, starting in 1979, from its previous steady 22% to about a quarter from 1980 to 1985. It remained constant in this period, but only because the Asian share was rising while the Latin American was falling.

The Latin American countries had a much larger, and earlier, fall in their trade with industrial countries, but from a higher level of about 75% in the early 1970s, to under 70% in the late 1970s, and about 60% in 1980–1. It has since recovered to over 70%, while their intra-trade has declined sharply. Intra-Latin American trade increased during the period, although at its highest it was only a quarter, and has since fallen back to about 20%.

In contrast, the share to industrial countries rose for the Asian countries in the late 1970s, when they were increasing their share of world markets, from under to over 60%, but has since returned to the old level. Oil exporters were more important markets for them before 1973, but only increased to 7%; this, and the subsequent fall, were offset by a fall and then a rise in the share of exports to other non-oil developing countries.

Developing country markets have been much more important for them than for Latin America at over 30% during most of the period, but they were least important in the late 1970s when their total market share was growing fastest. If the countries with the fastest growing exports are compared with those with rises in the share going to other developing countries in the period of rapid growth, seven of the 11 whose growth was faster than average had rising shares, compared with only six of the 13 that were falling, with the remainder in both cases equally divided between constant and falling. Thus the shares were highest for the faster growing exporters, but the diversity of results suggests that this does not explain the rise. There was less difference between the Asian and Latin American export market shares to developing countries in 1980 than before the period of rapid Asian growth. In the 1980s it was true for the Latin Americans as well that the relative importance of other developing countries fell as their aggregate performance improved. While the NICs, particularly Hong Kong and South Korea, have done well in intra-Asia trade, even in the last five years, there is no discernible pattern among the new NICs: Thailand's share to other developing countries fell in the 1970s, but rose in the 1980s; Malaysia's has tended to rise and Colombia's to fall, and only Peru had a rise in the 1970s and a fall in the 1980s. (Zimbabwe's share has varied for other, political, reasons.)

Most of the rise in trade with other developing countries has been intra-area trade, but the Latin American countries did have an increase in the share of their exports going to the Asian countries, particularly after 1980, when all Latin American imports were falling.

Because of the dependence of developing countries' export industries on inputs and capital equipment from the industrial countries (UNIDO, 1985), increases in output for this purpose tend not to give rise to proportional increases in the opportunities for exports from other developing countries to them. This could explain relatively slow rises in intra-trade when several countries within an area increase exports simultaneously.

In the early 1970s, the European Community (EC) was by a large margin the most important industrial country market with about a 30% share, followed by the US (23%) and Japan (9%). The EC share declined throughout the 1970s to around 20% in the early 1980s, while the US, which also fell in the 1970s, although only to 19%, regained its share in 1984–5. This is not surprising as EC imports in total have grown relatively slowly, and within this the share of intra-EC trade has risen. Japan (except for its peak year as an importer of manufactures in 1973) has remained below 10% (see Table 9.11). These results suggest that countries that export extensively to the EC have been at a disadvantage.

The one-third decline in the EC share appears in the figures for both Asia (from 18% to 12%) and Latin America (from 30% to 19%), and in the same period. In contrast, while Japan reduced its share of Latin American exports (to under 4% in the late 1970s, although this then recovered to about 5%), it has become a more important market for the Asian countries. At its highest, in 1979–82, it was over 20% and more important than the US, but it then declined slightly; it probably rose again in 1987–8. The US share of Asian trade rose slightly in the 1980s, but the principal change was its sharp rise (from 30% in 1981 to over 40% by 1985) in share of Latin American trade. Although there have been small increases in the importance of some of the smaller industrial countries, the principal change has therefore been much greater concentration, away from Europe in both areas, and in particular towards the US in Latin America. The corresponding Asian move towards Japan had gone much less far by 1985, but the rise in the yen since then appears to be raising its imports from Asia. Developing countries have, therefore, become much more vulnerable to changes in these two economies.

As with commodities, however, it is worth looking at the effects of different markets and of concentration of markets in more detail. If the markets taking more than 4% of a country's exports are defined as its 'major' markets, the US, Japan and the EC are all major markets for all the NICs and all the new NICs, and were so already in 1970 (with the minor exception of Japan for Colombia in 1970) (see Table 9.11). Thus all these countries have achieved diversification by major area. A few still have severe concentration (at least 40%) on one market, notably Mexico and Colombia on the US and Zimbabwe on the EC, but this is less common than in 1970. Most have large shares in at least two out of three of these industrial country markets, although seven of the 12 still send less than 10% to Japan; only Zimbabwe has this small a market share for the US, and none has for the EC. For the other 13 countries, only three had at least 4% to each of the three areas in 1970: Chile, Pakistan and the Philippines, joined by Sri Lanka in 1985. It is notable that these are all among the faster growing countries. Again, the share to Japan is low most frequently. The US also tends to be low for the African countries, and in general the Africans have less diversified patterns.

Some developing countries are large enough markets to be themselves major customers for some countries. Those which are major markets for at least two other countries are given in the table: three are Asian, helping to explain the high degree of Asian intra-trade noted earlier; South Korea is also an important market. Although China is at present 'major' only for Hong Kong, it is seen as potentially important for others, and the speed with which it has increased its share of Hong Kong trade is impressive: from under 1% up to 1978 to over a quarter. Brazil is important, though not 'major' as defined here, for several other Latin American countries. Although no OPEC countries appear in 1970 and 1985, Venezuela was important for several Latin American countries in the late 1970s, reaching over 10% for Colombia in 1981–2.

PROTECTION

The level of protection against ldc exports by the industrial countries is higher than that against exports from other industrial countries: it increased during the 1970s and is having identifiable effects (Page, 1987b). This growth, although not the discrimination, is a new feature of the period since 1974. During the 1950s and 1960s, tariffs were negotiated down and the restrictions arising from World War II and from the existence of trading blocs such as the

Sterling Area were removed, although some traditional areas of protection, notably agriculture, remained. Non-tariff barriers began to be formalised in textiles during the second half of the 1960s, in the series of measures that preceded the Multi-Fibre Arrangement. Although tariff escalation was identified in the 1960s as a potential problem for some of the industrialising developing countries, the main interest in protection as it affected them was in their own use of high tariffs to promote new industry.

It was only after 1974 that there was serious concern about the effect of protection on the potential for growth of developing country exports to industrial countries. The Tokyo Round of GATT negotiations (1975–80) produced a clear difference in results for developing countries, reducing the tariffs on their goods by much less than those on developed country exports, and non-tariff barriers began to become more severe as markets in the developed countries grew more slowly because of recession. Until the 1980s, although increases in the number of barriers, in the percentage of trade covered, and in the numbers of commodities subject to barriers were identified, developing country exports, as shown in the first part of this chapter, continued to increase particularly rapidly to the industrial countries. Since then, as such trade has grown more slowly, a series of studies (cf. IMF, 1983–6: Hughes and Newbery, 1984; Finger and Olechowski, 1986) have shown that the trade flows affected, in total or looking at individual products or markets, have grown less than would otherwise be expected. Textiles were particularly affected.

While the increase in coverage is most striking in manufactures, this is principally because many foods and other agricultural products were already severely restricted: this has long been one of the reasons for developing countries to wish to move from such exports into manufactures. The new situation, and expectations about how trade restrictions will change, in aggregate and among different products, markets and suppliers, must therefore be part of the background to looking at new policies for trade.

Tariffs on average are no longer high, and the GATT provisions for 'binding' (legal commitment not to raise a tariff above a declared level) restrict the possibility for increasing them except under defined 'exceptional' circumstances. Although there have been moves in the Tokyo Round of the late 1970s and the Uruguay Round which began in 1986 towards relaxing the criteria, and in particular towards permitting more discrimination among suppliers in defining an exceptional difficulty, this is not an immediate threat. There are, however, still some sectors in which tariffs are significant barriers, and many are products of interest to the industrialising countries. Although only 9% of total imports face a tariff of more than 10%, 21% of agricultural goods do. Only 6% of industrial countries' imports from other industrial countries pay rates above 10%, but 12% of those from developing countries, and 20% of their industrial goods, do (Finger and Olechowski, 1986). By 1983, average tariffs were 3%, but the highest were food (5%), textiles (8%), footwear (9%) and clothing (12%), and for each, developing countries faced higher rates than industrial countries (Laird and Finger, 1986). Imports into developing countries still face higher tariffs, although there has been little change since the 1970s (Anjaria et al., 1985). In recent years, there have been some moves to reduce them. Most are between 5% and 20%, but they vary much more widely, and in many cases are not subject to 'binding'. The goods most protected are similar to those protected by industrial countries.

Methods of measurement of non-tariff barriers, where most of the recent growth is found, are still being developed. They are not equivalent (in the non-technical sense) to a tariff in their form or, frequently, their purpose, because they are more tightly targeted on specific products and on achieving a specific level of imports (in value or market share). Techniques that find their 'tariff-equivalent', in the sense of that tariff which would achieve the same reduction of imports below the unrestricted potential and then use this to measure their effect, are not satisfactory, although these methods have given good indications of the magnitude of their price effects in the countries that have imposed them. Particularly from the point of view of countries whose exports are subject to them, measures such as the number of goods (incidence) or share of trade (coverage) are more relevant. (Even these require an agreement on what constitutes a barrier and fuller data than are at present available.)

Under various assumptions, the evidence of a significant rise between 1974 and 1979, particularly in manufactures and against developing countries, is persuasive (summarised in Page, 1987b). Since the early 1980s, UNCTAD and GATT have established more formal methods of compiling and analysing the data, and these suggest that the rise has continued, with a strong rise in 1982. In the 1970s, there was an increase in the number of goods and share of trade covered. Although this has continued, much of the increase since then may have been in tightness of control (partly because the 'base level' is now higher), for which satisfactory measurement is still lacking. On the UNCTAD measurements of coverage (UNCTAD, 1987), excluding fuels, industrial country barriers to imports rose from 20% in 1981 to 23% in 1986, but within this barriers to other industrial countries in 1986 were 21% and to developing countries, 26%. The highest barriers were to food (43% and 33% to developing countries). Chemicals were relatively low (13%), but other manufactures were high: iron and steel 64% and 55% for developing countries, and others 21% and 31% for developing countries. Within this textiles were 40% (61% for developing countries) and clothing 67% (78%). The only large change in the period was in steel, which rose from 30%. Barriers by developing countries are even less well documented, but on the same UNCTAD measurements, the incidence, the proportion of products rather than of trade covered, in 1986 was 73%, with food and other agricultural materials at about 80% and manufactures 72% (iron and steel 70%). They were highest in Africa (almost universal), and in Latin America (90%), while Asia[4] was 43%, nearer the level of industrial countries.

The discrimination against developing countries on both tariffs and non-tariffs is partly deliberate. They are not members of trading groups such as the European Free Trade Association or the European Community; agreements such as the MFA and barriers like Voluntary Restraints are targeted against specific countries. It is also partly the result of the goods in which they have large shares: textiles and clothing, and especially agricultural goods.

CONCLUSIONS ON GENERAL TRADE PATTERNS

Although the forecasts for the main medium-term path suggested in Chapter 2 (Table 2.1) do not suggest large differences in the growth rates of different industrial countries, they do suggest that the risk of the US and Japan falling seriously below their expected rates is greater, and that the European economies are, under either set of assumptions, likely to grow more slowly. The markets for developing countries thus offer potentially satisfactory growth, but with risks.

Clearly a high share of trade with the OPEC countries (or an ability to shift exports into these markets) had advantages in the 1970s. On the forecasts used here for the oil price, this will not hold in the future. A more general conclusion is that, unless there is a similar shock that sharply alters relative growth rates of imports of different areas or groups of countries, the ability to shift to such newly growing markets will be less important for fast export growth.

The trends in trade with other developing countries do not provide obvious lessons. Some of the successful Asian countries with rapidly growing neighbours have increased the share of these in their markets, but in general both Asian and Latin American countries appear to have achieved the most rapid increases in their exports when they were raising the share of their exports to the industrial countries.

With the exception of the oil exporters for some of the NICs, there is little evidence that switching to fast growing (or away from slow growing) markets was a major explanation of rapid increases in exports. This was particularly true of the Asian countries, which did not have large increases in intra-trade or a major shift to Japan in the fastest period of growth. The recent increase in Latin American exports, particularly of manufactures, to the US is an exception: it remains to be seen how secure this increase is. The switches that have occurred have led to diversification. The analysis of markets by country shows a clear progression from more concentrated markets, and less diversification among the major industrial country areas, for the lower middle-income countries to a much more diverse and less concentrated pattern for the NICs, with the new NICs in the middle. Diversification by country within areas may be more relevant to the flexibility and marketing questions to be raised in later chapters of this study.

Developing country intra-trade has tended to mean trade among the NICs and, to a lesser degree, the new NICs, and some exports from the other countries to the NICs. Other less advanced developing countries are almost inevitably smaller markets, and therefore less likely ever to represent major markets for the more advanced, either arithmetically or in the thinking of decision-makers. There does not, therefore, appear to be a large potential for a new type of exporting in which the NICs and new NICs export relatively sophisticated products 'down' to the less advanced countries. The exception is China. At present it is a major market for Hong Kong, where the relationship between the two 'countries' is also exceptional. China is also a potential exception more generally, however, because its size more than compensates for its low average income. But the evidence that intra-developing country trade is also, normally, intra-area trade suggests that, unless there is some growth in Latin American exports to Asia, China will remain important mainly for the Asians, both NICs and new NICs. Only Brazil is likely to be a major market in Latin America.

The implications of country composition for different types of export are mixed and the conclusions about the reduced need for flexibility in shifts among areas do not necessarily hold among commodities. Table 9.12 indicates that, while non-oil primary commodities have grown more slowly than average imports for all the major industrial countries, and this continues to be true in the 1980s, Japan has always had the highest share and the United States the lowest. For the Asian countries, therefore, the shift to the Japanese market has offset some of the difference between the growth of primary commodities and that of manufactures. For all areas, however, and Latin America in particular, the shift to the US reduces the potential for primary exports. The increase in the US share since 1980 corresponds clearly to an increase in the share of manufactures. The divergence between manufactures and other US imports has been much greater than usual in the last few years. It cannot be assumed that this unusual US growth of demand for manufactures will continue, especially as the dollar's value falls. The data available on tariffs and non-tariff barriers do not give strong indications that any industrial countries are particularly open or closed.

Overall, the growth of non-tariff barriers in industrial countries suggests that they may be less open than in the past to new increases in developing country exports, and the increase in the discrimination between developed and developing suppliers indicates that it may be more difficult for developing countries to increase their shares of these markets. The fact that on average developing country barriers, particularly to manufactures, remain even higher is an obvious constraint on shifting to such markets as an alternative. The patterns of trade change described in the first part of this chapter, the shift to industrial country markets when exports could grow rapidly, the higher importance of intra-trade among the Asian countries where the barriers are lower, the moves away from textiles and steel, are clearly logical in terms of the types and changes in restrictions that have been observed, and the evidence of detailed comparative studies is that there is a direct relationship. Some countries, particularly in Asia,[5] have compiled evidence on barriers against their own exports. This suggests a growing awareness of the problem.[6]

It is more difficult to increase export share within a controlled trade flow, where competition would have to be among developing country suppliers rather than between them and industrial countries: the evidence suggests that the latter was where most past increases were achieved. If it is not possible to increase shares, increases in exports of uncontrolled goods must be faster than growth in demand merely to maintain overall market share. If the increases in market share in new commodities which this implies in turn trigger new protective barriers, then countries may need to find new exports increasingly rapidly. The changes in export composition by past successful NICs already suggested that an export strategy needs to emphasise taking new initiatives, rather than only responding to underlying conditions or advantages or events. Increasing trade barriers reinforce this conclusion and may require stronger action. The lower the initial share of an exporter in potentially rapidly growing exports (manufactures and, particularly, machinery and transport), the greater the need for such a strategy because higher changes will be required for a smaller share of total exports to affect the total. The possibility that protection could increase (or decrease if the Uruguay Round is successful), and the probability that any changes will affect different products in different ways, introduce new difficulties into forecasting future market conditions. The new NICs, therefore, probably face a lower return from more slowly growing, more protected and more uncertain markets, and a greater need to take an active part in finding new opportunities than did the NICs.

NOTES

1. Aggregate African indices include Nigeria, which, because of its size, dominates them. This makes them much less suitable for inter-continental comparisons than the Latin American and Asian.
2. Kubo *et al.* find changes in structure, particularly of exports in an earlier generation of industrialising countries. 'The two periods . . . are those that begin and end the industrialization phase. In the earlier period, manufacturing growth and increases in manufactured exports are associated with large increases in machinery imports for investment, which leads to a negative effect on the change in the net trade balance. In the later period, increases in machinery imports for final demand are much less; and the effects of changes in manufactured exports on the trade balance are positive though changes in intermediate imports from manufacturing growth are the same in both periods' (Chenery *et al.*, 1986: 223).
3. It is important to remember that the countries in these lists are not 'all developing countries', but the middle to high income ones, and therefore not typical of their continents as a whole.

4. Bangladesh, Malaysia, Pakistan, Philippines, Singapore, South Korea, Sri Lanka and Thailand.
5. India, Malaysia, Pakistan, the Philippines and South Korea are reported in Anjaria *et al.* (1982), and more recent information on South East Asia is in ASEAN (1986).
6. This may not be a good measure of where it is most serious because existing exporters are more likely to be in a position to notice and complain about barriers than discouraged potential exporters.

Table 9.1 Growth of exports (annual average percentages)

	All goods				Manufactures[a]			
	1960–8	1968–73	1973–81	1980–5	1968–73	1973–81	1975–80	1980–5
World	7.3	9.7	3.3	2.3	10.2	5.7	7.1	4.1
Non-oil developing countries	4.6	9.0	4.8	7.7		8.8	14.0	9.4
Asia	5.5	14.3	4.0	7.9	19.9	11.9	16.7	10.1
Latin America	2.2	4.4	0.7	3.5	15.9	4.8	10.4	8.6
Africa	−1.0	22.7	−6.4	−3.9	9.8	−6.9	3.5	0.7
Newly industrialising countries								
Argentina	2.6	5.5	7.5		24.6	3.4	11.7	
Brazil	4.5	12.7	9.6	10.3	40.9	15.5	13.4	
Hong Kong		9.0	10.1	6.2	14.9	9.4	15.6	10.0
India	4.4	3.4	1.9	1.0	3.1	7.4	11.1	
Mexico	3.9	1.5	10.1	10.3	17.9	2.7	4.7	
Singapore			10.6	6.0	30.9	14.8	21.0	8.6
South Korea	33.6[c]	39.5	15.6	12.6	40.8	14.9	16.3	16.5
Taiwan	14.8	30.4	12.1	10.4	30.4[b]	12.5	20.5	13.2
New NICs								
Colombia	3.8	4.6	0.7	2.1	29.9	2.7	9.7	
Malaysia	5.5	6.8	4.5	3.2	12.7	22.7	18.2	
Peru	5.6	−5.3	−1.9	−0.6	−1.2	7.0	23.9	
Thailand	6.2	9.7	11.2	9.0	19.4	16.4	26.7	8.1
Zimbabwe		10.9	−1.8	−0.9		1.5	2.7	−5.5
Other middle-income countries								
Chile	1.2	−2.2	12.6			15.7	14.8	
Costa Rica	10.6	6.8	4.6	1.6	9.1	8.5	8.1	
Egypt	1.1	12.5	−1.2	7.1	4.0	−9.4	−15.0	6.4
Ivory Coast			−1.1	0.8	14.4	6.8	10.2	
Kenya	6.7	10.8	−2.2	−1.9		−3.1	−0.2	
Morocco	1.2	9.8	0.2	3.9	16.6	10.7	12.8	
Pakistan			8.4	6.7	12.7	3.5	6.8	9.1
Philippines	5.3	7.4	8.3	−0.6	24.1	12.8	22.4	
Senegal	0.7	−1.4	−5.1	3.9	17.6	1.0	−9.3	
Sri Lanka	2.0	−0.9	0.8	7.0	38.1	18.0	41.8	
Tunisia	4.6	6.4	2.7	−3.0	13.9	18.9	11.0	
Uruguay	3.1	−7.8	12.5	1.9		16.0	17.0	
Venezuela	−0.5	−0.9	−8.6	−6.9	18.6	17.1	23.3	

a. For most, estimated from values and UN unit value index for developing countries.
b. All goods.
c. 1963–8.
Sources: UN, *Monthly Bulletin of Statistics*; UNCTAD, *Handbook of International Trade and Development Statistics*; IMF, *International Financial Statistics*; IMF, *IFS Supplement on Trade Statistics*; national sources; author's estimates.

Table 9.2 Shares of developing countries in exports of manufactures (percentages)

	1970	1975	1980	1985
Shares in total exports of manufactures by developing countries				
Asia	52.4	62.8	71.8	73.8
Latin America	26.2	23.4	20.3	19.7
Africa	19.5	9.3	5.8	3.9
Shares in world exports of manufactures				
LDCs	7.0	7.4	10.0	12.5
Asia	3.7	4.7	7.2	9.3
Latin America	1.8	1.7	2.0	2.5
Africa	1.4	0.7	0.6	0.5

Sources: UN, *Monthly Bulletin of Statistics*; UNCTAD, *Handbook of International Trade and Development Statistics*; IMF, *International Financial Statistics*; national sources.

Table 9.3 Shares of sample countries in total developing country exports of manufactures (percentages)

	1970	1975	1980	1981	1982	1983	1969–73	1974–8	1979–83
Total value, US$ bn	12.8	34.9	104.8	115.1	112.9	125.6			
Newly industrialising countries									
Argentina	1.94	2.07	1.91	1.75	1.49	1.50	2.18	2.36	1.78
Brazil	2.86	6.36	6.31	7.03	5.95	5.75	3.43	5.75	6.31
Hong Kong	18.24	16.13	17.33	17.49	17.88	16.30	18.50	16.10	17.04
India	7.13	5.26	4.17	4.22	4.22	4.22	6.73	5.57	4.38
Mexico	3.28	2.45	1.63	1.88	2.26	2.22	2.60	2.36	2.02
Singapore	3.24	6.15	8.43	8.53	8.63	8.00	8.14	5.86	8.17
South Korea	5.04	11.88	13.08	15.01	15.95	16.23	6.75	13.87	15.15
Taiwan	8.87	12.38	16.66	17.48	17.51	17.98	11.17	14.35	17.17
Total	50.60	62.68	69.52	73.39	73.89	72.02	59.51	66.22	72.01
New NICs									
Colombia	0.51	0.88	0.74	0.70	0.66	0.33	0.79	0.88	0.64
Malaysia	0.83	1.89	2.30	2.00	2.42	2.76	0.89	1.62	2.34
Peru	2.48	0.98	1.52	1.22	1.28	1.00	1.99	1.23	1.37
Thailand	0.91	1.28	2.21	2.17	2.28	2.00	1.08	1.51	2.12
Zimbabwe		1.05	0.63	0.49	0.46	0.38	0.17	0.82	0.50
Total	4.73	6.08	7.40	6.58	7.10	6.47	4.93	6.06	6.97
Other middle-income countries									
Chile	0.39	0.37	0.39	0.25	0.30	0.30	0.35	0.38	0.31
Costa Rica	0.32	0.32	0.26	0.24	0.19	0.20	0.30	0.29	0.22
Egypt	1.62	1.29	0.30	0.23	0.21	0.29	1.53	0.97	0.29
Ivory Coast	0.23	0.38	0.33	0.20	0.20	0.17	0.24	0.27	0.23
Kenya	0.40	0.37	0.11	0.11	0.09	0.10	0.33	0.27	0.08
Morocco	0.40	0.56	0.55	0.56	0.63	0.62	0.50	0.53	0.59
Pakistan	1.77	1.64	1.20	1.28	1.22	1.50	1.96	1.49	1.31
Philippines	0.52	0.76	1.11	1.12	1.01	0.94	0.64	0.94	1.08
Senegal	0.23	0.20	0.06	0.08	0.10	0.10	0.21	0.14	0.08

Table 9.3 (continued)

	1970	1975	1980	1981	1982	1983	1969–73	1974–8	1979–83
Total value, US$ bn	12.8	34.9	104.8	115.1	112.9	125.6			
Sri Lanka	0.04	0.06	0.19	0.20	0.24	0.24	0.06	0.08	0.20
Tunisia	0.28	0.87	0.78	0.72	0.72	0.64	0.31	0.64	0.71
Uruguay	0.36	0.32	0.38	0.31	0.29	0.24	0.29	0.37	0.33
Venezuela	0.37	0.28	0.66	0.58	0.60	0.60	0.37	0.30	0.59
Total	6.93	7.42	6.32	5.88	5.80	5.94	7.10	6.66	6.03
Area totals for listed countries									
Africa	3.16	4.72	2.76	2.39	2.41	2.30	3.29	3.64	2.48
Asia	46.59	57.43	66.68	69.50	71.36	70.17	52.09	61.38	68.96
W Hemisphere	12.51	14.03	13.80	13.96	13.02	11.96	12.31	13.93	13.56
Total	62.26	76.18	83.24	85.85	86.79	84.43	67.68	78.95	85.00
Area totals, UN data									
Africa	19.54	9.27	5.83	4.47	4.71	4.40	17.69	8.08	5.17
Asia	52.40	62.79	71.79	73.51	74.39	74.40	56.80	65.94	72.82
W Hemisphere	26.19	23.43	20.31	18.72	17.11	18.86	24.53	22.81	19.24

Sources: UN, *Monthly Bulletin of Statistics;* UNCTAD, *Handbook of International Trade and Development Statistics;* IMF, *International Financial Statistics;* national sources.

Table 9.4 Share of manufactured exports in total exports (percentages)

	1970	1981	Most recent year
Non-oil developing countries	34	44	49 (85)
Asia	46	64	65 (85)
Latin America	22	21	30 (85)
Africa	35	22	26 (85)
NICs			
Argentina	14	22	22 (82)
Brazil	13	35	32 (83)
Hong Kong	93	92	90 (86)
India	45	59	
Mexico	30	11[b]	15 (84)
Singapore	28	47	50 (85)
South Korea	77	81	85 (85)
Taiwan	77	89	91 (85)
New NICs			
Colombia	9	27	13 (84)
Malaysia	6	19	25 (83)
Peru	31	43	44 (82)
Thailand	16	36	41 (85)
Zimbabwe	35	40	44 (84)
Other middle-income countries			
Chile[a]	82	55	
Costa Rica	18	27	24 (82)
Egypt	27	8	10 (85)
Ivory Coast	6	9	10 (83)
Kenya	15	11	11 (83)
Morocco	10	27	41 (84)
Pakistan	57	51	61 (85)
Philippines	6	23	24 (83)
Senegal	19	20	
Sri Lanka	1	22	27 (84)
Tunisia	19	33	42 (84)
Uruguay	20	37	36 (84)
Venezuela	2	4	4 (82)

a. Excluding copper: 15, 12.
b. 1980.

Sources: IMF, *International Financial Statistics Supplement on Trade Statistics*; UNCTAD, *Handbook of International Trade and Development Statistics*.

Table 9.5 Composition of exports by areas and markets (percentages)

SITC category	5 Chemicals	7 Machinery and transport	65 Textiles	67 Iron and steel	84 Clothing	Share of intra-trade in total Manufactures	All goods
		Share in exports of manufactures					
Total trade, 1985							
non-oil developing countries	8	32	8	.5	18		
Asia	4	34	9	3	22		
Latin America	15	32	5	11	4		
Total trade, 1981							
non-oil developing countries	9	26	11	5	15		
Asia	4	28	12	4	18		
Latin America	17	28	6	8	3		
Total trade, 1973							
non-oil developing countries	6	17	15	3	14		
Asia	4	19	19	3	20		
Latin America	26	16	7	5	4		
Total trade, 1969							
non-oil developing countries	7	9	16	4	10		
Asia	4	12	23	3	17		
Latin America	13	10	5	5	2		

Intra-trade, 1985							
non-oil developing countries	15	38	12	6	4	18	20
Asia	11	43	14	4	2	15	21
Latin America	24	24	5	6	4	19	15
Intra-trade, 1981							
non-oil developing countries	13	33	16	5	5	25	22
Asia	10	36	19	6	1	19	22
Latin America	17	36	5	6	4	37	21
Intra-trade, 1973							
non-oil developing countries	14	24	18	5	5	20	18
Asia	13	26	26	6	3	18	21
Latin America	19	28	8	8	5	25	17
Intra-trade, 1969							
non-oil developing countries	15	18	24	7	6	20	18
Asia	15	20	27	5	4	20	24
Latin America	20	18	8	9	4	27	18

Source: UN, Monthly Bulletin of Statistics; Definitions are UN; Asia excludes only Middle East; Latin America includes oil exporters.

Table 9.6 Composition of imports by areas and markets (percentages)

SITC category	5 Chemicals	7 Machinery and transport	65 Textiles	67 Iron and steel	84 Clothing
		Share in imports of manufactures			
Total trade, 1985					
non-oil developing					
countries	15	51	5	6	1
Asia	15	50	6	6	1
Latin America	18	55	2	4	3
Total trade, 1981					
non-oil developing					
countries	13	51	6	7	2
Asia	13	47	8	8	1
Latin America	13	56	2	6	2
Total trade, 1973					
non-oil developing					
countries	14	50	7	8	2
Asia	14	43	11	6	1
Latin America	16	52	3	9	2
Total trade, 1969					
non-oil developing					
countries	14	49	8	7	2
Asia	14	44	12	8	1
Latin America	15	52	3	7	1

Source: UN, *Monthly Bulletin of Statistics*; Definitions are UN; Asia excludes only Middle East; Latin America includes oil exporters.

Table 9.7 Characteristic exports of developing countries (percentages)

SITC 3-Digit level		Primary goods for which LDCs export at least 25% of the world total		Manufactured goods for which LDCs export at least 10% of the world total	
		1970	1982/83	1970	1982/83
331	Crude petroleum	89	80		
332	Petroleum products	47	42		
341	Gas	18	33		
071	Coffee	95	90		
283	Non-ferrous metal ore	48	57		
031	Fresh fish	29	42		
051	Fruit, nuts, fresh	44	43		
231	Rubber	76	58		
081	Animal feed	42	34		
281	Iron ore	40	45		
422	Vegetable oils, hard	83	84		
263	Cotton	65	41		
054	Vegetables, fresh	31	35		
242	Wood	47	49		
072	Cocoa	86	76		
011	Meat, fresh	21	14		
121	Tobacco	30	47		
042	Rice	39	52		
053	Fruit, preserved	30	39		
044	Maize	27	15		
061	Sugar and honey	72	72		
292	Vegetable materials	24	26		
421	Vegetable oils, soft	24	33		
221	Oil seeds	27	13		
074	Tea	88	84		
271	Fertilisers	44	68		
032	Fish, tinned	15	38		
075	Spices	90	84		
055	Vegetables, preserved	22	27		
841	Clothing			26	49
724	Telecom. equip.			6	23
729	Elec. machinery			5	15
735	Ships			4	24
851	Footwear			13	39
894	Toys			18	44
682	Copper			48	34
653	Textiles, woven			12	24
722	Electric power mach.			3	12
651	Textiles, thread			14	25
652	Cotton fabrics			34	33
631	Veneers			33	42
687	Tin			87	87
684	Aluminium			6	16
864	Watches, clocks			5	29
667	Pearls			15	16
831	Travel goods			19	59
513	Inorg. elements			16	18
521	Coal, petro-chems			39	52
725	Domestic elec. equip.			2	18
666	Pottery			2	18
821	Furniture			7	14
673	Iron, steel shapes			5	12
899	Misc. manuf. goods			37	30
656	Textiles, misc.			37	39
657	Floor covers			18	32
883	Plastic, misc.			13	17
661	Cement			21	27
611	Leathers			31	32

Table 9.7 (continued)

SITC 3-Digit level	Primary goods for which LDCs export at least 25% of the world total	
	1970	1982/83
045 Cereals	26	34
013 Meat, tinned	26	31
285 Silver and platinum	11	31
291 Crude animal matter	23	30

SITC 3-Digit level	Manufactured goods for which LDCs export at least 10% of the world total	
	1970	1982/83
561 Fertilisers, manuf.	7	16
681 Silver, platinum	14	21
698 Metal products	5	11
691 Metal structures	4	12
629 Rubber manuf.	4	11
671 Pig iron	16	24
892 Gold, silver	11	15
723 Elec. dist. mach.	6	15
632 Wood manufactures	14	25
697 Base metal	11	26
672 Iron, steel forms	3	14
655 Special textiles	6	14
733 Road vehicles, non-motor	5	13
731 Railway vehicles	2	13
844 Furs	17	44

Source: UNCTAD, *Handbook of International Trade and Development Statistics*, listed in order of total value of ldc exports.

Table 9.8 Concentration of principal exports (3-digit SITC)

Goods are classified as: advanced manufactures: all capitals; other manufactures: **bold**; new primary: *italic*; traditional primary: roman

	top 1	1+2	1+2+3	1+2+3+4	1+2+3+4+5	top 16	first	second	third	fourth	fifth
Newly industrialising countries											
Argentina	13.91	22.89	30.21	37.21	43.86	77.56	wheat	maize	cereal, nes	anim. feed	meat
Brazil	10.64	19.51	27.32	32.77	37.68	63.75	coffee	anim. feed	iron ore	petro prod	CARS
Hong Kong	32.39	42.17	50.43	57.12	60.92	83.15	Clothing	Toys	WATCHES	TELECOM	OFFICE MAC
India	12.67	24.89	33.83	40.13	45.06	69.52	crude oil	pearl	Clothing	iron	*frs. fish*
Mexico	58.98	62.89	65.24	67.46	69.28	83.56	crude oil	TELECOM	gas	EL. PWR. MAC	silv. plat
Singapore	26.96	34.82	42.05	47.07	51.32	62.89	petro prod	sp. trans	ELEC. MACH	TELECOM	rubber
South Korea	15.57	29.76	34.92	40.05	45.13	69.50	Clothing	SHIPS	Shoes	Text. woven	TELECOM
Average	24.45	33.85	40.57	45.97	50.46	72.85					
New NICs											
Colombia	50.71	61.27	66.27	70.12	73.31	85.56	coffee	petro prod	*frs fruit*	*crude veg*	**Clothing**
Malaysia	25.57	37.46	48.41	58.81	68.69	88.51	crude oil	ELEC. MACH	veg oil	rubber	wood
Peru	14.94	28.42	41.70	51.02	59.23	84.33	nonferrous	crude oil	copper	petro prod	silv. platinum
Thailand	14.19	26.06	33.15	40.24	47.14	78.97	rice	*frs veg*	rubber	sugar	**Clothing**
Zimbabwe	23.26	32.59	39.95	46.33	52.66	75.79	tobacco	pig iron	crude min	cotton	sugar
Average	25.73	37.16	45.90	53.30	60.21	82.63					
Other middle-income countries											
Chile	35.63	45.49	54.07	62.24	68.24	90.46	copper	iron ore	non fer met	anim. feed	*frs fruit*
Costa Rica	31.78	55.20	60.03	64.26	66.95	81.01	*frs fruit*	coffee	meat	**Clothing**	**Med. prod**
Egypt	51.46	65.25	78.01	83.07	86.41	95.78	crude oil	cotton	petro prod	**Tex. thread**	aluminium
Ivory Coast	26.06	48.09	58.14	67.52	70.69	88.77	cocoa	coffee	petró prod	wood	cotton
Kenya	25.95	49.84	66.75	70.59	74.19	90.24	coffee	petro prod	tea	cement	*pres fruit*
Morocco	25.16	38.76	47.03	53.98	59.09	87.56	fert crude	**In org chem**	*frs fruit*	**Clothing**	*frs fish*
Pakistan	12.77	24.43	35.58	45.33	53.55	87.72	rice	**Cotton fab**	cotton	**Tex. thread**	**Tex. prod**
Philippines	25.91	35.10	42.69	49.11	55.36	80.92	sp trans	veg oil	sugar	nonferous	**Clothing**
Senegal	23.54	42.69	56.94	67.90	76.87	92.97	*frs fish*	*frs fish*	**Fert crude**	tin fish	anim. feed
Sri Lanka	32.06	49.96	61.31	72.48	76.79	93.13	tea	**Clothing**	rubber	petroprod	*frs fruit*
Tunisia	42.04	58.97	68.02	73.39	77.08	91.15	crude oil	**Clothing**	**Fert. manu**	**In org chem**	petro prod
Uruguay	21.85	40.58	48.74	55.10	61.42	82.15	meat	wool	rice	**Clothing**	**Leather**
Venezuela	50.86	87.68	90.61	92.01	92.76	95.89	crude oil	petro prod	aluminium	iron ore	**Org. chem**
Average	31.16	49.39	59.07	65.92	70.72	89.06					

Table 9.8 (Continued)

	top 1	1+2	1+2+3	1+2+3+4	1+2+3+4+5	top 16	first	second	third	fourth	fifth
Area averages											
Africa	31.07	48.03	59.26	66.11	71.00	88.89					
Asia	22.01	33.85	42.49	50.04	56.00	79.37					
Latin America	32.14	47.10	53.80	59.13	63.64	82.70					
Average by group	27.11	40.13	48.51	55.07	60.46	81.51					
Average by area	28.41	42.99	51.85	58.43	63.54	83.65					
Industrial countries											
Germany	15.49	23.50	26.83	29.95	32.87	54.60	CARS	NONEL. MACH	Org. chem	PLASTICS	ELEC. MACH
Japan	21.49	27.59	33.62	39.54	44.18	73.79	CARS	SOUND REC	NONEL. MACH	TELECOM	ELEC. MACH
UK	16.04	21.21	26.32	30.21	34.03	58.89	crude oil	CARS	NONEL. MACH	petro prod	POWER MACH
USA	6.92	12.84	18.42	23.88	29.10	58.81	CARS	AIRCRAFT	ELEC. MACH	NONEL. MACH	OFFICE MACH

Source: UNCTAD, *Handbook of International Trade and Development Statistics*

Table 9.9 Export concentration indices

	1970			1983		
	No. Prod.	Diversi- fication	Concen- tration	No. Prod.	Diversi- fication	Concen- tration
NICs						
Argentina	35	0.764	0.222	143	0.721	0.212
Brazil	43	0.718	0.335	162	0.532	0.133
Hong Kong	8	0.781	0.342	125	0.732	0.305
India	41	0.653	0.139	160	0.579	0.183
Mexico	35	0.584	0.116	152	0.540	0.516
Singapore	59	0.606	0.295	173	0.503	0.255
South Korea	22	0.736	0.271	147	0.631	0.186
Taiwan						
Average	35	0.692	0.246	152	0.605	0.256
New NICs						
Colombia	3	0.773	0.622	113	0.744	0.488
Malaysia	31	0.792	0.371	158	0.633	0.280
Peru	74	0.872	0.350	120	0.688	0.237
Thailand	92	0.834	0.262	136	0.750	0.181
Zimbabwe	—			82	0.866	0.295
Average	50	0.818	0.401	122	0.736	0.296
excl. Zimbabwe				132	0.704	0.297
Other middle-income countries						
Chile	64	0.848	0.754	108	0.838	0.350
Costa Rica	81	0.755	0.398	107	0.754	0.379
Egypt	87	0.784	0.442	87	0.728	0.483
Ivory Coast	81	0.863	0.422	111	0.783	0.318
Kenya	76	0.813	0.336	104	0.816	0.340
Morocco	84	0.816	0.292	99	0.812	0.255
Pakistan	91	0.823	0.264	106	0.803	0.222
Philippines	78	0.855	0.324	131	0.743	0.255
Senegal	82	0.793	0.311	54	0.875	0.311
Sri Lanka	33	0.935	0.584	81	0.825	0.372
Tunisia	70	0.754	0.260	106	0.687	0.426
Uruguay	58	0.874	0.409	102	0.795	0.271
Venezuela	76	0.874	0.659	104	0.753	0.611
Average	74	0.830	0.420	100	0.786	0.353
Area averages						
Africa	80	0.804	0.344	92	0.795	0.347
Asia	51	0.779	0.317	135	0.689	0.249
Latin America	52	0.785	0.429	123	0.707	0.355
Average of groups	53	0.780	0.356	125	0.709	0.302
Average of areas	61	0.789	0.363	117	0.730	0.317
Germany	78	0.338	0.133	180	0.319	0.139
Japan	66	0.431	0.131	164	0.488	0.206
UK	78	0.310	0.098	179	0.255	0.146
USA	80	0.326	0.099	178	0.361	0.105

No. prod: Number of products exported at 3-digit SITC level (excluding <$50,000 in 1970 or $100,000 in 1983, or <0.3% exports). For both indices: the higher the number, the more concentrated. Diversification index: absolute deviation of country shares from world structure. Concentration index: normalised Hirschman index: difference between share of each product and level if all products had equal share.

Source: UNCTAD, *Handbook of International Trade and Development Statistics*.

Table 9.10 Export markets (percentages)

	1970			1975			1980			1985		
	Ind. countries	Oil exporters	Non-oil dev. countries	Ind. countries	Oil exporters	Non-oil dev. countries	Ind. countries	Oil exporters	Non-oil dev. countries	Ind. countries	Oil exporters	Non-oil dev. countries
Non-developing countries	62.7	2.3	21.8	58.1	5.8	22.2	56.6	5.9	24.4	59.0	4.9	24.9
Asia	59.9	3.8	29.9	59.2	7.4	28.7	58.9	6.4	29.3	57.7	4.1	33.1
Latin America	77.3	0.8	17.0	67.8	3.6	22.2	62.9	2.7	26.1	72.9	3.6	21.0
NICs												
Argentina	69.2	1.1	26.1	47.1	6.0	30.6	37.1	3.3	30.5	44.9	5.1	29.5
Brazil	76.1	1.3	18.0	60.2	7.6	23.5	57.3	7.3	28.6	62.4	9.6	21.0
Hong Kong	74.5	4.5	18.2	70.5	7.9	18.5	62.2	10.1	24.6	54.3	3.4	39.1
India	51.2	6.5	23.6	45.8	17.2	20.2	48.7	11.4	19.5	59.1	7.7	15.3
Mexico	71.7	1.7	9.0	73.4	2.4	15.9	85.4	0.5	12.1	88.3	0.3	7.8
Singapore	41.1	1.3	52.3	45.2	4.2	47.9	40.3	6.9	49.4	46.5	5.2	45.3
South Korea	86.6	1.9	10.6	76.6	6.6	15.1	64.2	12.8	18.3	70.0	6.2	20.1
Taiwan	67.3	5.6	16.2	67.6	5.9	18.3	65.1	5.2	19.9			
New NICs												
Colombia	79.1	0.7	12.6	74.9	6.2	17.1	75.5	8.4	12.9	87.8	3.5	6.7
Malaysia	56.8	1.9	34.6	58.5	2.4	33.5	59.5	2.0	33.5	54.6	1.8	39.8
Peru	86.8	0.5	9.9	58.6	1.0	23.0	63.6	1.9	27.0	71.5	1.8	17.8
Thailand	59.6	5.1	30.1	58.0	5.0	34.1	57.8	11.1	27.0	56.4	7.7	32.6
Zimbabwe	—	—	—	—	—	—	85.0	0.1	14.7	56.8	2.5	38.3

Other											
Chile	86.7	0.3	12.7	68.4	1.9	27.7	63.1	4.0	29.9	69.5	2.7	24.8
Costa Rica	72.9	0.0	24.1	68.7	0.5	30.3	62.9	0.4	36.2	70.8	0.7	24.9
Egypt	18.7	3.6	24.7	14.5	6.6	16.0	59.8	2.2	29.5	75.6	1.9	12.8
Ivory Coast	88.5	0.8	6.6	74.1	1.7	19.6	75.4	3.9	16.0	74.2	0.7	17.0
Kenya	42.7	1.2	47.5	40.8	1.9	45.8	43.5	2.7	41.5	54.0	1.2	35.1
Morocco	78.1	3.6	9.9	66.3	3.3	16.2	68.2	4.4	18.3	65.3	6.8	20.9
Pakistan	48.1	7.3	34.6	35.6	22.8	36.6	36.4	23.0	37.9	49.5	17.8	27.2
Philippines	91.0	0.2	6.9	86.5	3.5	8.2	75.2	3.9	15.7	73.7	1.8	21.8
Senegal	72.6	0.0	22.7	66.5	0.0	19.8	50.2	2.5	35.8	46.3	0.5	24.4
Sri Lanka	51.8	2.8	29.1	34.4	11.9	34.0	38.7	13.7	28.3	48.2	11.6	24.6
Tunisia	66.4	13.9	9.4	60.1	11.1	21.7	68.9	3.9	24.5	80.6	7.3	8.2
Uruguay	59.5	0.8	27.8	47.2	2.2	42.6	40.3	6.7	44.9	37.6	5.7	25.2
Venezuela	64.9	0.0	35.0	63.5	0.0	33.9	58.3	0.1	40.2	67.8	0.1	30.8

Source: IMF, *International Financial Statistics, Supplement on Trade Statistics; Direction of Trade.* Figures do not add to 100 because of trade with centrally planned economies and unspecified markets.

Table 9.11 Major export markets (percentages)

	US	1970 EEC[b]	Japan	US	1985 EEC[b]	Japan	1985 other major markets for at least two countries						
							Hong Kong	Singapore	Malaysia	China	USSR	Brazil	Spain
Newly industrialising countries													
Argentina	9	46	4	13	23	5					14	5	
Brazil	25	35	5	27	24	5							2
Hong Kong	36	21	7	31	12	4		3		26			
India	14	19	14	23	19	11					16		
Mexico	60	6	5	63	10	8						1	7
Singapore	11	16	8	21	10	9	6		16[a]				
South Korea	47	8	28	36	10	15	5						
New NICs													
Colombia	36	25	3	40	31	4							
Malaysia	13	19	18	13	14	25		19[a]				2	
Peru	33	36	14	36	22	10		8					
Thailand	13	18	25	20	18	13	4	8	5				
Zimbabwe		18		6	46	6							
Other middle-income countries													
Chile	14	54	12	22	32	10						6	
Costa Rica	42	19	5	42	19	0							
Egypt	1	12	3	2	58	10							
Ivory Coast	19	66	2	17	57	1							3
Kenya	6	27	1	7	40	1							
Morocco	2	68	2	1	51	4							
Pakistan	12	24	6	10	21	11	3			2			7
Philippines	42	7	40	36	13	19							
Senegal	0	68	1	1	38	4							
Sri Lanka	7	33	3	21	18	5							
Tunisia	1	60	2	7	63	0				1			
Uruguay	9	46	1	27	24	3						13	
Venezuela	38	12	1	41	16	3						2	

a. This includes a high but uncertain share of entrepot trade.
b. Ten members.

Source: IMF, *Direction of Trade.*

Table 9.12 Import structure of industrial countries (percentages)

	Primary ex fuels	Food	Agric. raw materials	Ores and metals	Manufact. SITC 5-8 ex 67-8	Chemicals SITC 5	Machinery and transport, SITC 7	Other Mfr. SITC 6&8 ex 67-8	Fuels
Japan									
1970	55.46	16.92	16.18	22.36	23.37	5.30	11.29	6.78	20.68
1975	37.91	17.88	8.86	11.17	17.36	3.56	6.61	7.19	44.33
1980	31.30	12.04	8.64	10.62	18.01	4.43	6.25	7.33	50.03
1985	30.67	13.92	6.68	10.07	24.21	6.33	8.70	9.18	43.75
France									
1970	36.47	14.79	6.81	14.87	51.40	8.07	25.24	18.09	12.11
1975	27.91	12.91	4.40	10.60	49.18	8.09	22.27	18.83	22.87
1980	23.06	10.28	3.77	9.01	49.97	9.23	21.32	19.42	26.60
1985	21.57	10.99	3.25	7.33	56.08	10.31	24.80	20.98	22.26
Germany									
1970	42.06	18.53	6.54	16.99	46.32	6.31	18.95	21.06	8.81
1975	31.80	16.29	4.71	10.80	47.93	7.03	17.58	23.32	17.65
1980	26.11	12.24	4.05	9.82	48.86	7.28	18.71	22.87	22.54
1985	24.40	12.15	3.51	8.74	53.44	9.10	22.64	21.70	19.89
UK									
1970	46.91	24.24	8.94	13.73	41.42	6.00	16.53	18.89	10.45
1975	34.11	19.29	5.36	9.46	45.37	5.88	18.85	20.64	17.92
1980	27.44	13.20	4.06	10.18	57.80	6.53	25.79	25.48	13.50
1985	21.58	11.86	3.45	6.27	64.64	8.37	31.65	24.62	12.37
USA									
1970	33.49	16.12	4.57	12.80	55.62	3.63	27.96	24.03	7.70
1975	23.91	10.84	3.08	9.99	46.25	3.82	25.01	17.42	27.25
1980	18.74	8.22	2.54	7.98	46.73	3.95	24.97	17.81	32.84
1985	15.08	7.03	2.12	5.93	67.03	4.45	37.83	24.76	15.52

Source: UNCTAD, *Handbook of International Trade and Development Statistics.*

10

SAMPLE COUNTRIES' EXPORTS

GENERAL POLICY AND PERFORMANCE

The *Zimbabwe* case study makes the point that a large role for trade has been characteristic of its economy since 1890, and was the basis of the colony's existence. Although its share in output fell under the sanctions during UDI (its phase of forced import substitution), it was still high. Trade has, however, grown more slowly than exports by all developing countries since then, although more than the average for African countries (see Table 9.1). Compared with other African countries, a high share (40% rising to 50% in the most recent years) is manufactures, about the same as the other countries in this study (see Table 9.4). The current Five-Year Plan has a target of 7% for export growth and assumes an underlying growth of 4% in the absence of policies of promotion. This is high compared with African or Zimbabwean past performance, but not for all non-oil developing countries or for the other new NICs. The Plan thus assumes an important autonomous improvement in export performance and intends a further strong impulse from policy. Given the large share of exports in output, such an improvement is argued to be of central importance in achieving its aggregate goals. Robinson stresses, however, that any policies or changes in export structure cannot be at the expense of other goals, rejecting in particular 'repressive' labour policies. The chosen changes – new commodities and new markets, and methods using government incentives – are discussed below.

The other countries (with the possible exception of Malaysia) were not as wholly dependent on exports of primary products, and all have gone through a phase of deliberate import substitution. Only Malaysia has a share of trade in output approaching Zimbabwe's level, but this is following a reorientation towards exports as part of its industrialisation strategy, which began in the early 1970s. It is noteworthy that Ariff cites the local example of the Asian NICs as one reason for this (and Japan could also be cited); the Latin

American and African countries would not have similar models, and their interpretation of the Asian model is less favourable.

Malaysia's exports grew rapidly, even faster than those of the Asian NICs, and manufactures have increased their share in the total from 6% in 1970 to a quarter. This is still, however, quite low for a country at the Malaysian level of industrialisation. This means that Malaysia does not consider itself 'export-led' in a way comparable with the Asian NICs. This could make trade at least arithmetically less crucial to its growth, and output has fluctuated much less than exports since 1970. The principal period of growth was the early 1970s; it has been slowing since then, falling below the world average in the 1980s, at least for total exports. The slowing is attributed by Ariff to the general poor world performance and to protection, but also to bottlenecks in domestic production capacity and to the relatively bad performance of individual commodities, discussed below. A simple return to past performance would be an improvement but, given the large change in Malaysia's relative trade growth, this cannot be assumed to follow simply from a revival of growth in world trade, especially one as small as is assumed in this study. The importance of government policy in turning towards export orientation, in obstructing it by its social policies and in assisting it by modifying these, is taken for granted. Multinationals help to explain the growth of trade in the 1970s and the reduction in growth of the 1980s.

For *Thailand,* the case study stresses that trade is of growing importance, but that, for both primary commodities and manufactures, this dates from the 1970s, much later than for the other countries discussed here. The expansion coincided closely with the general expansion in developing country exports, with Thai exports increasing slightly faster than the average, with slow growth in the first half of the 1970s, more rapid growth in the second half, and a pronounced slowing in the 1980s. The sequence for manufactures was similar, but these grew much faster than the average in the 1970s, particularly the second half, and slowed more in the 1980s. The share of manufactures in total Thai exports therefore rose from 16% in 1970 to 36% by 1980, and has remained at about that level (except when the value of other exports fell). The poor performance in the 1980s is attributed mainly to external factors, and expectations for the future are correspondingly low.

The high share of a single primary export distinguishes *Colombia* from the other countries, the other four new NICs and all except the oil exporters in the 26-country sample. Manufactures are still a much lower share of its exports (except when coffee exports fail) and the growth of its exports has been slower and much more erratic. It did have a period of relatively rapid growth of trade in manufactures in the first half of the 1970s, but has fallen behind since then. It is clear why diversification is a more important goal than growth for exports. Because of the importance of price and volume changes in a single agricultural commodity, its export volume growth is not closely related to that of aggregate world trade, but it is vulnerable on commodity prices.

Peru's exports grew at a rate comparable with the other new NICs in the 1960s, but then fell back, and after a severe fall in the second half of the 1970s were stagnant in the first half of the 1980s. This reflected the poor perfor-mance of its traditional primary exports; manufactures grew relatively rapid-ly, particularly in the late 1970s, but fell in the early 1980s. Although the share of manufactures appears relatively high, this is principally because of semi-processed metals; all 'non-traditional exports' were only about a quar-ter of the total in 1986, with the main rises in the early 1970s (from 3% to 10%) and 1976–9 (10% to 22%).

COMMODITIES

In terms of simple measures of numbers of commodities or diversification, *Zimbabwe* is less diversified than the average (see Table 9.9), or even than the normal lower-middle income or African country. It is not, however, as concentrated on a few major exports as many (see Table 9.8), and its high share of manufactures also suggests that the simple measures are misleading. The case study emphasises the 'volatility' of agricultural exports, but notes that a wide range have grown since Independence. Although manufactures can plausibly be expected to grow rapidly on the assumptions used for world trade, and to increase their shares of markets, their share in Zimbabwean exports is so small that it is outweighed by the slow growth expected for agricultural and metal exports (Table 8.1). The study therefore concludes that the targets of the Five Year Plan cannot be achieved because of the poor prospects for primary goods. The official stress on new exports has not yet been directed to particular products. Horticultural goods are often cited, and there are successful examples, but so are a wide range of other light industries, including textiles, footwear and others in which the NICs have achieved success in the past. As was seen in the previous chapter, such speciality goods have not been characteristic of the industrial countries or of most of the NICs, but there are some examples among the other new NICs. Improvements or further processing of existing exports including textiles and clothing, cigarettes and cigars, metals and paper are other possibilities, while chemicals and transport equipment would be possible new exports (UNIDO, 1986b). Only the last are in the categories which have been most successful in other countries' experience.

Malaysia is much more diversified than Zimbabwe at first sight (see Table 9.9), with a number of exports and a diversification index comparable to the NICs, but it remains very dependent on a small number of exports. One of these, electrical machinery, is not a primary commodity, however. Malaysia is the only one of the five sample countries with a machinery (SITC 7) product among its principal exports (a characteristic of all the Asian NICs), and telecommunications, other machinery and aircraft are all among its 16 principal exports, although each is only about 1% of the total. It has moved much closer to the composition characteristic of the NICs than have the other new NICs. The traditional Asian manufactured exports, textiles and clothing, were under 1% in 1970 and only about 3% by 1983. Malaysia's exports of electrical machinery share some of the problems of primary products, however. They are based on one product (semi-conductors) which can suffer the same type of temporary fluctuations as primary products through world over-supply (as happened in 1984–5) or changes in technology. And Malaysia's comparative advantage depends on 'depletable' resources: cheap labour[1] and tax concessions in the export processing zones.

The country has also undergone a process of structural change from dependence on one set of primary products to another: in 1970 its principal export was rubber (40%), followed by tin and other non-ferrous metals (23% each). This change explains much of the growth in the 1970s. Malaysia has not benefited from a particularly strong increase in demand for its existing commodities. The new commodities are also 'prone to price fluctuations', notably palm oil and wood which are both now among its five principal exports. The study notes problems with this dependence on primary exports, in addition to the direct effect of vulnerability to price fluctuations: domestic production over-responds to price changes, a suggestion that the variability of prices has effects on the structure of domestic production. Malaysian policy may have damaged its competitive position in its traditional primary exports, particularly rubber. Others were damaged by external demand, notably oil since 1983 and tin. No particular competitive advantage apparently exists for Malaysian agricultural exports (Ariff, 1984). More generally, the description of the changes in Malaysia's various primary exports indicates how variable in quantities and in markets these have been even over the period since 1980.

Ariff and Semudram are pessimistic about primary exports, volume and prices, expecting, with some variations, recovery from the present exceptionally depressed levels for a few and falls for others. Thus, diversification has not been a protection against a general depression even for Malaysia, where it extends to food, non-food agricultural products and metals. Government policy continues to stress 'resource-based exports', for example, new uses for rubber. Electronics components, in which Malaysia has established world leadership, are more promising, although there are risks to its position from rising costs (Ariff and Hill, 1985). The government is also promoting exports of the new Malaysian car, but the report argues that its competitiveness depends on subsidy.

Thailand's export diversification is close to average, and has moved in line with the other new NICs since 1970. It has, however, achieved a much lower than usual concentration on a few exports. The share of the top five fell from

98% in 1960 to 47% by1983, below even the normal range for the NICs, and the case study notes the large increase in the number of exports with a share of more than 1% in the total. Thailand is more like the usual Asian pattern than Malaysia, with a higher share of clothing (which is among the principal exports) and textiles (8% together), although electrical power machinery is also 4% of its exports. External conditions for its principal export, rice, have had an important effect on its total external position throughout the period studied.

The study stresses the structural change in Thai exports. Although food remains as important as ever, accounting for about half of exports, a higher proportion of this is processed, and other crude materials have been decreasing. Thailand rose from having a relatively low to a relatively high share of manufactures, with semi-processed goods in the 1960s being followed by finished goods in the late 1970s and 1980s. The study notes, however, that many of the manufactured goods are still based on natural resources and that primary goods remain important. Within the continued dominance of food, the structure has changed with the share of rice falling and large rises and falls in maize, tapioca and sugar. Thailand is an example of a country which has successfully pursued 'new', high-value food exports, with increases for fish products and fruits and vegetables. In other raw materials, rubber has declined steadily, but tin rose and fell. Electrical machinery has begun to rise rapidly since 1980, and particularly so in 1985 (the year in which Malaysian exports suffered), and other light industries include shoes and jewellery. But the country remains tied to resource-based exports, including these labour-intensive ones.

The improvement in rice exports has already been partially reversed, and there is a shift to new markets. Future prospects are poor, partly because of protection and other (principally US) producers' subsidies. Other food products have also suffered falling prices, and are expected to continue to do so. Although new markets have been found, these have proved to be temporary, again in some cases because of protection and subsidies. Non-food price prospects are also poor because of the world depression. Only the non-traditional food exports, which are still a small share of the total, have prospects of rapid growth. The main opportunities for exploiting new markets, which in the past helped to explain the rapid growth of textile exports, are over, it is argued, implying slow growth. Thailand is expected to maintain its labour cost advantage in electronics over the medium term, although the authors note that this is not permanent.

With the major exports expected to rise slowly, and fast growth only in the minor exports, the pessimistic picture looks similar to that of the other countries. But the Thai study suggests two reasons for modifying this: exports themselves are a higher proportion of output than in the past and their absolute contribution may therefore actually be higher, and there is still scope for diversification into new products and markets. Among the products where exports are more than a quarter of output are not only food, rubber and non-ferrous metals, but electrical machinery (a rise from 11% to 33% between 1975 and 1980) and miscellaneous finished manufactures (SITC 8, up from 19% to 49%). The study suggests that resource-based exports are particularly suitable for Thailand because of its relatively high resource endowment and because these are 'less subjected to protectionist restrictions'. The diversification which has been achieved is seen as a particularly important advantage.

Although *Colombia* is very dependent on its principal export, coffee, it does not have the dependence on a few other primary products observed for Malaysia, so that on broader measures it appears less of a contrast to the other countries.[2] An unusual feature of its experience is the fact that the main growth of non-traditional exports was before 1975, and that since then they have fallen back. The history of Colombian exports is therefore the history of coffee prices, and Echavarria stresses how variable those prices have been, and how they have differed from the average for commodity prices. The rise in prices in the mid-1970s led to an increase in the volume of production, and in productivity, because of the introduction of a new variety. Since 1979, coffee exports have moved in line with the international market, with a further growth in 1986. Although this increased dependence on a primary product and fall in the share of manufactured exports is clearly a contrast to the Asian industrialising countries, it is not unusual among the countries nearest to Colombia, the other Andean countries, where oil for Venezuela and Ecuador, and mining products for Peru and Bolivia, remain paramount.

The combination of high dependence and high fluctuations is considered a major risk. A boom on the scale of the 1970s is unlikely to occur again in the medium term, so average performance will be poorer than in the past. The increased importance of oil and coal is a potential problem because their prices are more vulnerable to world economic conditions; variations in the coffee price depend more on special factors in coffee production (the rise in the coffee price against the trend for other primary products in 1986, for example). There has been some recent success in non-traditional agricultural exports, but these are still minor compared with Thai exports. The study argues that the fall in manufactures after 1974 was not because of the general international decline or changes in domestic costs, but for particular reasons of marketing, that is, policy not demand or cost. This, and the recent success in some non-traditional primary products, could mean that better performance is possible. Official plans stress non-traditional, resource-based exports.

Peru's exports are not unusually concentrated by the conventional indices, and it is near the average for the new NICs with respect to the shares accounted for by its principal exports (see Table 9.8). As in Zimbabwe, however, these are all raw materials (or very lightly processed goods). There have been marked changes among these (see Table 7.3): oil became a major export only in 1978, and then declined (even before falling by two-thirds in 1986). Although copper has always been important, the other non-ferrous metals, silver, lead and zinc, have all become more important since the mid-1970s. Fishmeal was the principal export in 1970, fell sharply in volume (only partially compensated in prices) in the 1970s, with some recovery in the 1980s. In the 1970s, the variety of primary products protected the country from the worst fluctuations in prices of any one good but, since 1980, the prices of all its principal exports except zinc (and coffee in 1986) have fallen sharply; the metals, whose shares had increased, were particularly badly hit. The study suggests that demand for primary products will remain poor because of technological changes.

Nevertheless, it recommends promoting exports of some of the traditional primary products: those which face less protection (not sugar), those in which Peru has particular advantages (cotton and alpaca wool) or in which it can replace industrial country production (metals), and those which will fit into its own manufacturing potential (clothing). The stagnation in volume in the 1970s is attributed to supply difficulties, rather than demand; the completion of investment programmes permitted an increase in volume at the end of the decade, which coincided with a rise in prices. While the total world market is declining, developing countries' advantage within this may be increasing.[3] The paper notes, however, that boosting exports in this situation will be more difficult than in a rising market. Some growth in volume, and some recovery in prices (in line with the forecasts in Chapter 2), can therefore be expected in the next few years. Changed policies could remove constraints on supply (reducing substitution of food crops for cotton, for example), but little more can be done in the period covered by the study.

Manufactures rose sharply at the end of the 1970s after the introduction of subsidies, and their fall since then is attributed partly to protection, partly to reduced subsidies, and partly to domestic demand. Schuldt suggests increasing them and also new high-value food products, mentioning Asian as well as industrial country markets. These non-traditional products will depend on domestic measures to improve capacity and returns. They are seen as the principal means by which the trade balance could be improved in the short term. They would contribute to goals other than growth (and the balance of payments) by increasing industrialisation, employment and regional development.

MARKETS

Zimbabwe is as exceptional among the new NICs (or the NICs) (although not in comparison with other African countries) in its dependence on European markets as it is in its dependence on South Africa (Tables 8.2, 9.10 and 9.11), which took close to one-sixth of its total exports up to 1984, although this fell to 10% in 1985. It also has high trade with other African neighbours, at about 10%. The country study emphasises the risks of this pattern, especially in a period of unrest and uncertainty in South Africa: a useful reminder of the dominance of special or local problems over that of the more general problems presented in Chapter 2. Zimbabwe's choice of trading partners is closely limited by the transport links available, and improving and diversifying these is therefore one of the policies suggested in the paper.

Among the industrial countries, West Germany provided the highest market share in 1981, but this has remained flat at 8% recently, with a rise for the United Kingdom from 7% to 12% by 1984. Italy takes another 5%. Zimbabwe has also built up an unusual share of its exports to developing countries outside its region, with 5% going to the Far East (not including Japan), particularly to Hong Kong.

The case study notes the close correlation between types of export and particular markets. The potential of the southern African developing countries as markets is limited, it is argued, not only by their low demand but by type of product: they would not be suitable markets for Zimbabwe's traditional primary exports. The share of manufactures in the total is greater than average for both these states and South Africa and they are the only important markets for Zimbabwe's machinery. Tobacco is the principal export to the UK, and tobacco and other crude materials dominate trade with Germany. The manufactured goods that go to these markets are largely semi-processed products.

The likely shifts in areas suggest a diminishing share for manufactures. Exports to South Africa could fall. Increasing exports to the other African countries if trade with South Africa is cut off is a possible short-term move, but the medium-term policy is to prefer exports to hard-currency markets. If it were possible to replace South African exports to these countries, this would also imply increasing exports of primary products.

Malaysia has an unusually high proportion of exports to Japan, but up to 1986 this was largely in primary products including oil and gas; exports to Singapore are rubber and oil. There was an increase in exports to South Korea in the early 1980s. The US is the principal importer, with about half the market, for both of Malaysia's major manufactured exports: semiconductors and clothing. At least up to 1986, Japan had been a very small market for electronics and other manufactures, in spite of the important role of Japanese foreign investment in these in Malaysia.[4] Any exports of the Malaysian cars were expected also to be to the US and possibly the UK. Japan is not only a much less important importer for the Asian countries than the US is for the Latin American or the EC for the African, but it has been principally a market for primary goods (Lorenz, 1986). There is no apparent Malaysian policy to promote exports in specified directions, or to ASEAN countries in particular; market shares have remained little changed in the past.

Starting in about 1979, *Thailand* had a large increase in its exports to the US and a fall in those to Japan; the latter was particularly acute in 1984–5, the first years in which the Japanese market was less important than the US. The principal partner within the EC was the Netherlands (mainly tapioca), reaching 13% in 1980, but it fell to 7% by 1985 (after protective barriers were introduced). Thailand has maintained a high share to other Asian markets (about the average share for intra-trade by the Asian countries), particularly to Hong Kong, Singapore and Malaysia; that is, more to the NICs than to the other ASEAN countries. It does send about 5–6% of its exports to Africa. No areas are expected to offer particularly rapid growth in demand (in line with the general assumptions about world prospects), but the poorer South Asian and the African countries are suggested as good prospects because of the present small quantities going there.

Exports to Japan have remained mainly primary products, with the increase in manufactures going to other markets. Japan is an important importer of rubber, fish and tin, while the US is the principal importer of electronics and textiles, and processed food is also important. On textiles, the study suggests that this is because of traditional Japanese relationships with other suppliers, but the growth in Chinese exports is noted as an indication that the situation could change. Recent figures do show some Japanese imports rising. The EC takes some manufactures, especially textiles, but mainly primary products. Neither textiles nor tapioca offer good prospects in this area because of protection, which also limits Japanese imports of rice. Except for the recent possibility of greater Japanese openness to manufactured exports, the most promising steps seem to be in finding new country markets, not increasing the share in old ones, a similar conclusion to that for commodities.

Colombia, like other Latin American countries, is much more dependent on the industrial countries (88% by 1985) than on its area markets, and in particular on the US, but it also shows an unusually high share to the EC. About half its exports to the latter were to Germany, and these reached their highest point in 1978. The depression in the major Latin American countries makes the prospects for intra-regional trade still poor, but the most important explanation for its decline for Colombia is the fall in exports to Venezuela (which took 10% of Colombian exports in 1979 and 2% in 1985). With all developing country markets taking only 10% of the total in 1985, the immediate possibilities for increase here are not strong, and geography means that markets other than Venezuela are likely to remain of limited importance. The Andean Pact has not brought large-scale intra-trade, partly because of the poverty of some of the members even before the depression of the 1980s, but also because of the similarities of economic structure of the more advanced members, and the transport problems. Some of the other countries are also still at a stage where import substitution and developing an internal industrial structure seem more important than promoting regional trade (Puyana, 1982). There does not appear to be any policy of changing trade patterns.

Peru's exports were unusually dependent on industrial countries in 1970, but there was a sharp fall in the early 1970s, to about two-thirds (Table 9.10; 1975 was exceptional). Among the industrial countries, Peru has exported an unusually high proportion to Japan, although this has fallen slightly. Much of the increase was to other developing countries, mainly in Latin America; there was also an increase to the COMECON countries. The study stresses the scope for increasing intra-Latin American trade, especially the potential for Brazil. The areas for co-operation in the Andean Pact, including machinery and chemicals, are consistent with the products found to be important in intra-Latin American trade. The Pacific Basin countries are likely to be particularly important, and the study notes that Peru is well placed for acting as a link for other Latin American countries' trade with Asia as well as for promoting its own products there. Some of the increase in exports to other developing countries has been accounted for by Taiwan.

EXPORT POLICIES AND EFFORT

Zimbabwe provides some financial incentives to exporters, and the policy is to increase these. Robinson judges that this type of measure, although useful, is not sufficient because of 'inertia' in moving into export markets. He cites a variety of reasons for expecting an inadequate financial return to be a discouraging factor, including high domestic costs, and too-high domestic returns because of protected and monopolistic markets, but does not consider these to be the decisive obstacles. More institutional support is needed, particularly on marketing. He argues that producers will not look for opportunities without being trained to operate in more competitive and more uncertain markets, and also to treat export markets as being as permanent as domestic markets, and therefore worth continuing to service even in periods of difficulty. Below some threshold, exports are seen merely as occasional and opportunistic possibilities. This may be in part the result of the period of UDI in which exports were not a straightforward opportunity to increase sales. There also remain some problems peculiar to Zimbabwe, such as the restricted transport routes, but some of the obstacles to exports which he cites are barriers to entry which, on the evidence of the other countries, are a general problem of moving into exporting: the requirement of larger quantities, on a regular basis; the need to adjust to higher or different standards; markets with which a producer will necessarily be less familiar, and will lack the existing contacts and network of relationships that characterise national markets. Zimbabwe is introducing technical training for exporters.

The *Malaysian* study suggests that general assistance to firms has not only made exporting less financially attractive by reducing financial pressures, but has also made producers dependent on safe conditions in markets in which they enjoy not merely government support but protection from the disruptions of competition. The combination of policies to promote import substitution, and the very existence of extensive government intervention in the economy, together with the unsatisfactory nature of policies introduced to offset import incentives and to promote exports, also explain the poor export performance by purely domestic firms. The authors also note the difficulty of 'encounters with regulations in other countries, with which they are completely unfamiliar'.

The potential stimulus to export consciousness from the large number of foreign firms has been blunted because these are in export processing zones. The large share of multinationals in the past growth of exports is suggested as a reason for the failure of export orientation to spread to more sectors of the economy and give sustained growth. This suggests that stimulating exports by example, the type of effect attributed to the Asian NICs, may work more at the level of government policy than of private response. The success of multinationals illustrates another 'barrier to entry'. They have been more experienced in using financial incentives, and taking advantage of them. In spite of its much greater experience in exporting, Malaysia thus appears to have some of the same problems in 'developing exporters' as Zimbabwe. The government has also recognised the need to change the 'subsidy mentality'.[5] The study supports more effective measures to promote exports because of the importance of the static and dynamic economic gains, but also as a step to greater flexibility and more responsiveness to price. It suggests, however, that there are greater difficulties in a period of high protection.

The *Thailand* case study suggests that exports of manufactures were encouraged later than in other Asian countries because Thailand had readily available natural resource exports, and only when these failed after 1971 were others considered. The authors consider that a new point of difficulty for the present principal exports has now been reached, and the solution will require further diversification into new exports, and by implication, therefore, new rather than existing exporters. They do expect the presence of foreign investors to help producers learn to realise potential export opportunities.

One explanation offered for the decline in *Colombian* manufactured exports after the early 1970s is the direct effect of higher domestic demand 'crowding out' export demand for potential exports (Echavarria, in Grunwald 1985). On an aggregate scale, Echavarria considers a much broader view, that coffee booms produced a 'Dutch disease' phenomenon in which the resulting high exchange rate damaged other exports, but finds it only partially supported by the evidence. He emphasises the risks of being lulled into complacency about the adequacy of present exports because of the past good performance of coffee.

The *Peru* study suggests that changes in government policies, particularly on tariffs and exchange rates, have created a climate of uncertainty and given producers a short-term outlook This has deterred them from considering exports as a regular outlet, even when the policies have been designed to favour them. Except for the major primary products, most exports are disposals of temporary surpluses. Some are also directly related to debt repayments, in counter-trade deals. The Soviet imports and bank swaps for debt in 1987 (which were equivalent to 10% of total exports) were at least in part additional, but they are further examples of opportunism, and unlikely to provide bases for long-term exporting. The suggested solution is a clearer, more long-term policy on exports in order to reduce the uncertainty, and encourage the development of extra capacity directed at producing for export, with the strategy for exports tied more closely to a coherent policy for industrial and regional development. In the short term, however, the need to cover the external balance requires concentrating on the non-traditional goods which can be increased most rapidly. Protection in the industrial countries is expected to be a constraint on the choice of markets.

CONCLUSIONS

In spite of the importance of manufacturing within the sample countries, they all remain extremely dependent on a few primary exports for most of their export revenue. They have, however, all had important changes in the composition of their primary exports, usually at least assisted by policy intervention, so they do not fit the conventional picture of continued dependence on a traditional export. Even changing products and having a number of different primary exports (for example, for Peru) has not protected them from vulnerability to commodity price falls, so that strategies based only on primary exports seem insufficient to reduce risk. Diversification may remove the occasional possibility of large gains from a single product with special conditions (as in Colombia). Finding new exports is a primary objective for Zimbabwe and Colombia and important for all, with reducing vulnerability to price changes a key objective. (This means that simple measurements of diversification that do not take into account the difference between manufactures and primary exports or between 'traditional' and 'new' primary products are not good indications of export development.) These findings are supported by the observed differences among the patterns of exports of the NICs, the new NICs, and lower middle-income countries and the advantages of manufactured exports in projected growth, in prices and in promoting industrialisation and other goals. There are some cases of success with unusual primary products (as there are of failure with standardised manufactures such as textiles or even electronic components); the distinction between 'manufactures' and 'primary products' has therefore to be seen as a slight over-simplification.

Rapid recent growth of exports cannot itself prove either potential for growth or vulnerability to external conditions: in a single primary commodity (coffee for Colombia) it can be worrying, while in manufactures, particularly if these are a high share of total exports, it can point to a sustainable advantage. The possible divergence between good past performance and a good basis for future performance, and the additional benefits from certain types of product or structures of exports and domestic output, imply that a country may have a national interest in which products are chosen. This suggests a role for government strategic intervention, and the Colombian, Peruvian and Zimbabwean studies support this.

All the country studies stress that prospects for their principal primary exports are not good (and for Colombia, even that promoting coffee is a dangerous strategy), but several note that, although the growth rates of individual manufactured or non-traditional agricultural products may prove high, these are not a sufficiently high proportion of the total to give rapid growth without increases in traditional primary products as well. The most successful of these five countries, as was true for the larger sample, have moved from one commodity to another (whether among primary products or from them to manufactures). It is not possible to rely on good markets for existing products or improving the competitiveness of existing major exports (Colombian coffee in the 1970s is the major exception to this). The difficulty (in terms of economic, rather than industrial or market analysis) of extrapolating 'finding new products' into the medium term, instead of 'responding to demand' or 'improving competitiveness' in identifiable present markets or exports, makes such an analysis seem pessimistic. If there are reasons (as is argued for countries as different as Zimbabwe, Peru and Malaysia) for not expecting exporters to emerge with such new products, it is worrying. But it does indicate the type of strategy that is most likely to offer better than average results, although the 'average' is itself expected to be lower, and the Thai study in particular shows strikingly greater confidence in the ability to find new exports.

The question of which exports to look for at present is answered, officially at least, in all five countries as non-traditional but resource-based products. If labour supply is included in resources, the successes of the past support this, but this proviso indicates one limitation of such a strategy: it must be interpreted not as relying on traditional resources, but as a more active process of identifying newly significant ones. The Thai and Colombian (and more recently Zimbabwean) use of fresh products as industrial countries' tastes change and air transport costs become acceptable is as much an example of this as the use of the most traditional advantage, low-cost labour in the new industry of electronics. These conclusions imply that copying the particular goods which a successful exporter has already exploited may be the reverse of following his strategy of finding new opportunities. This does not mean that there is no scope for replacing other countries' production, but the returns to this may be temporary (as the Thai study recognises for low-cost, labour-intensive products) or low because the advantage comes from cost-competitiveness (as Peru notes for raw materials). It is also evident that finding and promoting new exports has been moved to a shorter cycle by the growth of protection (as shown in the rises and falls of some Thai agricultural exports).

The analysis of these countries' geographical distribution of exports shows some large changes in the past, and some pointers to future changes. The increases in the 1980s in exports to the United States could be vulnerable to exchange-rate changes, while the most recent trends indicate that the low levels of exports to Japan could rise. In the past, Japan has tended to take a higher proportion of primary goods than the US. Primary products have had a relatively high share in all the countries' exports to the EC, so its declining share is an additional indicator of poor prospects for these. The Peru study is the only one to stress an economic case for changing the direction of trade, and in particular searching for the areas most likely to offer growing demand for the products it wishes to promote (rather than responding to existing markets or finding new ones for existing products). This may be particularly necessary for the non-Asian countries. The latter are already well placed for an increase in Japanese demand or for the growing markets in the NICs. Colombia has shown less tendency to increase exports to Japan or to other areas outside Latin America.

The greater importance of intra-regional trade for the Asian countries is unlikely to change. Asian income is higher, the markets larger; they are more attractive to each other and potentially more complementary. The Peruvian and Colombian results confirm that only Brazil is a comparable 'pole' for Latin America, and transport realities make the Asian markets as accessible as the Latin American for Peru. Intra-African transport obstacles and costs may also help explain why there is some trade appearing between Thailand and Africa and between Zimbabwe and Asia.

The implication of the discussions in all the country studies of the need for particular efforts, going beyond financial neutrality or even financial incentives, is that the problem of increasing exports is not just one of price. It is necessary to encourage the emergence of exporters, rather than simply exports. The argument is that exporting is a skill and a type of activity that has to be 'developed', like other aspects of an industrialising country, and lack of this skill is a barrier to entry. This does not mean that the economic mechanisms do not work at all: countries that do not have obvious natural resource exports will export manufactures sooner than those that do; companies with better than average opportunities abroad (or worse than normal conditions in their own countries) will respond; experienced exporters of traditional products can respond.

The expectation that successful exporting means introducing new exports, not relying either on growing markets or improving competitiveness in existing products, implies that the advantages that a country may have need to be sought out. Potential exporters must learn: that they need to look for and develop opportunities; how to recognise them; how to develop them. The Malaysian comments on the failure to respond to the example of foreign investors suggest that active training may be necessary. This potential role for policy may exist during a significant period until the amount of local expertise in exporting becomes sufficiently high. (The scope of market information provided to Japanese or South Korean exporters by their governments is an obvious precedent.) If slower market growth and protection have increased the rate at which new exports and exporters must be found, some of the general barriers to entry cited, notably the need to become familiar with new countries' markets and regulations, may be more costly, so that the need for an extra effort to export may be greater. If a role for government assistance is accepted, as all the country studies do, this has implications for its amount and form, in comparison with previous successful industrialising countries, which are discussed further in Chapter 18.

NOTES

1. Ariff (1984) notes that 'labour-intensive exports which were strongly competitive in the early 1970s, have become less and less competitive over the decade, especially in estimates . . . where the LDC standard is used.'
2. This necessarily ignores the contribution of illegal exports which the Colombian study notes could be of the same magnitude as coffee, and which would alter this picture.
3. This is supported by analysis of primary product prospects in (UNIDO, 1987), which also expects that in the medium term more primary production will move from the industrial to the developing countries, if they can offer cost advantages.
4. There were some signs in 1987–8 that the rise in the yen might have changed the competitive conditions sufficiently for Japan to begin importing electrical, electronic and other goods from the South-East Asian countries.
5. Used of Malaysian manufacturers in a speech by the Prime Minister, *New Straits Times*, 8 November 1984.

11

IMPORT SUBSTITUTION

OR REDUCTION

IMPORT SUBSTITUTION AND DEVELOPMENT

If import substitution is seen as a way of removing (or mitigating) an external constraint on development (as is discussed more fully in Chapter 16), the result is intended to be a lower average ratio of imports to output. The type of product may not appear to be important in itself: what matters in the short run is that its production does not itself have a high import content. But the constraint may be a dynamic one. If the growth in a country's markets is persistently too slow to permit its exports to grow as rapidly as desired output (because world growth is too slow or its exports are primary products), then a change in import structure is important: the reduction must be in imports which have a relatively high marginal income elasticity or there must be a programme of repeated substitutions of lower elasticity products which achieves the same ends. It is this type of import strategy which offers a direct alternative or supplement to the symmetrical ones for exports explored in the previous two chapters (a series of new exports and preference for those with high income elasticities). The alternative to either external strategy, which is explored in the Peru and Zimbabwe studies, is to lower domestic income elasticities for imports by redistributing income, and by changing the composition of demand towards goods already produced locally. Thus although a study of the 'external constraints' may look first at the balance-of-payments role of import substitution, it is necessary even for this to consider also its sectoral form. The choice of which imports to replace is directly related to the expected or planned structure of the economy: the type of exports and the pattern of industrialisation or other structural change.

Chapter 9 showed that, at the aggregate level, there had been little change in the structure of imports in all developing countries, although there were minor differences between Asia and Latin America; the important differences in the balances for different areas came from the export side. In particular, imports of manufactures (excluding unprocessed metals) continue to be about 55–60% of total imports for all areas (see Table 11.1), which is not out of line with the figures for industrial countries, excluding Japan. The principal difference for developing countries is the dominant share of machinery and transport, higher for Latin America than Asia (see Table 9.6).

It is evident from Table 11.1 that, within these stable averages, there are quite large movements for individual countries. The present NICs appear to be more like the industrialised countries than are the new NICs, in their reduced dependence on non-electric machinery and transport equipment; the 'other' countries are different from both in still having high imports of more basic manufactures. The changes over the ten years of the table, however, do not show further movements in this direction. The apparent lessons from the aggregate data are the disparities among the successful countries and, as for exports, the significant role of machinery and transport products as characteristic of developed countries.

Most of the country studies make the distinction between substitution of relatively uncomplicated finished manufactures, largely for final consumption, and that of capital goods and the more advanced intermediate goods. The former, like substitution of local food production, may (if they have a sufficiently low import content) reduce the average dependence of the economy on imports, but do not necessarily lower the marginal propensities. As the lower income elasticity imports are replaced by domestic production, the marginal propensity to import may actually rise. This points to a need to progress to the more advanced products or to alternative strategies. The initial import substitution is of well-known, low-technology goods whose output is widespread (although there may be substantial intra-industry trade). The shift to the second stage can thus be seen to be from simple to more complex goods; from consumer to capital goods; from goods most of which will eventually be produced in most countries to those where choices are more necessary. The aggregate data for composition of exports (especially Tables 9.4 and 9.8) and imports (Table 11.1) suggest (and the country studies argue) that, while the new NICs have in general made the initial change, they have only started on the second, while the NICs have gone considerably further on the second. Zimbabwe and Peru still see possibilities in intermediate goods.

IMPORT POLICY IN THE FIVE COUNTRIES

The *Zimbabwe* paper sees the continuing dependence on imports of intermediate and capital goods as the significant constraint on the economy. The UDI period stimulated substitution of other imports; food self-sufficiency in particular was achieved at this time. Zimbabwe may still offer possibilities in the first stage of import substitution, although the intense pressures incurred in the UDI period suggest that new products may be limited quite specifically to those goods which could then be easily imported from South Africa. Robinson argues that intermediate goods should be the next target because these will produce the largest reductions in import content in the immediate future. Zimbabwe's share of machinery and transport goods (Table 8.5) is characteristically (for a new NIC) high. He also puts the case that some industries have a special role in development because of their own character-istics (for example the skill and technology contributions from the steel investment), while recognising that these are unquantifiable. The role of linkages with other parts of the economy is also emphasised both here and in other recent work on the Zimbabwe economy (Ndlela, in Mandaza, 1986).[1] The basis of the alternative strategy which Robinson proposes is to alter the structure of demand and output of the economy, and thereby reduce import dependence. The additional objectives of income distribution and rural development influence the choice of strategy.

Such changes would not operate directly on the present dependence on imports of capital goods (or machinery and transport equipment), or the marginal propensities with respect to individual components of national demand. They would extend the period during which the average dependence of the economy on imports can be reduced by increasing the share of 'first-stage' import substitutes and other domestic goods in demand. This would give time to build up the exporting skills discussed in the previous chapter (and to survive the particularly difficult external conditions faced at present in southern Africa). The more ambitious second stage is judged to be more suitable for a later period, after the next five years.

Peru's policy on imports in the 1970s was conditioned by the balance of payments (and later by anti-inflation policy), not by industrial policies. There were cycles of constraint, then easing. After the export boom at the end of the 1970s, with the external balance further improved by capital inflows, the controls and rates of tariffs were greatly reduced. The volume of imports rose more than 20% in 1980 and 1981, raising their share in GDP from 18% to 24%. After 1982, the liberalisation was again reversed. The period of liberalisation destroyed some manufacturing industry built up previously under protection. The strategy of the Garcia government from 1985 was to restrict imports principally by encouraging non-import-intensive demand (through income redistribution), and also using the considerable excess capacity resulting from the recession. The possibility of substituting new products is limited: the share of machinery and transport equipment in Peru's imports is already among the highest of the new NICs. For the future, the strategy envisages some additional food output in the medium term, and reductions in imports of intermediate goods. The latter accounted for most of the large rise in imports in 1986; food imports nearly doubled (Table 7.4), explaining much of the remainder. As in the Zimbabwe study, a less import-intensive industrial structure is proposed, but Schuldt stresses the interest-group pressures that have led to import intensity, and a high elasticity especially in periods of high growth.

The *Malaysian* study notes that the main phase of import substitution was in the early 1970s. This was true for food as well as for manufactures. There is now a high import elasticity because of capital and intermediate goods. Electrical machinery has a particularly high share for Malaysia in both imports and exports, indicating how the country has progressed to a later stage of import substitution than Zimbabwe. High levels of protection have encouraged some of the import substitution, although the authors note that it may be moderate by international standards. Ariff has argued elsewhere (Ariff and Hill, 1985: 16) that this may be because the government feared that general help to industry would be of most benefit to foreign and Chinese-owned companies. Government planners have also suggested that Malaysia is too small a market for many industries, and therefore not suitable for import substitution to the extent that the larger economies in Asia have been. Such arguments indicate the importance of national characteristics, economic and social. The authors of the Malaysia study nevertheless suggest that protection is now an obstacle to export promotion. The two policies are 'incompatible'. This is consistent with a price- and cost-based view of in-dustrialisation, which may be more suitable for a country like Malaysia which is passing the point at which exporters and industry have to be 'developed' as opposed to being simply stimulated.

The study implicitly rejects any special developmental objective for en-couraging particular import-substituting industries (at least at this stage of Malaysia's development). The government policy of the early 1980s took a different, more structurally based, view, arguing for a second stage of import substitution concentrating on heavy industry. This approach was behind its advocacy of the 'national car'. The study points out the damage to other parts of the car industry from favouring one firm. In shipping, however, it does see linkage and marketing advantages to import-substitution, implying that the industrial approach may be more suitable in new industries than in existing ones. A similar distinction seems to emerge for Thailand.

The *Thailand* study identifies the end of the 1970s as the end of the period of simple import substitution. It also comments on the change of industrial structure, away from consumer towards intermediate and capital goods, helped by protection. It emphasises, however, that the import structure was able to change relatively quickly during the 1960s while the first phase was in progress, but has remained more or less the same since then (allowing for the changing prices of oil imports). The level of protection has been relatively high; the bias against exports actually increased during the period when the study suggests that import substitution was becoming less easy.

A clear distinction is made between import substitution in the first stage when it may make 'a quick start of industrial development' and the current stage. For second-stage import substitution, the risk of high import content in intermediate and capital goods is greater. The need for high technology and a large domestic market is also greater, suggesting that the countries for which the second stage is suitable are more limited. It is also at this stage that the potential for conflict with export objectives appears.

Like the Asian countries, *Colombia* has completed the first stage of import substitution, but unlike them it has not yet had to choose what to do at the second stage. Echavarria points out the high level of capital goods imports, and that they have been growing rapidly, noting that unlike the case with other countries they have not been constrained in the 1980s. He suggests that further import substitution, using the new resources from coal and oil, is the path for the immediate future. This is not seen as a permanent strategy, but as a particular opportunity of this period, to build the base for future diversification of exports out of coffee.

In the longer run, he accepts the argument that some 'advanced' sectors (notably certain types of machinery) should be promoted for their special characteristics in development. Import substitution is thus suitable for a period in which there are special advantages (the availability of new resources) and special needs of the economy, but with more 'advanced' industry for export to follow.

CONCLUSIONS

The country studies suggest that the idea that there is a first stage of import substitution, followed by a period during which structural change becomes more complex and probably more difficult, is a useful way of looking at the new NICs' imports. After the first stage, average and marginal import elasticities may rise and eventually make import growth a constraint on further growth. The high level of imports of machinery observed for the middle-income group in Table 11.1, and the apparent lack of general changes in import composition for a prolonged period, are consistent with this analysis. During the first stage, it may be relatively easy to identify possible 'substitutions' as the goods will be already present with known markets. Moving beyond this stage means either choosing among various more advanced import-substituting industries, which may appear easier but involve high investment or import content, or identifying distant export markets with unfamiliar requirements; or, particularly for a small country, doing both at once. All the country studies suggest that the normal next step after first-stage import substitution (and with possibly a considerable delay) would be exports of some manufactures, with second-stage import substitution and more exports coming together as the country moves into a more developed or industrialised status. For a small country, second-stage substitution may never come on a large scale, while some industries may be brought forward for special reasons. The experience of the NICs (and the industrial countries), however, suggests that it is not a stage which an advanced country can omit.

It is clearly possible for a country to find itself leaving the first stage without being completely ready for the second, particularly if it has other economic or non-economic goals and social problems at the same time (Colombia, Peru, Zimbabwe), or if the first stage has been unusually rapid or early because of political factors (Zimbabwe) or policy (Thailand). This is an extension of the more traditional argument, that import substitution is a necessary first stage before export promotion because it gives experience in industrialisation, to include the need to acquire other types of 'expertise': in the process of industrialisation, or in marketing, or in choosing industries before relying on market- and price-based decisions becomes a feasible choice.

It is clear from all the studies that once the 'first-stage' import substitution has been completed, the decisions to be made have to be seen in the general context of industrial strategy. The proposals made in the different studies show how other national objectives can come into the decision, including income distribution and industrialisation. If the development of economic decision-making and responses has been sufficient by the end of the first phase, and a large role for private decision-making can be and is assumed, it becomes important to have at that point prices that can provide useful guidance. If this has not yet happened, or if non-economic or structural objectives are important, then prices may be less significant as signals.

It is important in an economic analysis to note a further problem (which Robinson brings out most clearly, but which lies behind the uncertainties in the other country studies), once the first stage has passed. After the first stage, reducing import dependence may come from changes within sectors, substituting parts of an industry, altering products to suit a changed market if there is income redistribution. This makes economic specification of the policy or analysis of its effects difficult as much depends on technologies or the new consumers' behaviour.

NOTE

1. In contrast, other approaches to Zimbabwean import substitution (UNIDO, 1986b) concentrate on identifying particular products with known markets which could be produced in Zimbabwe, an approach more characteristic of the initial stage of import substitution.

Table 11.1　Structure of imports of manufactures (percentages)

Shares in total imports of:	Manufactures ex 67+68			Non-elec. machinery, SITC 71			Elec. machinery, SITC 72			Transport equip, SITC 73		
	1975	1980	1985	1975	1980	1985	1975	1980	1985	1975	1980	1985
Newly industrialising countries												
Argentina[a]	48.51	71.69	67.18	13.06	18.61	14.91	4.07	11.88	9.34	3.39	9.74	7.46
Brazil[a]	52.21	38.48	31.87	20.13	10.36	6.69	7.76	5.75	5.37	3.81	3.37	3.42
Hong Kong	61.62	72.02	75.74	6.01	7.17	8.22	8.62	10.52	12.69	2.22	4.41	3.04
India[d]	38.34	32.61	31.43	9.53	6.99	8.49	3.69	2.28	2.61	2.41	4.02	1.75
Mexico[e]	67.89	68.88		22.03	23.41		6.31	6.36		17.06	16.20	
Singapore	49.70	50.51	52.98	12.17	10.46	10.69	9.75	12.06	14.59	4.26	6.86	5.98
South Korea	45.93	38.65	53.41	11.68	10.43	11.47	7.05	7.23	9.87	7.53	4.72	13.11
Average	52.03	53.26	44.66	13.52	12.49	8.64	6.75	8.01	7.78	5.81	7.05	4.97
New NICs												
Colombia[a]	73.20	63.39	64.22	17.58	17.22	16.77	6.74	8.00	8.80	14.67	12.34	9.81
Malaysia[b]	56.73	60.81	64.31	13.88	13.21	13.45	10.07	15.62	19.81	8.71	10.00	9.49
Peru[c]	59.66	67.15	72.10	20.14	23.02	21.69	5.05	7.72	8.80	7.37	9.75	13.66
Thailand[a]	59.03	45.30	53.65	17.66	10.41	14.27	5.86	7.18	9.21	11.26	7.18	5.89
Zimbabwe[c]		64.32			11.04			7.18			13.03	
Average	62.16	60.19	63.57	17.32	14.98	16.55	6.93	9.14	11.66	10.50	10.46	9.71
Other middle income countries												
Chile[d]	52.98	57.76	65.99	17.27	11.75	12.13	5.97	8.24	8.18	9.45	13.38	16.63
Costa Rica[c]	71.00	63.14	55.92	13.25	10.06	5.98	5.18	7.09	5.45	8.53	6.96	3.17
Egypt	43.18	51.11	52.13	7.50	12.36	12.15	4.27	5.46	6.08	8.69	9.51	6.78
Ivory Coast[b]	63.83	50.38	54.46	14.76	9.37	7.83	5.40	5.19	5.55	10.64	6.97	11.43
Kenya[b]	58.55	50.63	45.16	14.04	12.89	10.92	5.29	4.25	5.70	11.01	10.87	6.31
Morocco[a]	47.56	40.72	36.97	14.79	12.75	10.00	4.24	3.63	4.56	9.72	4.86	5.26
Pakistan	42.38	49.04	47.10	11.76	10.75	12.51	6.11	3.32	4.84	5.96	11.31	9.76
Philippines[b]	52.65	42.35	40.65	18.15	12.27	11.30	4.50	4.83	6.12	9.20	6.75	3.88
Senegal[d]	54.28	46.01	38.12	12.37	10.02	8.08	4.37	5.16	3.90	9.23	8.14	5.86
Sri Lanka[a]	26.67	48.87	52.82	4.75	11.13	8.66	1.84	4.67	7.14	1.99	9.09	8.33
Tunisia[a]	60.08	51.75	59.64	16.98	11.79	15.29	5.59	4.90	7.03	9.88	6.61	8.68

Table 11.1 (continued)

Shares total imports:	Manufactures ex 67+68			Non-elec. machinery, SITC 71			Elec. machinery, SITC 72			Transport equip, SITC 73		
	1975	1980	1985	1975	1980	1985	1975	1980	1985	1975	1980	1985
Uruguay[a]	44.34	52.13	45.79	9.91	12.84	7.95	3.49	4.54	7.13	5.50	12.84	3.43
Venezuela[d]	72.97	72.70	72.12	26.52	20.73	19.92	7.20	10.56	9.53	14.38	11.54	13.99
Average	53.11	52.05	51.30	14.00	12.21	10.98	4.88	5.53	6.25	8.78	9.14	7.96
Area averages												
Africa	46.78	50.70	40.93	11.49	11.46	9.18	4.17	5.11	4.69	8.45	8.57	6.33
Asia	60.31	61.70	52.80	17.77	16.44	11.78	5.75	7.79	6.96	9.35	10.68	7.95
Latin America	48.12	48.91	52.45	11.73	10.31	11.01	6.39	7.52	9.65	5.95	7.15	6.80
Average by group	55.77	55.17	53.18	14.94	13.23	12.05	6.19	7.56	8.56	8.37	8.88	7.55
Average by area	51.74	53.77	48.73	13.66	12.74	10.66	5.44	6.81	7.10	7.92	8.80	7.03
Industrial countries												
Germany[a]	47.93	52.02	53.44	6.90	7.07	9.05	5.02	5.35	6.31	5.66	6.28	7.29
Japan[a]	17.36	18.01	24.21	3.55	2.71	3.71	1.74	1.94	2.97	1.32	1.61	2.03
UK[a]	45.37	57.8	64.64	9.57	10.06	13.49	4.36	5.27	8.11	4.92	10.45	10.04
USA[a]	46.25	46.73	67.03	7.25	6.75	10.58	5.13	6.04	9.46	12.63	12.18	17.79

a. Last year is 1984.   d. Last year is 1981.
b. Last year is 1983.   e. Last year is 1979.
c. Last year is 1982.

Source: UNCTAD, Handbook of International Trade and Development Statistics.

12

EXCHANGE RATES

The question of how responsive to price signals these economies are (because of their level of development) and should be (in the presence of objectives other than growth and efficiency) affects the country studies' views of the role of exchange rates. The most striking feature is how little attention the studies give to the exchange rate as a tool, and the implication (made explicit in the Peru study) that governments also tend to consider it only when it forces itself on their attention. When it is used, it is frequently to manage inflation or costs, not to alter trade volumes.

This is not far from the traditional view that the dependence of developing countries on prices and markets over which they have little control limits the effectiveness of the exchange rate as a tool, while their extensive controls and taxes on imports and exports make it a misleading signal. Any structural or other objectives that reduce the role of prices generally in determining economic decisions further marginalise the role of the exchange rate. Even the NICs have found it difficult to define the appropriate strategy (particularly in the unsettled conditions of the mid-1980s).

The increasing importance of interest and amortisation payments, which are (unlike returns on foreign investment) fixed in foreign currency, has introduced a new consideration in exchange-rate policy for most countries. Unlike most imports of goods and services, they are fixed in volume as well as in foreign-exchange price. Devaluation therefore raises their cost in local currency immediately by the full amount of the exchange-rate change and there is no later downward adjustment. This, of course, makes the conditions under which a devaluation can eventually improve the balance on external payments more restrictive by effectively increasing the average inelasticity of payments. (If imports are substantially higher than exports, which would not be unusual in a country accumulating debts, the size of the problem is increased.)

All the countries examined here have forms of managed or floating exchange rates. They are nominally based on baskets of other currencies but, as the baskets are not generally made public and the rates are not fixed, this specification is of little interest except as a guide to those who fix the rate.

In *Zimbabwe*, it is argued that imports and other payments are so controlled by other means that devaluation has little effect. On exports, it could affect profitability, but this would not necessarily lead to volume increases where they were wanted, and therefore selective subsidies are more appropriate. This is consistent with the study's general view of the need for intervention, and in particular the weakness of the response by new producers to market incentives. The existence of the controls and subsidies makes it impossible to analyse meaningfully the effect of the apparent overvaluation of the exchange rate: presumably if the rate were different, the same import and export results would be achieved by appropriate changes in the controls.

In the *Colombian* strategy, the exchange rate is again relegated to a minor role (it could improve the competitiveness of some minor agricultural products), while the tariffs on imports, the government's role in allocating income from the major (legal) exports, and arguments for a strong structural and regional role for government policy in the future leave little scope for a major exchange-rate effect. The still high share of primary exports in the total also makes the traditional presumption that external prices are exogenous, likely to hold.

Malaysia also has a relatively low share of manufactures in total exports, but its second highest export (electrical components) is extremely price-sensitive, and some of its other primary product exports are more subject to price competition than a standard commodity. The government has had an exchange-rate policy, and the authors of the Malaysia paper argue that the rate can (and by implication should) be used as an instrument 'to redirect resources'. The rise in the real rate in the early 1980s hurt, and the depreciation since then has helped, manufactured exports. However, Malaysia's debt and interest liabilities (discussed in Chapter 15) are explicitly seen as a limit on the use of the exchange rate by the financial side of the government.

The *Thai* exchange rate was tied to the dollar until 1984 (although the rate had been changed in 1981), and was floated as well as devalued thereafter in order to give the possibility of a policy. The study suggests that since then it has been held down to promote Thai manufactured exports. The high level of protection against imports suggests that the exchange rate is unlikely to be the decisive influence on their level.

In *Peru*, the exchange rate has received more attention, in the 1970s, and again under the Garcia government, but for its effect on inflation rather than on the trade balance. Schuldt suggests that it has been repeatedly left unchanged, and thus liable to become overvalued, until the IMF has intervened. Except during the period of liberalisation of imports in 1980–2, the volume of imports has been controlled directly. Economists and government have been sceptical about the benefits from devaluation to traditional exports. Subsidies to non-traditional exports have limited the effect of the anti-inflationist tendency to overvalue. In 1982, real devaluation was used, unsuccessfully, to improve the balance of payments. The effect of devaluation on the cost of basic consumption is high (and obvious) because of the high proportion of food in imports; so political pressures limit its use. The 'heterodox' model formalised these observations into an expectation that devaluation was deflationary because the negative effect on output through income was greater than any positive effect through exports (Alarco, 1987: 153). The Garcia government has maintained multiple exchange rates (12 official ones in late 1987, with effectively more as these were combined with different foreign exchange controls), moving together. The lowest legal rate was about half the highest, and the parallel market rate a third. The system supplemented tariffs and subsidies to favour non-traditional exports over primary, with subdivisions within each, but the (on average) over-valuation reflected the fact that the principal concern was inflation, not relative prices.

The country studies do not treat the exchange rate as an important variable in future strategies. The only country in which devaluation is suggested as a tool for promoting manufactured exports, Malaysia, faces the obstacle of high debt payments, and still has a high share of primary exports.

13

INDUSTRIALISATION

The process of industrialisation in developing countries is beyond the scope of this book, and has recently been studied in great depth (Chenery *et al.*, 1986). Two questions, however, are closely linked with the impact of (and strategy for) the external sector: first, whether 'industrialising', in aggregate or in particular sectors, should be seen as itself an essential part of development, not simply as an outcome of changes in demand in a growing economy. Second, what 'comparative advantage' means in a country that is assumed to be changing its structure, and how it can be applied to choice of new sectors to develop. World changes in technology and preferences are also changing the relative importance of existing advantages and entrepreneurs' initiatives. The view that the country studies take on these questions strongly influences their perception of what strategies are available as well as choices among them.

THE SPECIAL CONTRIBUTION OF MANUFACTURING

The Chenery study shows that industrialisation is characteristic of countries that have developed. What is surprising is that the question needed to be asked. Development and industrialisation have traditionally been synonymous, and the history of the present 'industrial' countries (the old conventional view still sets the terminology) and the NICs emphasises it. It was only the strong emphasis on exports (and perhaps the success of OPEC) in the 1970s that raised doubts.[1] Chenery (p. 351) cites four characteristics of manufacturing:

1. high income elasticity;
2. tradeable and substitutable goods;
3. productivity gains through reallocation of resources and specialisation;
4. a source of technological change.

The first is the traditional reason for expecting the share of manufacturing to rise as a result of growth. The other three restore to manufactures some of the gains attributed in the 1970s to trade and 'openness', implicitly in any product (see Chapter 16). Earlier development economists probably took the third and fourth characteristics for granted (certainly most policy-makers in the present or earlier developing countries would do so), and the second is a necessary condition for these.

If these are accepted as structural, empirically observable characteristics of manufacturing, a growing industrial sector is significant in itself for development. It may ease those structural factors which impede growth directly or through reducing the responsiveness to prices and other market signals, so that industrialisation becomes a strategy, not a response to demand. It may be a necessary ingredient in an export-based strategy. It is important to distinguish the characteristics (and advantages) of a growing manufacturing sector from those of a large one. Although a large sector offers more scope for reallocation and flexibility, an established sector of any economic activity may have rigidities; between two countries with similar present structure, the one with the shorter history of manufacturing may have some advantages. On the other hand, the advantages of technological change, and perhaps those of specialisation, may be cumulative, and therefore work in the opposite direction. Kubo et al. found between 1953 and 1973 a 'mild inverse relation between the initial share of manufacturing in GDP and the rate of industrialisation' (Chenery et al., 1986: 190), although the sample included countries reaching industrial country status (South Korea, Taiwan and Singapore had the highest rates).

The definition of new NICs for the present study was based on the share of manufacturing in output. The Chenery book found that a rise (from 19% to 36%) was typical of 'structural transformation', and Table 13.1 shows this clearly. The developed countries are at about 30%, with signs now of a decline in the share, and the NICs (except India) are at around a quarter. The countries chosen for this study are at the upper end of the range for the next category; the least developed countries, especially in Africa, are well below this. The only difference from comparisons in the earlier chapters based on trade is the higher share for Latin America than Asia, particularly in 1970. A large industrial structure is thus longer established there. Only among the new NICs is there a consistent increase in the shares over the last 15 years (although less for the Latin American countries). Among the NICs, the Asian countries show more of a rise than the Latin American. All these are consistent with Kubo's findings.

The *Zimbabwe* study assumes that the exploitation of technologies through industrialisation is central to growth, but suggests two reasons for not giving it priority in the next few years. The first is Zimbabwe's relatively advanced degree of industrialisation for its income level (following the import substitution under UDI). The implication is that this permits other goals, including those of rural development and redistribution, to be pursued without serious damage to long-run structural development. The second is the poor prospects for trade, especially in southern Africa, in other words that one of the normal benefits of industrialisation is reduced, changing the trade-off in favour of the other goals. Zimbabwe is thus an example of a country where other structural factors are believed to affect the potential benefits of further industrialisation.

Whether to industrialise is no longer an issue in *Malaysia*. The 1986 Industrial Master Plan assumes that its share will continue to increase (industry grows at 8.8% against 5% for the economy as a whole). Ariff and Semudram question the level of industrial targets, however, because of the external constraints on the growth of exports.

The share of manufacturing fluctuates in *Thailand* because of changes in the value of agricultural output, but it has risen strongly (Tables 5.1 and 13.1). The study questions the success of the government's policy of industrialisation, noting the strong dependence on imports; but only to propose a different emphasis, on exports rather than import substitution, not to suggest an alternative to industrialisation.

In contrast to Zimbabwe and the Asian countries, *Colombia* has not seen an increase in manufacturing's share in the last 15 years, and Table 6.6 shows that in the last ten years industry has grown more slowly than agriculture. As the study points out, this poor performance was unusual by Latin American standards, and by Colombian as well, and the reasons lie in poor performance by industry, not policy choice or exceptional performance by other sectors. Echavarria attributes it to poor industrial structure, itself the result of lack of government policy. Industrialisation is needed to diversify the economy out of dependence on coffee.

Peru has had the largest share of manufacturing in output of the new NICs, but no significant change in the period (Table 7.6), with even a slight fall in the worst years of the 1980s depression. The expansion of the economy in 1986 was based in part on the substantial idle capacity in industry, but although manufacturing did expand at twice the average rate (close to 19%), this only restored its level of output to that of 1976, with a slightly lower share. Expanding industry for both export and domestic sales is part of the present government's programme. Aggregate growth is seen as an important means of reducing unit costs, and also of increasing employment and decentralisation, but the balance of payments situation has also brought a concern for finding sectors that can be a permanent basis for exporting, and these are expected to be mainly in industry.

Although Zimbabwe and Malaysia, where manufacturing has already gone furthest, especially for countries of their size, see temporary limits on the exporting opportunities of industry, all the countries agree (effectively without even feeling a need to justify it, except in Colombia) that increasing the share of industry is the normal and expected mechanism of growth or development. The reasons for wanting (or assuming) industrialisation lie in dissatisfaction with the prospects for primary production as well as in the particular advantages of manufacturing identified in this chapter, although clearly high income elasticity and the gains from reallocation of surplus labour to industry are also seen as important advantages. The element of diversification (for its own sake, not merely as a way of securing new or different technologies or allocation advantages) also favours industry in all countries for the long term, although not in Zimbabwe in the immediate future.

CHOICE OF SECTORS

Although the Chenery book finds 'higher productivity growth associated with export expansion than with import substitution' (Chenery et al., 1986: 358), the evidence on the role of different sectors within manufacturing is more mixed than that for country differences. There is support for the view that this is associated with a progression of industrialisation from import substitution to export expansion. There is a wide variation in the performance and contribution to productivity of different types of industry (Chenery et al., 1986, ch. 7).

There may, therefore, be scope for increasing productivity by switching among sectors or by encouraging the development of particular sectors. This could come as a response to external trade and this is one of the arguments for an export-based development, discussed further in Chapter 16. But if it is assumed that underdevelopment implies less than perfect flexibility and response to market and profit signals, or if a change in industrial structure also promotes other objectives then, as with industrialisation in total, sectoral change should be treated as actively contributing to development, not merely a response to growth and markets. In an unindustrialised country, where 'increasing output' is more likely to mean 'producing a good for the first time' than in an industrial country, barriers to entry may be a limit more frequently, and marginal changes may be suitable less often. The country studies consider a variety of advantages from particular sectors. If these can be identified, the effectiveness of trade in promoting the preferred sectors can be examined. The basic question (and there are differences in view among the country studies) is which associations among sectors or between industries and other effects are causal, and in which direction.

The Chenery study also looks at the question of linkages. If there are industries which as suppliers or users of intermediate inputs have a particularly strong effect in encouraging other sectors, this would suggest another role for a sectoral strategy. This is closely associated with the view taken on an external strategy because the assumption behind analysing linkages is that there is something different and stronger about the effect of a domestic industry, compared with imports or exports of the same products. To examine this it is necessary to look in detail at individual industries rather than taking an input–output approach.[2]

In the Zimbabwe study, Robinson advocates more awareness of linkages. He argues that government policy (on local content or procurement requirements) is necessary; companies must be encouraged or trained to respond to technical challenges. This suggests that, in addition to looking for industries that encourage such responses, it is possible to develop the ability to respond in industries that are already present. (It is more dynamic than the conventional view of immediate import saving as a reason for procurement rules.) The discussion of the Zimbabwean steel industry looks at inter-industry linkages, attributing the growth of engineering and capital goods industries directly to the availability of domestic steel (at subsidised prices). The alternative of developing the same industries on the basis of imported steel is explicitly rejected; it might not have the same subsidy (because of reluctance to subsidise imports), and would lack the advantages of direct contacts and co-ordination between the steel supplier and its customers. Because of the broad import substitution under UDI, completely new sectors are less likely to be needed than in most developing countries. The problem of developing interactions among existing industries is therefore the most important.

The Malaysian study looks in detail at the choice of which sectors to emphasise. Although an increased emphasis on heavy industries (steel, petrochemicals and cars) followed the government's shift to a policy of second-stage import substitution in the early 1980s, the authors of the study do not support this, preferring the allocation advantages from export orientation. The size of the Malaysian market is seen as a constraint on any industry that does not have export potential; by implication, therefore, domestic linkages are less important than in a larger country. The Malaysian study does not see any particular advantage in linkages beyond the potential general externalities of technological diffusion, preferring to emphasise a broader trade orientation. In contrast to the arguments in the Zimbabwe study, the description of the lack of domestic or export markets for the steel industry does not suggest any linkage advantages to compensate for the costs. The study criticises the establishment of a car industry as well, on the grounds of its high costs, and does not suggest any potential gains which would explain or could justify government efforts to establish it. As was seen in Chapter 9, cars and metals are characteristic of industrial country exports, but this does not necessarily imply that, particularly in smaller countries, these structures should be copied precisely, or indicate whether they are results or causes of development.

The Malaysian plan looks for growth in natural resource-related industries. The authors consider these likely to be particularly vulnerable to protection at present, but appear to share the general Malaysian belief that this is where future opportunities lie (cf. Chee, 1981). Although this is usually interpreted to mean processing industries, it can also include those needed to produce the machinery to extract and process the resources. This assumes not only that Malaysia is more competitive in resources than other producers (as the products are not, in general, facing rising demand) but also that it can be competitive in the related machinery (even taking into account the existing capacity in countries whose production it is displacing) or that there are particular advantages in producing the capital equipment near to where it is to be used. If the latter, however, then the opportunities for sale would presumably be limited to Malaysia, and this is in conflict with the usual criterion that products need to be exportable to be viable in a country of Malaysia's size. An alternative extension which has started to occur is to invest abroad in related industries.

The Malaysian study also looks at the income distribution effects of different types of industrialisation: it finds that export-oriented industrialisation is labour-intensive, consistent with the target for a further increase in employment, but that the income effects are more ambiguous. It is particularly hesitant to draw conclusions about relative incomes in the Free Trade Zones, but considers their employment-creation effects the overriding factor.

The conclusion seems to be in favour of little change in the present structure of manufacturing industry, with continued emphasis on manufacturing for export, based on 'footloose' labour-intensive industries, but with a long-term intention of moving more into industries using Malaysia's other natural resources when prospects for these improve. The assumption, therefore, is of a response to given opportunities of supply and demand, with specialisation in a few sectors, not an unconstrained choice of sectors.

The Thailand study suggests ending the protection of inefficient import-substituting industries, and taking advantage of the allocation gains from moving into export industries. The assumption is that these will be less capital-intensive and less import-dependent, so improving the macro-balance of the economy. Like the Malaysian study, it proposes more emphasis on resource-based industries, and suggests that as these are in general not in competition with those in industrial countries the risk of protection will be less. (There are obviously some exceptions to this assumption including feedstuffs and other agriculturally based industries.) No particular advantages are put forward which could justify emphasis on particular sectors, rather than on those which would contribute most to net output and net balance of payments gains, but the fear of protection suggests a constraint on the allocative gains from trade.

The Colombian study quotes the criteria developed by Chenery, of labour intensity, static comparative advantage, linkages and import intensity, which favour metal products, machinery and equipment (but excluding cars) and basic metals. (This is broadly consistent with the trade patterns found in Chapter 9.) Echavarria's use of these criteria, and his emphasis on other goals in addition to growth, are consistent with a sectoral approach to industrialisation. The choice should be based on industrial and other domestic (regional, distributive) criteria, not on the implications for the external sector. There appears to be no general consensus on which industries Colombia should develop, although there is on the need for structural change.

The concern for export potential, and also such goals as employment and decentralisation, have brought a new interest in restructuring *Peru's* industry and favouring particular sectors, but there is also support for a more responsive approach. Government policy has so far not gone beyond helping exporters (in aggregate), because the 'investment' stage of the 1985–90 plan was to follow the initial increase in use of existing capacity and this was never reached. Schuldt suggests some criteria based on general economic objectives. Subsidies to fixed capital and high working capital costs encourage capital intensity (especially when the exchange-rate system works to favour imported capital goods). A policy of increasing employment requires the opposite, particularly in a country where one major sector, mining, is necessarily capital-intensive. Using a more sectoral approach, Schuldt argues for more processing of natural resources, to permit development from semi-processed to final goods, and from domestic production (perhaps through local intra-Andean Pact exports) to more general exports. He suggests that this would give varied types of product (some would be mass consumption, others luxury, others investment goods) and this would train producers to look for (and adapt to) different markets.

Exporting has to be seen as part of the strategy because of the small size of the domestic market. The sectoral strategy thus derives from a traditional emphasis on natural advantages combined with the perception of special advantages from manufacturing in 'developing' entrepreneurs, not from a sectoral approach *per se*.

The discussion of the potential advantages of different sectors in the Zimbabwe, Colombia and Peru papers suggests various reasons for sectoral advantages, but none of the country studies is willing to identify which sectors have them. The problem is that they are non-quantifiable advantages, to motivations or inter-industry links, or to regional policy. Even where there are economic advantages which should be exploited without special promotion or policies (such as substitution of labour for capital), what cannot be modelled or quantified (beyond any effect from subsidies) is why the industries do not respond themselves. The presence (or absence in the case of Malaysian steel and cars) of special advantages can be seen in retrospect, but, except by looking at existing successful countries (which is probably the explanation of the establishment of steel and car production), there is little scope for economists to identify them. To bridge this analytical gap, the emphasis, for example, in the Zimbabwe study, on the need to teach industries to respond to incentives, or for the government to provide opportunities to respond, is a useful approach. The Peruvian combination of this with natural resources provides some insurance against completely inappropriate choices. The Colombian study sees a need for the government at the present stage of the country's development to encourage a wide range of potentially successful industries.

The Malaysian discussion of general forms of technology spread is in line with the perception that, at least at the early stages of industrialisation, a spread of sectors and incentives, without trying too hard to identify 'best' industries, may be fruitful. At a later stage, which at least Malaysia and Thailand have reached (and possibly Zimbabwe, but other reasons call for a pause there), more care in choosing industries is necessary. Implicitly, both the Asian studies assume that this is a choice mainly for industrialists or investors, not for governments or academic researchers, in other words, that the requirement to learn to take decisions has been successfully met. The Thai study then looks only for efficiency and output criteria. Both suggest that appropriate decisions are likely to lead to more attention to the presence of natural resources (including labour for labour-intensive manufacture).

TECHNOLOGY TRANSFER

The introduction of a new sector must introduce new technologies and new approaches to production, so the simple case for manufactures' contribution to technology is easily made.[3] As long as sectors of manufacturing which are important in most industrial countries are still absent from a developing country (as the import composition data discussed in Chapter 11 show is true for our five countries) this case remains a valid argument for more industry. At least historically the dynamic case, that technological progress was greater in manufacturing than in primary sectors, was correct. The transfer of technology, not simply of techniques but of the knowledge and ability to use them, is unquestionably an element of development.

The country studies do not look for advantages from particular industries, but probably all accept technology as one of the general reasons for industrialisation. The Zimbabwe study assumes that industry in general makes important contributions to technology, and to the technological development of the labour force. This may be a particularly important argument at the early stages of industrialisation when labour forces lack any experience of industrial work, and publicly provided vocational training is lacking. Like the need to train entrepreneurs in appropriate responses, raising even 'unskilled' labour to a minimum level is a prerequisite for treating the factors of production in terms of 'normal' economic responses to markets and price signals.

The Malaysian study emphasises the role of a general spread of technology from industries, including those in the Free Trade Zones where there may be no direct supplier–purchaser link. The authors include knowledge of markets in this.

COMPARATIVE ADVANTAGE

The industrialisation and sectoral objectives discussed in the first half of this chapter are one influence on the composition of trade. What can be sold or bought on acceptable terms is the other. As stated earlier, the Malaysian, Thai and Peruvian studies base their industrial strategies on natural resources. The assumption that what is needed is to 'identify' rather than 'choose' or 'create' appropriate industries is a crucial difference from the Colombian and Zimbabwe approach. Echavarria explicitly rejects the notion of static comparative advantage, arguing that 'future comparative advantages are acquired by present policies'. Robinson also emphasises, in his discussion of exporters' behaviour, the need to create the appropriate responses. The contrast should not be pushed too far. The Asian emphasis on natural resources includes looking for new uses and ways of marketing them. The Peruvian study emphasises new stages of production and markets for resource-based industry. All three stress encouraging or training potential exporters to find and develop resources effectively, while the searching for advantages by Colombia and Zimbabwe is subject to competitiveness. Nevertheless, the two approaches are representative of two different current approaches to trade.

One area for choice arises from the findings outlined in Chapter 9. That there are different patterns for Asian and Latin American exporters of manufactures and, for each, different patterns in the trade with different classes of customer countries, makes it clear that there is no simple definition or pattern of which industries are most appropriate for all developing countries, and that it is possible to exploit the existence of different commodity opportunities in different markets to change a country's aggregate commodity composition. Especially for the advanced sectors of manufactures, machinery and transport equipment, the major increases for the NICs came from industrial country markets. Further, the choice for exports need not be identical to that for all industry. Research on multinationals (which are responsible for, or involved in, a high proportion of these countries' trade in manufactures) suggests that, while they may differentiate among goods in choosing which to export from developing and which from industrial countries, they also differentiate within products between the quality necessary for domestic sales and those for export (to any market) (Page, 1986b). The labour (particularly skilled labour) and capital content of the 'same' product may therefore differ between markets even for the same producing country. There are thus a wide variety of possible interactions among the choices of specialisation available to a developing country.

The data on concentration in Chapter 9 indicate that widening the range of choice is characteristic of development. Kubo *et al.* found that

> The process of industrialization is associated with structural changes beyond a simple increase in the share of manufacturing in output. Changes in the structure of final demand, in international trade, and in the use of intermediate inputs all contribute to the evolution of an economy. Although some basic long-run forces are common to all countries, differences in initial conditions and in the choice of a development strategy affect how these three components interact and the rate at which the process unfolds. (Chenery *et al.*, 1986: 223)

If choices can be made, then criteria for choice are necessary. The substantial changes observed in structure, particularly the growth in exports in the categories previously most characteristic of industrial countries, and in intra-industry trade, are an indication of why the literature on revealed comparative advantage is even less useful in describing developing countries' trade patterns than it is for developed. The analytical content of comparative advantage comes from its focus on potential gains from trade: it is a criterion for choice between two (or more) possible changes to a country's existing pattern (or between the existing one and an alternative). In contrast, only if there is no potential gain can the present pattern 'reveal' comparative advantage, even with present resource endowments and industrial structure. If a country is not realising potential trade or industrial efficiency gains (for the reasons of inadequate response suggested in earlier chapters or because new opportunities have opened up), then its present pattern will only 'reveal' that lower-than-potential pattern. If it is expecting to change its structure because of growth or planning to change it to promote growth or some other objective, the present pattern is likely to be even less appropriate as a guide. The concept is an unsatisfactory way of evading the need to introduce analysis of production characteristics into choice of industrial strategy.

The more traditional and analytical approaches of trade theory ask what resources are abundant or scarce in the exporter and its potential customers, and suggest that allocation gains from trade can come from an appropriate choice of industry in the light of this analysis. For this to imply a change in structure, there must be an implicit assumption that the resources have changed or that existing opportunities are not already being correctly exploited. If the remedy is simply to respond to the changes or to remove obstacles, the analysis remains within economic choices. This is the approach behind support for resource-based trade, and fits with an interpretation of the NICs' success which stresses the role of policy in supplying information, credit and other prerequisites for efficient markets. But there remain considerable practical difficulties in a country which (by definition) is undergoing structural development.

One is to identify by means of economic analysis basically industrial characteristics. The broad range of possibilities of what can be considered 'resource-based' has already been discussed. The question of what is a resource is not unambiguous and fixed. A new resource can appear, either because of other exogenous changes or because of innovation in finding new uses. An existing resource can become more, or less, valuable for similar reasons. The potential for horticultural trade, for example, which appears to be an entirely 'resource-oriented' potential export for developing countries still wishing to specialise in primary production, is new because of changes in storage and transport technology and in demand patterns in high-income countries. These changes are at least in part the result of research and promotion by potential producers. The advantages of large supplies of unskilled labour in the electronics exports of South-East Asia depend on current patterns of demand and production methods, and also on product-development that took advantage of the labour supply once it had been identified. Different types of labour have corresponded to other products and production technologies in the past, and future shifts in demand (for example, to less standardised products or to services) could change the potential gains from this 'resource'. If structural change is being pursued for other reasons, as discussed in the first part of this chapter, all these judgements must be made in a way consistent with the evolution and achievement of the new pattern.

A second practical problem is forecasting the external influences on actual or potential resources, and seeing the results of a country's own structural changes. It is not possible to rely entirely on previous industrialising countries' experience, because not only the external conditions but also the domestic conditions are different. These include the existing industrial and other economic bases, which could affect the choice of model country, and the various general differences, of size, social characteristics or pressure groups, for example, discussed in Chapter 19. They also include the labour supply, both quantity and quality. The findings of other studies (e.g. Bradford, 1987b), that some countries with abundant natural resources did not go through a phase of exporting labour-intensive goods, are not surprising if labour is simply one natural resource which a country may or may not have in abundance, relative to others. The particular characteristics of labour in some South-East Asian countries – of abundance relative to other natural resources (and this includes countries where it was simply less scarce, such as Singapore), with a basic minimum of training (relative to most African countries) but low-cost (relative to countries where industry is longer established, for example in Latin America) – are unlikely to be generally available.

But if, as the country studies suggest, the problem is not exploiting or creating new opportunities but rather that potential gains from sectoral change or greater efficiency in sales or production within sectors exist but are not exploited, then the need is for a more fundamental type of development. Identifying the appropriate criteria for choice of industry cannot then be assumed to make implementing that choice automatic.

If the potential for structural change is introduced as a modification to analysis of present comparative advantage, it and the more choice- (or deliberate policy-) oriented view of trade come together. The findings (discussed in Chapter 17) that there may be common elements in a sequence of development, in particular that a 'substantial industrial base' (Kubo *et al.*, in Chenery *et al.*, 1986: 224) may be a precondition for exports of manufactures, are consistent with the emphasis in the Colombian study on creating conditions for future comparative advantage. The significance of the stock of capital and of certain types of infrastructural capital in increasing the potential for future industry is not a new idea. If this is extended (cf. UNCTAD, 1987: 127) to include 'knowledge accumulated or generated by individual enterprises through learning and experience, through acquisition from other enterprises or entities, and through R and D', and if the arguments presented in the earlier part of this chapter for expecting technology to be transmitted particularly strongly through expansion and diversification of manufacturing are accepted, this becomes another reason for seeing manufacturing as a part, not a result, of development.

The interesting question is not whether potential exports are fixed by comparative advantage or completely at the discretion of the country's planners, but how much weight choice should have and whether this is changing. The importance which the country papers (and previous research on the NICs) attach to creating an ability and a commitment to respond to export opportunities, at the firm and the national level, indicates the crucial role of attitude and initiative, and not simple availability to meet demand. If a product or industry attracts such characteristics, either through private initiative or because other government policy goals identify it as a priority area, this is itself an advantage. It may not be sufficient in a completely inappropriate industry to outweigh other disadvantages (steel in Malaysia) but it should be included in the balance (steel in Zimbabwe). The experiences of the NICs do show examples of industries that were not considered appropriate which have become competitive (steel in Brazil).

It is possible that we are now observing such a significant increase in the importance of high technology and differentiation in industrial goods, which implies a decrease in the share in their value accounted for by natural resources and unskilled labour, that the role of resource-based comparative advantage is being seriously weakened. It has been argued that this could reduce the role of developing countries generally in trade; what is more certain is that it could change their freedom to make choices.

It is clear that the question which this study asks, namely, which goods a country should concentrate on in the medium term, for exports or for import substitution, is not a trivial one to be answered by mechanical measures of revealed comparative advantage or alternatively by copying previous countries' choices. There is a real choice, which is bounded by the objectives and strategy of the country, the expectations of changes in national and external conditions, technical industrial characteristics and the country's resources. The choices made now will in turn affect the conditions for future decisions. Wrong choices certainly exist, but there may be more than one set of 'right' choices.

NOTES

1. In 1982 it was possible to write (Puyana, 1982: 274) that Latin American countries had 'abandoned the definition of industry as the strategic sector for development, to which end the remaining sectors should be adjusted. Today they are moving toward a more "classical" economy and seem more inclined to accept, in the international division of labor, their vocation as natural providers of primary materials, foodstuffs, and light manufactured goods.'
2. The latter can assume that domestic linkages are different from those to exports or imports by specifying or estimating different coefficients on inputs, but does not explain such differences.
3. The new primary exports do not appear to have this effect.

Table 13.1 Share of manufacturing in total output (percentages)

	1970	1980	1983/4
Newly industrialising countries			
Argentina	33	25	30
Brazil	24	26	26
Hong Kong	28	22	21
India	13	15	14
Mexico	24	23	24
Singapore	20	28	25
South Korea	21	28	28
Average	23	24	24
New NICs			
Colombia	16	17	17
Malaysia	12	21	21
Peru	24	28	25
Thailand	16	20	21
Zimbabwe	19	23	24
Average	17	22	22
Other middle-income countries			
Chile (83 est)	26	21	21
Costa Rica	18	19	23
Egypt	19	30	24
Ivory Coast	13	12	17
Kenya	11	11	11
Morocco (83 est)	16	17	17
Pakistan	15	16	18

Table 13.1 *Continued*

	1970	1980	1983/4
Philippines	23	24	25
Senegal	16	15	18
Sri Lanka	16	17	13
Tunisia	8	12	12
Uruguay	19	22	20
Venezuela	16	16	19
Average	17	18	18
Area averages			
Africa	15	17	18
Asia	18	21	21
Latin America	22	22	23
Average by group	19	21	21
Average by area	18	20	20
Germany	41	37	36
Japan	36	30	30
UK	28	24	22
USA	26	23	22
UNCTAD categories			
Developed	30	27	25
Developing	18	18	18
America	23	24	23
Africa	10	8	10
North Africa	13	9	11
Other	8	8	9
Asia	15	16	16
S. and S.E.	16	21	21
Major exp. mfrs	26	27	26

Sources: UNCTAD, *Handbook of International Trade and Development Statistics*; national sources.

14

FINANCING AND INVESTMENT

THE ROLE OF EXTERNAL FINANCE

The quantity and forms of external finance available for the non-oil developing countries have suffered changes in the 1970s and since 1982 at least as significant as those in trade, and there are strong reasons for expecting that if more 'normal' conditions now follow, they will be different from those of the 1970s. The reduction in the total supply of new finance, present and projected, will be the major influence on their growth as a group. Combined with the rise in interest rates, this has sharply reduced the ability to finance trade deficits: for all non-oil developing countries, the trade deficit fell from an average of around $60bn in 1978–82 to about $20bn by 1984 (see Table 14.1) and they were in surplus in 1987. The change was smallest for Asia but there was a clear break in the previous trend. This was also true for Africa, although with a larger fall. The main change was for Latin America which accounted for $30bn of the change, and which moved from an external savings contribution of about $10bn to a transfer of domestic savings abroad of over $20bn.

The share of imports financed by exports which had remained at about three-quarters during most of the 1970s, even with the impact of the oil price rise, started to rise in 1982 and reached 90% by 1984–5. Here there is a sharp contrast between Asia and Latin America: for Asia, the ratio had started to rise in the early 1970s, and it has fluctuated around 100 for the last ten years. In contrast, Latin America had been able to reduce the ratio through borrowing during the mid-1970s, but the shift to repayment can be seen in the rise above 100 since 1983. For both areas (in aggregate) external finance is no longer making a contribution to total savings.

The change in the types of finance available implies a change in its destinations, so that the effects of the reduction are unevenly distributed among countries. It may also require changes in the pattern of development or institutional organisation within economies to fit the objectives and methods of the remaining providers of finance.

The criteria for how much and what types of external finance developing countries should use are not well established. The question of whether it should be treated as different from other forms of savings is frequently dealt with in terms of the relevance of so-called 'two-gap' models. The issues raised by these (which have been used in some of the country studies) are discussed in Chapter 16 on the special role of an external strategy; the arguments are based on whether there are types of investment or capital good which specifically require external financing. But there are other reasons for treating external finance separately from other saving. The obvious one, that it is (normally) denominated in foreign currency, is crucial in a period of large changes (and fluctuations) in exchange rates. It may have particular costs to an economy because the forms (loans or investment by multinationals, for example) in which it is available are different from those of domestic capital (perhaps deposits or taxes). The financial costs may be dependent on the conditions in industrial countries (monetary stringency or expectations of profit) and variable, and there may be non-financial conditions attached to it (loans from official lenders or private investment).

The costs will be different for different countries because in practice different forms are available to different countries: in principle, official flows on non-commercial terms to the poorest; more costly official flows to the less poor; private flows on normal commercial terms to the most advanced. Particular economic and political conditions, and past histories, mean that what is actually available for a given country may be very different from any of these, and changes in the supply of the various forms have moved the boundaries between the country groupings sharply in the last 15 years. The position of countries which are in transition from one category to another is particularly uncertain. The costs must, therefore, be compared to the general benefits, in so far as the finance adds to the supply of saving and permits increased investment, but also to any special benefits of the different forms of foreign capital.

There are various reasons for expecting developing countries to make use of external financing which have different implications for the most suitable amounts or forms. On a non-economic or welfare-economic basis, it can be argued that transfers of resources to other countries are desirable simply because they are poorer or because their poverty suggests that the marginal utility gained from the resources transferred will be greater than the loss in the donor country. The countries in this study have passed the point at which they can expect aid as relief for 'the poorest', but they could still expect assistance to permit them to grow more rapidly relative to their trading partners than they could using only their own resources for investment. In addition to a direct need for extra savings, they may need external finance to compensate for the balance of payments effects of relatively fast growth, and to compensate for their disadvantage if they are expected to suffer a fall in their terms of trade for structural reasons. These arguments all suggest a long-term transfer of resources, with only limited opportunities for capturable private direct returns to the flows; investment in infrastructure could provide a return, but only at aggregate level.

Any country may need temporary external finance to give it the liquidity to absorb short-term fluctuations in revenues and payments. Developing countries may need more than industrial countries if the fluctuations are greater, or because they are poorer and therefore less able to cope with change from their own resources. If they are to be encouraged to concentrate on long-term development by shielding them from the impact of temporary cycles in the developed countries (the conventional assumption of the 1960s and 1970s before adjustment, and the ability to adjust, became objectives), they may require more medium-term finance for this purpose. This can be treated as potentially repayable (subject to the usual doubts about distinguishing trends from fluctuations), although again probably on a national rather than project basis.

If their faster growth or relative scarcity of capital raises the return on capital above that in industrial countries, there are clear efficiency and allocation benefits from investing in them. Lack of information or preference for familiar customers may discourage this, effectively constituting barriers to entry.

The role of public sector finance is clearly greatest for poverty-motivated flows and that of the private sector for identifiable high-return opportunities. If the long-term returns are high enough, and alternative investment returns low enough, there can be a role for the private sector in development finance, and, depending on the length of the cycles and the nature and imperfections of the capital markets, the private sector can provide finance for fluctuations.

The existence of imperfections in capital markets and of limits on public sector allocations, however, means that the supply of funds may be wrong, not merely in total, but in the proportions suitable for any of these purposes, and it may vary over time for reasons unconnected with conditions in the developing countries. They may, therefore, need to adapt to changes in the supply unrelated to their needs, or to use resources suitable for one purpose for another. Countries' own attitudes to the proper roles of public and private finance within their economies will also make finding a satisfactory match between demand and supply more difficult. The long-term nature of development and even the 'medium-term' duration of a cycle, such as the oil price rise of the 1970s or the depression of the 1980s, means that changes in what is available may occur in the middle of a country's need of a particular form of finance.

Some changes have increased the flows to the developing countries, at least as a group. There was a shift in the late 1950s or early 1960s to regarding the first two types of transfer, aid to the poor or for development, as normal.

Previous relationships with the independent developing countries had been mainly commercially-based, and to a great extent this was true also with the colonies in the 1950s (Clark, 1981: 84). There has been growing acceptance of some forms of finance for fluctuations caused by changes in agricultural prices or supply.

The establishment of the International Monetary Fund in the 1940s marked acceptance of the international need for smoothing more general types of fluctuation, but until recently there was no presumption that the costs of adjustment to fluctuations were greater for the developing countries and no provision for medium-term fluctuations.[1] Even these positive changes had adjustment costs for individual developing countries in adapting their domestic institutions and policies to meet the criteria and forms required by donors or lenders. The changes that occurred after 1973 and particularly after 1982 have involved cuts as well as reallocations of finance, with more serious effects on developing countries.

The much more general access to a new form of finance, commercial bank lending, in the 1970s, coincided with a substantial increase in investment in developing countries as a group. In the 1960s (IMF, 1985b: 190-3), external financing accounted for about 10% of gross investment, rising to 12% by 1967-72. Between 1974 and 1981, it rose to over 16%. Total investment in these countries rose from 20% of GDP in the 1960s to more than 25%. The extra external financing was thus equivalent to about 40% of the rise in investment. By 1984, both ratios had fallen back to their pre-1970 level. The Inter-American Development Bank (1987: 23) argues that the access to bank finance was a 'key factor' in raising the investment rate in Latin America from 19% of GDP in the 1960s to 23% in the 1970s, and the loss of access helps to explain the fall to 16% in 1984-6, when Latin America had moved into trade surplus (see Table 14.1).

THE CRUCIAL DIFFERENCES AMONG THE DIFFERENT FORMS

The flows available to developing countries differ in several characteristics relevant to a choice of external strategy, including how far they are exogenous rather than demand-driven, how far their use is under recipient control or directed by the lender or donor, whether they go to the public or private sector, and which industrial or other uses they can finance, as well as their financial conditions, cost and other terms.

Official flows, including grants and loans, have been seen by their recipients as relatively low-cost, with low interest rates, often fixed rather than variable, and frequently relatively long term, but subject to heavy (and probably increasing) conditionality on their use. They are basically determined from outside but (except in cases of political pressures) fairly stable.

Direct investment[2] is also normally long-term and stable, and although its cost is likely to be higher than official flows, this is tied to the outcome of the investment, which reduces the risk of exogenous changes. It has, however, additional costs and benefits which may impinge on government targets other than growth and financing. It is effectively entirely under the control of outside decision-makers and therefore offers little opportunity for sectoral control by the recipient. It is usually directed to the private sector in the recipient country. This means that the effects of an increase in its share of the total on both the sectoral development of a country and its general economic structure may be greater than for any other form of external finance.

The sectoral effects, and also its contribution to technology and development of the labour force, may interact with other goals of the host government. Contribution to general technology, as discussed in Chapter 13, comes from the type of product produced and the need to meet standard quality criteria. The view that investors produce simpler products in developing countries because of the lower levels of income does not appear to be supported by the evidence, at least for middle-income countries. While the market for advanced goods may be relatively smaller, it is in such products that foreign companies see their advantage over domestic producers. They would reject making a lower quality in order to protect their international reputation. Once the early stages of import-substituting industrialisation are passed, foreign investment in manufacturing is most frequently found in electrical and electronics products, or other high value-added consumer or engineering goods, roughly corresponding to the more advanced sectors whose importance was found to increase with level of development.

The type of company that makes foreign investments is not a typical industrial country company. Most investment is by a few large, technically advanced, by definition internationally-oriented, companies. This means that they are more likely to have access to high technology and to export markets than the average company in either their own or the host country.

The issue of transfer of more specific technology is difficult to consider at an aggregate level. As most companies explicitly see technology, and in some cases marketing, as being their principal advantage in and contribution to another country, it must be assumed, in most cases, that direct investment is more than an inflow of external saving. It appears to be difficult to produce new products still under development at a distance from where design is taking place, and this is normally the home country. Some very specialised and consumer-specific products may be difficult to produce abroad. For most companies, the technology eventually exported is the most recent fully developed. Because of cost and quality criteria, and the informed demand from developing country markets, it is not normal to use older technologies (although a few examples of deliberate hoarding of technology can be found). Slower growth or smaller markets may, however, make replacement investment less frequent and most new development takes place in the home country. The average level of technology may therefore be below that in the developed country, but the lag is strictly limited. Developing countries' access to a choice among multinationals further limits companies' freedom to offer lower technology. This could change if changes in technology are tending to increase the proportion of products falling into the very specialised category; some electronics companies do see this as a trend.

Although investment is increasingly discussed in terms of the capital needs of the developing countries, and seen as a form of financing, it is unlike either official flows or the developing country-initiated bank borrowing discussed below, in that the quantities and directions are decided on the basis of commercially-based judgements of specific opportunities, and not on the needs or policies of the countries as a whole. There is therefore no reason to expect its movements to correspond to the overall balance of payments changes of recipient countries. The questions of what does motivate it and whether it lies at all within the control of recipient countries have therefore become of serious concern.

It has become conventional in recent studies to distinguish among three motives for foreign investment: to develop (and normally export, with or without some processing) a natural resource; to meet local market demand; or to use a developing country's labour resources to produce more cheaply goods for a company's home (or other developed economy) market. In practice, these three are not as sharply distinguished by companies as by analysts. The third should probably in fact be considered an aspect of the first, as large supplies of cheap labour are not a characteristic of all developing countries, and are an exhaustible resource.

Most investment is either in natural resources, or to meet local demand. For the major foreign investor of the last 15 years, the United States, most investment in developing countries has been in chemicals, transport equipment and minor industries in Latin America, while machinery was important in Asia. For Japan, metals have been important in Asia and Latin America, with textiles and chemicals also important in Asia. (The UK, with a declining share in investment, has been more concentrated than the other countries in non-manufactures and, within manufactures, in food.)

Most investors are at least potentially interested in both the local market and exports, although the increased tendency to look at the costs and returns to individual activities of a firm may have increased the opportunities perceived for the third, cost-reducing type of investment in recent years. The characteristics of a country that attract foreign investors have therefore to be looked at against both criteria together. It is not possible to assume that production for a company's home markets can be attracted by quite low labour costs, while investment to satisfy the host market requires relatively high incomes to provide the market. The latter is more important. Even when making investments for one motive, companies normally consider the prospects for others, as a possible precaution against risk, and they use their position within a country to look for further opportunities. This is particularly true for countries where investors believe that the most important import-substitution opportunities have already been exploited (and they would agree with the country studies that these include the countries discussed here). While they would make an investment initially for the domestic market, some possibility of exports in the longer term is likely to be required.

Once an investment has been made, companies are reluctant to withdraw from a country completely, even if current returns would no longer justify new investment. They would lose their position within the country. Most companies choose countries for the long-term characteristics of the economy as a whole, not merely the particular opportunity in which they invest, and these change infrequently. These explanations are closely tied to the importance of familiarity with a country in making investment decisions. Initially, this may be gained from exporting to the country. It reduces the appraisal costs of a new or additional investment. It may also reduce running costs, if it includes knowledge of how to deal with local private and governmental institutions and acquiring appropriate contacts. It can extend to familiarity with a country physically close to the location of an existing investment. It also appears to be the case generally that companies' criteria for reinvestment of profits are less strict, and more open to local initiative, than for new investment, so that expansion of an existing operation is easier than new establishment.

All these arguments mean that the number of countries which existing foreign investors even consider as possibilities for new investment is in practice extremely limited and rarely changes. Those with real prospects of attracting significant amounts number under ten. In the survey of investors in Colombia, Peru, Malaysia and Thailand, the only countries mentioned (other than the ones they were already in) were Malaysia and Thailand, Singapore, seen as the ideal model by most investors, Taiwan, South Korea and Hong Kong (in the short term), and Brazil and Mexico (only by investors already in Latin America). India, China and Bangladesh received isolated mentions.

Because of the experience and size of the companies that account for most foreign investment, they do make their own decisions about individual investments and about the long-term conditions of the countries. Evidence on their expectations shows informed differences of opinion. The economic characteristics most often mentioned by the survey of foreign investors included factors directly affecting the investment such as infrastructure, labour supply and cost, and trade policy, and general characteristics such as the size of the market, its recent and expected performance and the structure of the economy, both domestic and external. Both the aggregate income and income levels per capita were considered important in countries of the size of the new NICs, and the former was one reason that only projects with an export potential were considered. For some investors, even small countries with good export prospects could be 'too small' to consider because of the high fixed costs of making the initial appraisal.

The size of the agricultural sector was one aspect taken into account, although some considered a large agricultural sector to be evidence of social stability and others emphasised its economic vulnerability. The size and maturity of industrial sectors were also ambiguous in their impact: infrastructure (and an experienced labour force) were an advantage, although not essential, but maturity could mean rigidities and more regulation.

Foreign investors when interviewed have strong views about the political and social characteristics that are desirable, but these are not correlated precisely with the current conditions in the countries in which they invest. This is partly because of the dominance of long-term over short-term considerations, partly because familiarity with a country appears to increase tolerance of problems that would inhibit a new investment, and partly because of a preference (especially on the part of US and UK investors) for giving most weight to economic factors; investors consider themselves most competent to assess these. German and Japanese investors put more weight on other factors and this could lead to changes in the direction of investment as the latter's share in the total is rising. The importance of ability to export implies that the prospects of a country's neighbours are also a significant but uncontrollable factor in influencing foreign investment.

The implication of these criteria is that foreign investment will tend to go to established recipient countries, but for these it will be a relatively stable flow rather than an economic response to changes in the conditions or medium-term prospects of the country. This suggests that investment flows may in many cases be an inadequate way of exploiting the possible higher returns to capital in developing countries (suggested above as suitable for private financing).

The data in Table 14.2 are consistent with a strong effect of these motives in contributing to stability and concentration of foreign investment. In the past, the more long-standing economic development of Latin America and its proximity to the major foreign investor gave it the highest share of foreign investment (two-thirds in 1969-73). This share fell in the latter 1970s, but has only fallen to below a half since 1983. Most goes to the NICs. But more detailed examination shows that a few countries account for almost all the investment and explain the apparent area and group changes. Until 1983, Brazil and Mexico dominated the total. Although their share fell from 60%, it was still 40% in the 1979-83 period. Singapore and Malaysia account for another 20-25% of the total. The only other countries which have had shares of more than 5% (excluding temporary fluctuations) have been Argentina, Hong Kong and Egypt.

A few other countries have shown some ability to increase their share during this period, including Thailand and Colombia, and perhaps Tunisia. The importance of experience in and performance by neighbouring countries tends to favour Asian countries, with some prospects in the medium term for Latin American, but much less for African countries.

The limited number of countries which both the survey evidence and data on past investment suggest can attract investment implies that there must be considerable caution about the prospects for success in spreading investment to new countries. Government policy can take advantage of some of the characteristic motives, for example, by making access to domestic markets dependent on export performance or (the most important factor mentioned by foreign investors) protecting the domestic market. Even investors planning to export consider this important in the short run while they are establishing production. Among the improvements to infrastructure which can be effective, and less costly than physical investment, may be legislation on protection of technology (patent and copyright law). Lack of such protection clearly inhibits investment specifically in software development, which was mentioned as one of the possible new areas of investment, and has deterred technology transfers. More general incentives such as tax privileges were not seen as important by most investors (except as indications of a favourable attitude). The inertia of investors suggests that tax incentives for keeping investment in a country are likely to be less necessary than for attracting it, at which point they may turn the balance. Easing administrative and regulatory systems which affect the operating managers who make the decisions on reinvestment may be more effective. But overall, the evidence is that a country's long-term stability and medium-term economic performance are the important determinants of new investment, in addition to existing investment.

In the late 1960s and early 1970s, there was a move into *commercial bank finance* partly because of the inadequate levels of aid flows, but also because bank loans are seen as avoiding some of the disadvantages of aid on the one hand, and investment on the other. Bank lenders imposed less strict conditions or supervision of projects or general policy than official lenders, thus reducing the costs of adjustment and some of the indirect servicing costs. In contrast to direct investment, the finance went to the government which could then allocate it in accordance with its priorities. At the time, direct investment and bank borrowing were seen as complementary. Much of the direct investment that occurred was also financed by bank lending: companies as well as countries were looking for alternative forms of investment which separated the capital-supplying function of foreign investment from that of technology and management. The low level of real interest rates at the time also altered the balance of choice between equity and loans.

Particularly after 1973, bank lending was, at least for relatively advanced developing countries, available almost on demand. Because it could arise at the initiative of the borrower, it was not restricted to traditional recipients and, as new lenders, banks were more ready to consider new clients. As real interest rates fell in the late 1970s, it became suitable even for long-term development finance, on the criteria discussed above. This view ignored the problem that these rates were variable. They had no direct relationship with the actual or expected rate of return on the investments which they financed, and therefore the ability to service the debt was subject to two uncertainties: the outcome of the investment and financial terms in the industrial countries. The risks of instability of supply were also probably underestimated because this kind of finance was an unfamiliar flow. There was also a failure to realise that the banks' more arm's-length approach, which permitted them to lend to a large number of countries without detailed knowledge of individual borrowers and with fewer conditions than either public lenders or direct investors, meant that risks were also treated on an aggregate basis, by area or even for 'sovereign countries' in relation to other types of borrowers. Therefore, stability of flows to individual borrowers depended not only on their own performance but on that of all others in their area or classification, thus increasing the uncontrollable external uncertainties.

HOW THE DIFFERENT TYPES WERE USED, 1970–85

Table 14.3 shows the principal types of finance used by all developing countries.[3] Bilateral aid tended to cover the major part of the deficit of developing countries before 1973, and if OPEC aid is added, this remained true until 1977. It then fell sharply, to between a quarter and a third in 1980–2, but by 1985 the contraction in the deficit meant that it was roughly equal to it. The reason for the fall was the failure of aid to expand as rapidly as developing countries' imports.[4] Even including OPEC aid, the real value was almost unchanged between 1970 and 1980 (or 1984), although there was a rise in 1985. Flows from the World Bank and the IMF have risen much more, although not by enough to raise total official finance to its share in financing before 1973.

Direct investment could have been depressed, like national investment in industrial countries, by the low level of demand and capacity utilisation, but until 1981 it kept pace with the growth in bilateral official flows, although, like them, it covered a falling share of the total current balance. (This and the private financial flows columns of Table 14.3 are in net terms; the public sector ones are published in gross terms.) It did fall in 1983, but only from the exceptionally high levels of 1981–2, and the inflows since then have been at or above the 1980 level.

The major part of the extra financing needed during this period came from the banks, using international medium-term loans (Tables 14.3 and 14.4). In the early 1970s, private lending was at a level similar to that of the bilateral flows or direct investment. By 1976 it was the major source of finance, and remained so until 1982, although from 1978 (Table 14.3) a major part of new lending was accounted for by refinancing past debts. In 1983, following the first stages of the debt crisis, it contracted sharply, and has fallen in each year since then. In 1981–2 and 1985, there were rises in the use of bond finance, and in 1986 this remained important relative to the depressed level of bank loans, but, overall, bonds were of minor importance.

The change in the composition of financing is shown clearly in the measure of the 'grant element' of total lending to developing countries (which takes account of the degree of concessionality of the terms of the loans).This declined in the 1970s as private finance increased its share in the total, and effectively disappeared in the peak years, but rose sharply in 1985 when bank financing fell significantly below public finance. Interest payments on private loans have risen, with the level of debt and with the rise in interest rates (see Table 14.5). Compared with capital inflows and the trade balance, they first became a conspicuous cost in the late 1970s; by 1983 they exceeded new net inflows; and by 1984–5 they more than accounted for the deficit on current payments.

The remaining columns of Table 14.3 show the conventional forms of short-term adjustment finance: use of a country's own reserves and use of IMF credits. Although for individual countries reserves have been an important response to unexpected changes, taken overall this cannot easily be seen. This is a pointer to what will become obvious in examining the individual countries: they have faced financing crises at various times, aggravated by, but not necessarily simultaneous with, those found by looking at developing countries as a group or at the major countries. The use of IMF credits does correspond more closely to the periods when there have been unanticipated increases in deficits: in 1974–6, with repayment following shortly after; then in 1981–3; again the flows of the years following show the effects of repayments by the first borrowers, although the increase in total IMF funding permitted continued net lending until 1986.

How developing countries responded to the financing needs of the 1970s is relevant to analysing their future prospects, first, because the consequences have important effects on the present positions of many of the countries; second, because it illustrates the risks of making incorrect assumptions about the external sector; and finally, because countries' own experience at that time and their interpretation of other countries' experiences are an important influence on their choices of strategies for the future.

In the 1970s, the export volume of non-oil developing countries rose by about 5.5% a year, about one point faster than in the 1960s. Import volume rose by about 4% p.a. in both periods. Between 1980 and 1985, export volume rose by 7–8% while imports rose by about 1%. For the period of the major rise in the current deficit, 1973–81, export volume rose at a rate of 4.8% and imports at 3.5%. The increased need for financing, in aggregate, was therefore more than accounted for by the downward shift in the terms of trade (the rise in the oil price) whether or not the period of the rise in other commodity prices and high inflation of the early 1970s is included in the comparison. Export performance was not worse than before and imports did not expand more rapidly. The composite measure of the purchasing power of exports (changes in export volume adjusted for the terms of trade) developed by UNCTAD shows the constraint imposed by the terms of trade on imports, and therefore on growth, starkly: it rose by 4% in 1960–8, then by 9% to 1973, and by less than 2% for the rest of the 1970s. Over the whole period 1970–85 it rose at 4% p.a. There were, therefore, two financing problems: long-term, the average rise was too low to permit the volume of imports to expand even as rapidly as target rates of output growth (6%); and short-term, there were sharp changes in the rate at which it rose which, without compensatory finance, would have required corresponding changes in growth rates.

From 1973 to 1981 the developing countries were faced with the problem of first, correctly identifying the nature of the oil price rise as temporary or permanent; then, choosing whether to adjust to it by altering the rest of their external balance appropriately (increasing exports or reducing other imports) or to finance a deficit. In considering the feasibility of each option, they had to make assumptions about the response of the industrial countries, as export markets and as suppliers of their finance, to the same questions. Given their judgements on all these, they then had to reconcile their desired response with the largely exogenously determined supplies of total finance and the different forms.

If the shift in the terms of trade was temporary and reversible, as commodity price fluctuations had proved to be in the past, a temporary and repayable form of finance (a loan, with as low an interest rate and as few conditions as available) could be appropriate. If it was not expected to be reversed but was expected to be temporary (the belief that the oil price would be eroded by inflation and weakening of the cartel, but that the early 1970s level had been as low as could reasonably be expected), then a temporary increase in non-repayable transfers to the developing countries with or without some temporary adjustment on their part would be the correct response; it would be important not to create obstacles to a return to a 'normal' path when the oil price returned to 'normal'. If the rise was a permanent step-change in the terms of trade, there was a need for a permanent new flow of financing.[5] In all cases, adjustment, with real income costs, in the developing countries was a possible alternative to financing; in the last case, this might be eased by short-term finance to slow the adjustment. Adjustment would avoid the financial costs attached to any financing option, and the financial risks of making the wrong judgement. It would have severe real costs, and would have been inconsistent with the view held then that developing countries should follow a long-term path, and be helped to avoid (or compensated for) exogenous shocks. It could have effects on the level of capital accumulation, extending beyond the period of the terms-of-trade crisis.

There was an additional difficulty. Finding new financing methods for countries in temporary or medium-term trade disequilibrium in order to permit orderly adjustment to permanent changes and to avoid (or damp down) the transmission of temporary fluctuations in the trade balance to domestic economies, and redefining the criteria for deciding which countries should adjust in various circumstances, were already among the priorities of the attempt to reform the international monetary system that was under way at the end of 1973. The moves to reform had been prompted by growing dissatisfaction at the inflexibility of the fixed exchange rates and limited provision for temporary finance of the 'Bretton Woods' system, ending in the breakdown of fixed exchange rates first to frequent devaluations, culminating in that of the dollar in August 1971, then to floating rates in 1972–3. The problem of large imbalances among the industrial countries was starting to appear endemic. If the concern over existing methods of financing or resolving imbalances was justified, about which there is little dispute, then the oil price rise came at a time when the system was particularly ill-adapted to find and implement a proper solution to the medium-term problems which it posed.[6]

Most analysis in 1974 correctly (as it appears in 1988) assumed the second case: a temporary rise in oil producers' terms of trade which would be eroded but not reversed. As the OPEC producers were assumed to be unable to increase their spending on imports as rapidly as their income, the assumption was that they would have a surplus available to finance developed or developing country oil-consumers' deficits. Then, even before the terms of trade were returned to normal, pre-1973, levels, their imports would rise (adjustment through exports would take place in the consuming countries) sufficiently to restore trade equilibrium. If the investments the oil producers had made in the interim (directly or through the alternative 'recycling' mechanisms by financial institutions), were productive, servicing them would not impose a continuing net burden on the economies of the borrowing countries, although the rise in exports would be a one-off loss.

Most of the developed countries, however, adjusted their demand downwards at the time of the first oil price rise to eliminate their new deficits as quickly as possible. Following the second price rise, the developed country response was more general and more rapid because of the difficulties incurred by those that did not adjust in the first period. This made adjustment by the developing countries more costly, as their traditional export markets were growing less than normal, and the potential returns to new investment were lower, but it also meant that a higher than expected share of the OPEC surplus was available to finance slow adjustment, or perhaps to avoid it altogether. The unexpectedly rapid rise in the oil producers' imports reduced the financing problem, although increasing the short-term transfers to them.

The initial reaction was that the decisions on how long it would be acceptable to prolong developing countries' adjustment and on the allocation of the finance to permit this should be controlled by the major countries and by the international organisations which had been set up to deal with international adjustment. This did not happen, principally because of the decision of the oil producers not to 'recycle' their surplus through the multilateral agencies or through official loans to the major countries, but to use commercial banks and direct loans to deficit countries. There was no mechanism for regulation by the official decision-makers of the 'recycling' of the funds deposited in the commercial banks, and the preferences of OPEC as lenders would have precluded any such attempt.[7]

The result was that the only new source of finance available was OPEC's preferred asset: arm's-length liquid deposits. This would have been appropriate to the needs of the developing countries (and to the normal role of commercial banks) only if the oil price rise had proved to correspond to the first case, namely a temporary and reversible change in the terms of trade, which would have permitted repayment of the loans following the completion of the cycle. The deficit countries had to decide if the costs of using the 'wrong' form of finance were less than those of making the 'wrong' response, namely of making a real adjustment and harming long-term development in response to a temporary, second-case, difficulty. The data in Table 14.3 suggest that most chose bank financing, although as the analysis of individual countries will show, the actual shifts among different forms by different countries were complex. In most cases they used it only for the medium-term (roughly five-year) period appropriate for a temporary shift, not as a new source of long-term finance.

LONG-TERM CONSEQUENCES OF THE 1970S FINANCING STRATEGY

The way in which the 1970s deficits were financed, the use of commercial finance at variable interest rates, failed to meet the criterion of avoiding a continuing burden. It left a major cost on developing country payments which increased the need for external financing in the future. By the end of the period, interest payments were a major part of the current deficit, and thus even the average apparent increase in purchasing power of 4% over the period was severely reduced. Interest payments rose from about 0.5% of GDP in the first half of the 1970s to 1% by 1979 (Table 14.5). By 1985, they had doubled again to over 2%, and current projections (summarised in Page, 1987) are for the ratio to remain at about 2.5% for the medium term. Relative to exports, the ratios have risen from about 3% to 10%.[8] The effect of this is to increase the need for imports or exports to adjust to any change in external conditions, because this proportion of external payments is now fixed (it is completely inelastic to relative price changes or exchange-rate changes).[9]

The rise has affected countries at all levels of development: there is a difference between the Asian countries and the rest, but even for them, a doubling in the 1970s, followed by a further near doubling in the five years to 1985 to 2% of GDP is unprecedented. The Latin American increase was to 4.7% for the countries in this sample or 3.8% for the World Bank's measure of all Latin American countries, from a similar initial level. The African countries had an intermediate rise, to over 3%. It is notable that for all groups (and almost all countries) the increase in the five years 1980–5 was the largest, whether compared to GDP or exports: although individual circumstances and policies were important, as shown in Chapter 15, there is no question that there is also a general change. A comparison of individual countries shows that the area differences are characteristic, not statistical accidents, except in the group of new NICs which includes one of the highest Asian ratios, for Malaysia. The Philippines, which could be considered to fall into the same category, has an even higher ratio on the export measure. Among the NICs, the highest ratios and increases are for Argentina, Brazil and Mexico, and among the 'others' for Costa Rica and Uruguay, but also for some African countries, including the Ivory Coast and Morocco. South Korea, although it has a high ratio for an Asian country, is one of the few to show a smaller increase in the last five years than in 1975–80.

These data suggest that the problem of a heavy continuing cost of servicing past borrowing goes very far down the income level, to countries at all stages of development. The new NICs and the other middle-income countries have ratios now as high as the NICs; this means that the former have a severe fixed burden on their external payments which the latter did not have at similar levels of development. This affects the willingness of lenders to increase lending exposure, but also that of countries to increase their liabilities. The country studies show clearly that policy-makers are much more conscious of the costs of borrowing. A borrower in the early 1970s[10] who could have made reasonable estimates of normal loan-servicing costs would have found only one or two countries with a ratio as high as 2% of GDP, or 10% of exports. The averages are now above these; the range goes over 5% of GDP, with several countries making payments of more than a quarter of exports. The increases in the five years to 1985 show how rapidly a country's situation can deteriorate.

For the non-oil developing countries as a group, the crisis in financing in the early 1980s arose partly out of the direct impact of the unforeseen recession on external trade and on views about future trade prospects, but also from the strains caused by the mismatch between the types of finance needed and those available. The reversal in the terms of trade in favour of non-oil developing countries which would have permitted repayment did not happen (instead, the recession imposed a further deterioration). The need to maintain and roll over an increasing quantity of nominally medium-term debt increased countries' external vulnerability to changes in financial markets. Two major changes in these in the 1980s, namely, the sharp falls in new supplies of funds and the rises in interest rates, helped to make it essential to look again at the problem of finding an external financing strategy.

The stagnation of export revenues in the 1980s reduced the ability of the borrowing countries to increase their debt-servicing costs precisely at a time when they had recently increased their level of debt because of the second rise in oil prices and when interest rates were high and (in real terms) rising. The loss of confidence in future growth rates of trade reduced the expected rate of return on past as well as potential investments, and therefore lowered their appropriate level of indebtedness, making it more difficult or impossible to justify new borrowing as an alternative to adjustment, on the criteria suggested above. The banks were faced with a new, and much lower, assessment of the appropriate share of the developing countries in their lending, by criteria of the absolute or relative rates of return which such loans could attract and the security of their prospects, and simultaneously with declining new deposits from OPEC (as their surplus fell) which reduced their total supply of funds. The difference between official. and bank lending, namely, that the banks did not regard lending-on the OPEC funds to developing countries as in any way different from other lending, and therefore were not willing (without compulsion) to continue it when it ceased to offer an acceptable return and level of risk, became important for the first time. The fact that banks (more than private direct investors) treated 'country-lending' as a category where risks in one country affected assessments of others also became evident. The costs of using an 'unsuitable' form of deficit financing thus increased significantly.

There was, overall, a contraction in world savings ratios as the OPEC surplus declined, raising real interest rates to 4–5%, not merely above the 1970s level of around 0 but above the 1950s–1960s level of 2%.[11] The way in which this crisis has been managed is not the subject of the present study, but it is necessary to note how what has been done or the way in which it has been done could have long-term effects.

The cost of servicing past financing increases the need for finance, but it also means that the cost of such new finance is treated as a much more important constraint than it was in the past, and the risks of instability of costs, in particular from the variable interest rates on bank lending, are now seen as a much greater risk than was true in the past (see Table 14.6). The banks' perceptions of risks and costs have been similarly altered, and a higher expected return is therefore likely to be required, relative to other possible lending, to compensate for higher perceived risks of non-repayment (including delayed payments) and lower effective liquidity. The involuntary reschedulings required of them since 1982 mean that medium-term lending has the new risk of proving to be unintended long-term lending.

Even at the end of the 1970s, before 1982, there was a reduction in lending by the principal continental European countries (which had about 40% of the total in 1978 but just over 30% by mid-1983) and an increase in the shares of the United States and United Kingdom, as these continued lending. This shift has probably continued in the rescheduling since then. One result is that the latter countries have dominated the renegotiations of debt, and the types of arrangement applied. Their banking systems and regulations have affected the nature of the process, and their views on appropriate policies have affected the types of solutions considered. The possible (not yet in 1988 actual) increase in Japanese banks' role could alter this share. Borrowers may see risks in this vulnerability to the views of particular creditors as an element in borrowing decisions (as it was in their choice of banks over official lenders in 1974–5).

The role of official lenders has increased not merely in quantity and share, as discussed above, but because of their role in co-ordinating their and the banks' response to debtors in difficulties. They took on (at least from 1982 to 1986) the role that they had been unable to sustain in 1974–6 of directing the allocation of all types of flows, and establishing conditions for their use. The bank lending that was recorded after 1983 was largely in response to official pressure or subject to countries' accepting official conditions. This type of lending is therefore no longer as different in its conditions from official finance as it was in the 1970s. Even a transition back to private flows, therefore, would imply differences in the nature of financing from that of the 1970s.

FINANCING PROSPECTS

The margins of error for historic series of deficits and capital flows make attempts at forecasts even of broad orders of magnitude hazardous. The ability of countries to attract different types of financing varies widely, and the ability of those providing the flows to alter the total quantities and the allocation of flows from year to year and from country to country is much greater than the plausible range of outcomes of a trade or output forecast. Nevertheless, some view must be taken of the direction of changes, in totals and in the components, as a background for looking realistically at possible financing strategies. A rise in the oil price like that in 1974 or 1979–80 is not forecast (see Chapter 2), so that a sudden change in international savings rates is not expected. Alterations in the major countries' balances among each other could have effects on the rest of the world, but the forecasts that are now most generally accepted do not assume any major changes.

The prospects for bilateral and multilateral official flows do not suggest any large changes in the 1990s. The low performance of OECD flows in the 1970s and 1980s and the declining ability to increase spending on development assistance on the part of the OPEC countries could suggest a lower outcome, but the rise in multilateral programmes could compensate for this.

On the basis of the 1987 forecasts by the IMF and World Bank, it seemed reasonable to expect all official flows to rise by under 5%, about in line with past growth rates, although this may prove optimistic. The concern of developing countries over their levels of indebtedness, however, may be restricting their willingness to use even concessional finance. As was seen in Table 14.5, even the lower middle-income countries have seen their interest payments rise to levels that would have been high for a NIC in the early1970s; for the poorest countries even concessional interest rates and loan terms become heavier burdens in the face of falling prices and volume for exports. Increased use of official flows could be constrained on the demand as well as the supply side.

Slow growth in general and the absence of good trading prospects for the developing countries suggest that there is no reason to expect returns to investment to rise sharply in developing countries, in absolute terms or relative to other possible locations of investment, although some revival from present very depressed levels could come as capacity limits are reached, in manufacturing industries for local consumption and primary, especially non-agricultural, commodities. It is less certain that export-oriented manufacturing, in particular labour-cost-reducing investments will recover to the level of the late 1970s and early 1980s. Such investment is more characteristic of periods of depression or recession than of expansion (even if this is at the slow rate expected for industrial countries), and the possible changes in technology and industrial structure discussed in Chapter 13 could make it more necessary to produce near the research centres or near markets, or could reduce the importance of low labour costs. The investor with the largest increase in investment in the 1970s, Japan, has moved towards making a high share of its investments in other developed countries. It is also possible that some of the increase was a once-for-all response as companies identified ways of 'unbundling' their production. On the other hand, the change in exchange rates, in particular the rise in the value of the yen, may give Japanese investors the same need to counteract high domestic labour costs that US firms had in the earlier period. There is already some evidence that they are beginning to change their strategy and import back into Japan from their subsidiaries, a practice which was virtually unknown until 1987.

The recovery of profits in developed countries in 1985–6, which is partly the result of their improved terms of trade with the oil and non-oil developing countries, suggested that, in contrast to bank finance, there could be an increase in supply. However, the uncertainties on external payments created by the debt crisis could have affected investors' views of the risks of foreign investment in general, although the evidence is that they are less subject to such broad views than bankers. There are also potential policy constraints. Protectionist forces have led to complaints about transfers of production abroad; the trade protection discussed in Chapter 9 has affected export prospects which are one of the motives of foreign investors.

On the developing countries' side, there is probably greater willingness (or eagerness) to accept foreign investment than in the past, so demand is less likely to be a constraint than for bank loans, but the evidence is that their attitudes or policies can have little effect in increasing flows. After a general move in the early 1970s towards greater regulation of the activities of foreign investors and the sectors in which they were allowed to operate, there was a relaxation which began in 1976–7 and intensified in 1983–4. This was related to the general fashion for a more open attitude to external forces, but also reflected a greater interest in improving access to new technology and a growing confidence in ability to control what were seen as the unacceptable aspects of foreign investment. The return to looking towards industrialisation as an essential part of development may therefore help to explain the change in attitude; foreign investment offered access to both general technology and the specific industries, especially in engineering, which were seen as characteristic of more developed countries. The success of Singapore among the NICs was taken as an example of how investment could make a contribution to development.

The growing use of joint ventures and of other alternatives to traditional direct investment, such as technical contracts or turnkey arrangements, has encouraged developing countries as well as foreign investors to consider the potential costs and benefits of foreign investment more analytically, and provided evidence on them. The existence of even a few cases of arm's-length technology fees or sales of semi-processed parts gives a yardstick for a 'reasonable' price for this component of a foreign investor's return. At the level of particular investments, local participation can give an outsider (which has frequently been the host government itself) access to the accounts.[12] (Similarly, foreign investors have acquired, since the early 1970s, experience in dealing with government restraints, and therefore of making realistic estimates of their costs, and are less likely to reject them because of the risk of unknown costs.) This increase in knowledge applies even to countries which have not yet had substantial foreign investment. The international negotiations about codes for multinational behaviour, while failing in their immediate objective, have led to exchange of information among countries, and organisations such as the UN Centre for Transnational Corporations have built up information. All these have increased bargaining confidence.

The banks are not expected to return to significant net lending in the medium term (although a net outflow of capital is not assumed). This aggregate judgement could include continued net lending to a few countries, but does not suggest any major changes from the 1986 patterns. Borrowers, lenders and the regulatory authorities are all concerned about the consequences of 1970s lending.

These forecasts, for every flow to grow at or below its rate in the past, combined with the effect on the borrowers' attitudes to the costs and risks of using external finance in the past and the lack of any form that is both stable and available on demand, suggest that external financing, either medium-term to meet exogenous shocks or long-term for an investment programme, is likely to be lower in the future than in the 1960s, as well as much lower than in the 1970s.

Its cost will probably remain high, and might rise. The shift back towards a managed, if not fixed, exchange-rate regime by the industrial countries in 1987–8 has been accompanied by some rises in interest rates. The difficulties of asymmetry of adjustment, with more pressures on deficit than surplus countries to take action, and the reluctance to accept devaluation for fear of inflation, which characterised the last years of the pre-floating period, were never resolved. If the international monetary system now returns to those conditions, interest rates could remain high and subject to upward pressure.

NOTES

1. The only longer-term facility in the 1970s was the Oil Facility, most of which was used by the industrial countries.
2. Much of this section is based on a survey of foreign investors operating in Malaysia, Thailand, Colombia and Peru, reported more fully in Page (1986b).
3. The problems of data for the past are much more serious for finance than for trade. The data for current balances are more unreliable because they include invisibles, where recording problems and differences of definition (particularly on interest and other investment returns) are much more significant. The capital components are also less subject to direct recording than trade flows; definitions and reporting conventions vary (even for treatment of official flows). Data on bank and investment flows are published by a variety of national and international sources, but there is considerable disagreement among different sources. For example, the data shown in Table 14.3 for bank lending (from OECD) show various divergences from those in Table 14.4 (from the World Bank), and both are different from those obtained directly from individual countries. The major changes can be accepted with some certainty, and the figures have been improving, because of the increased interest since 1982.
4. As noted for debt measurement, there is much less agreement on the conventions of analysis of capital flows than that of trade. To measure the real value of aid to recipients, the conventions of domestic analyses suggest deflating by their import prices. The alternative of using inflation in the developed countries, measured by prices of manufactures or GDP deflators, is inappropriate if is assumed that deficit financing is needed to contribute to the costs incurred by the countries, which include imports from other areas (in the 1970s, a basic difference is the weight given to the oil price). If the financing is measured against a domestic gap between saving and investment, consistent with the development view of assistance or the two-gap model assumed in some of the country studies, this might suggest an investment goods price as the more suitable deflator, but data problems would be insuperable (particularly at aggregate level), and import costs at least give a useful measure of balance-of-payments support.
5. If the oil price was assumed to have moved on to a permanently rising path, this would require a growing flow, but this view only started to appear, even in the

macroeconomic forecasts with the least industrial content, after the second price rise in 1980, and there was no basis for it on previous experience or energy conditions.

6. That it coincided with the US preoccupation with the domestic non-economic problems arising out of Watergate further weakened the possibility of official responses.

7. The power of the OPEC countries in dealing with individual countries and the impossibility of co-ordinating the response of the industrial countries, whatever their interest in combining, had been demonstrated in the first two months of the oil crisis when co-ordination broke even in the face of actual oil shortages.

8. The choice of whether to measure debt-servicing payments or interest costs against exports or GDP depends on the purpose. The approach of looking at ratios to trade flows may indicate the ability of a country to adjust quickly to external circumstances, and provides a useful comparison with other trade relationships. A larger trade flow permits a more widely distributed adjustment. The ratio to exports does not, however, measure the overall effect on the economy or the ability to sustain a cost in the long term. What may appear to be low cost measured against a relatively large trade flow may have a severe impact if trade overall is more important than the average, and the reverse will also be true. Any simple ratio can be only a rough indicator because the composition of the trade flows and the flexibility and productivity capacity of the domestic economy all affect the outcome.

9. At the limit it could alter the direction of a country's response to a devaluation by effectively reducing its import elasticity by the servicing ratio.

10. It would in practice have been impossible to look at these ratios because data were not collected or published. This is in itself a measure of the change in what influences decisions.

11. For interest rates as for capital flows, it is impossible to identify a 'right' deflator. Conventionally, a measure in the industrial countries where they are determined is used. From the point of view of countries paying them, their own export prices indicate the real cost.

12. Stricter requirements for company accounts have also helped.

Table 14.1 Trade balances and ratios

	Trade balances			Exports/imports		
	Non-oil developing	Africa	Asia	Latin America	Non-oil developing	Asia	Latin America
	$ million				Percentages		
1969	−7,145	141	−4,008	−852	73	74	94
1970	−9,343	−200	−4,856	−1,201	77	78	94
1971	−13,122	−1,452	−5,360	−2,558	72	75	86
1972	−10,890	−807	−4,149	−2,510	76	84	83
1973	−11,756	−467	−4,266	−1,235	80	89	92
1974	−29,024	−938	−10,903	−5,153	73	87	89
1975	−41,572	−4,930	−13,996	−11,469	67	83	80
1976	−26,198	−2,915	−6,412	−8,026	77	100	86
1977	−24,441	−3,716	−6,855	−5,897	79	101	88
1978	−41,076	−7,099	−14,817	−9,064	76	103	88
1979	−46,011	−5,084	−19,350	−7,154	75	95	87
1980	−66,194	−7,997	−27,589	−11,223	75	94	87
1981	−79,370	−10,401	−32,643	−12,166	75	94	85
1982	−56,652	−9,651	−26,415	104	80	95	96
1983	−36,724	−6,229	−25,831	21,122	87	100	118
1984	−22,934	−6,085	−20,982	27,703	92	110	115
1985	−31,504	−6,347	−32,225	24,109	89	99	110

Note: Ratio is for trade of each with rest of world.

Source: UN, *Monthly Bulletin of Statistics.*

Table 14.2 Foreign investment

	Value $ million							Percentage shares in total of sample			
	1970	1975	1980	1982	1983	1984	1985	1969–73	1974–8	1979–83	1983–5
Newly industrialising countries											
Argentina	11	0	788	257	183	268	977	0.80	2.07	5.23	6.59
Brazil	131	1,190	1,544	2,534	1,373	1,556	1,267	36.13	35.81	21.44	19.36
Hong Kong	0	100	374	652	603	682	−216	0.00	3.14	6.61	4.93
India	6	−10	0	0	0	0	0	−0.22	−0.12	0.00	0.00
Mexico	323	609	2,186	1,655	461	390	492	24.37	15.90	17.54	6.20
Singapore	93	611	1,028	1,178	1,062	1,125	1,075	10.14	14.04	11.99	15.05
South Korea	38	53	−7	−76	−57	73	200	2.03	1.77	−0.15	1.00
Taiwan	61	35	124	71	130	131	257	3.62	1.62	1.16	2.39
Total	663	2,588	6,037	6,271	3,755	4,225	4,052	76.87	74.23	63.81	55.53
New NICs											
Colombia	39	35	51	337	514	561	729	2.44	0.94	2.65	8.33
Malaysia	94	349	934	1,397	1,261	797	685	8.10	9.70	11.65	12.66
Peru	−70	316	27	48	38	−89	−54	−0.41	3.01	0.66	−0.48
Thailand	43	86	187	189	348	400	162	4.02	2.46	2.28	4.20
Zimbabwe	0	0	2	−1	−2	−2	−2	0.00	0.00	0.01	−0.03
Total	106	786	1,201	1,970	2,159	1,667	1,520	14.16	16.11	17.25	24.67
Other middle-income countries											
Chile	41	50	170	384	132	67	112	1.22	1.23	2.75	1.44
Costa Rica	26	69	48	26	55	52	67	1.97	1.38	0.51	0.80
Egypt	0	8	541	285	471	713	1,175	0.00	2.24	6.99	10.89
Ivory Coast	29	0	95	48	38	0	0	1.76	0.70	0.62	0.17
Kenya	14	16	78	86	55	60	77	0.81	0.70	0.77	0.88
Morocco	12	0	89	80	46	47	47	0.62	0.62	0.67	0.65

Pakistan	20	25	59	66	31	60	140	0.81	0.37	0.70	1.07
Philippines	-29	97	-106	16	105	9	-14	0.06	2.90	0.42	0.46
Senegal	5	7	13	0	0	0	0	0.52	0.34	0.04	0.00
Sri Lanka	0	0	43	64	38	33	30	-0.01	0.01	0.52	0.47
Tunisia	16	45	235	339	186	115	109	1.92	1.86	2.36	1.89
Uruguay	0	0	290	-14	6	3	-8	0.00	0.94	1.17	0.01
Venezuela	-23	418	55	253	86	42	106	-0.71	-3.62	1.43	1.08
Total	111	735	1,610	1,633	1,248	1,201	1,841	8.97	9.66	18.93	19.80
Area totals											
Africa	76	76	1,053	837	793	933	1,406	5.64	6.45	11.45	14.45
Asia	326	1,346	2,636	3,557	3,521	3,310	2,319	28.54	35.90	35.18	42.23
Latin America	478	2,687	5,159	5,480	2,848	2,850	3,688	65.82	57.65	53.38	43.32
Total of above	880	4,109	8,848	9,874	7,162	7,093	7,413	100.00	100.00	100.00	100.00
All non-oil developing countries		5,300	9,100	12,200	8,900	9,400	10,400				
Difference		1,191	252	2,326	1,738	2,307	2,987				

Source: IMF, *International Financial Statistics, World Economic Outlook,* estimates.

Table 14.3 Current balance and principal capital flows ($ million)

	Current balance	Change in reserves[a]	Net dir. foreign invest.	Bilateral aid OECD	Bilateral aid OPEC	IBRD/IDA loans to 30 June	IMF credits	(World Bank) Banks Net lending	(World Bank) Banks Interest payments	All, grant element %
1969						1,407				
1970	−7,859	−1,751		4,789		1,992	−475			
1971	−9,815	−1,449		4,865		1,637	58			
1972	−6,433	−5,460		5,360		2,180	329	1,119	419	31.9
1973	−6,709	−7,866		5,716	1,810	2,570	165	3,061	567	27.7
1974	−23,259	−2,220	4,200	6,205	2,854	3,074	1,356	5,691	934	23.4
1975	−32,452	1,020	5,100	7,406	5,900	4,503	1,595	7,131	1,565	21.0
1976	−18,038	−11,088	5,300	8,982	5,000	5,149	2,005	8,063	2,288	21.0
1977	−14,694	−13,937	5,300	8,632	4,000	5,637	−82	13,215	2,601	18.6
1978	−26,822	−14,013	5,300	9,251	6,600	6,582	−119	16,759	3,377	18.6
1979	−42,097	−10,717	7,100	11,919	5,000	7,543	448	22,592	5,451	14.1
1980	−66,513	−38	9,600	14,421	6,866	8,788	755	22,670	8,658	7.3
1981	−80,443	2,781	9,100	15,218	6,113	9,444	4,574	20,036	13,389	8.5
1982	−62,906	3,860	13,600	15,594	4,222	10,225	4,285	24,837	16,703	−1.3
1983	−33,397	−4,475	12,200	15,833	3,861	11,365	8,574	28,412	20,222	1.3
1984	−19,091	−12,077	8,900	16,296	2,548	12,034	2,702	18,560	20,017	7.3
1985	−21,139	5,936	9,400	17,480		11,590	4,636	15,381	21,730	7.7
1986		−4,495	10,400	20,812		14,776	2,864	8,352	24,346	13.2

a. A positive number indicates a fall.
Sources: IMF, *International Financial Statistics World Economic Outlook;* OECD, *Geographical Distribution of Financial Flows to Developing Countries;* World Bank, *Annual Report World Debt Tables;* UNCTAD, *Handbook of International Trade and Development Statistics.*

Table 14.4 Measurements of commercial bank borrowing ($ million)

	Bonds, internat.	Bonds, foreign	Euro-Bank loans	World Bank financial markets		
				disburse-ments	repay-ments	net
1969						
1970				2,063	944	1,119
1971						
1972	408	339	2,344	4,572	1,512	3,061
1973	388	700	4,530	6,929	1,238	5,691
1974	92	730	7,389	9,625	2,494	7,131
1975	179	466	8,068	10,869	2,806	8,063
1976	880	909	11,121	16,349	3,134	13,215
1977	2,080	1,268	11,662	21,173	4,414	16,759
1978	1,809	1,561	23,761	34,538	11,946	22,592
1979	1,545	1,094	36,334	37,647	14,977	22,670
1980	1,018	507	28,532	32,967	12,931	20,036
1981	2,945	878	37,634	39,556	14,719	24,837
1982	3,156	451	30,274	41,910	13,498	28,412
1983	1,660	549	23,852	29,976	11,417	18,560
1984	2,252	834	18,910	25,930	10,549	15,381
1985	5,720	1,417	14,080	22,106	13,754	8,352
1986	2,517	1,467	6,866			

Sources: OECD, *Financial Statistics*; World Bank, *Debt Tables*.

Table 14.5 Ratios of interest payments to GDP and exports (percentages)

	Interest/GDP ratios				Interest/exports, goods and services				
	1970	1975	1980	1985	1970	1975	1980	1985	highest year
Newly industrialising countries									
Argentina	0.6	0.7	1.6	5.7	5.6	7.4	7.5	33.6	33.6 1985
Brazil	0.3	0.7	1.7	3.0	4.3	8.6	18.0	21.5	25.3 1982
Hong Kong	0.0	0.0	0.2	0.1	0.0	0.0	0.1	0.1	0.1 1985
India	0.3	0.3	0.2	0.4	8.9	4.4	3.0	5.6	8.9 1971
Mexico	0.6	1.0	2.2	4.5	7.4	13.0	15.8	25.2	25.2 1985
Singapore	0.3	0.5	0.9	0.9	0.3	0.3	0.4	0.5	0.6 1978
South Korea	1.0	1.4	2.2	2.6	5.1	4.8	5.8	6.5	6.9 1982
Average	0.4	0.7	1.3	2.5	4.5	5.5	7.2	13.3	33.6 (highest)
New NICs									
Colombia	0.6	0.9	0.8	2.3	4.3	5.2	4.8	15.7	15.7 1985
Malaysia	0.6	0.7	1.0	3.9	1.2	1.4	1.7	6.3	6.3 1985
Peru	0.6	1.2	2.9	0.9	3.5	10.9	11.2	3.9	13.2 1978
Thailand	0.2	0.2	0.8	1.6	1.4	1.2	3.1	5.9	5.9 1985
Zimbabwe	0.3	0.1	0.2	2.4	1.1	0.2	0.6	7.0	8.9 1984
Average	0.5	0.6	1.1	2.2	2.3	3.8	4.3	7.8	15.7 (highest)
Other middle-income countries									
Chile	1.0	2.3	1.8	7.1	6.1	8.5	7.7	21.4	21.4 1985
Costa Rica	0.7	1.2	2.8	10.1	2.5	3.9	10.6	26.3	42.5 1983
Egypt	0.7	1.4	1.6	1.8	5.6	6.9	6.0	8.5	11.9 1978
Ivory Coast	0.8	1.5	3.8	7.2	2.0	3.7	9.7	13.0	16.6 1982
Kenya	0.8	0.7	1.9	2.5	2.3	2.2	6.4	9.4	9.7 1982
Morocco	0.6	0.5	3.4	4.1	3.3	2.5	18.8	15.3	20.6 1981
Pakistan	0.8	0.9	1.0	0.9	9.5	7.6	7.5	8.4	9.7 1978
Philippines	0.3	0.4	1.1	2.6	1.8	2.2	4.6	10.5	10.5 1985
Senegal	0.2	1.0	2.0	1.8	0.8	2.7	6.4	6.0 n.a.:	(est for 1985)

Sri Lanka	0.6	0.7	0.8	1.9	3.1	3.2	2.5	6.6	6.6	1985
Tunisia	2.6	0.8	2.5	3.0	5.4	2.6	6.4	8.8	8.8	1985
Uruguay	0.6	1.3	1.0	6.0	5.4	8.3	6.6	21.2	21.2	1985
Venezuela	0.3	0.4	2.1	2.8	1.4	1.0	5.5	8.2	9.9	1983
Average	0.8	1.0	2.0	4.0	3.8	4.3	7.6	12.6	42.5 (highest)	
Area averages										
Africa	0.9	0.9	2.2	3.3	2.9	3.0	7.8	9.7	20.6 (highest)	
Asia	0.5	0.7	1.0	1.8	4.5	3.6	4.0	6.5	10.5 (highest)	
Latin America	0.6	1.1	1.9	4.7	4.5	7.4	9.7	19.7	42.5 (highest)	
Average, groups	0.6	0.8	1.5	2.9	3.5	4.5	6.4	11.2		
Average, areas	0.7	0.9	1.7	3.2	4.0	4.7	7.2	12.0		
World Bank averages										
Developing countries	0.4	0.6	1.2	2.2	3.0	3.3	5.8	9.6		
Asia	—	0.6	0.6	1.2	1.3	1.6	2.2	3.7		
Latin America	—	0.7	1.9	3.8	4.1	6.0	10.2	18.7		
Interest rate on private finance	7.5	8.6	12.6	9.1						
Real: deflated by:										
US CPI	1.5	−0.5	−0.8	4.7						
Non-oil ldc exp. p.	3.5	1.8	−6.5	15.9						

Source: World Bank, World Debt Tables.

Table 14.6 Interest rate on long-term loans from private creditors

	1978	1979	1980	1981	1982	1983	1984	1985
Non-oil dev. countries	9.5	11.5	12.6	13.9	12.3	10.6	11.0	9.1
Asia	9.6	10.2	13.1	12.4	11.0	9.6	9.7	8.8
Latin America	10.0	12.1	13.3	15.9	13.8	11.6	12.7	9.9
NICs								
Argentina	10.0	12.2	14.3	12.5	11.5	12.5	n.a.	9.9
Brazil	10.2	11.5	13.6	16.3	13.1	11.6	13.3	10.4
Hong Kong	8.5	10.0	7.8	7.9	7.8	9.5	12.5	n.a.
India	12.7	15.4	15.5	11.8	10.2	10.3	9.6	9.5
Mexico	10.4	12.3	12.6	16.4	15.0	11.7	12.3	9.8
Singapore	11.0	9.5	9.7	11.7	10.5	9.6	9.5	10.5
South Korea.	9.7	11.3	13.7	13.7	11.6	10.2	9.9	8.7
New NICs								
Colombia	8.6	11.9	15.4	14.4	13.0	9.7	11.5	9.8
Malaysia	9.2	8.7	14.1	13.9	12.5	9.8	9.9	9.0
Peru	9.1	11.8	10.6	15.6	13.1	11.4	11.7	10.5
Thailand	8.9	10.4	13.8	13.7	10.9	9.0	9.5	8.6
Zimbabwe	2.4	2.0	18.2	13.6	9.8	8.8	7.3	9.1
Other								
Chile	10.7	13.2	14.3	16.2	13.6	12.5	13.3	9.7
Costa Rica	10.3	12.5	15.2	17.3	15.6	11.6	12.8	9.4
Egypt	10.1	9.4	10.3	9.9	10.0	10.3	10.1	10.0
Ivory Coast	9.2	10.8	12.9	16.9	14.4	11.4	12.3	12.6
Kenya	7.9	10.6	9.3	14.9	9.3	9.2	8.6	10.4
Morocco	9.7	11.1	13.4	13.7	11.9	10.5	10.9	10.8
Pakistan	8.9	11.2	10.9	17.5	13.9	10.4	9.7	8.5
Philippines	9.1	10.5	14.2	14.5	13.4	9.9	9.8	9.8
Senegal	8.7	9.4	11.8	10.1	8.4	4.0	11.1	9.9
Sri Lanka	6.1	9.6	8.9	15.0	8.8	9.6	8.8	10.4
Tunisia	8.9	9.7	9.8	10.3	9.6	9.8	7.9	9.5
Uruguay	10.5	8.4	13.2	14.5	12.8	12.2	12.2	11.5
Venezuela	7.9	13.4	12.6	18.3	17.6	11.6	n.a.	n.a.

Source: World Bank, *World Debt Tables*.

15

HOW EXTERNAL FINANCE
IS USED

What appeared in the previous chapter as the aggregate financing problem, namely, unchanged or improved real trade performance but unfavourable terms of trade, applies directly to only a small number of countries. This is not surprising because, as we saw in Chapter 9, adjustment through higher exports was achieved by only a few countries, and was, at least partially, at the expense of the market shares of other developing countries. Analysis on a country basis points to differences in trading performance, in timing, in the choices between adjustment and finance, and in the types of finance available and used.

The evidence from the NICs and the other middle-income countries indicates that only countries with access to large flows of official finance, or the few which are small and have large inflows of foreign investment, can maintain continuing deficits. The only country that has successfully used commercial borrowing to sustain a deficit over a prolonged period is South Korea, which has been able to increase its exports at an exceptional rate and thus meet the rising debt-servicing cost. Even using commercial finance as a stop-gap measure, whether to meet a temporary external shock or to finance a period before official flows can meet a more permanent external deterioration, leaves a lasting burden of interest payments, particularly for countries whose exports are growing slowly. Only some Asian countries with very rapid export growth have managed this successfully. This was partly because the years 1978–82, when most countries did their temporary commercial borrowing, were followed by a period of particularly high interest rates (Table 14.6), and then by exceptionally low inflation (in prices of traded goods) which increased the cost of financing existing debt even after borrowing stopped.

It is notable that there were considerable variations in the interest rates paid, which did not correspond to a division between persistent and new borrowers or to one between the different classes of countries: the Latin

American countries and a few of the others paid significantly higher rates than even the heaviest Asian borrowers. This is surprising as most loans are based on the same international rates, and the variations are larger than estimates of the conventional spreads on loans. Robinson attributes the high rates paid by Zimbabwe to inexperience. This is consistent with high rates for some of the other new borrowers, and low rates for the more experienced Asian NICs and new NICs, but it does not apply to Latin American borrowers. Official lending from Japanese sources may have been denominated in yen and carried lower interest rates, but this is unlikely to have applied to commercial loans until very recently. The Asian borrowers, including the new NICs, have tended to use bonds more in the last few years, sometimes refinancing bank debt with them. This reduces the interest rate and in some cases has extended the term of borrowing. It may also reduce the role of the banks as creditors and be a move towards a less conditional form of finance.

THE NICs

Hong Kong[1] did not face a major increase in its trade deficit until 1978. By 1982 (with a fall in imports only in that year) the deficit had been reduced, although there was a further large rise in 1984 (Table 15.1). These changes coincided with large rises in the volume of its imports. To meet them, it borrowed commercially, in the first period using banks but switching to bonds in the second. It has received no significant aid flows throughout the period. It did begin to receive foreign investment in the 1980s, and this became temporarily as important as loan finance. The low and temporary nature of its deficits has meant that its interest costs are still small relative to its total external payments.

Singapore had large changes in its current deficit only in 1974 and 1980–3. The second period was one of relatively slow export growth and rapid import growth. In each case, it required one year of reduced imports to adjust: 1975 and 1985. In normal years, its deficit has been entirely covered by net investment inflows (Table 15.2), although it has had some official credits. Since 1978, it has increased its borrowing on capital markets, with a switch to bonds in 1985 when it was making heavy repayments of previous borrowing. This has led to a rise in its interest payments, although they are still small relative to new inflows.

Taiwan has had a surplus on its current balance except in 1974–5 and 1980; these deficits can be explained by changes in the terms of trade. It cut imports in 1975, 1982 and 1985. Although it did borrow heavily from 1974 to 1983, this has now been reduced, so that it is probably making net repayments, while foreign investment has been low relative to its surplus. It has not, therefore, as a normal practice relied on foreign capital inflows, although transfers were important in the past (Table 15.3).

South Korea is the only country among the NICs to have avoided financing problems while relying heavily on bank finance (Table 15.4). It had large increases in its deficit in 1974–5 and 1979–81, with the latter brought down to near balance by 1986 when its trade moved into surplus. Changes in the terms of trade account for the deficits, and the recovery after 1981 came from its faster-than-average increase in export volume, with a reduction of imports in 1980. In the early 1970s, bilateral assistance was still sufficient to finance nearly half its deficit; although this has diminished, World Bank loans remain a significant inflow, but they did not increase in response to the deficit increases. To meet these, South Korea used IMF credits and its reserves, but it also borrowed commercially from 1974 and maintained a high level of borrowing even when the balance improved. This was partly to meet the growing level of repayments ($1.5bn by 1985). Like Hong Kong and Singapore, it began to change to the bond markets in the 1980s.

South Korea has thus used combinations of official (World Bank) and commercial bank finance for both long-term financing and (substituting the IMF for the World Bank) meeting short-term fluctuations. As a result, its interest payments have become a significant burden on its payments (Tables 14.5 and 15.4). It has been able to do this without debt-servicing problems because it increased its exports sufficiently rapidly. As indicated in Chapter 9 (Tables 9.1 and 9.3), no other country has been as successful in increasing its export share. The other South-East Asian NICs have avoided borrowing. Singapore is one of the four developing countries receiving substantial foreign investment; Taiwan has remained in surplus; and although Hong Kong has now started to use borrowing, it has combined this with increased direct investment. Only South Korea now has a heavy interest burden from past financing. All made import reductions, but only for brief periods, not affecting long-term rates.

India has had deficits regularly only since 1980, following the rise in its import prices in that year. It remains principally dependent on official inflows (see Table 15.5), and was able to increase these (from the IMF) after 1980. It started to use commercial finance in 1980, and the increase in all forms of finance has led to a large rise in its interest payments, although they are still small relative to income. Its import growth rate has been halved since 1980 after remaining at about 4% p.a. in volume (the average for developing countries) since the late 1960s.

Mexico had a current deficit until 1982 (see Table 15.6), with a rise in 1974–5, and a much larger increase in 1980–1, in spite of massive improvements in its terms of trade in both periods. Imports grew extremely rapidly during the 1970s, at over 9%. They were reduced by more than 50% by 1983, to a ratio to GDP comparable to that in the early 1970s. Although Mexico has been one of the major recipients of foreign investment, this was never during the last 15 years a major source of finance for the deficit. Mexico was also one of the largest recipients of World Bank assistance, and received some bilateral official finance. Its principal major continuing source of finance, however, was commercial borrowing which financed its deficit until 1978. In that year, roughly five years after the first rise in its deficit, repayments doubled to $4bn, interest payments started to rise steeply and the net inflow began to fall. There was a brief recovery in 1981, but from 1983 a trade surplus was required to finance the outflow as interest payments became much higher than net new inflows, in spite of temporary official finance from the IMF. Although the borrowing has now ended, Mexico is left with a ratio of interest to exports of 25% and of 4.5% to GDP, more than twice the developing country averages, although as recently as 1980 its ratio to GDP was the same as that of South Korea.

Brazil had a large rise in its deficit in 1974 (see Table 15.7) which was never significantly reduced in the 1970s, although imports were low throughout this period. There was a further rise from 1979 to 1982, which was then eliminated by 1984, by means of large falls in imports. Although fluctuating, exports have grown on average at over 10% throughout the 1960s to 1980s. The terms of trade, which fell in every year except two from 1974 to 1982, and have since risen slightly, are the principal explanation for the balance-of-payments problems. Although Brazil has been the largest recipient of foreign investment, it has not been its principal source of finance. Official flows have been important in long- and short-term finance, but rose most after the current balance had started to improve in 1983. The major source of additional finance was commercial borrowing. (Like Mexico, Brazil used bonds only in the late 1970s, and has not done so in the 1980s.) This expanded rapidly in the mid-1970s, and further in 1978, but the rise in repayments and interest payments meant that it ceased to make a net contribution in 1980. In most years since then there has been a net outflow, financed by a large trade surplus since 1983. Brazil's interest costs are similar to those of Mexico.

Argentina (see Table 15.8) had a current deficit in 1975, but has had one regularly only since 1979. Although export performance has been erratic, the principal influence has been an almost uninterrupted decline in the terms of trade. The improvement in the current balance since 1980 is the result of a cut of over a half in import volume. Commercial borrowing began even before the country moved into persistent deficit, and was the principal source of finance, but it did not rise when the deficit reached its peak in 1980–1: to finance this Argentina had to use first its reserves and later official flows from the IMF. From the late 1970s, Argentina did start to receive some foreign investment, but it was not a major source of finance. The early rise in borrowing meant that interest payments began to rise in 1980, and from 1981 they exceeded net new inflows,[2] and Argentina's costs of servicing existing debt are greater than those for Brazil and Mexico.

The three Latin American NICs were thus similar in their pattern of financing to South Korea, but were unable to increase exports rapidly, either while they were borrowing regularly or when they faced erratic difficulties.

All therefore reduced imports sharply. But because the costs of debt servicing are fixed exogenously relative to exports, this cannot remove or reduce the continuing burden of financing.

By the mid-1980s, only Hong Kong and India among the NICs had significant external financing (current deficits), very different from the expected position of developing countries, as outlined at the beginning of Chapter 14.

OTHER MIDDLE-INCOME COUNTRIES

Among the countries which are less advanced than the new NICs, the *Philippines* moved into deficit on current balance in 1974 (see Table 15.9), saw a steady deterioration until 1982 in spite of exceptionally high export volume growth in the 1970s, and then eliminated the deficit by 1985. The improvement since 1982 results from a 40% cut in import volume. Foreign investment is not an important source of financing. Official financing is still significant, but the major increase in the 1970s came from commercial borrowing; this has fallen back since then. The country's period of use of bonds was the same as the Latin American; it did not join the major Asian borrowers in the 1980s. Interest payments started to rise in the 1980s, and equalled new inflows after these began to fall sharply. The country is left with high interest costs, especially relative to exports which have performed poorly in the the 1980s. The ratios have doubled since 1980 in spite of the decline in new borrowing.

Sri Lanka is in persistent deficit, but the magnitude rose briefly in 1974–5, and then more lastingly after 1979 (see Table 15.10). These two changes were immediate results of falls in the terms of trade, although the 1970s was a period of very rapid import growth and export stagnation. Since then, exports have grown, though not particularly rapidly, while imports have been held constant. Since 1979 Sri Lanka has received significant amounts of foreign investment for its size, but this has only financed about 10% of its deficit. The major source of finance remains assistance, both bilateral and, since 1979, multilateral. This rose almost enough to cover the additional deficit, but some commercial borrowing was necessary between 1979 and 1984. In spite of the large proportion of official financing, interest costs rose rapidly in the 1980s, although Sri Lanka's ratios remain slightly below the present high averages.

Pakistan has a large persistent current deficit, although rises can be seen in 1974 and 1979. Although exports grew rapidly, imports increased at an average of 16% p.a. in the 1970s (see Table 15.11). This slowed down in the 1980s, but without significant falls. Throughout the 1970s, most of Pakistan's financing came from official inflows (including from OPEC), although there was a small steady inflow of foreign investment. In 1979, however, OPEC aid declined, and OECD aid stopped rising. Although there was some increase in multilateral financing, this was not until 1982, with a further rise in 1985. The gap was met from commercial borrowing. Unusually, the change in Pakistan's circumstances was triggered as much from the financing as the trade side. Debt-servicing costs are not large relative to its income and have not risen sharply.

Chile is also normally in deficit, with a large increase, beginning in 1978 and falling back after 1981 (see Table 15.12). This followed very high increases in the volume of exports in the 1970s, which outstripped a high growth of imports. Imports were reduced sharply after 1981 (as with the other Latin American countries, by almost 50%). The principal explanation for the rise can be found in the terms of trade, with falling export prices aggravating rising import prices. Although there was a large increase in foreign investment from 1978, most of the increased inflow came from commercial borrowing.[3] Interest costs rose surprisingly rapidly: except for IMF loans in the early 1980s, Chile had little official finance and appears to have paid exceptionally high interest rates (perhaps because the government was forced to take responsibility for loans which had originally been private). As a result, even without unusually high borrowing, it moved from an average level of debt-payment ratios to one of the highest between 1980 and 1985.

Costa Rica (see Table 15.13) has had a high deficit, increasing in 1974 and again from 1978. This was earlier than the normal, and the correction also began earlier, from 1981, helped by a 40% cut in imports. Although import growth has been modest, exports have also risen slowly (by 2% and 4% respectively in the 1970s), while its terms of trade fell. For its size, Costa Rica has had a significant inflow of foreign investment, covering about a quarter of its deficit until 1977, when a decline in investment coincided with a rise in the deficit. Official flows were smaller, until 1983, and there was only a brief period of high commercial borrowing in 1978–80. Partly because of exceptionally high interest rates (aggravated by the continued slow growth in exports), this was sufficient to leave the country with very high interest ratios.

Uruguay (see Table 15.14) has had a 'conventional' pattern of rough current balance until it moved into deficit in 1974–5, then recovery, a further increase in the deficit in 1979–81, and then a reduction. Exports have generally grown quite slowly, although there was a period of rapid rise at the end of the 1970s and early 1980s. Although imports also grew slowly, this was not enough to compensate for a continuing fall in the terms of trade. Since 1980, imports have been cut by more than a half. Official inflows have not been a significant source of finance. Although there was a short period of foreign investment between 1978 and 1980, the main continuing inflow was from banks. This led to a build-up of interest payments after 1980 to a surprisingly high level: the debt outstanding appeared to rise much faster than new borrowing.

Although it is a traditional oil exporter, *Venezuela* (see Table 15.15) is included in this study because it shows some of the same characteristics as the non-oil middle-income countries. It had a rapid build-up of debt-servicing costs, like the other Latin American countries. Although it has been in surplus during most of the period, it borrowed heavily between 1976 and 1982. Bank loans were the only major source of external financing: in consequence, it has high interest payments and ratios. The temporary deficits were the result of maintaining a rapid growth of imports in periods when the value of exports fell. Venezuela was thus also risking the use of commercial borrowing as an adjustment mechanism for a temporary problem. The servicing costs remained a serious cost after imports had been adjusted; these have now fallen to the usual Latin American 40% from their peak in 1977.

Egypt (see Table 15.16) had large deficits in most years between 1975 and 1985. Although it became an important oil exporter during the 1970s, imports increased exceptionally rapidly (with a cut in 1979–80). The principal source of finance has been official inflows. OPEC was important until 1978, but then fell sharply. By 1980–3 bilateral OECD and multilateral financing had increased and, with foreign investment, which began to be important in 1978, these have become the major source of external finance. It was between 1977 and 1982 that Egypt's commercial borrowing was high. The heavy reliance on external financing gave it high interest ratios, but they have not increased greatly in recent years.

The *Ivory Coast* (see Table 15.17) had its major rise in current deficit from 1978, but has been in deficit for most of the last 15 years. Since 1984, however, it has moved almost into balance. Exports rose at only a little over 5% in the 1970s, while imports expanded at 6%. Since 1978, it has had to reduce its imports by a half. Until 1975, the principal external financing was from official sources, but this did not rise rapidly when the deficit increased: the Ivory Coast received IMF financing in 1981 and an increase from the World Bank in 1981–2. It increased its commercial borrowing from the mid-1970s, reaching the highest levels in 1980–2. Interest payments, therefore, rose rapidly after 1980 (aggravated by a relatively high average interest rate), and are well above the average.

Kenya (see Table 15.18) has always been in deficit. This showed a 'normal' increase in 1974–5, but it also rose in 1978, before the impact of the oil price rise, and remained high until 1982. There has been exceptionally slow growth of exports throughout the period, with the 1985 level slightly below that of 1972. Although imports were nearly as sluggish, the deficit was aggravated by a persistent adverse movement in the terms of trade. Although Kenya has had a little foreign investment, its main source of finance has been bilateral official finance. This did not, however, finance the increased deficit between 1978 and 1981, and it borrowed commercially. This brief period led to some increase in its relative interest costs; the ratios are made worse by the poor performance of exports.

Morocco (see Table 15.19) has had a large deficit only since 1976. A large rise in its export prices in 1974–5 encouraged a large rise in import volume, which did not fall back as export prices were reduced and the terms of trade became less favourable. Since 1979, imports have been restrained. Official finance from bilateral and multilateral donors has financed most of the deficit. Morocco has borrowed commercially for short-term periods, when the deficit increased (in 1976–7, and again in 1981), until an increase in official finance followed (in 1979 and 1982). Since 1982, OPEC finance has fallen sharply. The temporary use of commercial credits was sufficient to cause a steep rise in interest payments, especially from 1980. Morocco's ratios are now among the highest for the African countries included in this sample.

Senegal (see Table 15.20) had a significant increase in its persistent deficit in 1978 and again in 1980. It is probable that the recovery in the current deficit after 1982 continued in 1983 and 1984, and there were small falls in the trade deficit in those years. Although exports fluctuate widely, there has been little change in volume over the last 15 years. The small gain, which was offset by the unfavourable terms of trade, was not sufficient to finance a slow growth of import volume; imports were reduced after 1977. The principal source of finance is bilateral official inflows, although there has also been continuing finance from both the World Bank and the IMF. Senegal undertook only small borrowing from the commercial markets. Its ratios therefore reflect the costs that can arise even from using official financing and with very low import growth.

Tunisia (see Table 15.21) only moved into serious deficit in 1975–6, but since it has shown little change. It benefited from the oil price rise, but the volume of its exports (with fluctuations) has changed little since the early 1970s. Although the rise in its terms of trade permitted rapid import growth during the 1970s, this stopped, and there was some contraction after 1979. Official flows have been the principal source of finance, and in most years were almost sufficient. When the deficit was at its highest levels, however, Tunisia also had to borrow commercially, especially after 1977. Interest payments did not rise as much as in other countries, as it paid a relatively low rate, but its ratios are high by Asian or pre-1980 standards.

Most of the *lower middle-income countries* have remained in deficit, in the conventional pattern for developing countries, but only by relying on official finance. Foreign investment has been significant for a few, but has not displaced official flows as the principal source of finance. The principal long-term problem has been persistently declining terms of trade, in some cases aggravated by sluggish export volumes. This has left them in a vulnerable position when import prices have risen exceptionally. Such rises have imposed a need for temporary extra financing which official flows have not normally met. Official flows have also been slow to respond to new longer-term needs, and these gaps too have been filled by bank finance. Relying on commercial finance, even for short periods (in most cases for 4–5 years around 1978–82), has led to severe rises in interest costs. The interest payments have then remained a serious burden after the need has passed. This is partly because the temporary falls in terms of trade have not normally been matched by rises, but also because some countries have used the rises to increase imports. The normal expectation that borrowing costs will become less of a burden as income rises has been frustrated because interest rates rose and export incomes (and GDP) have been seriously constrained by the world depression. The countries have been forced to cut imports; there has been no reduction in interest costs relative to exports. Even persistent heavy reliance on official finance has led to serious interest costs for some. The Latin American countries and some African ones have tended to suffer much more drastic cuts in their imports than the Asian, which have been able to adjust sufficiently by holding them constant.

THE NEW NICs

The intermediate countries have relied on various proportions of grants, official loans, direct investment and commercial borrowing, not on a single source. This has given them the appearance of greater ability to choose how, and how much, to finance.

Zimbabwe (see Table 15.22) has had a current deficit since 1979, reflecting the post-Independence surge in imports, which was not matched by an increase in exports and not sufficiently offset by an improvement in the terms of trade (trading costs were reduced because of the removal of sanctions), and also the rise in foreign investors' remittances. It has relied mainly on official financing, but this was slow to build up, particularly from multilateral agencies, and the interim need was financed by commercial borrowing (in 1981–3). This led to a rapid rise in the interest/GDP ratio, from 0.2% to 2.4% between 1980 and 1985.

Robinson explains the deterioration of the current deficit as occurring initially mainly because of the rise in domestic output and the need to replace capital equipment after the years of sanctions. In subsequent years, external factors, the decline in the terms of trade and in demand for exports, became progressively more important. Since then, other negative external factors have included the effects of South African restraints on transport. Following independence, there was a major mobilisation of official capital to finance rebuilding the economic structure. Although the data quoted by Robinson imply slightly higher figures for official inflows than appear in Table 15.22, he notes that they were 'slow to materialise' and less than the targets. The government's efforts to increase inflows after 1983 can be seen in the Table.

Most of the aid has been directed towards agricultural projects and infrastructure (Mandaza, 1986: 133) (including electricity), not towards industry.

The Plan targets do not anticipate a large increase in inflows, which is in line with the general forecasts of Chapter 14. The discussion there of the motives and concerns of suppliers of capital suggests that Zimbabwe's political rhetoric of socialism could be expected to be a negative influence on both official flows and foreign investment, but less so on commercial borrowing. The Zimbabwe study notes some cases where bilateral flows may have been affected. The other political uncertainties in the region could have serious consequences, which are not explicitly included in the forecast.

As an ex-colony, Zimbabwe started with a high stock of foreign capital, and Robinson notes that the restrictions on repatriation during UDI ensured reinvestment and supplemented domestic savings. Since then, net investment has been negligible. Foreign capital made a major contribution to mining and to manufacturing. The Plan expects major inflows of investment, as a result of 'economic recovery, aided and influenced by the economic programme of this Plan', and the government appears to believe that it is a targetable variable. Robinson suggests, on the basis of the explanations for foreign investment given in Chapter 14, that this is unlikely. He does argue, however, that if it offers technology and marketing skills, it would be desirable to increase it, subject to controls on its activities. Regulation is more important than actual ownership which, he suggests, is still given too much symbolic importance by the government, while the need to secure training at all levels is neglected. This analysis suggests that official policy in Zimbabwe is at the stage in its attitudes to foreign investment where the NICs, and perhaps some of the new NICs, were in the early 1970s, namely, of distrust of both the foreign investor and the national ability to deal with him. In these circumstances, alternative forms of foreign participation became popular. These may be suitable for Zimbabwe, but the discussion in Chapter 14 suggests that they may be less readily available than they were in the 1970s. On the other hand, information to enable Zimbabwe to acquire greater confidence may be more available. But, as Robinson suggests, attracting foreign investment should not be given great priority as long as Zimbabwe's poor markets and doubtful export prospects discourage it; remittances have been restricted.

Robinson notes the high growth in debt: reducing it is a target of the current Plan. The increase after 1980 was not entirely the passive result of external needs: comparison of Zimbabwe's servicing ratios with those of other countries (cf. Table 14.5) led to the conclusion that Zimbabwe was 'under-borrowed' and therefore to a willingness to incur more debt in order to increase development financing. It was unfortunate that this coincided with the period of high world interest rates and then with an exceptional need to borrow because of Zimbabwe's own external difficulties. Robinson also notes the relatively unfavourable terms which were obtained (shown for interest rates in Table 14.6). He suggests that Zimbabwe can sustain the present debt-servicing cost, which would fall, given the borrowing envisaged in the Plan, even on low export growth figures. He argues that it would be undesirable to prevent more rapid development by cutting the level of imports; in particular if, as he expects, exports fall below those expected in the Plan, this shortfall should be covered by borrowing. This is clearly a more risky strategy, but if the costs can be met, and it did lead to lower import requirements in the medium term, it would meet the criteria for external financing considered in Chapter 14. He does, however, raise doubts about whether new official finance could be obtained under these circumstances, and therefore suggests rescheduling.

Both Robinson and government officials in Zimbabwe argue that the reluctance to borrow is because of the high perceived risks: although countries at its stage of development have borrowed in the past, the reluctance is understandable given the much higher costs of debt service already incurred by Zimbabwe, and the rapid increases in these costs during the last five years. The reluctance may even extend to rescheduling existing loans (as a sign of potential uncreditworthiness). These constraints on willingness to use foreign finance are a long-term effect of the debt crisis.

The prospects for large increases in foreign capital inflow therefore do not appear promising. Even the Plan does not expect changes in official flows. Foreign investment is likely to be difficult to obtain, particularly in forms acceptable to policy-makers. The Plan is cautious about using debt finance. Only in altering the amount of borrowing is there any real possibility of a choice of strategy, and Robinson's arguments for borrowing more would imply little more than not reducing its contribution to domestic saving. The reduction in private financial flows and the increasing proportion of official finance could have sectoral effects as well as the macroeconomic effect on the level of investment, giving a bias towards agriculture.

Malaysia (see Table 15.23) was normally in surplus until 1979, except for a deficit in 1974–5. After 1980, it had large deficits, which were reduced in 1984 and 1985. Until 1980, there had been exceptionally rapid export growth, which resumed in 1984; although there were also falling terms of trade in 1980–2, this pause in export volume was the principal reason for the deficit. Malaysia has had large inflows of foreign investment; although these increased after 1980, it was not by a sufficient amount to finance the new deficit, and they declined sharply in 1984–5. Malaysia had borrowed from the banks in 1974–5 to meet the first oil deficit and increased its borrowing again in 1978. Since then, this has been the main source of finance (bilateral official flows have been significant, but not as large as foreign investment). Like the Asian NICs, Malaysia moved to more use of bonds instead of loans in the 1980s, including the borrowing to refinance existing borrowing in 1985. This helped to reduce servicing costs. It has thus relied on all forms of finance, but has needed to use loans to meet a temporary external financing problem. In spite of its long record of high exports and foreign investment inflows, its interest costs rose sharply, and its interest ratios are now much higher than even the present ratios of the old Asian NICs, although there was only a short period of slow export growth and heavy borrowing. Ariff and Semudram note that the interest rate on yen loans has been much lower than on dollar, but most of Malaysia's exports are still denominated in dollars and it is therefore vulnerable to yen revaluation.

The requirement to reduce the share of foreign ownership, especially in favour of native Malays, has led to joint ventures becoming the usual form of direct investment, with other new forms also becoming more important. The authors stress the growing importance of technology agreements; it is clear that technology is now regarded by policy-makers as a major contribution of foreign investment, along with sectoral and marketing effects. It is not seen purely in financial terms. The requirements of greater Malay participation in all levels of employment have probably been a deterrent to foreign investment because they affect not merely ownership but also the operations of companies. Effectively, they have reduced the supply of qualified labour, which is a disincentive precisely to the type of investment Malaysia was attracting. The survey evidence (Page, 1986b: 97) also suggested concern about religious conflicts.

Ariff and Semudram note the potential conflict between the New Economic Policy and promoting foreign investment, and suggest that the NEP will have to be modified. The relaxation of its rules from 1986 may lead to a rise (especially as they make expansion by existing companies easier, as well as new investment). Malaysia has a record of active government promotion of foreign investment through tax and other measures which rivals that of Singapore. In terms of economic criteria, it has suffered from rising costs for the labour which is one of its competitive advantages.

Ariff and Semudram accept that the country 'has reached a point at which it has become increasingly difficult to obtain loans' from official sources at low interest rates; also it wants more financing for industry, for which official loans are less available. Like Robinson for Zimbabwe, they question whether the government, which froze official borrowing from commercial sources, has become too cautious (developed a 'phobia') about borrowing to meet productive investments, which could finance their own repayment or temporary difficulties. They argue that 'there is no economic rationale for such behaviour' and that the government should not become more concerned with the costs of servicing than with development. To meet temporary external difficulties borrowing should be preferred to sacrificing development targets.

They do not, however, advocate borrowing as a long-term solution because of its high fixed costs. In the past, the rise in commercial lending helped to finance the increase in government investment associated with the NEP as well as temporary gaps. They express concern at the borrowing by state enterprises, as they may be unable to repay out of their own income. Interest has become a major component in the invisibles account, with public sector interest outstripping private after 1980. By 1985, interest payments exceeded new borrowing. Malaysia's experience well illustrates one reason for the growth in caution, even about borrowing for temporary needs: its ratios were still small compared to other countries in 1985, but the fall in export value led to a sharp increase by the end of 1986. The authors also suggest that Malaysia ceased to be able to refinance using bonds, with lower interest rates, after 1985, because of doubts about its creditworthiness.

The Malaysia study argues that increasing foreign investment is a realistic target; Malaysia is one of the four major recipients, and in spite of some reasons for caution appears to meet most of the criteria of foreign investors discussed in Chapter 14. Private flows may be needed for balanced investment. As in Zimbabwe, agriculture has been the main beneficiary of multilateral official flows, followed by infrastructure, which was the main destination of bilateral loans; industry received a relatively minor share.

Thailand is still at the stage of having a persistent balance-of-payments deficit and access to large official inflows (see Table 15.24). The explanation of its need for increased financing is also similar to that of the poorer middle-income countries: a persistent deterioration in the terms of trade. The deficit started to rise in 1975, and was highest in 1979–81 and 1983, with some recovery since then. The fall in 1983 was explained by a fall in exports; except for that year, they have grown extremely rapidly throughout the period (an important difference from the average African commodity producer). Although imports have grown, they have risen less rapidly than exports except in 1983, and they were reduced in the early 1980s and after 1983.

Until 1974, official flows financed the deficit, but they did not rise rapidly enough after 1975 although they remained the major source of finance until 1984. Foreign investment has been another important source, especially since 1980, but only covering about 15% of the deficit. The additional deficit, particularly in 1979–80 and again in 1985 when foreign investment and multilateral financing both fell sharply, has been covered by commercial borrowing (like other Asian countries, Thailand shifted to bonds in the 1980s). Borrowing increased with the rise of the government's role in the economy, unmatched by an increase in financing from official sources, and also with the emergence of a gap in investment financing. This was partly because of controls on the pricing of state enterprises. The loans have gone mainly into infrastructure (Tables 5.15 and 5.17), financing the state enterprises, but the study also notes the quantity going into military spending. Neither provides exports directly to finance their servicing. Interest payments rose from 1980, but Thailand has lower ratios than the average because it has had rapid export growth, and only used bank borrowing for extra, not regular, finance. The government has now put a ceiling on new borrowing.

The study notes the extra cost of commercial borrowing (especially since the rise of the yen) and the rise in its impact on the current balance.

The authors of the study accept the case for external saving to finance part of a developing economy's investment and to provide other benefits, but they argue that more caution is necessary because of concern over debt-servicing difficulties; alternative public-sector pricing policies could increase domestic financing. They suggest that the most important reasons for wanting direct investment are the linking of costs to returns on the project; the probability of reinvestment; and the technology and marketing advantages of a link to a multinational. Most investment has been in manufacturing, especially the machinery and engineering sectors identified as important to industrialisation. The study indicates that Thailand has met the criteria for both labour-using and import-substituting foreign investment, with investing for export now beginning to be more important. Most new investment includes exporting. Thailand does have an investment promotion programme, although it is less intensely organised than the Malaysian, and the principal obstacles, according to the survey evidence, come from administrative difficulties and inefficiencies. It could benefit from Malaysia's rising costs.

Colombia (see Table 15.25) has normally had a current balance surplus, with deficits in 1973–5, but it moved into severe deficit in 1982–3, and has reduced but not eliminated this. Export volume has never grown particularly rapidly, but because of the coffee booms discussed in the country study, there have been relatively favourable terms-of-trade movements (except in 1975 and 1981). Imports grew rapidly until the early 1980s; they have been cut since then, but not as drastically as in other Latin American countries. Inflows of foreign investment increased sharply after 1981 so that they have become as important a source of external financing as official flows, and sufficient with them to cover the reduced deficit. Between 1979 and 1983, however, the principal, immediately available source of finance for the deficit was commercial borrowing. With Colombia paying at the above-average interest-rate level common to Latin American countries, this increased its payments sharply from 1980, raising its interest ratios quickly to the average for the new NICs.

Colombia has been regarded since the early 1970s, when it took a leading role in the tight restrictions imposed by the Andean Pact, as unfavourable to foreign investment (in contrast to the South-East Asian NICs and new NICs), and Echavarria questions whether the policy changes since then have been sufficient to change this, as the country has no special economic advantage or large market to offer. Like other Latin American countries (and Zimbabwe) it clearly has a different basic attitude towards foreign investment, starting with an assumption that it is beneficial only if it is properly directed, while the Malaysian and Thai policy-makers start with the assumption that the most efficient decisions can be made by the investors, although some constraints may be necessary. Echavarria does not, therefore, expect it to make a major contribution to financing. Colombia has tried to promote investment, particularly in order to get access to technology. There has been an increase in investment, and the survey evidence suggested that, although new investors were deterred, existing investors considered the risks acceptable. But even if Colombia's own growth prospects remain relatively favourable, the economic uncertainties in the rest of Latin America make export prospects difficult for an investor to assess, and the political situation has deteriorated.

Echavarria argues that Latin American countries have traditionally used foreign savings to increase domestic investment; the position after 1982, when loans were no longer available, was an abnormal departure from this. He states that Colombia deliberately chose not to use foreign borrowing in 1972–8 when it was freely available, partly because of its income from coffee, but also because it did not want greater government intervention in the economy (the reverse of the Malaysian and Thai situation where increased government intervention led to greater use of debt finance). After that time, the government was prepared to take a more active role, and debt increased at a rate similar to that of the rest of Latin America until 1982, and continued to rise thereafter when Colombia was one of the few Latin American countries still able to borrow.

The Colombia study puts most emphasis on trade in its external strategy. It points out that having high reserves was important to surviving the 1980s recession and does not suggest other forms of external financing for either permanent or temporary support, in spite of its stress on the potential gap in saving. In the past, Colombia has used borrowing for financing fluctuations, with official and investment finance for the continuing deficit. Even with this combination, its servicing costs have become a major burden. Although Echavarria accepts that borrowing in the past was the correct reaction because it was used for investment, in contrast to the Asian and African studies, the cautious Latin American argues against taking risks: 'in a very unstable international economic situation conservative and cautious policies always pay.'

Peru (see Table 15.26) has had a persistent deficit on its current balance, with increases in the mid-1970s, and again in 1981–2. The deficit was then eliminated, but the fall in the surplus in 1986 signalled its reappearance. Export volume and the terms of trade fell throughout the 1970s, although exports levelled off after 1978. The high level of interest payments has been another explanation of the persistent need for financing, cited by Schuldt as a major problem since 1970. Import volume did rise in the early 1970s (attributed in part to a build-up of military purchases) and in 1980–1, but it has now been reduced, by the customary Latin American 40% since 1981. The rise in the 1980s followed the increase in export value to its highest point.

Official finance has been an important source of finance, but not sufficient to cover the deficit, although it increased sharply between 1982 and 1985.

There was some foreign investment in the mid-1970s, when new oil and mining investments were made, but it was never a significant part of external finance, and it gave rise to large remittances after 1979. These were an important additional cost to the balance of payments in that period (Alarco, 1987: 190). Up to 1983, Peru used commercial borrowing as a principal regular source of finance, and for additional finance when the deficit increased. At the end of 1986, most of its debt was to official lenders (two-thirds to governments and multilateral lenders, and a quarter to commercial banks). The period when export value did increase exceptionally (the late 1970s to 1980) was not used to repay previous borrowings, except on a minor scale in 1981, so that the strategy did not apparently distinguish in practice between a normal deficit and financing fluctuations; it used all available finance at each point, and the reaction to each increase in need was to use bank and reserve financing. Rebuilding reserves has been a declared objective, but has not been followed consistently. After 1984, there was no new private or World Bank lending, and no net direct investment.

The result has been that interest payments (and amortisation) have been a serious cost to Peru throughout the period. Schuldt notes that its average servicing to export ratio was over 25% for the decade 1977–86 (Table 7.5). Interest payments alone were over 10%. Peru thus has long had the problem which the other new NICs have been facing since the early 1980s, of managing an external strategy with already high debts and debt-servicing costs. As it has not been able to increase its exports as rapidly as South Korea, the use of bank borrowing has meant that it has been in permanent difficulty on the balance of payments.

The country study suggests that continued external financing will be necessary, but will not be available. The level of debt servicing required on past debts is too high (the decline in recent years is the result of lower payments, not lower liabilities). Paying all the due interest payments would absorb 6% of GDP and 30% of exports (the actual ratio in 1987 was 28%). Paying only the interest, and only on multilateral institution lending, would take 11% of export revenue.

The prospects for new inflows are considered to be poor. The only realistic possibility is judged to be official financing. World Bank lending stopped because Peru had not serviced existing debt and passed more than six months into arrears in 1987. Negotiations have started to find a solution. It is possible that bilateral credits could be negotiated (if Japan, which has a relatively high level of trade and foreign investment in Peru, considers this a reason for giving it part of its proposed programme of aid). Some foreign investment was considered possible as recently as 1987, to develop further mineral resources, but only in the medium term, and by 1988 government policies and behaviour, and the internal security situation, had made this improbable. The country's general economic situation is deteriorating. There was little investment for local sale even in the early 1980s when the situation was better and the government changed legislation to promote it. Increasing investment from the NICs is an objective, but the same constraints apply, and outflows, including to other Latin American countries, are now the problem.

For short-term financing, there is no obvious source. Peru is unwilling to accept IMF finance, even if it were available. Rebuilding reserves to make the country independent of the need for external finance would require a period of unusually high external receipts, which is unlikely on the prospects defined in the study.

The only solutions so far have been to limit payments abroad. The government announced a 10% limit on debt repayments relative to exports in 1985, and followed this in 1986 with a two-year suspension of private investment remittances. The study argues that the original 10% limit was set arbitrarily, on the basis of the minimum that could be taken seriously. Since then, however, the government has developed what Schuldt considers a (the first) major strategic approach to debt repayment, defining priorities among creditors and types of debt according to the criterion of those most likely to provide new finance. These are the official lenders, bilateral and multilateral, and short-term trade credits (which have always been serviced). For commercial banks, other solutions involving reduced repayment are proposed, including the conventional menu of debt settlements: exchange for long-term bonds or equity; trade swaps; and, for the smallest debts, writing off. Buying back the debt at a discount becomes increasingly desirable as the discount rises, but would require adequate reserves.

The country study does not offer any solution to the financing problem, and at the economic level it is not clear that one exists. Reducing imports does not reduce the burden of debt against exports or against domestic output (it may increase the latter if output falls). The 'heterodox' policy assumption that it is possible to increase output with constrained imports by restructuring the economy was at best a medium-term solution, and cannot bring the ratios to acceptable levels quickly. And even that required a continued inflow of finance, which was not available.

CONCLUSIONS

Apart from Peru, the five new NICs have all used official inflows or foreign investment, or a combination of both, to finance their *long-term deficits* (or have stayed in surplus). They have had difficulties when they have tried to continue to fund deficits as their access to official finance has declined with their growing maturity, and foreign investment has not (fully) taken its place. Their experience (especially that of Peru) confirms that the use of commercial finance is inappropriate as a continued source of external finance. A country that is becoming too advanced to attract substantial official flows, and which is not a recipient of foreign investment, effectively cannot run a persistent deficit. The evidence on what determines foreign investment suggests that it cannot (except to a very limited extent) be 'attracted'. The appropriate level of external deficit, therefore, is defined not by the type of criteria introduced at the beginning of Chapter 14, but by exogenously determined access to official and investment flows. The problem may be compounded: if a country cannot increase its growth either through exports or through domestic restructuring (which may require investment), this will make it unattractive to foreign investors. Peru offers a discouraging example of the vicious circle of inability to develop without finance or to obtain finance without development.

None of the countries has found an alternative to commercial bank finance for the major part of *short-term* financing needs. Reserves or IMF finance are sometimes available, but are not adequate on their own. The long-term financial flows do not respond to temporary needs. But all have found that temporary bank finance has left the borrower with a severe burden. This suggests a heavy permanent cost from having to meet temporary fluctuations, and therefore a strong incentive for trying to avoid them. This is especially true in a period of low expected exports and high interest rates which increase the costs of servicing the debt and, in the absence of high inflation, keep them high. It has not proved practical to rely on repaying debt from future favourable shocks not only because these have been rare, but because some of the episodes of bank borrowing have been to meet changes in long-term deficits to which the sources of long-term finance have not responded sufficiently rapidly.

The source of external finance is also a constraint on the structure of investment to be financed from it. The Zimbabwe and Malaysia studies both note that the shift to a higher proportion of official finance means more investment in agriculture and infrastructure, and less in industry. Thailand expects more foreign investment to mean more in manufacturing. The question of public or private investment is relevant to Colombia, Thailand and Malaysia; more bank borrowing has been associated with higher investment by their public sectors. For Peru, the need for any form of external finance makes these questions secondary, but they do suggest a possible conflict between its least unpromising sources (official) and its programme of restructuring the economy.

Zimbabwe concludes that it can still expect some public flows, and Malaysia expects to be able to attract foreign investment, as it has in the past. The authors of both studies consider that their countries should still accept the risks and costs of using commercial borrowing for temporary adjustment, rather than the costs to development of cutting imports, but note that their governments are taking a more cautious attitude. The Thailand and especially the Colombia papers share their governments' cautious view of increasing borrowing, but do not see an urgent need for finance. Peru simply accepts that there is a financing gap, and that finance must therefore be found, even if neither the government nor the country study paper can find it.

NOTES

1. The status of Hong Kong as a colony, and of Taiwan as unrecognised by the international institutions (and therefore absent from their published statistics), implies that analysis of their balances of payments may reflect differences in definitions, but the basic trends and composition can be accepted.
2. The World Bank figure for net inflows in 1982 is inconsistent with the breakdown from the OECD.
3. Chile is one of the countries with serious divergences between World Bank and OECD borrowing figures: both show the rise after 1978, but the World Bank shows a steadier series in the earlier 1980s and a sharper fall in 1985.

CURRENT BALANCE AND PRINCIPAL CAPITAL FLOWS

Table 15.1 Hong Kong ($m)

	Exports Imports cif	Net dir. foreign invest.	Bonds, Internat.	Euro- Bank loans	Interest payments
1969	−279	n.a.	0		
1970	−391	n.a.	0		0
1971	−516	n.a.	15		0
1972	−419	n.a.	0	10	
1973	−584	n.a.	0	125	0
1974	−811	n.a.	50	81	0
1975	−739	n.a.	24	543	0
1976	−354	154	0	100	0
1977	−831	144	128	16	3
1978	−1,952	252	0	629	4
1979	−1,990	362	0	798	7
1980	−2,679	374	0	1,472	37
1981	−2,957	1,088	124	2,442	29
1982	−1,681	652	72	1,259	15
1983	−1,836	603	63	733	12
1984	−3,736	682	186	553	10
1985	−2,378	−216	934	331	18
1986			505	830	

Source: for Tables 15.1–15.26, see Tables 14.3–14.4.

Table 15.2 Singapore ($m)

	Current balance	Net dir. foreign invest.	Bilateral OECD aid	IBRD/IDA loans to 30 June	Bonds, internat	Euro-Bank loans	(World Bank) Net lending	Banks Interest payments
1969	−191	38	14		0		6	0
1970	−572	93	27	16	0			0
1971	−724	115	28	0	10		11	1
1972	−492	1,900	27	10	51	0	53	1
1973	−518	265	23	0	30	0	30	4
1974	−1,032	572	20	32	0	0	14	8
1975	−687	611	10	25	12	0	10	9
1976	−568	651	10	0	141	0	109	9
1977	−296	335	11	0	57	0	149	18
1978	−453	739	5	0	25	100	−11	38
1979	−736	941	4	0	25	350	115	37
1980	−1,507	1,028	9	0	0	280	18	48
1981	−1,378	1,378	18	0	36	360	122	64
1982	−1,206	1,178	18	18	125	247	195	66
1983	−819	1,062	12	12	70	197	159	73
1984	−727	1,125	39	39	0	371	432	85
1985	−253	1,075	22	22	105	173	−177	110
1986					344	41		

Table 15.3 Taiwan ($m)

	Current balance	Net dir. foreign invest.	Bilateral OECD aid	Euro-Bank loans
1969	−34	51	4	
1970	1	61	3	
1971	171	52	0	
1972	513	24	−26	
1973	600	62	−26	10
1974	−1,114	83	−18	205
1975	−589	35	−20	143
1976	292	64	−21	301
1977	911	44	−17	409
1978	1,639	110	−17	138
1979	181	122	−14	668
1980	−913	124	−5	592
1981	519	91	−6	410
1982	2,248	71	−8	865
1983	4,412	130	−5	287
1984	6,976	131	−1	12
1985	9,195	257	−2	0
1986	16,105			50

Table 15.4 South Korea ($m)

	Current balance	Change in reserves[a]	Net dir. foreign invest.	Bilateral OECD aid	IBRD/IDA loans to 30 June	IMF credits	Bonds, internat.	Bonds, foreign	Euro-Bank loans	(World Bank) Net lending	Banks Interest payments
1969	−549	−162	−3	328	83	0	0	0		59	4
1970	−623	−57	38	268	55	0	0	3		38	7
1971	−848	173	56	305	92	0	0	12		115	9
1972	−366	−90	63	351	58	0	0	0	100	47	14
1973	−307	−362	93	263	203	0	0	0	48	76	29
1974	−2,020	608	105	221	92	135	0	19	300	347	39
1975	−1,888	−504	53	213	298	120	0	0	326	453	70
1976	−310	−1,189	75	181	325	96	74	0	979	412	113
1977	12	−997	73	172	444	−10	72	0	796	557	137
1978	−1,085	203	61	136	439	−78	0	56	1,665	823	227
1979	−4,151	−195	16	100	397	−125	44	0	2,639	2,099	377
1980	−5,321	34	−7	117	544	545	0	48	2,047	1,308	711
1981	−4,646	243	60	326	390	563	280	43	3,148	2,293	1,036
1982	−2,650	−126	−76	15	470	−89	100	42	2,927	1,550	1,256
1983	−1,606	461	−57	10	672	203	442	105	3,171	1,530	1,157
1984	−1,371	−407	73	−35	769	207	729	327	3,239	2,367	1,295
1985	−887	−116	200	−8	556	−59	1,328	372	2,990	2,785	1,332
1986		−362			626		425	308	1,118	—	—

a. A positive number indicates a fall.

Table 15.5 India ($m)

	Current balance	Change in reserves[a]	Bilateral aid OECD	Bilateral aid OPEC	IBRD/IDA loans to 30 June	Change in IMF credits	Euro-Bank loans	(World Bank) Banks Net lending	(World Bank) Banks Interest payments
1969	-230	-244	753		193	-230		-7	3
1970	-393	-80	753		267	-10		6	3
1971	-640	-179	847		243	0		8	6
1972	-154	26	445		472	0	0	-11	6
1973	-529	-33	457	235	564	609	10	-19	5
1974	1,206	-179	602	209	442	209	0	-10	3
1975	-147	-61	820	500	840	-345	0	1	2
1976	1,571	-1,703	725	134	894	-320	0	3	2
1977	2,107	-2,080	482	219	750	-152	50	67	2
1978	659	-1,554	670	17	1,282	0	55	21	8
1979	48	-1,006	769	72	1,492	339	50	56	10
1980	-1,785	488	633	-68	1,660	320	79	252	14
1981	-2,698	2,251	931	-100	1,711	1,620	1,043	272	23
1982	-2,524	378	471	-20	2,165	1,420	342	436	106
1983	-1,953	-622	750	-104	2,151	222	694	584	141
1984	-2,311	-905	634	0	2,722	281	607	795	237
1985		-578	516	0	2,347	72	174	611	273
1986			0		2,368		1,080		

a. A positive number indicates a fall.

Table 15.6 Mexico ($m)

	Current balance	Change in reserves[a]	Net dir. foreign invest.	Bilateral OECD aid	IBRD/IDA loans to 30 June	Change in IMF credits	Bonds, internat.	Bonds, foreign	Euro-Bank loans	(World Bank) Net lending	Banks Interest payments
1969	−592	−1	297	17	65	0	45	26		308	83
1970	−1,068	−75	323	20	147	0	20	0		144	134
1971	−836	−184	307	4	75	0	30	20		238	133
1972	−916	−224	301	2	277	0	80	97	402	311	150
1973	−1,415	−184	457	10	200	0	61	116	1,178	1,338	227
1974	−2,875	−78	678	16	309	0	0	50	1,478	2,054	430
1975	−4,042	−145	609	9	360	0	87	197	2,151	2,962	660
1976	−3,408	195	628	10	315	371	276	153	2,140	4,096	879
1977	−1,854	−461	556	6	257	138	757	591	2,895	4,194	1,066
1978	−3,171	−193	824	8	470	−211	346	342	6,217	3,957	1,562
1979	−5,459	−230	1,332	49	552	−163	225	138	10,488	3,211	2,535
1980	−8,162	−888	2,186	55	300	−136	300	54	5,858	4,395	3,553
1981	−13,899	−1,114	2,537	102	1,081	0	1,727	617	7,899	8,732	4,453
1982	−6,218	3,240	1,655	142	657	222	1,419	183	6,510	7,072	5,746
1983	5,419	−3,079	461	136	888	1,039	0	0	5,095	2,443	6,009
1984	4,240	−3,359	390	75	576	1,100	0	0	3,800	509	6,837
1985	540	2,366	492	123	598	609	0	49	0	257	6,918
1986					904	616	313	0	0	0	—

a. A positive number indicates a fall.

Table 15.7 Brazil ($m)

	Current balance	Change in reserves[a]	Net dir. foreign invest.	Bilateral OECD aid	IBRD/IDA loans to 30 June	IMF credits	Bonds, internat.	Bonds, foreign	Euro-Bank loans	(World Bank) Net lending	Banks Interest payments
1969	-336	-399	241	132	75	0	10	1		-9	26
1970	-837	-531	131	131	205	0	16	0		289	69
1971	-1,638	-554	215	114	160	0	0	6		436	69
1972	-1,690	-2,437	570	87	437	0	121	0	597	1,179	96
1973	-2,157	-2,227	1,341	56	425	0	25	36	842	1,197	214
1974	-7,562	1,144	1,268	118	242	0	25	0	1,605	2,372	387
1975	-7,008	1,236	1,160	116	426	0	0	35	2,120	2,315	614
1976	-6,554	-2,508	1,372	78	498	0	159	34	3,288	3,123	665
1977	-5,112	-704	1,687	58	188	0	604	252	2,341	3,247	815
1978	-7,036	-4,634	1,882	76	705	0	541	395	5,215	6,152	1,406
1979	-10,478	2,860	2,223	54	674	0	364	371	6,397	5,695	2,392
1980	-12,806	3,197	1,544	58	695	0	225	92	5,299	3,628	3,626
1981	-11,751	-835	2,313	207	844	0	0	61	6,798	5,444	4,528
1982	-16,312	2,676	2,534	162	722	550	40	61	6,844	4,876	5,262
1983	-6,837	-427	1,373	94	1,458	2,094	0	0	4,629	3,913	4,428
1984	42	-7,153	1,556	140	1,604	1,541	0	0	6,500	5,937	4,457
1985	-273	903	1,267	64	1,523	433	0	0	0	254	5,373
1986					1,620	-118	169	0	0		

a. A positive number indicates a fall.

Table 15.8 Argentina ($m)

	Current balance	Change in reserves[a]	Net dir. foreign invest.	Bilateral OECD aid	IBRD/IDA loans to 30 June	IMF credits	Bonds, internat.	Bonds, foreign	Euro-Bank loans	(World Bank) Net lending	Banks Interest payments
1969	-230	248	13	15	107	0	0	86		4	34
1970	-163	-130	11	-5	60	0	50	20		68	37
1971	-391	341	11	2	152	0	0	0		223	42
1972	-227	-121	10	-1	0	189	0	0	236	204	62
1973	715	-836	10	10	0	21	0	0	87	136	90
1974	117	5	10	12	0	-132	0	0	476	307	122
1975	-1,287	856	0	5	0	214	0	16	34	-171	142
1976	651	-1,157	0	7	0	237	0	0	896	1,239	125
1977	1,126	-1,709	145	9	320	-111	43	0	828	251	175
1978	1,856	-1,812	273	10	165	-419	199	68	1,273	632	302
1979	-513	-4,422	265	18	96	0	262	154	2,127	1,933	335
1980	-4,774	2,669	788	32	237	0	25	139	2,390	1,651	584
1981	-4,712	3,451	944	29	68	0	150	45	2,769	537	794
1982	-2,353	762	257	24	400	0	0	0	1,241	3,435	1,034
1983	-2,436	1,334	183	28	100	1,174	0	0	1,750	1,207	1,131
1984	-2,495	-71	268	26	0	-75	0	0	0	130	1,790
1985	-954	-1,881	977	31	180	1,213	0	0	3,700	2,975	3,235
1986					545	136	0	0	17		

a. A positive number indicates a fall.

Table 15.9 Philippines ($m)

	Current balance	Change in reserves[a]	Net dir. foreign invest.	Bilateral OECD aid	IBRD/IDA loans to 30 June	IMF credits	Bonds, internat.	Bonds, foreign	Euro-Bank loans	(World Bank) Net lending	Banks Interest payments
1969	-253	23	6	76	59	14	0	11		-13	4
1970	-48	-119	-29	41	22	29	0	0		9	12
1971	-2	-114	-6	64	40	5	0	0		-12	20
1972	5	-171	-21	156	12	-11	50	0	61	14	17
1973	473	-513	54	214	165	-8	0	0	149	-52	7
1974	-208	-466	4	133	208	110	17	0	853	85	15
1975	-923	145	97	160	268	211	0	367	223	117	30
1976	-1,105	-283	126	161	318	103	93	37	873	520	44
1977	-753	118	210	144	438	67	75	141	705	434	65
1978	-1,094	-284	101	165	396	93	100	76	1,830	549	76
1979	-1,496	-487	7	170	412	185	0	67	1,829	692	133
1980	-1,917	-596	-106	205	533	105	0	69	1,261	808	221
1981	-2,096	780	172	331	453	-125	30	0	949	474	347
1982	-3,212	1,178	16	276	503	108	0	0	1,053	869	322
1983	-2,751	141	105	359	183	-184	0	0	494	668	391
1984	-1,268	145	9	356	254	279	0	0	0	402	453
1985	8	-13	-14	438	151	137	0	0	925	446	478
1986		-1,113							0		

a. A positive number indicates a fall.

Table 15.10 Sri Lanka ($m)

	Current balance	Change in reserves[a]	Net dir. foreign invest.	Bilateral OECD aid	IBRD/IDA loans to 30 June	Euro-Bank loans	(World Bank) Net lending	Banks Interest payments
1969	-133.9	12.0	-1.8	46.3	0.0		3.2	0.7
1970	-58.8	-3.0	-0.3	43.3	0.0		-3.7	0.7
1971	-36.3	-7.0	0.3	46.5	0.0		-0.9	0.6
1972	-32.6	-9.0	0.4	48.9	0.0	0.0	-0.7	0.6
1973	-25.2	-28.0	0.5	42.2	6.0	0.0	-1.0	0.5
1974	-135.9	9.0	1.3	58.2	0.0	0.0	-0.5	0.5
1975	-109.3	21.0	0.1	100.0	28.5	0.0	-11.3	0.2
1976	-6.5	-35.0	0.0	95.0	25.0	0.0	0.5	0.1
1977	135.8	-201.0	-1.2	119.0	33.2	0.0	-0.2	0.1
1978	-67.7	-105.0	1.5	216.0	33.5	0.0	-0.2	0.0
1979	-228.5	-119.0	46.9	232.0	68.0	50.0	-0.1	0.6
1980	-657.2	271.0	43.0	296.0	151.5	53.3	87.7	4.2
1981	-445.6	-81.0	49.3	287.0	167.0	174.0	167.0	21.1
1982	-549.0	-24.0	63.6	305.0	128.7	110.9	232.4	41.4
1983	-466.2	54.0	37.8	347.0	32.0	31.5	75.4	60.4
1984	6.5	-214.0	32.6	319.0	67.1	42.5	56.3	67.1
1985	-556.3	60.0	29.8	334.1	134.0	0.0	-15.7	68.1
1986		98.0			85.0	20.9		

a. A positive number indicates a fall.

Table 15.11 Pakistan ($m)

	Current balance	Change in reserves[a]	Net dir. foreign invest.	Bilateral aid OECD	Bilateral aid OPEC	IBRD/IDA loans to 30 June	Change in IMF credits	Euro-Bank loans	(World Bank) Banks Net lending	(World Bank) Banks Interest payments
1969	-348	-85	21	290					1	3
1970	-667	142	23	385		96	-36		3	2
1971	-482	7	1	361		48	2		21	2
1972	-241	-92	17	275		50	74	0	0	2
1973	-68	-191	-4	208	18	63	36	0	-19	11
1974	-917	20	4	265	328	111	136	0	58	4
1975	-1,049	52	25	375	243	126	145	8	14	5
1976	-780	-126	7	352	821	172	73	0	18	6
1977	-723	17	15	375	59	205	21	27	106	10
1978	-719	41	29	379	45	122	-17	6	-10	13
1979	-1,114	195	62	418	18	164	-71	110	28	17
1980	-921	-283	59	339	289	165	-61	136	209	31
1981	-914	-225	107	421	63	202	374	206	-5	44
1982	-802	-248	66	400	74	310	409	291	450	77
1983	25	-1,004	31	254	54	304	213	267	-118	92
1984	-1,196	938	60	303	-41	306	-138	131	137	83
1985	-1,106	228	140	428	0	678	-15	283	-181	62
1986		98				650	-190	168		

a. A positive number indicates a fall.

Table 15.12 Chile ($m)

	Current balance	Change in reserves[a]	Net dir. foreign invest.	IBRD/IDA loans to 30 June	Change in IMF credit	Euro-Bank loans	(World Bank) Net lending	Banks Interest payments
1969	89	−134	85				129	6
1970	−26	−46	41	19	2		68	21
1971	−190	172	−42	0	41		38	17
1972	−458	73	0	0	43		55	3
1973	−465	−25	0	0	10	0	69	12
1974	−384	81	12	14	101	0	1	23
1975	−641	−15	50	20	191	0	−95	61
1976	148	−349	−1	33	80	125	−21	33
1977	−551	−21	16	60	−102	227	339	42
1978	−1,088	−664	177	0	−18	1,201	709	129
1979	−1,189	−848	233	0	−168	683	841	190
1980	−1,971	−1,185	170	38	−56	919	243	347
1981	−4,733	−90	362	78	−74	2,288	63	383
1982	−2,304	1,398	384	0	−42	1,194	953	455
1983	−1,117	−221	132	128	600	1,315	1,344	444
1984	−2,060	−267	67	0	173	.780	1,538	813
1985	−1,307	−147	112	287	309	1,085	513	852
1986				456	243	0		

a. A positive number indicates a fall.

Table 15.13 Costa Rica ($m)

	Current balance	Change in reserves[a]	Net dir. foreign invest.	Bilateral OECD aid	IBRD/IDA loans to 30 June	Change in IMF credits	Euro-Bank loans	(World Bank) Net lending	Banks Interest payments
1969	-50	-9	24	13	34	0		2	2
1970	-74	13	26	11	0	0		-7	3
1971	-114	-13	22	13	33	0	0	12	2
1972	-100	-13	26	15	8	0	11	8	2
1973	-112	-8	38	15	24	23	10	25	4
1974	-266	6	43	14	41	12	46	30	8
1975	-218	-7	69	17	39	2	40	47	12
1976	-202	-47	63	12	18	-2	54	51	11
1977	-226	-95	63	14	42	-4	221	105	13
1978	-363	-3	47	34	34	26	252	83	34
1979	-558	75	42	26	30	-1	182	249	41
1980	-664	-27	48	23	29	46	0	179	85
1981	-409	14	66	30	0	-10	0	95	73
1982	-272	-95	27	59	25	99	215	4	32
1983	-317	-85	55	217	0	-36	0	130	432
1984	-256	-94	52	186	84	33	0	26	128
1985	-327	-101	67	239	0	-16	0	64	202
1986		-17							

a. A positive number indicates a fall.

Table 15.14 Uruguay ($m)

	Current balance	Change in reserves[a]	Net dir. foreign invest.	IBRD/IDA loans to 30 June	Change in IMF credit	Euro-Bank loans	net lending	(World Bank) Interest payments	Banks Debt outstanding
1969	−19	15							
1970	−64	5		6			10	7	100
1971	−64	−6	0	22	8		−9	10	111
1972	59	−49	0	11	18		6	5	95
1973	37	−32	0	0	22		4	10	123
1974	−118	20	0	14	−2	0	−5	9	126
1975	−189	22	0	0	40	0	91	14	225
1976	−74	−117	0	52	39	130	104	27	327
1977	−167	−146	66	0	28	82	76	40	402
1978	−127	−30	129	10	−26	60	54	38	458
1979	−357	29	216	27	−119	230	45	42	504
1980	−709	−61	290	98	0	35	93	50	599
1981	−461	−46	49	30	0	116	163	79	758
1982	−235	314	−14	40	96	167	244	97	992
1983	−60	−91	6	45	142	30	319	129	1,304
1984	−129	73	3	0	−15	240	384	182	2,099
1985	−108	−40	−8	64	128	0	34	253	2,111
1986				45	45	45	88	244	2,226

a. A positive number indicates a fall.

Table 15.15 Venezuela ($m)

	Current balance	Change in reserves[a]	Net dir. foreign invest.	Bilateral OECD aid	Bonds, internat.	Bonds, foreign	Euro-Bank loans	(World Bank) Net lending	Banks Interest payments
1969	-220	-11	224	10	0	8		89	4
1970	-104	-107	-23	3	13	0		142	19
1971	-13	-460	211	6	0	0		186	25
1972	-100	-210	-376	5	40	0	264	224	35
1973	861	-633	-85	5	8	0	129	31	62
1974	5,810	-4,094	-343	2	0	2	50	-180	79
1975	2,171	-2,369	418	1	0	0	200	-192	62
1976	254	279	-889	-17	0	0	1,129	883	30
1977	-3,179	389	-3	-10	105	333	1,650	1,925	133
1978	-5,735	1,700	67	-18	382	307	1,810	2,346	354
1979	350	-1,285	88	6	174	0	2,887	3,110	565
1980	4,728	716	55	15	132	0	2,936	1,388	1,167
1981	4,000	-1,560	184	13	95	196	1,278	758	1,224
1982	-4,246	1,585	253	14	35	0	3,943	398	1,594
1983	4,427	-1,064	86	15	0	0	220	961	1,692
1984	5,418	-1,258	42	15	0	0	0	-697	1,416
1985	3,086	-1,350	106	13	0	0	48	-620	1,356
1986					0	0	0		—

a. A positive number indicates a fall.

Table 15.16 Egypt ($m)

	Current balance	Change in reserves[a]	Net dir. foreign invest.	Bilateral aid OECD	Bilateral aid OPEC	IBRD/IDA loans to 30 June	IMF credits	Euro-Bank loans	(World Bank) Net lending	Banks Interest payments
1969	124	24	0	2		0	51	0	-10	3
1970	0	-23	0	31		0	-2	0	-10	1
1971	-63	17	0	13		0	27	0	118	3
1972	38	5	0	5		30	-50	0	35	7
1973	370	-208	0	19	556	51	49	0	-30	12
1974	12	8	0	106		44	39	230	92	16
1975	-786	58	8	250	2,181	227	-34	0	41	22
1976	-1,431	-46	61	428		222	127	118	60	29
1977	-1,200	-191	98	617		268	103	250	301	43
1978	-1,220	-61	298	860	606	241	76	54	77	70
1979	-1,542	-37	1,211	1,012	145	323	-62	13	41	84
1980	-438	-517	541	1,187	10	421	-147	186	-4	86
1981	-2,136	330	747	1,105	-14	287	-78	46	-36	87
1982	-1,852	18	285	1,237	-25	465	-42	226	199	70
1983	-411	-73	471	1,241	-24	350	-6	45	197	75
1984	-2,081	35	713	1,651	-45	458	-3	48	-102	88
1985	-2,245	-56	1,175	1,681		263	-6	59	-68	78
1986						70	-11	0		

a. A positive number indicates a fall.

Table 15.17 Ivory Coast ($m)

	Current balance	Change in reserves[a]	Net dir. foreign invest.	Bilateral OECD aid	IBRD/IDA loans to 30 June	IMF credits	Euro-Bank loans	(World Bank) Net lending	Banks Interest payments
1969	20	7	12	37		0		9	2
1970	−34	−45	29	37	19	0		8	4
1971	−86	29	15	40	28	0		32	5
1972	−78	2	15	37	18	0	0	7	6
1973	−196	−1	51	49	16	0	74	101	12
1974	−61	23	0	52	28	14	63	7	19
1975	−307	−37	0	72	77	−1	50	115	28
1976	−249	26	45	76	57	14	148	93	33
1977	−179	−108	15	75	64	−11	296	522	58
1978	−839	−263	83	86	121	−16	162	591	107
1979	−1,383	301	75	139	52	0	227	522	153
1980	−1,827	127	95	152	33	0	605	631	248
1981	−1,411	2	33	91	133	372	506	501	300
1982	−1,012	16	48	102	375	108	465	560	361
1983	−909	−18	38	140	32	138	20	−13	299
1984	−107	14	0	114	251	−26	0	76	305
1985	100	1	0	111	141	30	153	59	256
1986					340	1	0		

a. A positive number indicates a fall.

Table 15.18 Kenya ($m)

	Current balance	Change in reservesª	Net dir. foreign invest.	Bilateral OECD aid	IBRD/IDA loans to 30 June	(World Bank) Net lending	Banks Interest payments
1969	−32	−70	16	43	0	2	4
1970	−5	−50	14	47	0	−9	3
1971	−112	49	12	58	0	1	3
1972	−68	−31	14	60	0	15	4
1973	−126	−31	0	76	39	5	4
1974	−308	40	0	99	41	−1	5
1975	−229	20	16	104	18	−1	5
1976	−126	−102	42	137	−41	22	3
1977	26	−247	54	121	10	99	7
1978	−662	170	32	187	75	97	8
1979	−500	−275	78	284	52	215	21
1980	−887	136	78	277	10	197	63
1981	−723	261	60	363	138	75	67
1982	−518	19	86	333	75	−65	84
1983	−134	−164	55	339	−37	−91	55
1984	−195	−14	60	294	106	−103	43
1985	−211	−1	77	329	−55	−115	38
1986					75		

a. A positive number indicates a fall.

Table 15.19 Morocco ($m)

	Current balance	Change in reserves[a]	Net dir. foreign invest.	Bilateral aid OECD	Bilateral aid OPEC	IBRD/IDA loans to 30 June	IMF credits	Euro-Bank loans	(World Bank) Net lending	Banks Interest payments
1969	27	−29	4	73						
1970	−124	−26	12	74		76	37		13	2
1971	−60	−32	16	118		45	−9		8	4
1972	47	−63	9	87	0	58	−28	0	20	3
1973	97	−27	2	76	9	72	0	0	2	5
1974	226	−150	−14	82	96	136	0	0	−11	6
1975	−525	39	0	171	44	63	0	200	114	5
1976	−1,398	−115	38	147	99	150	134	409	233	8
1977	−1,855	−38	57	159	40	166	6	702	488	17
1978	−1,338	−113	48	180	421	85	86	620	835	77
1979	−1,521	61	38	169	452	349	−26	627	519	147
1980	−1,420	158	89	188	345	204	117	450	688	255
1981	−1,844	169	59	209	229	223	134	573	370	436
1982	−1,878	12	80	230	29	276	419	160	96	506
1983	−892	111	46	190	7	308	51	44	608	406
1984	−988	58	47	248		266	71	0	−31	400
1985		−66		318		208	199	0	452	308
1986						538	−163	0	−104	260

a. A postive number indicates a fall.

Table 15.20 Senegal ($m)

	Current balance	Change in reserves[a]	Net dir. foreign invest.	Bilateral aid OECD	Bilateral aid OPEC	IBRD/IDA loans to 30 June	IMF credits	(World Bank) Banks Net lending	(World Bank) Banks Interest payments
1969	−48	10	3	44				8	0
1970	−16	−16	5	26		0	0	0	0
1971	−26	−7	10	25		0	0	10	1
1972	11	−9	13	37		18	0	7	1
1973	−101	26	5	46	1	30	0	65	4
1974	−66	6	7	63		7	0	33	10
1975	−56	−25	36	83	9	30	30	16	13
1976	−93	6	25	82		34	0	29	12
1977	−68	−9	−6	89		24	1	3	13
1978	−236	15	6	122	10	37	25	68	18
1979	−249	0	13	149	1	32	5	45	24
1980	−442	11		182	5	52	37	45	31
1981	−480	−1		215	9	103	50	−19	24
1982	−400	−3		189	10	20	36	23	12
1983	−400	−1		212	45	32	13	14	8
1984	−400	9		245	23	62	4	3	14
1985		−1		196		24	40	39	15
1986						67	26		

a. A positive number indicates a fall.

Table 15.21 Tunisia ($m)

	Current balance	Change in reserves[a]	Net dir. foreign invest.	Bilateral aid OECD	Bilateral aid OPEC	IBRD/IDA loans to 30 June	Euro-Bank loans	(World Bank) Banks Net lending	(World Bank) Banks Interest payments
1969	-48	-1	6	105		21		-8	5
1970	-53	-23	16	98		36		-6	6
1971	7	-88	23	90		56		7	5
1972	-4	-75	31	101	7	14	0	-6	4
1973	-59	-84	57	117	8	47	0	2	4
1974	48	-111	49	124	56	64	0	13	4
1975	-170	33	45	114	12	57	0	3	6
1976	-407	14	110	150	26	94	145	41	5
1977	-580	15	93	164	31	67	195	279	11
1978	-476	-92	89	253	59	99	154	288	31
1979	-308	-136	49	151	73	171	12	258	76
1980	-354	-11	235	158	42	153	40	89	107
1981	-454	54	291	162	35	161	0	32	110
1982	-758	-70	339	150	15	149	205	27	99
1983	-693	39	186	157	5	135	130	208	74
1984	-734	161	115	141	0	141	17	46	93
1985	-536	174	109	122		28	136	126	85
1986									

a. A positive number indicates a fall.

Table 15.22 Zimbabwe ($m)

	Current balance	Change in reserves[a]	Net dir. foreign invest.	Bilateral OECD aid	IBRD/IDA loans to 30 June	Change in IMF credits	(World Bank)		Financial markets	
							Disburse-ments	Repay-ments	Net lending	Interest payments
1979	-109	-151	0	12	0	0	100	3	97	7
1980	-244	85	2	112	0	0	53	29	24	8
1981	-636	44	4	137	0	44	240	35	205	24
1982	-709	29	-1	142	0	-2	336	42	293	77
1983	-460	65	-2	185	241	159	631	321	309	85
1984	-100	30	-3	243	96	56	75	125	-50	89
1985		-48		214	10	8	95	191	-96	80
1986		-13			0	-30				

a. A positive number indicates a fall.

Table 15.23 Malaysia ($m)

									(World Bank)		Financial markets	
	Current balance	Change in reserves[a]	Net dir. foreign invest.	Bilateral OECD aid	IBRD/IDA loans to 30 June	Bonds, internat.	Bonds, foreign	Euro-Bank loans	Disburse-ments	Repay-ments	Net lending	Interest payments
1969	239	−107	80	28	22	0	10		36	7	29	5
1970	8	−59	94	23	55	0	0		2	28	−27	8
1971	−107	−139	100	38	32	0	0	76	97	6	90	8
1972	−246	−152	114	44	60	25	0	0	124	5	119	14
1973	105	−368	172	39	124	17	0	140	29	24	5	21
1974	−480	−272	374	83	110	0	0	425	86	43	43	29
1975	−444	91	349	93	104	0	0	200	411	61	349	27
1976	580	−948	381	57	131	10	0	130	271	118	153	77
1977	436	−380	400	59	86	43	0	1,138	430	283	147	74
1978	108	−459	500	67	132	20	120	118	917	600	316	70
1979	929	−672	573	90	50	30	122	1,083	532	311	221	94
1980	−285	−472	934	106	182	0	0	1,475	655	40	615	151
1981	−2,486	289	1,265	117	152	0	0	2,310	1,650	35	1,614	241
1982	−3,601	330	1,397	104	143	750	67	1,071	2,600	146	2,453	423
1983	−3,497	−16	1,261	145	70	541	344	714	2,335	156	2,180	531
1984	−1,671	61	797	299	90	950	191	59	1,651	337	1,314	801
1985	−723	−1,189	685	203	331	1,741	261	849	2,910	2,612	298	911
1986		−1,215				0	43					

a. A positive number indicates a fall.

Table 15.24 Thailand ($m)

	Current balance	Change in reserves[a]	Net dir. foreign invest.	Bilateral OECD aid	IBRD/IDA loans to 30 June	IMF credits	Bonds, internat.	Bonds, foreign	Euro-Bank loans	(World Bank) Net lending	Banks Interest payments
1969	-200	36	51	64	47	0				0	0
1970	-250	69	43	70	13	0				0	0
1971	-175	36	39	58	42	0				0	0
1972	-52	-175	68	48	81	0	0	0	0	0	0
1973	-47	-244	77	56	149	0	0	0	0	5	0
1974	-88	-551	189	64		0	0	0	10	0	0
1975	-607	79	86	71	0	0	0	0	5	13	2
1976	-440	-119	79	71	228	78	0	0	100	23	3
1977	-1,101	-15	106	84	108	4	0	0	183	94	7
1978	-1,153	-196	50	149	232	96	25	44	242	45	12
1979	-2,086	-166	51	279	285	63	130	46	287	340	25
1980	-2,070	283	187	305	542	-57	0	46	905	628	71
1981	-2,569	-172	288	316	326	523	55	44	707	607	149
1982	-1,003	194	189	272	634	-4	20	43	306	479	251
1983	-2,874	-69	348	340	393	206	195	59	309	354	303
1984	-2,109	-314	400	357	153	-117	173	111	757	3	279
1985	-1,537	-269	162	386	113	229	800	62	341	118	270
1986					93	-32	0	0	468	930	245

a. A positive number indicates a fall.

Table 15.25 Colombia ($m)

	Current balance	Change in reserves[a]	Net dir. foreign invest.	Bilateral OECD aid	IBRD/IDA loans to 30 June	Euro-Bank loans	(World Bank) Net lending	Banks Interest payments
1969	−175	−53	50	100			−8	3
1970	−293	6	39	122	128		2	4
1971	−455	1	40	94	153		7	3
1972	110	−121	17	83	65	90	107	3
1973	−55	−207	23	116	125	170	107	10
1974	−361	85	35	71	542	8	52	20
1975	−108	−44	35	62	88	116	122	34
1976	207	−626	14	58	80	138	14	30
1977	440	−646	43	31	281	43	135	30
1978	322	−619	66	52	355	85	−20	46
1979	492	−1,478	103	29	312	888	429	91
1980	−206	−987	51	32	518	662	469	135
1981	−1,961	90	228	43	550	1,026	753	246
1982	−3,054	880	337	53	291	584	481	384
1983	−3,003	1,960	514	36	78	444	402	288
1984	−1,401	537	561	42	464	331	386	294
1985	−1,390	−231	729	37	708	1,052	139	376
1986		−1,101			700	50		

a. A positive number indicates a fall.

Table 15.26 Peru ($m)

	Current balance	Change in reserves[a]	Net dir. foreign invest.	Bilateral OECD aid	IBRD/IDA loans to 30 June	IMF credits	Euro-Bank loans	Disbursements	(World Bank) Repayments	Financial markets Net lending	Interest payments	Debt outstanding
1969	3	−51	6	30	0	28		55	19	36	17	238
1970	185	−154	−70	38	30	−18		3	29	−26	12	156
1971	−34	−85	−58	33	0	−6		71	74	−3	20	250
1972	−32	−62	24	32	0	30	151	126	28	98	9	231
1973	−192	−84	70	72	75	−17	628	400	148	253	28	487
1974	−807	−399	58	63	0	−16	362	624	134	490	61	979
1975	−1,535	500	316	53	174	0	454	463	31	432	125	1,401
1976	−1,072	136	170	54	60	184	350	443	51	392	124	1,788
1977	−783	−68	54	72	0	21	144	446	177	269	152	2,076
1978	−164	−33	25	120	124	129	0	174	154	21	186	2,177
1979	953	−1,131	71	175	111	158	551	572	214	359	245	2,500
1980	−102	−459	27	177	148	−18	369	365	504	−139	322	2,313
1981	−1,729	780	125	187	287	−86	929	838	839	−1	302	2,200
1982	−1,609	−150	48	144	302	262	1,066	1,232	474	759	318	2,902
1983	−871	−16	38	236	123	48	450	761	85	676	243	3,816
1984	−221	−265	−89	242	31	−23	0	534	80	454	175	4,161
1985	125	−197	−54	286	14	27	0	116	3	113	16	4,360
1986	−1,055					27	0					

a. A positive number indicates a fall.

PART FOUR

THE ROLE OF THE EXTERNAL SECTOR IN DEVELOPMENT

16

HOW IMPORTANT ARE EXTERNAL INFLUENCES AND CONSTRAINTS?

CRITERIA FOR ANALYSIS

The emphasis of the traditional analyses of the NICs was on their 'openness' as the explanation of their success, and by implication, on the central importance of a country's policy towards external variables and influences as a determinant of economic performance. This chapter attempts to re-examine the ways in which 'openness' may explain performance, but more broadly to look at the interaction among domestic forces, external variables and policy.

Except by assuming (unrealistically) that the other two never change, it is meaningless to ask how important any one of these three is in absolute terms. It is self-evident that the more external conditions vary, the greater will be their role in explaining variations in performance; more specifically, the more depressed they are, or the stronger is an international tendency like protectionism, the more likely they are to be a binding constraint on a country's performance. Conversely, the more a country can (by policy or market response) adapt to new conditions, the more independent will its performance be of external forces. The more effectively its government is willing and able to intervene in normal conditions, the smaller may be its reaction to changes.

If a country's objectives are complex, the analysis needs to look beyond simple aggregate measures of growth to indicate either the success of external policy or the size of its impact on an economy. The fact of extensive government involvement in economic decisions and, in the countries studied here, particularly in their economic relations with the rest of the world, means that separating the roles of government policy and the impact of external events requires information or assumptions about how policy reacts to such events. Two themes come clearly from the country studies: that the external influences are seen as a constraint on (or in better times a stimulus to) aggregate domestic performance, not the basic explanation for it, and that structural change must come from internal structural changes (and probably policy); it is not a response to external stimuli. At both the macroeconomic and the structural level, better-than-average (for current conditions) external performance can be seen as a result, not necessarily an explanation, of good domestic performance.

If, as has been argued in Part three of this study on trade and financing, there are fundamental changes in the external conditions affecting industrial-ising countries, this is a reason for starting the analysis there, but a response directed at the particular export or financial flow that is changing may not be the appropriate adaptation to a long-run change. As some of the country studies argue, the appropriate response may be to reform or restructure some other part of the economy, possibly because the unfavourable change makes some existing weakness even less tolerable than before, rather than acting directly on the external side. On the other hand, government intervention has been heavy on the external side, and the policy and administrative reasons for this may remain convincing, so policy to offset any unfavourable change may frequently be directed to trade and capital flows, whether or not these are the immediate source of the problem or areas of serious weakness in the economy. The balances between what can be done to offset short-term difficulties and what should be done to promote long-term objectives, under changed circumstances, and between how much performance depends on external influences and how much on a country's own resources, are very sensitive to the views that a country takes about other (including non-economic) goals or constraints.

The interpretation may also be sensitive to systematic biases from the type of observer. If one is comparing a number of countries which are all facing the same change in external circumstances, it is the extent to which all have needed to adapt, even if in very different ways, which attracts attention. The authors looking at individual countries, however, see external circumstances in the context of all the changes as well as the continuing problems that their countries face; the adaptations that were made, and those which they believe should now be made, are reactions to the whole set of conditions facing a country, not a simple response to the changes in the supply of financial resources or the growth of world trade. Both interpretations are valid.

For the authors of the *Malaysia* study, it is industrialisation policy that is crucial, with exports seen as a part (a necessary one) of that. Like the Zimbabwe study, it emphasises the dependence of a small economy on its trading partners. *Thailand* also treats external demand and financing effec-tively as part of total demand and saving, with no special importance in themselves, and indeed for both it emphasises the existence and availability of domestic substitutes.

Echavarria stresses the importance that external demand has had for *Colombia*, but he points out that in earlier work, on Colombian history up to

1980, he had found little importance for trade. Even in 1980, reserves were sufficiently high for the changes in the external situation not to affect the economy immediately. The principal external trade shocks which he identifies since then are not the international ones, but the large movements in the coffee price and in Venezuelan imports.

The *Zimbabwe* study gives great importance to policy for the external sector, but within a more general strategy. The external sector is significant because of its size and many of the 'normal' effects discussed in Part three. Robinson argues that 'the key element' in Zimbabwe's strategy for the medium term is 'the management of the economy's links with the outside world', in this case reducing import dependence, but that 'policies in the area of trade and financing cannot themselves constitute a strategy to achieve overall socio-economic development goals'. External policy must be constrained by the objectives of redistribution of income.

For *Peru*, the specific shocks which Schuldt identifies as important in the 1970s originated in domestic excess demand, but in 1981 the combination of the fall in export prices, followed by volumes in 1982, and the reduction in tariffs and in restrictions on imports in line with a policy of opening the economy produced a severe external shock. The resulting policy changes also damaged export promotion; existing subsidies were restricted or eliminated. Even this shock, therefore, arose from government policy as well as from the external situation itself. The trade and financing difficulties since then have meant that the external position was a constraint on any policy. To lift it, the paper argues the need for industrialisation rather than an external policy.

The Peruvian analysis is fundamentally different from the others. Like Zimbabwe, it takes the country's 'dependence' on the industrial countries for granted: the particular explanations for different external crises may be domestic or external, but external constraints on trade and financing are always binding. For this reason both studies put reducing this dependence as an important goal in itself. For Peru, however, the dependence is at least as much on deliberate policies abroad as on international economic forces, on industrial countries' use of monetary policy to reduce inflation and on the deliberate transfer of adjustment costs to the developing countries. The response must, therefore, also be a political one: reducing dependence, a policy limit on debt repayments, and reform of the international monetary system all have a part in this.

THE SPECIAL CONTRIBUTION OF THE EXTERNAL SECTOR

It is uncontroversial that a country with a relatively large external sector will grow faster if its exports grow rapidly because of the direct effect on output, and because of the effect of relaxing any balance-of-payments constraint on imports and through them on investment and long-term growth. The results of comparing export growth and general performance sketched in the next two sections of this chapter are therefore surprising because of how weak the association seems rather than because of its existence. The analytical problems, and in many cases the confusion, arise because much of the literature on the significance of the external sector moves beyond these static associations. One direction is to argue (or assume) that raising exports is the only (or best) way of stimulating growth: whether because it is impossible to raise other, domestic, sources of demand directly or because a balance-of-payments constraint is binding on them. A more radical addition to normal trade analysis is to argue that external demand contributes to development not simply by increasing growth but by stimulating behavioural or structural changes (discussed in the following two sections on productivity and responsiveness). Such arguments may be based on the effects of some types of export. For manufactures, this in part raises the structural issues of industrialisation discussed in Chapter 13. In conventional terms, opening trade should raise a country's income (welfare) by permitting it to change the composition of its output to a more efficient structure, along a given production frontier. If it removes some financing or investment constraint, it may also permit the country to move to a higher frontier. But if trade is to have the third, stimulating, effect, this implies, first, that some behavioural inadequacy, an underdeveloped ability to perceive or respond to existing opportunities, is holding the country to a point below its physically determined production frontier (which would be in line with much of the country discussion here) and, second (usually implied rather than stated), that external demand is the only or best way of curing this situation.

For primary products, and for the total size of the external exposure of a country, exposure to the risk of large changes is also an issue. Effects from this raise behavioural issues, of what is the response to such risks and what modifications in response come from increased or reduced exposure to risk.

Understanding the significance of external events thus raises issues on the relative importance of demand and supply factors, and on the dynamic economic and non-economic interactions between external conditions and domestic responses.[1] Trying to examine these issues empirically adds, at each stage, the question of how far what is observed is a direct result of the external conditions, and how far it has been modified or attenuated by government policy responses.

Whether the government is one of the actors, and whether this is considered good, bad or neutral in its impact on the economy, is central to the interpretation of the evidence and to the policy conclusions to be drawn. This should be separable from the questions of whether trade has effects, beneficial or harmful, on an economy, and how these can be strengthened or mitigated; in practice, views about whether it is beneficial for a country to adapt to changes in external conditions and about the appropriate role of government action tend to be too closely related to encourage clear analysis.

To test the arguments for the third type of effect of the external sector, of improving response, it is necessary to examine what they are asserting about behaviour, and what type of evidence would be relevant. Unfortunately, such examination is not possible using the conventional data on external and domestic performance available here for the large sample because the basic studies from which the view that external strategy is crucial, and an open one the most favourable, is derived are not sufficiently clear in their behavioural assumptions. It is for this reason that the country studies focus particularly on the interactions between external and domestic factors. The studies also heighten the awareness of all the conditions affecting a country in addition to any external changes, which is essential to identify other straightforward economic explanations.[2]

EXPORTS AND GROWTH

The aggregate data for the countries studied here support the conclusion reached by all other studies, that countries with an above-average growth of manufactured exports tend to have an above-average GDP growth, but the relationship is by no means close.[3] Table 16.1 shows that while there was some association, especially for the NICs and the new NICs during the period 1973–81, this was already diminishing in the second half of the period; the data for more recent years are inadequate. The contrast between the apparent association for the more advanced countries and the more random results for the other middle-income countries suggests that any explanation must explain a step-change from one pattern of growth for which manufac- tured exports are not particularly important to another where they are; this could be as simple as an increase in the share of manufactures in total exports and output. As the discussion in Chapter 9 suggests, a few Asian countries effectively explain the apparent relationship; excluding them leaves a much less clear result. The evidence cannot justify putting a large analytical weight on differential performance. At the aggregate level, particularly the last four lines of the table which include all developing countries, there is a potentially important association between changes in aggregate export performance and changes in growth rates. Equally clearly, the divergences show a large role for special conditions in individual countries.

Zimbabwe has had below-normal export and GDP growth (until the most recent period), so that the emphasis of the country study on the need to change this is understandable. In contrast, Malaysia has had exceptionally good performance, and the country study emphasises the relationship. Thailand had above-normal export and GDP growth in both periods, and a study quoted in the country paper (Ajanant et al., 1984) confirms that export demand became increasingly important in the second half of the 1970s, but that domestic demand is the principal source of growth. Both Colombia and

Peru are most dependent on, and vulnerable to, exports of primary products, not manufactures.

SECTORAL EFFECTS

The evidence in Chapters 9 and 13 clearly shows that developing countries that have higher incomes have industrial structures and patterns of manufactured exports that are closer to those of the industrial countries, although still significantly different from them. The question of which way the causation runs among these three (and other) factors is not answerable at this level of aggregation, and needs to be considered at the country level; and that the changes in domestic structure seem greater than those in trade pattern suggests that it would be easier to justify a conclusion going from domestic structure to trade composition.

PRODUCTIVITY EFFECTS

The traditional argument for an effect from the external sector on the general performance of an economy is that of improved efficiency of allocation of resources arising from specialisation according to comparative advantage. This assumes either that prices are already operating as correct signals or that they are altered to remove distortions, so that greater external openness is necessarily associated with reduced domestic price distortion. This is now questioned in developing countries.[4] It also assumes that there are no other objectives which could conflict with that of higher output, and therefore require intervention.[5] Even if long-term growth is the critical objective, the arguments in Chapter 13 that particular patterns of output, or sectoral development, provide a better base for long-term development suggest one limit on allowing the external sector to determine these. Another reason comes from the discussion of the size of the economies and the role of risk. Short-term efficiency and comparative advantage arguments may suggest a high but risky degree of specialisation. Any national advantages from diversification in itself and in sectoral development could be external economy reasons for reducing the direct transmission of market signals from the external sector.

Productivity arising from reallocation would in any case be only a transitional effect. Some of the literature on the importance of openness attempts to extend it to a dynamic one. Krueger (1983: 53) explicitly tries to extend it in two ways. The argument that 'export promotion permits the rapid expansion of the most successful new firms and industries' is an implied series of efficiency gains, as firms move into new markets. Although it is thus merely a prolonged allocative gain, for a small country moving into world markets it may be sufficiently prolonged to provide years of growth.

Krueger then extends this to x-efficiency (efficiency in the more popular sense of how well a firm performs relative to some standard of best practice). While recognising that 'little is known about the dynamics of productivity increase; it is not at all clear the extent to which increases in output per head are achieved within existing plants; by new higher-productivity firms driving out older ones; and by competition among firms', she suggests that

> firms in an exporting environment are generally confronted with international competition and do not face the sheltered domestic markets they face under import substitution . . . In a monopolistic setting, for example, it might with fairness be asserted that productivity growth could be slow because of the absence of a competitive spur or because the entrepreneurial skill of management was poor, or for other reasons.

This spells out what many of the arguments for external competition simply assume: that increased competition produces improved productivity as a response. It takes the case for openness outside economics to the traditional behavioural argument over whether increased price competition encourages a producer: because a threat of a loss or lower return is a more powerful incentive than the prospect of an increased return within static market conditions; or discourages him: by reducing long-term security and short-term returns. In the absence of an agreed and measurable concept of 'open policy' (and comparable data on productivity) it is not resolvable by economic analysis.

There is a related argument which appears plausible, namely, that exporting, especially to markets which are more advanced, imposes certain standards of quality or other types of performance and thus has a type of training effect on productivity. It is supported by the attitudes of foreign investors in developing countries who make a clear distinction between quality acceptable for domestic consumption and that necessary for exports, even to other developing countries (Page, 1986b). But their reason (to preserve the reputation of the company in world markets) suggests that this attitude may not be a result of exporting. It may instead be part of the general change in practice to seeing exporting as normal (and therefore reputation as important), that must itself be created to make rapid export growth possible. It embraces two types of training effect: the conventional one, improving the quality of labour, and one in line with the broader definition of improving the quality of strategic decision-making discussed in Chapter 13.

These productivity arguments assume that an export strategy will be based on new, probably manufactured, exports, and not simply responding to growth in traditional markets for traditional exports. This is in line with the conclusions about the experience of successful exporters and about potential exports in the country studies and in Chapters 9 and 10. If a country is at a stage where its potential exports are those intensive in natural resources (including unskilled labour), producing import-substituting manufactures for the home market might better serve an objective of increasing the ability to offer high quality production. A contrary argument for expecting more systematic improvement in the quality of labour from concentration on exports would be as follows: if exports are based on the characteristics of the labour force and the production for home demand on the composition of that demand, there may be more systematic production links among potential export industries. The evidence from the Chenery (1986) study discussed in Chapter 13 does not appear to support any general distinctions of this sort; differences among industries and among countries are too strong.

If the productivity arguments for exports are valid, they would be reasons for encouraging a level of exposure to external markets determined not by whatever was implied by neutral policies, but by the level which captured all the benefits, which would have no necessary relation to that implied by world prices. This reasoning treats exports as instruments in achieving structural, domestic changes. For some countries, for some purposes (or in some periods, as is treated more fully in Chapter 17) other policies or targeting other markets might serve the purposes more effectively.

The Zimbabwe study sees such effects as coming instead from choice of sector. But it also suggests a role for a much more active policy to develop awareness of the possibilities and requirements of exporting. Both the Colombia and Peru studies also see this as a need, and consider the tendency to see export markets simply as markets for temporary excess production as a major behavioural deficiency. The other two studies take awareness of exports for granted. None would therefore accept a mechanical dependence on exports to change attitudes. The industrial policy (the movement out to a production frontier) must come from the country itself.

Although Krueger, as cited above, did not find a correlation between success and specific policy actions, she did for the direction of policy (Krueger, 1983: 204). The cases where export promotion measures were introduced independently of other policy changes, however, are not treated separately; on the contrary, the association of aids to exports, including devaluation, with other government action is one of the advantages cited for them.[6] One of the associated government incentives given particular emphasis is commitment to a long-term policy, in other words a reduction in risks for the potential exporter. The argument does not specify why a reduction of risk in this way should have advantages over other methods, such as a guaranteed home market, or how seeking advantages from risk reduction is consistent with the role of external markets in exerting pressure for productivity improvements by increasing the risks of losing markets, although one reason could be that the latter are by their nature less threatening to economic decision-makers than policy changes. There are a number of countries (including some of her case studies) which have moved away from export promotion, so that such a commitment may not in practice be seen as genuine by economic decision-makers.

EXTERNAL DEMAND AND RESPONSE TO CHANGES

The ability to respond to (and indeed to anticipate) changes is clearly an essential part of dynamic productivity for economic decision-makers, and it is arguable that spreading it is a basic element of what may be called development. The history of successful exporters in Chapter 9 does suggest that an ability to respond to new markets and to find new products is an essential element of success, but it is not clear whether there could be causation in the opposite direction as well. If ability to adapt can best be improved through practice, then increasing the number of changes, or the rate of change, facing decision-makers may improve their long-term prospects. But there may be more structural factors determining it which need to be altered. The level of development already reached, or the time during which a country has been industrialising, may lead to the existence of industrial or other economic interests which must be satisfied.

One argument for an effect from external demand is that external demand changes more often (Balassa, 1981: 26). With respect to fluctuations, this is contrary to the normal presumption that a large number of countries will smooth effects. The faster growth and greater structural change in developing countries in recent years are also reasons for doubting whether industrial country markets offer more challenges than home markets. In the 1970s and the first half of the 1980s, the instability of demand growth in industrial countries and the variability of primary prices increased. Although the consensus forecasts for the medium term (as always) do not show such fluctuations, the perceived possible range of outcomes must now be greater than in the late 1960s or early 1970s, if expectations are determined by recent experience. In some countries (including the sample countries), however, domestic outcomes and conditions have also become much more uncertain than in the past, and it is arguable that for private decision-makers the uncertainty of domestic policy changes is greater than that from external economic changes. It is indeterminate whether domestic or external dependence should be regarded as the greater risk. For governments, who can make the policy changes, the perception must be that domestic uncertainties are smaller or more manageable.

The international responses to the major international economic crises of the last 15 years, in particular the three oil price changes and the debt crisis, suggest that international co-ordination is unachievable (whether or not it is desirable), and therefore that if intervention to mitigate external effects or protect a long-term strategy from them is desired, it must be at a national or country-grouping level. The withdrawal of industrial countries behind protectionist barriers and their own exchange-rate regime, the Louvre agreement, and the revival of interest in regulation of international monetary arrangements, suggest a move in all countries towards rejection of the attitude that external shocks are unavoidable. As was suggested in Chapter 2 with regard to protection, this growing reluctance to adapt could itself stem from greater shares of trade and external financing which increase the size of external effects. The contrast between the withdrawal behind barriers by the industrial countries and the continuing use of export strategies by the NICs may hint at a disadvantage in ability, or willingness, to adapt for countries with a long industrial background compared with those with more recent industrialisation. This could suggest different responses between those countries now industrialising from a long-existing base and the others.

These trends indicate that exposure to maximum change may not be desired by governments, but also that external exposure may not be the best way of increasing productivity. It is important to remember that learning to adapt is not an end in itself. An ability to adapt is important partly to allow a long-term programme for an industry or country to continue in the face of unexpected changes. Changes in patterns of output may be designed to affect the long-term ability to respond flexibly, while continuing to grow; adapting to short-term problems could hinder this. The potential long-term financial cost of exposure to external risk was discussed in Chapters 14 and 15. These conflicting considerations make it difficult to see *a priori* whether a need to become adaptable should lead to a presumption in favour of exposure to external conditions, particularly if countries' flexibility or ability to adapt also arise from differences in their initial conditions.

The recent history of Zimbabwe, before Independence and in current southern African trading conditions, suggests that it is more exposed than normal to risks from dependence on foreign trade, and some protection from the risks might therefore be indicated. The Malaysia study emphasises the increased exposure to variations in foreign demand during the 1980s. Although arguing that the fluctuations were not 'detrimental', it does not suggest that they were beneficial, and notes the ways in which the government has intervened to reduce them. Thailand and Colombia also emphasise how external finance and government intervention have been used to reduce the impact of external changes. Peru has seen large effects from changes in government external policy as well as from purely external factors, and the study considers this vulnerability harmful rather than stimulating.

The ability to respond to change and the types of 'productivity' raised in the preceding section suggest an objective seen as important in several of the country studies, that of developing 'exporters' rather than exports. The contrast between an economy where there are many entrepreneurs looking for new activities and markets and one where many are at best prepared to respond to clear opportunities may be a better description of the difference between the NICs and the rest than more mechanical ones.

INCOME DISTRIBUTION

Income distribution can be affected by the pattern of industry or the pattern of incentives, and therefore could depend on the choice of strategy. In particular, encouragement of exports on the basis of the advantages of low-cost labour, and maintenance of a low exchange rate, could affect the income of different types of labour. The direction of these effects, however, when combined with the potential training and other productivity effects and (if the policies are successful) with increased demand for such labour, is not predictable. Those country studies that consider income distribution as one of the policy goals are more concerned with other groups, in particular with rural populations. The studies suggest that the distributional implications of different strategies are (or should be) an important criterion (and, as discussed in Chapter 17, judge the NICs' performance accordingly), but indicate that the particular conditions of each country determine what effects can be expected.

The distribution of income and wealth is an important objective or constraint for government policies, including trading strategy, in most of these countries. Therefore the outcome for distribution must be an acceptable (and intended) consequence; it would be wrong to analyse it as an uncontrollable additional effect of any policy. Studies of changes in income distribution in the NICs are inconclusive.[7]

The Peru study gives a particularly comprehensive description of how the different interests explain the formulation of policies and the changes in them, but this underlies the discussions in the other papers, particularly Colombia and Zimbabwe. In this sense, namely, the political necessity of satisfying interests, external policy is always subordinate to domestic goals even in countries where it appears to be most constraining (the Peruvian policy on debt is an example of the need to 'break' the constraint when there appears to be a fundamental contradiction between the two).

IMPLICATIONS FOR POLICY DIRECTED AT THE EXTERNAL SECTOR

The evidence from the past, even for the periods of rapid trade growth, in favour of special advantages for exports and therefore for trade policy, is not strong. It is not possible to say whether the countries which succeeded did so because of special effects from trade, or because they were able to alter their economies in such a way as to be able to respond to and create opportunities which, in the period to which most of the studies quoted in this section relate, were frequently in trade. Most of the economies had rapid growth and transformation in domestic demand as well.

Robinson's arguments for import substitution in *Zimbabwe*, with exports seen as necessary 'as a means of relaxing constraints', are given entirely in terms of the domestic development strategy, not of a special role for the external sector.

Echavarria argues that for *Colombia* the prospects for export income from coal and oil (and the coffee revenue available in 1986) should be used as an opportunity to develop into new sectors, in new exports, and through encouraging domestic industry and agriculture. He also stresses the need explicitly to avoid allowing fluctuations in coffee revenue to overwhelm the economy and planning for other sectors, a case where the effects from one of the additional results of exports (exposure to changes) are large enough to justify a special external policy. In particular, he suggests that a more consistent policy on both other exports and import controls is necessary. He also argues that active search for external revenue has become a need for Colombia because of the change in the world external financing situation. External policy thus does not have a central role for either Zimbabwe or Colombia, but this is because of the particular difficulties or opportunities facing these countries, not because of general characteristics of external demand.

The Colombian experience also indicates how even a country with an extremely important external sector treats external policy as a suitable tool for various domestic goals: in particular, the use of the exchange rate (and in some cases import controls) to reduce inflationary pressures. Peru also offers examples of this.

The perceived impossibility of increasing external financial resources for *Peru*, combined with the heavy dependence on capital and intermediate good imports, means that the Peru study does put strong emphasis on improving the trade position. Import substitution is seen as difficult for specific, product-related reasons in the short term, but desirable in the medium term. Because simple consumer import substitution and traditional exports offer few opportunities, the analysis focuses on the possibilities for non-traditional exports. The strategy is thus explicitly presented as the best available means of raising resources for development, not as the result of assigning a special position to exports of manufactures in development. Peru is the only one of the countries to have tried a policy of complete openness to imports, apparently as a consequence of direct application of the type of arguments for trade discussed in this chapter.[8] The results of its increased vulnerability to fluctuations from the external sector without adequate finance to mitigate them do not offer an encouraging example.

EFFECTS OF TARGETING THE EXTERNAL SECTOR ON THE ROLE OF GOVERNMENT

The Krueger (1978) position is explicitly for export-promotion policy (by price-oriented means): 'the alternative of a strictly laissez-faire regime is not explored [because no government has followed it]; rather the comparison is between two conscious active policies to encourage growth' (p. 284), i.e., between import substitution and export promotion. The additional effects from exports thus apparently come more from the nature of the policies used to promote them (prices) than from the fact that the goods are going abroad.[9] A more extreme policy position is that no policy is better than any policy. This is the position taken by Balassa (e.g., 1982: 48). Unlike Krueger, he rejects the view that the successful exporters intervened, and appears to favour a very restricted role for government. Arguments against intervention, in addition to those of allocative efficiency and comparative advantage, are that even if special advantages or disadvantages exist, the possible mistakes by developing country governments or harm from inefficient administration would be more damaging.

The fact that there was intervention in some NICs appears indisputable. If any of the arguments for special effects (favourable or unfavourable) from trade are accepted, this could be a reason for intervening to encourage or avoid them. The traditional argument in international trade theory, that other types of domestic intervention are preferable if the objective is to promote specific industries or manufacturing in general, is not relevant here because the issue is specifically whether external factors rather than industrial policy are important and, if so, how to harness their peculiarly external effects on the economy.

If the extent or form of government intervention in the economy is regarded as important in itself, then the type implied by different external strategies becomes an important factor in the choice. Increased trading exposure may lead to greater involvement in negotiations about products with other governments, which may require far more sectoral and microeconomic intervention in domestic policy (administering trading arrangements or standards, for example). Avoiding trade involves more drastic, but perhaps less discriminatory, controls. The same is true of external financial exposure, especially as official flows, and official renegotiations of commercial flows, have increased their relative importance. Avoiding government intervention, or even choosing the form it takes, may not be feasible in areas where more powerful trading partners or creditors intervene. The effect of trade on government is not an issue in any of the country studies, partly because they all see trade policy as only an element in other policies.

The role of the external sector may also have a more direct impact on government; taxes on trade have traditionally been regarded as among the easiest, administratively and perhaps also politically, to collect. Fluctuations in trade, therefore, may have an immediate effect on government as well as traders. Malaysia in 1986 and the central role of coffee in Colombia are obvious examples, but this is an additional reason for avoiding fluctuations for all the countries.

EXTERNAL FINANCING AND GROWTH

The increase in the real aggregate supply of funds to the developing countries in the 1970s was associated with an increase in their average difference from industrial country growth rates (the growth rates of the developing countries fell less), as would be expected if the balance of payments is a binding constraint. The additional finance permitted them to be 'de-linked' from the old pattern of only a slight difference in growth rates. In the more traditional development terminology of 'two gaps', it helped to fill the gap left by domestic savings which were inadequate to finance desired investment and output growth. The fall and expected continuing low level of external finance are, under such a model, significant reasons to expect markedly slower growth in the future. The discussion in Chapter 14 suggests that available capital inflows are not amenable to influence by the recipient, and that the risks even of accepting what may be available have become more serious. This channel of external influence may therefore be a more important exogenous determinant of the domestic economy than in the past.

This does not mean that the additional argument used for export promotion, that it improves access to the international financial markets (for example, Krueger, 1978: 285), is valid. Various effects of the trade regime on supplies of other types of finance, including aid and foreign investment, are argued, mainly suggesting that a less controlled regime is most attractive. This is not supported by the evidence in this study. As was noted in Chapter 14, only South Korea (and Brazil, if it is considered successful) of the successful exporters relied heavily on bank finance, while many of those who used it heavily were not successful exporters. There is no evidence in the stated objectives of the bilateral aid givers to support it.[10] Foreign investors normally prefer a protected market as most invest for local sales rather than to compete for exports, and even those that do export have their own ways of encouraging efficiency in their subsidiaries without relying on the uncertain effects of exposure to external competition (Page, 1986b). The exception may be access to multilateral institutional finance. This is now tied to policies which are derived from the studies quoted here, as seen in Peru's experience.

For those countries (broadly those in Latin America) which have depended on foreign capital for a significant long-term contribution to total national savings, the conclusions from Chapters 14 and 15 that middle-level countries cannot do this, and that it cannot be regarded as normal for them to be able to rely on temporary external finance to avoid temporary trade changes or to give extra time to adjust to permanent changes in the supply of external finance, are of central importance to development strategy. The country studies all, therefore, consider the question of the supply of savings, and most start from the assumption that there is a gap between domestic saving and desired saving (to be filled if possible from foreign saving). This raises the question of whether the traditional two-gap model which emphasised the special contribution of foreign saving to development is still relevant. Malaysia and Thailand look at foreign financing primarily in the context of the problem of increasing the total supply of saving. The arguments for giving it a more crucial role are developed most fully in Echavarria's paper on Colombia, but the Zimbabwe and Peru papers also argue for particular needs for some imported goods which therefore require some contribution from foreign financing. If this is valid, then foreign financing, as was argued above for exports, has a contribution beyond the purely macroeconomic. To the extent that the increase in external financing in the late 1970s went principally to the public sector, this is another route by which a greater role for the external sector might actively increase the role of government in the economy, rather than merely accommodating it, as in the Malaysian case.

Although *Zimbabwe* considers it necessary to increase the rate of investment, its pessimism about foreign sources of finance leads to the conclusion that exports must be the principal means. The Peru study is very conscious of the policy constraints on multilateral official finance, but it is the lack of access to all external finance which is crucial. ˙

Malaysia did face a problem of inadequate domestic savings in the early 1980s, arising from the decline in tax buoyancy and also the shift to a countercyclical policy in managing exposure to external fluctuations, combined with the increase in their size. Foreign finance was the chosen answer, and it probably also financed increased investment. Although the study argues that this may have been over-used in 1980–2, it suggests that it may now be being under-used. The impact of past events on perceptions of risk is, therefore, the important constraint on exploiting the trade and financing advantages from the external sector.

The study of *Thailand* sees some problems from excessive domestic demand, and points out some areas in which revenue could be mobilised (public sector prices, for example). But it also argues that there are particular difficulties in increasing domestic saving because of the poor tax base. External borrowing seems, therefore, to be seen as a simple substitute for domestic, and it has had an increasing role since the 1971–6 Plan when the government began to take a more active role; its share in total saving increased again in the 1980s. Since 1980, as the debt-service ratios have increased, government investment has had to be compressed. The study's conclusion, that the use of external finance should be reduced, is based purely on its possible costs, not any special characteristics relative to the domestic alternatives.[11] As in Malaysia, shorter-term foreign finance enabled the government to increase its intervention, and the choice between using it or not is still available, and to be made on cost grounds; both traditional roles of the foreign sector remain feasible.

In *Colombia*, there has been a particularly unstable external sector (because of its vulnerability to a few primary product prices) so that domestic (public) savings have compensated for foreign fluctuations. The presence at various periods (most recently 1986) of considerable foreign revenue from temporarily high export prices effectively reverses the external financing problem to one of where to assign the surplus, including how to divide responsibility between the producers and the government; long-term foreign saving has not been important as a substitute for domestic saving, but medium-term has been an important buffer between world conditions and the Colombian economy. The suggestion is that an ability to compensate for the foreign fluctuations which are the necessary cost of high dependence on primary exports is (at least) a desirable condition for relying on them. In Colombia, the policy recommendations of reducing dependence on coffee would thus move the economy simultaneously away from the external sector as the source and financier of fluctuations.

For Colombia, Malaysia and Thailand, although in very different ways, the availability of foreign finance has been an important explanation for the activities of the public sector in stabilisation and investment. If foreign finance provides a type of saving to which the government has preferential access, this can have an important developmental effect. It permits the government to allocate saving according to a programme. Stabilisation could reduce the perceived risks of other investors, which (unless the training effects of change and instability are given a high weight) must increase investment and should increase the relative weight of long-term returns. Under current conditions, probably only Malaysia has sufficiently rapidly growing exports and adequate access to foreign credits for this to remain important.

Although the Colombia study notes that external surpluses are less likely to be available in the future, and the other two comment on the increased concern about the risks, none of the three countries has yet faced the drastic change in the availability of funds assumed in the world prospects outlined in Chapter 2, or already facing many other debtor countries. Their policies, and those suggested for them, may not yet therefore have fully adjusted to the changes and the conclusions implied by the analysis of Chapter 14 and 15. Peru has suffered since the 1970s from the absence of any cushion, whether access to finance or own reserves, against external shocks (or the impact on the external sector of domestic changes in demand). This has meant that policy there has been more dominated by the need to make short-term adjustments. While the results have been complicated by other problems, they do illustrate difficulties that may become more prevalent as other countries face the need to manage external trading exposure without access to medium-term finance.

CONCLUSIONS ON THE ROLE OF THE EXTERNAL SECTOR

There has been a shift in perceptions within industrialising countries towards emphasising the role of the external sector (as observed by Echavarria). Since

1980 export markets and the supply of external savings have become constrained, and therefore can no longer be taken for granted. The practicality of treating exports (and imports) as the outcome of a policy of industrialisation or other domestic goals, or as determined by the ability to create new exports and exporters, and of taking the risk of specialising in promising products, depended on a cushion of available external finance in order to prevent short-term domestic or external shocks from having a serious impact on a planned programme of development. This 1960s and 1970s model has been replaced at the policy (and economic analysis) level by emphasis on adjustment, and destroyed at the practical level by the more severe external shocks and less adequate financial resources outlined in earlier chapters.

The shocks and the growing variability in external trade and financial flows in the 1970s had already started to change perceptions. Until the 1980s, however, governments had been able to blunt the impact of external shocks, even the largest and even in Peru (Alarco, 1987: 136). The rise in interest costs and the fall in expected export growth were serious blows. A final change which must be recognised, however, is the emphasis on exports and on particular policies derived from studies of the NICs by the multilateral institutions. Their strong advocacy of increasing trade, directing policies at trade, and a price-led approach to policy, was a new type of external influence on developing economies reinforced by their control of a growing share of the diminishing pool of finance. Although most economic work on the NICs and other developing countries since the early 1980s has noted the uncertainties, country differences and limitations on the type of role found for an 'export strategy' in the 1970s writings (as cited and discussed above), the official publications of the World Bank (particularly *WDR*, 1985, 1987) and the IMF remain exceptions, and such views probably also influence some bilateral lenders.[12] As their role in external finance increases, and the role of external finance as a constraint on development itself increases, their views must affect policy and the relative importance given to external policy, even if policymakers in the countries concerned are not convinced by them. The external sector is certainly now an important constraint.

The analytical difficulty in treating exports or external exposure as having a special role, in other words, as being a substitute development stimulus for a government unable to manage industrialisation (or other structural change) by domestic policies, lies in the inconsistencies of trying to combine in the same model the traditional benefits of open markets with developmental, supply-side problems. The former assume that exports follow demand, with gains coming from changes among sectors, each of which is already efficient in terms of its own production. The latter assume that sectors or firms are not operating efficiently in terms of either internal production or finding markets, and are, for some reason, unable to respond properly to market incentives. If the second set of problems exists, then the first mechanism is unlikely to work properly. It is not merely a question of starting with rigorous assumptions and relaxing them: the first, traditional, results depend on the ability of factors of production to move efficiently to new patterns of production, and the second assume that they need to be 'developed' before this can happen.

Even if open markets do improve allocation, there is not a permanent effect on 'development' because the inefficiencies in production and the difficulty of moving to a composition of output that offers more long-term growth, including the need to adapt to future changes, are not resolved. The export strategy can only 'work' if it accomplishes the developmental shift in attitudes and productivity, so that the country remains responsive to external changes. If exports are the only way of transforming the economy, and if once they have moved a country to its production frontier future growth depends on external demand, even this does not offer a mechanism for catching up, only for growing at the same rate as a developed country. Any special advantages from exports must be balanced against the special disadvantages of external financing. Its costs and its supply are determined externally, in constrast to domestic financing, so that a country vulnerable to exports loses the ability to choose when to adjust and when to finance a shock.

If the problem is to change the productivity (i.e., the behaviour) of decision-makers in the developing countries, then, as the original studies of export orientation point out, little is known about how this is done. There can certainly be no presumption that one type of structural change: from domestic to export demand, will work better than another: for example, to particular types of output. Still less is it acceptable to argue that a change to exports does have such unquantifiable effects, while considering only measurable economic benefits from other changes. The need to study, rather than assume, how decision-makers respond to a challenge should not need stressing. The presence of long-term objectives for the structure of the economy on the part of governments further reduces the presumption that only one solution is effective.

The experience of rapid growth in developing countries (and in their exports) in 1986 is important precisely because it suggests that there are important possibilities of increasing exports from developing country efforts in the absence of explanatory factors on the side of demand or relative price.[13] The lack of understanding of how this happened, however, is a reason for caution about accepting a purely structural approach that returns to treating the external sector as an unconstrained cushion, particularly in the light of the high financial costs incurred in the early 1980s. The country strategies and analyses of their prospects need to find a balance between the economically clear arguments from trade theory and the more difficult territory of industrial and behavioural change discussed, albeit inadequately, in Chapter 13.

NOTES

1. A distinction is made between the comparative static effects of changing a country's external policy or exposure and the possibility of dynamic ones from having a 'more open' policy. These may not be fully separable if behavioural effects mean that an open economy builds up pressure for a change back (the argument that increased external exposure leads to increased demands for protection, for example) or against one (the argument that it alters the behaviour of entrepreneurs from rent-seeking, and therefore protection-seeking, to profit-seeking). These are not explored in the present study.
2. Balassa (1981a: 23), for example, includes three countries with internal shocks in his sample of seven inward- oriented countries in comparing performance with five outward-oriented economies in the 1970s, although it is clear that these countries had substantially lower growth than the 'unshocked' inward-oriented countries and therefore bias the comparison.
3. Although Krueger's (1978: 299) conclusion was that 'Why the export-growth strategy should appear to be so much more effective is not entirely understood', her analysis found (p. 273) a coefficient of only 0.1 when regressing output growth on export growth; the size seems surprisingly small, given simply the normal relationships expected between one component of demand and output, and not an argument for putting special weight on it. The coefficient for the policy regime, the main focus of the study, was insignificant.
4. Bradford (1987) finds 'no general association between degrees of price distortion and inward versus outward orientation' (p. 312), and in particular a tendency to have more negative real interest rates among the more outward-oriented and successful.
5. Bhagwati (1978: 90 et seq.), for example, argues against quantitative restrictions on the grounds that they make allocation different from that of the market. As this is their purpose, it does not seem a sufficient argument without passing judgement on the reason for preferring a different allocation.
6. It should be noted that what Krueger calls liberalisation (p. 93) is in part a matter of arithmetic rather than of policy change. A devaluation reduces the estimated effect of a quota because this is measured by the difference between the (esti-mated) local price of the externally produced good and the home price, and devaluation raises the price of the foreign good. There is thus liberalisation even if there is no change in any of what are normally considered to be trade restraints, even if they continue to be strong enough to be binding or potentially to influence behaviour.
7. Cf. World Bank (WDR 1987: 87), which points out that 'an outward-oriented strategy can improve the distribution of income' and quotes examples in both directions.
8. Cf. Schuldt (1981) for the direct role of the World Bank in encouraging the adoption of liberalisation in 1980.
9. The analysis even attempts (p. 287) to define some protection against imports as market-based export promotion if industries receive 'sheltered positions in the domestic market' although they 'compete satisfactorily in the international market'. This is not valid; the domestic protection is an export subsidy because if there are economies of scale it permits lower pricing by reducing or removing the risk element in required returns.
10. Bhagwati (1978: 14) notes an opposite effect: one reason for the fact that all developing countries intervene in trade is that aid-tying requires some form of import licensing by source.

11. This role of external financing as an easy alternative to politically difficult mobilisation of domestic saving could suggest a systematic relation between its use and the supply of domestic saving, and has been used as an argument against it (especially against aid). Bradford (1987) analyses externally and internally-oriented countries, and finds little difference; the differences in other factors affecting domestic saving and in investment ratios make any simple relationship unlikely. Looking at differences in the same country in different periods, as some of the country studies do here, is an alternative approach. It is not even clear what the sign or direction of influence might be: rather than a substitution effect, higher saving through higher foreign saving could increase growth or expectations of it and therefore investment and hence domestic savings. But higher domestic savings could also permit the economy to grow and attract foreign saving.

   It is, however, unclear what policy implication could be derived if a relationship were found: unless domestic saving is considered to have some special function, if an alternative source of saving is available at lower (economic or political) cost, it seems desirable to use it. Avoiding it because it is 'easy', like promoting exports because foreign markets are 'difficult', could only be justified in the context of a 'cold-shower' model of development which suggested that the challenges from normal world conditions are insufficient to stimulate economies to mature.

12. Cf. Bradford (1986: 124) 'It is not a helpful circumstance to have our premier international financial institutions wedded to a single model of a successful development policy or to a narrow definition of an effective stabilization program.'

13. The lack of explanations by the international institutions is discussed in Page (1987).

Table 16.1 Relationship between exports of manufactures and GDP growth

	GDP growth			Growth of exports of manufactures relative to ldc average		
	1973–81	1975–80	1980–5	1973–81	1975–80	1980–5
Newly industrialising countries						
Argentina	1.1	1.4	−2.1	−8.4	−2.2	
Brazil	5.9	6.8		3.6	−0.6	
Hong Kong	8.5	11.1	5.7	−2.4	1.6	0.7
India	4.1	3.4		−4.4	−2.9	
Mexico	6.6	6.6	1.6	−9.1	−9.3	
Singapore	8.2	9.0		3.0	7.0	−1.5
South Korea	7.6	7.5	7.5	3.1	2.4	6.3
Taiwan	8.0	10.5	6.1	0.3	5.6	0.8
Simple average	6.2	7.0		−1.8	0.2	
New NICs						
Colombia	4.6	5.4	2.0	−9.1	−4.2	
Malaysia	7.7	9.2	5.1	10.9	4.3	
Peru	2.6	1.7	−0.5	−4.9	9.9	
Thailand	7.1	7.6	5.3	4.4	12.4	−2.0
Zimbabwe	3.3	0.9	5.1	−10.3	−11.3	−14.8
Simple average	5.1	4.9	3.4	−1.8	2.2	
Other middle-income countries						
Chile	3.7	7.5	−0.4	15.7	14.8	
Costa Rica	3.9	5.2	0.3	−3.3	−5.9	
Egypt	8.4	6.7		−21.2	−29.0	−3.7
Ivory Coast	6.2	6.8		−5.0	−3.7	
Kenya	4.5	5.8	2.7	−14.9	−14.2	
Morocco	5.2	5.1		−1.1	−1.1	
Pakistan	5.9	6.1	6.3	−8.3	−7.1	−1.0
Philippines	5.8	6.2	−0.9	1.0	8.5	
Senegal	2.5	1.4		−10.9	−23.3	
Sri Lanka	6.9	5.5	4.7	6.1	27.8	
Tunisia	5.9	5.8		7.1	−3.0	
Uruguay	4.2	4.5	−3.1	4.2	3.1	
Venezuela	3.5	3.3	−1.3	5.3	9.3	
Simple average	5.1	5.4		−1.9	−1.8	
Averages by area						
Africa	5.1	4.6		−8.0	−12.2	
Asia	6.9	7.3		1.5	6.0	
Latin America	4.0	4.7		−0.7	1.6	
Areas using UN data						
Africa	3.6	3.6	0.9	−18.7	−10.5	−9.5
Asia	6.0	6.8	6.4	0.0	2.7	0.0
Latin America	4.6	5.3	0.6	−7.0	−3.6	−1.5
All non-oil developing countries	4.7	5.3	2.5	actual growth rates		
				11.8	14.0	10.1

Sources: IMF, *International Financial Statistics*; IMF, IFS, *Supplement on Trade Statistics*; UNCTAD, *Handbook of International Trade and Development Statistics*; UN, *Monthly Bulletin of Statistics*.

17

THE NICs AS EXAMPLES TO
THE NEW NICs

The 1970s studies of the NICs looked at export promotion as an alternative to import substitution in seeking faster growth. In addition to the doubts about the actual impact of export promotion (and about growth as a goal), more recent analysis of the experience of the NICs suggests that import substitution and export promotion are not alternatives. They may be appropriate at different stages of a country's development or under different external or domestic conditions, or for different sectors simultaneously. If this is so, the questions of whether they must conflict as implied by the traditional approach, and of how to move from one to the other, become important. There are also other lessons from the NICs which are being drawn by observers and decision-makers in the new NICs.

IMPORT SUBSTITUTION AND EXPORT PROMOTION AS A SEQUENCE

The countries that did show high rates of growth of manufactured exports in the 1970s were those which already had a high share of manufacturing in total output, following a period of import substitution (Melo *et al.*, in Chenery *et al.*, 1986). In the context of trade outcomes as an aspect of industrialisation, the arguments for expecting import substitution to come first are related to those for infant industry protection. For an individual industry, it can be argued that it needs to develop skills, both conventional training and managerial or entrepreneurial skill; perhaps to reach a minimum level of output, if there are economies of scale; and to start in a market which is 'easier' both because of lower direct costs, better transport, etc., and because it is more familiar.[1] This could be extended to a country either by aggregation, namely, a country will have relatively more new industries and fewer mature ones at earlier stages of development, or because of the additional role of linkages among industries in strengthening all of them for moving into foreign markets (emphasised by Chenery, in Chenery *et al.*, 1986) and the need for a general development of attitudes. A country may also need a certain level of physical infrastructure for individual industries to be able to compete on equal terms in world markets. Whether these are from the public sector or financed by the early industries to permit their own development, they require a minimum capital accumulation from domestic markets.

The policy implications of such a sequence depend partly on the costs to the rest of the economy of developing an industry, or industrialisation in general, compared with the size of the eventual benefits (and, therefore, how long the sequence lasts). They also depend on whether industrialisation or structural change is itself an objective, in which case if import substitution is a necessary phase, its costs also are inevitable. The sequence might not, however, be necessary for a country without such an objective and with natural resource-based exports and a special advantage which can compensate for the lack of a developed infrastructure. The more important these are, the less importance a country may give to the whole question of a strategy of industrialisation or to planning and incurring the costs of the sequence.

The importance of attitudes, however, suggests that the choice between import substitution and export promotion may not be entirely a matter of economic linkages and necessary sequences. The results of the country studies have emphasised the need for individual industries to develop the perception that exporting is a possible option. But this was also true for countries. Before the success of the NICs and the studies of that success, the choice for developing countries was seen as between specialising in primary production for export, while importing most manufactures, and developing an industry for the home market. The argument put forward above for a sequence, that only countries that had already achieved substantial development could have the necessary economic (or socio-cultural) structure for exporting manufactures, was unquestioned (Pazos, 1985: 63). The issue was whether a country could accelerate the process of development through deliberate industrialisation (by means of protection) or, indeed, whether it was essential to do so because it could not depend on primary exports to grow sufficiently to permit industrialisation. There were no counter-examples of countries that were still clearly 'developing countries' but competing against 'industrial countries'.[2]

The fact that the present 'new NICs' (and outside advisers) can now see successful developing country exporters of manufactures means that they may consider the possibility of this at an earlier stage in their development, or without waiting for the natural process, if there is one, of the sequence. That the NICs have succeeded indicates that the strong version of the need for a sequence – namely, that a complete developed economy structure must precede competition with other developed countries – cannot be valid; but their own histories of import substitution support the weaker version – namely, that some period of domestic-based industrialisation is necessary. The strong version may have made two common errors: first, of confusing the average level of skills, both general and specific, in a developing country with the maximum available levels (the latter may permit some industries to succeed); and second, of overemphasising the difficulty of transferring technology and training. It may also have underestimated the contribution that can be made by faster growth, through its effect in reducing the average age of capital goods and thus raising productivity and the potential advantages from cheap labour (Pazos, 1985: 63). The first two judgements would also apply to prospects for the next generation of NICs. The last, however, cannot be assumed if world growth is slower, and the amount by which growth in developing countries exceeds it is smaller. And large supplies of labour are present only in some countries.

There is another potential constraint. If successful exporting, (and rapid industrial development), requires efforts to move into new products to make structural change, and in some cases to contend with strong interest groups, there may be a limit to the time during which this can remain a principal national goal, and therefore during which countries will consistently out-perform the average. The decline in the relative export (and output) growth of some of the early NICs (and of the industrial countries before them) could be because of this type of reduced competitiveness, possibly reflected in part in rising labour costs no longer matched by productivity gains (cf. Bradford, 1987b). The successful developing countries have been able to postpone this until they have made the transition to export growth and gone some way to changing the composition of their exports and output in the direction of the pattern characteristic of development.

If world growth is slower, it may be more difficult to sustain the efforts over what is likely to be a longer period. A country still dependent on primary products may face particular difficulties in making the transition if upward fluctuations in their price periodically reduce the incentive. The Colombia study suggests that this may be true there, although Echavarria argues strongly that this complacency is an error. Malaysia may have moved into a period of determination to grow in the 1970s, perhaps helped by the internal pressures which generated the NEP. Whether the renewed social pressures in 1987 strengthen or weaken the external performance, and what effect discouragement from poor expectations for the world economy may have, are difficult to determine. For Zimbabwe, the pressures and opportunities from the political and military situation in southern Africa could lead to a turning point in perceptions of external opportunities, but this could be in either direction. In contrast to the 1970s, the current tide in economists' interpretations of success is in favour of intervention, which affects choice of policy.

The countries in our sample are not, of course, monolithic. The interests of different groups within them (stressed particularly in regard to Colombia, Peru and Zimbabwe) are affected by the choice of different types of industry, and changes in groups' political influence can, therefore, also lead to changes in external strategy. This has certainly explained the alternation, rather than sequence, in Peru, and can help to explain changes between greater and lesser enthusiasm for industrial development in the other countries. A more stable sequence may only be possible where interests are less divergent or one is more dominant, perhaps in Thailand.

The success of the NICs has affected attitudes in the next generation, particularly among the Asian countries, because of their close contacts (Ariff and Hill, 1985: 233). At the time which the country studies identify as the beginning of the turn towards exports, in the early 1970s, the success of the Asian NICs was starting to be apparent and to be studied; world trade was growing at its fastest rate; and the decline in protection had become sufficiently well established to be taken for granted. In contrast, the examples nearest to Colombia and Peru are Mexico and Brazil (and Colombia for Peru), with periods of successful exports but also long periods of import substitution. Therefore, Peru and Colombia do not regard import substitution as necessarily an obstacle to a successful export strategy.

MOVING FROM IMPORT SUBSTITUTION TO EXPORT PROMOTION

If import substitution normally precedes export promotion, it is necessary to analyse how the transition happens. Does it build up forces which then help turn the economy outwards, or are the policies to promote substitution (and the interest groups helped by it) so different that the transition requires major force, or are exports merely a possible next step? Much of the analysis of the 1970s which assumed a choice between import substitution and export promotion suggested that they were incompatible, and indeed that both the policies that promoted import substitution and the type of industries which resulted were harmful to export prospects. The fact that successful countries have accomplished the transition suggests that these difficulties are not insuperable, and there are good arguments for why the reverse could be true. The potential to grow more rapidly through the specialisation made possible by international trade, once the initial 'maturing' process has been completed for an industry or country, is the traditional force which would lead towards exports. It has probably characterised the NICs' development.

The transition may be actively sought because a country has reached the limit of substituting imports (as determined by markets) and wishes or is forced to increase 'unsubstitutable' imports (goods which require levels of technology or natural conditions that are not present) more rapidly than its traditional primary exports can grow. If the 'easiest' substitutions are made first, then a country (or industry) may reach a point where even if exporting is intrinsically more difficult, the costs are less than the next stage of import substitution. Payment of debt interest can be treated as a particularly inelastic (and unsubstitutable) import payment. These conditions are likely to arrive sooner the slower is growth in external demand for traditional exports, and the greater the share of essential imports in the total; they are likely, therefore, to be more common now than in the past, particularly in the new NICs where import substitution has already been extensive. Combined with the effect of the example of the NICs on perceptions of possible policy, this suggests that the transition to exports may be attempted at an earlier stage or more rapidly than in the past, so that the possibility of conflicts between the two policies is a more serious problem.

These conflicts can arise for several reasons. The short-term costs imposed by a policy of industrialisation, particularly if it is encouraged by tariffs or other import restrictions which raise other industries' costs rather than by subsidies, can clearly hinder export performance in the short run. In the long run, the new industries should become efficient suppliers to the exporters. These are conventional temporary costs of the allocation of resources to industries which are not currently the most productive, and acceptable if they will be offset by future benefits or if they are a necessary one-off cost of development. They are a permanent cost only if the type of industrialisation chosen proves not to be a correct path to development or it is badly managed. A second line of argument (the corollary of that favouring exports discussed in the previous chapter) is that protection reduces the incentive to use resources efficiently within an industry. This is again a question of reactions and behavioural assumptions. On the other side, it has been argued that a protected market can attract competitive companies within a country, thus lowering costs (Pazos, 1985: 65). This would provide an additional mechanism for moving from import substitution to exporting if it speeded the development of an industry. In a small market, at least, it is unlikely. A final behavioural reason for expecting poorer performance is 'rent-seeking': if an industry can improve its returns more easily through seeking protection than by increasing normal productivity or expanding sales, it will divert its efforts to that end. This implies that what appears to be a policy of promoting industry or import substitution as a national goal may in fact be one of yielding to particular interest groups.

If the sequence is for the economy as a whole (as assumed in the earliest development models) then initially there are no exports of industrial country-type goods for the costs from short-term inefficient allocation to affect, and the principal concerns are the behavioural ones. Under these, in addition to the conventional discouragement of productivity, a long period of import substitution may discourage the search for export opportunities that will be needed in the long run. It is difficult to see how this can be avoided. Domestic industrialisation is a necessary preparation for exports (or it can be imposed for political reasons as in Zimbabwe under UDI). But if it is accepted that some industries may be ready to export while the economy is still 'developing', finding methods of encouraging new industry without raising the costs of 'mature' industries becomes more important. The arguments from trade theory for promoting industries directly through subsidy rather than through protection, which may damage both the costs of other industry and the welfare of consumers, are relevant here.

The problem for the new NICs may be that trying to develop exports earlier than in the past, especially if this becomes necessary for reasons outside conditions in production or trade, for example to reduce dependence on current financing or to meet the costs of past finance, makes balancing these costs and incentives more difficult. The traditional arguments that protection may divert scarce resources away from the most productive uses come into effect if the same limited supply of entrepreneurs must allocate their efforts between a high and subsidised return on domestic markets and more risky and unknown export markets.

COMBINING IMPORT SUBSTITUTION AND EXPORT PROMOTION

The new NICs, particularly the Asian ones, have consciously tried to combine the two within a broader industrial strategy. They all also distinguish between two stages of import substitution: light industry and then intermediate and capital goods. This provides a model of how the export promotion of the first-stage products can be occurring while the second stage is only beginning. Because many intermediate and capital goods fall into the second stage, its costs to exports are high and direct. The Malaysia, Thailand and Colombia studies would all put their countries in the second phase of a three-part sequence: consumer and light industry import substitution; new exports; second-stage import substitution of intermediate and capital goods. The Malaysian study suggests that the government is following the Korean example in moving directly to the second stage, but that for Malaysia the costs are too high. It argues that Malaysia should concentrate at present on exports. Later, second-stage import substitution may be possible, although the country's small size may always restrict its scope. The more severe constraints on trade and financing faced by Zimbabwe and Peru do not allow them to take this progressive approach. Both see a need to increase import substitution (concentrating on intermediate goods) at the same time as promoting new exports. Their immediate needs leave no real choice about which products or how to combine the two policies, and increase the risks of conflicts between them.

HOW THE NEW NICs THEMSELVES SEE THE NICs

The new NICs, as shown in the country studies, do see the NICs as examples, but look at their whole experience. Ariff and Semudram find 'no empirical or theoretical basis which suggests that export-oriented industrialisation is more conducive to economic growth than import substitution'. The possible conflict between export promotion and other goals concerns them all. Robinson argues that 'Zimbabwe's political economy would anyway not countenance the sort of labour-repressive measures needed seriously to compete in the range of products and markets which formed the basis of the export expansion strategy of the first generation of NICs'. The Peru and Colombia studies would share these doubts, while Thailand and Malaysia take a more favourable view of the Asian NICs' experience.

In the studies of the four countries that have not suffered severe debt crises, it is clear, as was discussed in Chapter 15, that the avoidance of crises, and of heavy financing costs, has become a major priority, with even the apparently technical choice between refinancing and rescheduling loans a major issue in both Colombia and Zimbabwe. The costs and the loss of control over policy-making incurred by Mexico and Brazil (and Peru) are clearly influencing behaviour. The Colombia study strongly emphasises the contrast between the 'cautious' policies of the Colombian governments and those of the other Latin American countries in incurring debt. While recognising the South Korean example of the successful use of debt, it suggests that the risks taken were too great. The Peru study, in contrast, sees external finance still as a necessary part of any long-term plan (although it accepts that Peru is unlikely to be able to obtain it in the short run). This difference in attitude, with the most affected debtor the most ready to accept further debt, and the comments on South Korea in Echavarria's paper suggest that the current financial lessons from the NICs may be as disputable as those from their 'export-led growth'. Borrowing like exporting is not intrinsically good (or bad), but can only be successful if it is part of a more general strategy. Borrowing and export promotion face greater costs, and greater potential conflicts with other parts of a strategy, than in the past.

All the new NICs are more aware of the potential costs and risks of following the NICs' policies than the NICs were 15 years ago. They seem more afraid of the dangers and less impressed by their 'success' than are some of their outside advisers.

NOTES

1. As noted earlier (Chapter 14) this is an explanation given by foreign investors for following a sequence from satisfying a domestic market to considering exports (Page, 1986b).

2. 'Perhaps the most important lesson that has been learned from the experience of the successful exporting countries is that identification of industrialization and the development of new industries with the import substitution policy is fundamentally mistaken' (Krueger, 1983: 51). Her study does, however, recognise that for individual industries, the home market usually comes first, and only exceptionally is production exclusively for export.

18

THE ROLE OF GOVERNMENT

It is impossible to separate analysis of the role of the external sector from that of the role of the government because they interact at every point. This chapter examines how the policies that have been followed, the philosophy behind them and the practicalities of implementing them, have modified the role of the external sector. Unstated assumptions about the appropriate role of the government in setting alternative goals to (or constraints on) economic efficiency and growth lie behind some of the 1970s studies of the role of an export strategy. The actions of a government in economic planning, its reactions to changes in external (or domestic) conditions and how it administers and implements its policies are inevitably all factors affecting the impact of any sector of the economy, but particularly that of one where active intervention is as common and traditional as trade or external capital movements. In all the countries considered here, the governments also participate actively in production or trade, and some of their non-economic roles (notably in military spending) are important enough to have a significant economic impact. A final potential influence is on the behaviour and response to incentives of economic agents.

ATTITUDES TO GOVERNMENT

The *Zimbabwe* study is strongest in expecting the initiative for economic changes to come from the government, and assuming a major role for government in shaping development. This may in part be the result of the need to transform the economy rapidly to meet sanctions before Independence (Kadhani, in Mandaza, 1986) and then the present regional constraints. It also reflects the socialist views of the government: it accepts public and governmental goals as appropriate criteria for economic choice and not necessarily subordinate to private. The need to improve regional and rural–urban distribution of income and economic growth is also accepted as an important constraint on any economic strategy or development path.

In *Colombia*, the appropriateness of some role for the government in defining the framework for economic development, and particularly for the role of trade and foreign capital, is not questioned, but there are different views on its extent.[1] Colombia has explicitly accepted government intervention to regulate the economy since 1936 and a role for government planning since 1945 (Ocampo, 1987: 299). The country study sees the government's role as supplementing or replacing private sector investment rather than taking a strong initiative. The way in which the export market for coffee is administered shows how in an economic choice, namely, how to allocate the revenues among the government, the regional development funds and the producers, all participants accept some prior claim for the private-producer interests, but also intervention by the government, to smooth the price changes and take at least part of the revenue from 'exceptional' high prices. The study notes the greater right of the government to allocate the revenue of the new mining industries because they are government-owned (this derives from the centuries-old government right to the subsoil). On capital flows, control is accepted as the norm, with relaxation of controls considered to be a concession. For industrial policy within the country, indirect intervention, through prices and taxes or subsidies, is in practice the only form normally considered, rather than direct industrial control or 'targeting'. It is notable that the study finds it necessary to justify each type of domestic government action, but takes intervention in the external sector for granted. The Zimbabwe study assumes a right of the government to intervene at any point.

The *Peru* study suggests that there also the external sector (trade, capital and exchange rates) is considered an unquestionable area for government action, while other intervention may need explanation and justification. The same range of policies as in Colombia is traditional. As in Zimbabwe, however, current government policy, of transforming the structure of the economy and the distribution of economic power, implies a more active role.

There is also more direct participation, reflecting the greater traditional importance of the mining sector, as well as President Garcia's more comprehensive approach. Some of the price intervention (notably the multiple exchange-rate system) has in practice been more disaggregated than in Colombia. As in Colombia, such policies as export promotion have normally been pursued by these and other financial instruments, not through industrial promotion, or even through providing appropriate infrastructure. Internal transport and ports, for example, which are major areas of policy in Zimbabwe, Malaysia and Thailand, are severe problems in both Colombia and Peru. In both, particularly at present, the pressures for regional and rural–urban distribution are important, non-economic reasons for much of the government's intervention.

The political need to resolve income differences between Malays and Chinese was a basic element in the *Malaysian* New Economic Policy which has set the frame for economic intervention. This has meant acceptance of quite detailed regulation in the operations of companies, but not for reasons of industrial strategy. The role of the government as planner may be seen as less central than in Zimbabwe, although it has an accepted role in such initiatives as export promotion through the Free Trade Zones and determining the pace of import substitution, and there has also been more direct intervention than in Colombia or Peru to encourage particular patterns of industrial development through investment incentives. Although the country study questions the choices that have been made, the right of the government to choose is accepted. The study does suggest that the government may now be moving to a less active role, partly because of a change in philosophy, but also because of its diminished revenue. On foreign capital, the government's role is seen more as a regulator and promoter than as the basic policy-maker as in the Latin American countries.

The *Thailand* study probably suggests the least active role for government in determining the structure and nature of development, and this has been characteristic of the country, but the authors stress the need to provide infrastructure and incentives to invest. Although as in the other countries there has been import protection, the contribution of tariffs to revenue has been seen as an important reason for their existence, and special treatment has come more in response to demands from industry than as part of a general industrial strategy. The authors of the study argue against protection because it alters incentives away from the most efficient sectors. They suggest that state enterprises' pricing and spending decisions should be related to economic criteria. This apparently less interventionist approach, however, fails to take account of the extensive *de facto* control through administrative intervention which, with perhaps greater implicit national consensus on goals, has made overt structural planning less necessary as a means of mobilising the economy. It is also important that there has been no serious non-economic problem requiring a particular change in the pattern of development, as in all the other countries.

INTERVENTION TO MODIFY EXTERNAL INFLUENCES

Increasing the control of the government over the economy, and specifically over disturbances from outside, is seen as an appropriate goal for *Zimbabwe*. It is one of the purposes of import substitution, for example. Countercyclical intervention (stabilisation) is therefore regarded as desirable, but it has probably not been a major explanation of the extent of, or changes in, government intervention.

For the other four countries, intervention for this purpose has led to a substantial increase in the role of government since the mid-1970s. The availability of foreign finance for public borrowers, both central government and public corporations, has simultaneously increased the government's direct responsibility for a large share of the external balance and its share of domestic investment. This increased role for stabilisation policy is partly the result of the increased instability of external demand, leading to increased concern over its impact on the domestic economy. It could be regarded as part of the process of 'developing', as these countries have moved away from dependence on official finance towards greater vulnerability to private, less stable, forms. Their transition period has coincided with a change in the assumptions about the appropriate treatment of developing countries within the international economic system. The emphasis has switched from 'compensating' them for fluctuations in their external accounts to expecting them to 'adjust' to these, as is expected of industrial countries, through their own actions to finance or absorb the fluctuations.

The *Malaysia* study suggests that, at the end of the 1970s, the government took countercyclical measures against the recession but, especially in the early 1980s, also increased spending in response to higher revenues. These both appear to represent a change of direction from concentrating on the development (or other policy) roles of public spending. The fact that it did not act to reflate the economy in 1986 was the result of insufficient resources, not of a change of policy.

The *Thai* study notes the slow response of the government to changes in external conditions. It has itself acted in a conventional countercyclical way to stabilise demand (as government revenue is highly trade-dependent), although not to stabilise investment or the conditions facing individual industries.

The increase in stabilisation activity by the *Colombian* government has been permitted to lead to a significant structural change in the shares of public and private investment. Echavarria emphasises that public sector action is important specifically in replacing investment by the private sector, rather than demand in general. The shift in policy from the priority of growth to a need also to look at stabilisation came after 1974.

The severe external instability faced by *Peru* in recent years has made government stabilisation particularly desirable. Private companies now lack the resources to ride out unstable periods. Schuldt argues that Peru must reform its relationship with the international system, and that the system itself needs reform because the same constraint, the lack of external financial resources, has meant that the government has been unable to intervene so that its stabilising role has in practice been much smaller than in Malaysia or Colombia. In the 1970s and early 1980s, its own changes in policies led to major shocks from the trading sector.

GOVERNMENT PLANNING

Zimbabwe has a formal macroeconomic development plan, setting out economic and social goals, and the economic structure which it considers necessary to achieve them. There is no serious controversy about the appropriateness of planning. The more important issues raised in the country study and by other observers are only whether the targets are appropriate and attainable, and whether the Plan uses effective means of intervention and is realistic in its assumptions about what it cannot control. The study's proposals include intervention in the choices of which sectors to develop; regional, employment and income distribution policies; and policies for the external sector.

The *Peru* study considers the programme of President Garcia to be the first 'coherent' national plan because it was based on a set of consistent (although 'heterodox') assumptions about how to combine growth, price stability and a sustainable balance of payments, and made clear the structural choices between industry and primary production, the need for regional development and the macroeconomic outcome. After the first year, it attempted to mobilise private support by sectoral co-ordination ('concertación'). By late 1987 the approach was questioned, partly because difficulties on the external account suggested that the assumptions on which it was built had been wrong, but also, at least in part, because its implementation appeared to have become erratic. Even under this strategic approach, however, implementation has remained largely indirect as in traditional intervention, through credit controls and exchange rates, for example, and unexpected results have been met by further modifications of these, and not by industrial planning.

Malaysia has had a series of medium-term plans, as well as the 20-year programme of the NEP, but planning other than that for public expenditure itself is seen by the country study as 'indicative', namely, statements of expectations about the behaviour of the external sector and the response of the private. The transfer of wealth and income planned under the NEP is a substantial exception to this, but it was expected to occur outside changes in the productive structure of the economy, on the assumption that the distribution of increases in income could be separated entirely from production decisions. As the country study shows, it has affected industry directly, by imposing compliance costs, and may have affected its composition indirectly through its impact on foreign investment; the costs have also been a drain on public sector resources. Any sectoral effects, however, have not been planned. The promotion of Free Trade Zones, however, has resulted in growth of specific (electronics and textile) industries.

For *Colombia* government planning has meant planning of its own expenditure, with concentration on agriculture and infrastructure. The plans have had no long-term objectives for the structure of the economy. Echavarria argues for a continuation of this, with some intervention in industry where the private sector will not invest, but still no industrial policy for the development of private industry. Instruments such as trade policy have been used countercyclically to help in the stabilisation of prices and foreign-exchange earnings against the fluctuations in coffee. Even the advocacy of a diversification of exports away from coffee treats structural industrial intervention as appropriate only as an additional instrument in reducing the economy's vulnerability to external fluctuations.

ADMINISTRATION AND REGULATION

The Malaysia, Thailand and Peru studies all consider the extent of administrative intervention an obstacle to private decisions, but it is also provides a potential mechanism for government control. All establishment of and changes in industrial activities come under supervision, and in Malaysia and Thailand this is used to encourage firms to comply with government policies (even if these involve other aspects of a company's activities). Export promotion, regional policy, Malayanisation and the activities of foreign investors (Page, 1986b) are all examples. The potential importance of such continuing supervision by government makes it difficult to measure the total impact of government policy in economic changes, especially as the extent and effectiveness of its use fluctuate. But it must modify any view that the government's role is as limited in Malaysia and Thailand as the country studies imply.

In *Peru*, it is the delays which administrative requirements and inefficiency impose on economic decisions, for example, to set up new activities in response to demand, which are most stressed; action to remove these could be a significant way of reducing costs and improving the efficiency of markets (Alarco, 1985: 198–201). Yet the Garcia government established new organisations to promote its plan objectives, including a new export promotion agency, and commissioned two (foreign) companies to supervise trade. Such controls as import licences and the multiple exchange-rate system remain major administrative costs even for activities which are encouraged.

In *Malaysia*, the regulation stems in part from the detailed provisions of the distributive aspects of the NEP. The Free Trade Zone policy also requires detailed documentation of companies' sales and purchases. The country study points out the need for all industry to be licensed as a major channel of influence, and also notes the growing use of financial intervention. The acceptance of such controls (and of the use of those imposed for one policy to supervise the implementation of others) does give significant scope for implementing policy goals without more obvious direct intervention. The study points out, however, how inefficient a means this is: it imposes costs from delays, and it is also uncertain and subject to change. Like Peruvian studies, it suggests that the existence of a large number of regulations leads to evasion, and this further increases the uncertainties affecting private industry.

Administrative delays and obstacles are also important in *Zimbabwe*, although inexperience rather than excessive regulation is seen as the problem.

By their nature, such controls are very difficult to compare internationally: entrepreneurs may be particularly aware of them in economies which are, in fact, becoming more flexible, and, therefore, where existing constraints start to be binding or to appear anomalous. It may be precisely in those countries where they are most pervasive that they are invisible. The views of foreign investors, who could be assumed to have some opportunity to compare, ranked the countries from least to most difficult to operate in as follows: Malaysia, Colombia, Peru, Thailand (Page, 1986b: 102–3). (Zimbabwe was not included.)

The fact that all the countries regard extremely detailed controls as legitimate, even if unproductive, suggests that the need to use them would not be seen as a fundamental obstacle to any type of policy. Lack of instruments, therefore, does not explain the absence of detailed industrial or sectoral policies in some of the countries. They are, however, regarded as extremely costly, directly and in delays to industry, and therefore an inefficient instrument, and to be avoided. This argument would be consistent with the view that developing countries do not have the administrative capacity to implement detailed plans, but the evidence on inefficient private response suggests that this does not imply the usual conclusion: that decisions should therefore be left to the market. An alternative response is direct intervention by the public sector, discussed in the next section.

Since they are not designed as instruments of national sectoral plans and each country finds them costly and ineffective (the Malaysia study, in particular, strongly advocates their reduction), it is not clear why these controls proliferate. Inexperience could explain why they are implemented slowly or inefficiently. Those operating them are unfamiliar with them, and as a corollary have little confidence in their own judgement. In a changing structure, new types of decision will need to be made, for which existing regulations may not have been designed. Inexperience could, however, also help to explain why they are perceived as a particularly serious problem: a new industry (or industrialist) is more likely to be facing each regulation for the first time and with limited experience of similar regulations. It could also help to explain why some are imposed: if there is no experience or confidence in predicting how economic agents will behave, it may seem better to direct them, or at least to keep fully informed about what they are doing, than to take risks. Regulations may also be perceived both as a particular problem and as especially necessary when growth is slow. Any cost is more important when revenue is growing more slowly, but the risks of a wrong decision may be even more costly.

DIRECT PARTICIPATION BY THE PUBLIC SECTOR

The Colombia and Malaysia studies both emphasise the increase in the share of investment accounted for by the public sector, attributing much of this to the 'stabilisation' policies, which became, through recession, permanent increases in public spending. In Malaysia, the operation of the Malayanisation policy also contributed, by creating funds held in trust for Bumiputera workers. In all the countries, public sector corporations have been important in infrastructure and in some industrial (and mining) sectors.

Particularly in Malaysia and Thailand, public sector corporation borrowing abroad has been one way in which foreign saving has been mobilised, but it is difficult to distinguish how much this should be treated as an independent influence on the corporations, and how much attributed to central government financing policy. The government clearly has the means to control it.

In Thailand, the larger part of government debt was incurred by the state enterprises. They required outside financing, from abroad or from the government, because their prices were held down while they were expected to undertake major investment. External financing was thus used principally to finance energy, communications and transport, and water utilities. These are clearly in line with a strategy of public investment complementary to the private sector. The study argues that this investment should now be reduced to limit further increases in external debt: the electrification programme, for example, is now being cut back. This is not seen as a deliberate reduction of the government's role.

In these two countries, the governments have used public ownership to promote elements of an industrial development policy, particularly import substitution of heavy industry and, at least in Thailand, regional policy. In Malaysia, the government is reducing the share of public sector enterprises through privatisation. Like the reduced role for stabilisation policy, this is the result of the pressure of lack of financial resources for the government.

Mainly through its participation in mining companies, the Peruvian government is the country's principal exporter, while the operation of the coffee market, supplemented now by coal and oil, gives the Colombian government a dominant role in trade there. In Peru, the public sector industries do not appear to have been mobilised to contribute to the government's industrial programme, for example, to implement its efficiency, industrial or trade policies. Their size alone makes this a major gap in the programme, but it also fails to mobilise their potential roles as an example.

The large size and the range of industries in the public sector of the five countries suggest that, except perhaps for Colombia, there are no important doctrinal constraints on using direct government action to achieve economic sectoral goals. In Peru and Zimbabwe, government participation has included entering sectors where the private sector was already active, not merely investing in new industries or infrastructure. The problems and opposition that this has created have related to the methods used (e.g., the banks in Peru) or the efficiency (questions about the benefits of buying existing firms rather than using government resources for new investment in Zimbabwe), not the principle.

THE EFFECT OF GOVERNMENT ON BEHAVIOUR

'Getting the signals right' does not ensure that economic agents respond to them; government intervention might be able to act to ensure or increase the private sector's response, in other words, intervention to improve market functioning. The Malaysia study suggests that the reverse can also occur: excessively detailed government intervention and suppport make the private sector less able to operate without direct assistance or the accompanying international protection. The Malaysia and the Thailand studies put most emphasis on removing the inefficiencies and active disincentives imposed by government activities on the private sector. The other studies would put more weight on encouraging changed behaviour. They emphasise the role of the government in setting an example in its own activities in the economy. They would approve trying to improve responses but cannot see feasible means of doing so. The strongest suggestions are for more information about exporting and about the markets themselves for example, and training.[2] The discussion in Chapter 14 of the potential role of foreign investment suggests that it could provide a model or improve behaviour through its expectations or requirements, a special aspect of the external sector's contribution.

An argument used against government intervention is that it can reward and encourage corruption. The argument that any controls can encourage 'rent-seeking' behaviour, for example, pressure for import protection once the principle of controls on trade is accepted, is clearly simplistic. As with the parallel arguments against permitting any private economic decisions, because these could always be used to conspire against other interests, it is not helpful to conclude that any government action must be avoided because it is always possible to imagine a way of gaining a private advantage through special treatment. What is necessary in both cases is to have sanctions (which can be traditional or legal) against such behaviour, or a system that rewards its avoidance. When there are delays and administrative difficulties and users too inexperienced to use the normal methods efficiently, the pressures for corruption may be greater, so that it may be an inherently greater problem in developing countries, or it may be greater in depressed economic conditions when the rewards for conventional economic actions are reduced. This suggests that, in the countries where public corruption is a problem, private combinations may also be difficult to control, so that it is not clear what conclusion about the role of government intervention can be drawn.

CONCLUSIONS

All the country studies accept that their governments do and should intervene. There are differences in the extent and forms which are acceptable, and other countries and economists would show a much wider range of views, illustrating one of the basic themes of this study, namely that the choice of strategy does not depend only on the economic situation and purposes. What forms or extent of intervention are 'acceptable' cannot be determined without considering whether policies or goals are seen as of comparable importance with economic growth. Economic efficiency and government policies and measures are potential tools, which are not desirable or undesirable in themselves. There are also differences and doubts about what is possible, some for practical reasons (administrative competence, for example), but some because of disagreements over behaviour. Are price and other incentives the only methods available or the only ones necessary to alter behaviour, in particular towards industrialising or exporting, or is something more like training, or even compulsion, appropriate? These differences affect how the studies move from the question of what could and should be done in the abstract, to what it is reasonable to suggest should be done by the existing governments under actual economic and other pressures.

Except perhaps for Zimbabwe, in all the countries there are implicit limits on what type of government intervention is normal, and what needs special justification. These are not the same or ranged along a simple spectrum from more to less, so that they set different types of limits on how a country's objectives can be achieved. Particularly in Colombia and Peru, there is greater implicit acceptance of intervention in the external sector than in the rest of the economy. This could help explain the emphasis on the external sector as a major lever on the economy by those who oppose government intervention as well as those who support it.

The major direct role of governments, through public sector corporations, trade and external financing, implies that even if macroeconomic intervention were removed (or neutral), governments would retain a high degree of responsibility for external performance. They could choose to behave and respond to external changes like private firms, but this could fail to meet any public interest goal which might explain why intervention occurred in these sectors in the first place.

The question of how well prices can function, and how easy it is to improve this in the short run, must be an important constraint on assumptions about the appropriate extent of government intervention to direct the economy. If it is not possible to rely on economic agents to respond to economic incentives, and, as was discussed in Chapters 16 and 17, if it is not possible to predict with confidence their response to general government policies, then a government with detailed objectives for the economy may have no alternative to detailed intervention. But in countries like Peru and Zimbabwe, the public and private sectors may experience the same external obstacles (and exhibit the same weaknesses) in contributing to structural development. If government structural and sectoral planning is impossible, whether for administrative or political reasons, the goals may need to be recognised as unachievable until either public or private mechanisms are improved.

The external situation has had an important effect on the role of the government. The fluctuations on trading accounts led to an increased role for stabilisation policy, and as the trend deteriorated, to a permanent shift upwards in public investment. In the 1980s, as public sector access to external finance has contracted, this has been reversed, and governments have in some cases withdrawn from whole sectors, as well as reducing aggregate investment.

NOTES

1. The extent to which the Colombian and Peruvian authors take a significant impact of government policy for granted can be seen in the organisation of their studies: by administration, not by topic, with individual politicians frequently named.
2. Implicitly, doing research itself requires a belief that persuasion and information must be effective means.

19

COUNTRY-SPECIFIC
CONDITIONS INFLUENCING
THE CHOICE OF
STRATEGY

In each country study there are special factors that the authors consider to be crucial limits on the choice of strategy. Although by definition they cannot be applied directly to other countries, they indicate some of the types of 'other influences' which decision-makers must take into account. Outlining some indicates the limits of any general recommendations.

SIZE

Recent work on successful growth during the recession has stressed the importance of the economic size of countries and differences in industrial structure. Demand factors: the relative importance and stability of domestic markets; and supply: for example, diversity of resources, are suggested as important (e.g., UN, 1987; UNIDO, 1987; Roy, 1987). In all five countries, the limited size of the domestic market is seen as an important reason for looking towards an export strategy once the first stage of import substitution has been achieved, but the market, and particularly the population size, are most stressed in Malaysia. This is also receiving increasing attention in Colombia. Table 19.1 shows that the five countries are all smaller than those NICs which developed on the basis of home markets. The comparison with the South-East Asian NICs is more mixed; they are of a similar range of size, excluding the extreme cases of Hong Kong and Singapore. The survey of foreign investors found that they considered that, for the types of production that interested them, only industries with at least the potential for export could offer sufficient return in these countries (Page, 1986b). This suggests that a purely locally-based industrialisation would be more costly in these countries than in the larger NICs, and also that they will have access only to a more limited range of foreign investment.

There is some reason on the basis of these rough comparisons for the Malaysian emphasis on the absolute size of its population as a problem in itself. Malaysia is the smallest of the most advanced new NICs, and even allowing for its higher per capita income, its total market is substantially smaller than that of Colombia or Thailand. Only Zimbabwe is well below the NIC range on this measure: its forced early import substitution gave it a relatively advanced production structure for its level of income.

Malaysia and Colombia are approaching the GDP per capita levels of the NICs, but the others are comparable with the other middle-income countries included in this study. It may, therefore, be more difficult for the latter to adjust to, rather than finance, external shocks.

EDUCATIONAL DIFFERENCES

With the possible exception of Malaysia, the countries all have relatively high rates of literacy for their income levels, and this could help ease the process of rapid change and adaptation which is a necessary part of successful industrial development. Only in Zimbabwe are absolute shortages of particular levels of technical or managerial labour seen as a regular constraint on policies or how they are implemented, although there are particular shortages in all five countries. The perceptions of foreign investors about the general levels of basic training (corresponding to ability to adjust to unskilled industrial work) would rank the Latin American countries above, and the African significantly below, the Asian. Although they also cited differences in attitudes as important to success, these are clearly not unchanging characteristics of countries. (South Korea was cited as a country where the move to successful industrialisation was linked to change in attitudes to work.)

LOCATION AND GEOGRAPHY

The Zimbabwe study includes drought and relations with South Africa as principal risk factors, on a level with the general external situation. They make reduced external vulnerability an even more important objective, and specifically increase the risk, and therefore reduce the expected return, of export-based strategies. More than usually risky natural conditions, which are characteristic of Peru as well as Zimbabwe, also make a country more vulnerable to changes in the availability of finance for temporary fluctuations in its external account.

The direct effects on trade deriving from location in Asia, Latin America or Africa were discussed in Chapters 9 and 10, and on private investment in Chapters 14 and 15, but there may also be effects on what countries consider to be the development examples to be followed. Although all the countries now look at the Asian NICs, contacts among political and economic decision-makers are closer within Asia, and the demonstration effect works more directly. A progression is seen from the success of Japan, to the NICs, to the new NICs, with the new NICs recognising similarities in external markets and internal conditions (for example, large supplies of labour). For the Latin American countries, familiarity with the success of Brazil is greater, and offers a different model of industrialisation, while the differences in local external conditions and in the domestic structures of their own economies make it more difficult for them to see the Asian NICs as a close example. The Colombia study explicitly considers Colombia's policies and performance in the context of other Latin American countries.

The fact that the Asian countries appear more frightened by the experience of Latin American borrowers than reassured by the success of South Korea seems to contradict this, but it may in fact come from the same cause. They may be more aware of the risks of South Korea's position in the early 1980s, and the efforts it made to reduce its deficit, and more deterred by reading descriptions of countries in debt crisis than is a country like Peru which has already survived more than one such crisis. The Latin American and Zimbabwe studies also show more concern than the Asian about the possible social problems of the 'cheap' labour model of export-based industrialisation. The more complex conditions and arguments may be more visible to the NICs' neighbours. In Africa, it is difficult to find any near model of successful industrialisation or successful external policy. The conditions of the Latin American and Asian countries appear very different. Any choice of strategy, therefore, must, as in the Zimbabwe study here, be based more on judgements derived from theory about how economic systems should be managed, and faith that the elements that these assume (industries with particular characteristics, responses by different actors) will emerge, and less on example.

POLITICAL AND ECONOMIC INTERESTS

The Peru study gives particular attention to how economic policy has changed in response to the particular interests of those in power, emphasising the instability in policy on some fundamental prices in the economy resulting from the alternation in power of those with interests in primary exports and industrialists. It is notable that the industrialists, looking mainly towards the domestic market, and requiring political support from urban workers, take the protectionist, import-substituting position. They do not yet see sufficient export opportunities for an 'open' strategy, which was favoured by the traditional primary exporters, to be a serious alternative. (Foreign investors in Peru shared this view, and their support for protection.)

In Malaysia, the NEP reflected a clear conflict between the interests of the government's supporters and some well established commercial and industrial interests. In Thailand, similar motives may have strengthened government resistance to imposing import barriers (Ariff and Hill, 1985: 93). It was the NEP's emphasis on growing sufficiently to produce a radical redistribution of wealth through the allocation of additional income which placed economic growth at the centre of Malaysia's objectives, and, as the end of the 20-year period approaches, puts increasing weight on short-term growth and efficiency rather than structural or longer-term objectives.

In some circumstances, therefore, a change of government can make a change of external policy easier. Depending on the conditions (or interpretations), this can result in the disadvantages of instability or the advantages of transition to a new pattern. Simple analysis of economic interests, however, offers an incomplete explanation of the policies followed. It is clear that real differences in view about the results of different policies are major explanations of the governments' choices. Peru's move away from protection between 1980 and 1982, when the interests supporting the government and the performance of the economy both suggested the opposite policy, may be attributed to misapplication of lessons from research on the NICs.[1] Extensive protection had been established in Malaysia (and Thailand) even before there was a substantial industrial interest to support.[2] The import-substitution recommendations of an earlier generation of development economists may be responsible. The import-substitution policy of Zimbabwe has been supported by pre- and post-Independence governments representing very different economic interests, but with the same political problem of a strictly limited number of friendly potential trading partners.

REGIONAL POLICY

In Peru and Colombia, the unequal income distributions (international comparisons are notoriously difficult, but both claim to be the worst in the world) are stressed as an overriding reason for urgent policies to increase total domestic demand and to alter the structure, and regional distribution, of production, under the threat of political upheaval and violence. In Zimbabwe, income redistribution is also seen as an essential step, although the country study bases its emphasis more on the country's declared objectives than on such threats. In all three, reducing inter-regional inequalities and increasing rural incomes are seen as essential parts of such a strategy. The countryside has the poorest areas, and in Colombia and Peru this is where the major guerrilla forces control some areas.[3] The studies propose various ways of reconciling this set of requirements with the goal of industrialisation (including regionally-based industry in Zimbabwe and Peru, and leaving regional development to the public sector and industrialisation to the private sector in Colombia). The Colombia and Zimbabwe studies also put weight on investment in housing as an important area of infrastructure for development with direct benefits to the poor. Although the types of investment proposed have clear economic and developmental benefits, the need to look at regional distribution is a constraint on the policies and resources available to promote industry. Although regional initiatives exist in Malaysia and Thailand, they are less important. As Table 19.1 shows, the more industrialised countries have a more urban population; Malaysia and Thailand are exceptionally rural for their income levels.

CIVIL VIOLENCE, WARS AND DRUGS

For all the countries these are an immediate and serious problem which can only be noted superficially here. In Colombia, armed civil conflict has been a problem for the last 40 years. The intensity has varied; in 1987 it was increasing. Opposition to the whole political system, conflicts between political parties and the interests of the drug traffickers have all been elements in it. In Peru, guerrilla activities have increased in the 1980s, but there was a period of military government (and high military spending) in the 1970s and spending had again become a major cost in 1982–3. In both countries the violence has been against both particular governments and the system. The NEP in Malaysia originated in open conflicts between the Malay and Chinese populations. The immediate pressure was removed, but in recent years the policies and the fruits of slower economic growth have failed to satisfy either side, and in 1987 conflict again erupted, aggravated by differences among Malays. In Thailand, there have been persistent difficulties on the borders, and a strong military presence in governments. As in Peru, military spending made a large contribution to the growth of borrowing in the late 1970s. Zimbabwe has been in civil or international conflict since the early 1970s, and the country study presents the current situation as one of the major constraints on policy.

The conflicts have high direct costs to the government and to the external accounts, and constrain industrialisation by requiring priority for other objectives (regional development in Colombia, Peru and Zimbabwe; spending on transport and reallocation of exports in Zimbabwe; short-term growth and restrictions on ownership and employment in Malaysia). The fact that all the new NICs in this study are being affected in this way may not be a coincidental extra burden on their development.[4] The external problems of Thailand and Zimbabwe are not directly related to their levels of development, but the strains of structural change do put additional pressure on existing internal conflicts or inequalities, and if growth is slowed (or reversed) by poor external conditions, this increases the scale and the duration of the pressure. The failure of the NEP to reach its targets by 1990 is the most visible sign of this, but the increase in violence within Peru after 1980 and in Peru and Colombia in 1987–8 also coincides with serious deterioration in their economic prospects. In Peru, President Garcia's argument that 'external debt and the poverty that leads to and encourages violence are tightly related' was one of the reasons for imposing the 10% limit on debt-servicing.

CONFIDENCE TO DEVELOP

The new NICs do not and cannot, therefore, single-mindedly seek industrialisation and growth. And these problems, which arise out of their own national backgrounds, or from conflicts which are inherent in development, are made worse by poorer possibilities of growth, while the returns to concentration on development are now poorer because of lower economic expectations for the future. On the other hand, the success of those countries that did become the NICs and the unexplained revival of developing countries in the poor conditions of 1986 cannot be adequately explained by demand or existing structures. The final factor that must be considered is countries' confidence or determination to find the opportunities that constitute success. Like the more specific questions of finding industrial or export opportunities discussed in earlier chapters, this is not a question that can be analysed in an economic study.

The change in Peru to a focused, structural plan, with a greatly widened debate about long-term strategies and quite specific export suggestions, had promising elements, but the collapse of support for the government and the disappointment of expectations may make confidence even harder to revive in the future. In Colombia, Malaysia and Zimbabwe the lack of confidence in choosing industries to encourage (whether in the private sector or the public) appears worrying, but Colombia still has a range of choices and the resources which give it time to choose, and Malaysia's repeated success in new products and rapid recovery in 1987–8 suggest that it may now be able to rely on investors to respond to or create opportunities. For all four, however, the need to contend with immediate violent conflicts makes it difficult to give priority to economic strategy. Thailand faces a range of possibilities, with fewer immediate distractions.

NOTES

1. In South Korea the government has been able to promote exports in part because it could resist pressure by industrialists to increase protection.
2. This inadequacy of 'political economy explanation of protection' is cited in (Ariff and Hill, 1985: 94–5).
3. In Colombia, the first local elections in 1988 made the problem particularly urgent.
4. It was not a bias from the choice of countries; on the contrary, the study attempted to avoid countries where political and military problems were likely to overwhelm any long-term thinking about economic strategies.

Table 19.1 Characteristics of the countries' population

	GDP $m	Population million	GDP per capita $	Literacy (%)		Urban population (%)	
	1985	1985	1985	1960	1980	1965	1985
NICs							
Argentina	65,920	30.5	2,130	91	93	76	84
Brazil	188,250	135.6	1,640	61	76	50	73
Hong Kong	30,730	5.4	6,230	70	90	89	93
India	175,710	765.1	270	28	36	19	25
Mexico	177,360	78.8	2,080	65	83	55	69
Singapore	17,470	2.6	7,420		83	100	100
South Korea	86,180	41.1	2,150	71	93	32	64
New NICS							
Colombia	34,400	28.4	1,320	63	81	54	67
Malaysia	31,270	15.6	2,000	53	60	26	38
Peru	16,850	18.6	1,010	61	80	52	68
Thailand	38,240	51.7	800	68	86	13	18
Zimbabwe	4,530	8.4	680	39	69	14	27
Other middle income							
Chile	16,000	12.1	1,430	84		72	83
Costa Rica	3,810	2.6	1,300		90	38	45
Egypt	30,550	48.5	610	26	44	41	46
Ivory Coast	5,220	10.1	660	5	35	23	45
Kenya	5,020	20.4	290	20	47	9	20
Morocco	11,850	21.9	560	14	28	32	44
Pakistan	28,240	96.2	380	15	24	24	29
Philippines	32,590	54.7	580	72	75	32	39
Senegal	2,560	6.6	370	6	10	27	36
Sri Lanka	5,500	15.8	380	75	85	20	21
Tunisia	7,240	7.1	1,190	16	62	40	56
Uruguay	4,380	3.0	1,650		94	81	85
Venezuela	49,600	17.3	3,080	63	82	72	85
Low income	587,020	2,439.4	270	34	52	17	22
Lower-middle income	509,630	674.6	820	39	59	27	36
Upper-middle income	930,330	567.4	1,850	61	76	49	65

Source: World Bank, *World Development Report*.

20

CONCLUSIONS

SUMMARY OF RESULTS

To assume a conventional common objective – growth – as in many comparative studies is not a reasonable simplification; it obscures many of the explanations of performance and policy. The choices of development strategies and the instruments available for them are affected by non-economic goals, and growth must be considered to be one among other economic objectives which may be part of development. National stability, changes in the distribution of wealth and economic power and altering the structure of the economy were all basic objectives.

The performance of the countries which were most successful in exporting cannot be explained as a response to changes in external demand, or as a result of opening their economies to external demand or other macroeconomic policies. The process was more active: finding new potential for exports, and changing industrial structure to meet it, and repeating this process continuously. They moved to more rapidly growing markets and then to newer markets. The success did not depend, therefore, either on external circumstances (having the right markets or products) or on the conventional policy recommendations. These could only give a once-off gain, from acquiring the benefits of trade specialisation, unless we can find evidence that there were dynamic benefits from exposure to external price signals which explain the changes in trade and industrial structure.

The success was achieved in manufactured exports: for the most advanced, in machinery. The share of primary products in their exports fell, although even for the most advanced there are still important differences from the pattern of exports of the industrial countries. Diversification of both products and markets was normal.

The need for an active approach to the structure of output was supported by the evidence on import substitution and industrialisation generally. There were clear patterns of differences in structure among countries at different levels of development. The industrialising countries took these as objectives, not merely aspects of growth. As industrialisation proceeded, the importance of choosing industries became important with no general answers to the questions 'which industry?' and 'which exports?'.

During the 1970s and 1980s, the successful NICs did not, in general, rely on external savings, and particularly not on commercial bank lending, to finance a major part of their investment (except for South Korea). The countries that did, and those which used external finance only in response to shocks to their trading balances, borrowed for a relatively short period, usually three to four years between 1978 and 1983. They found that even this limited exposure imposed continuing high costs on their economies, which could not be reduced during any subsequent revival of their external position. This was partly because some financing needs proved to be less temporary than expected, but more significantly because the only type of finance available was unsuitable on account of its high cost. Bank finance cannot substitute for reserves as a source of immediate liquidity for payments imbalances because it carries a high real interest rate and this is not matched by a financial return in the developing country, only by the avoidance of loss. (Monetary conditions in the creditor countries and prices on world commodity markets aggravated this result.) Official loans and foreign investment are not sufficiently quick to respond to provide liquidity.

By looking at a range of countries, not merely the successful NICs, and at other characteristics of the case-study countries in addition to their external sectors, this study has attempted to establish not only what structures or policies can be successful, but also more general characteristics of the relationship between a country's performance and its interaction with external factors. The country studies and the chapters looking at the general results give different points of view. In analysis, it is necessary to balance two approaches: emphasis on the effects from outside and, associated with this, on the possibility of finding general rules for successful external strategies, and, secondly, confidence in a country's own efforts, development from inside, with responses to external crises seen in the context of national circumstances. In policy, this balance is still important, but it may be that the confidence is itself an important factor in success.

WHAT AN EXTERNAL STRATEGY CAN ACHIEVE AND MUST AVOID

It is now increasingly clear from recent studies that the original conclusions concerning the NICs were wrong about what they did (overemphasising the role of market pricing), about how common among developing countries their basic economic characteristics were (in particular, large supplies of surplus labour), and about how successful they were. The increases in the shares of their exports in world markets and, at home, in the share of manufacturing in their output, have been slowing or ceasing. Newer interpretations (Chenery et al., 1986) emphasise the importance of domestic industrial strategy, with good external performance as one aspect or result of their general development success.

The earlier work had put export success in a much more central position as an engine of demand and efficiency, with growth (and, by implication, development) following as results. The early simple criticisms of this approach, however, were also misinterpretations. The argument that following the example of the NICs would produce a 'fallacy of composition' as too many developing countries flooded world markets with unwanted surpluses of identical manufactures made the same error about the nature of the NICs' example. Their achievement lay in developing their economies so successfully by finding products in which they had advantages that they were able to compete with more developed countries. A similar process now of finding a successful strategy would certainly produce different products (although the emergence of common patterns of industrial structure suggests that complete rejection of their choice of industries and exports in favour of non-industrial products would be risky) and probably a different balance between external and domestic demand in different countries. There is no general formula of choice of macroeconomic policy or of a range of products which will guarantee success. The NICs' achievement, and example, was in devising their individual successful strategies; their good fortune was in doing this in a period when the world economy offered high rewards to success, and generous financing for temporary setbacks.

One theme that emerges is the importance of how a country, and the economic decision-makers within it, respond to demand. The way in which successful exporters have adapted to new demands shows 'flexibility, that is, the ability to shift resources rapidly from an export where sales are proving difficult to an export or import substitute where profit opportunities are now superior' which may be attributed to a requirement to respond to changes in international prices (World Bank, 1987: 150). But the way in which they have moved to new products, industries and markets shows supply-based initiative, not simple shifts in response to marginal changes in prices. The discussion in the country studies of the difficulty of securing such responses suggests that ability to respond in this way should be considered at least as much a result as an instrument of development. The argument that recognising new opportunities and price advantages is a skill which needs to be developed in individual entrepreneurs or companies is convincing. In a rapidly industrialising country, a high proportion of industrialists and potential exporters will be inexperienced.

This does not mean that prices cannot be effective. In the primary sector where producers are experienced and the transmission paths of price signals from consumers (including export markets) to producers are well established, the country studies do not find sluggish responses to prices. (Malaysia and Colombia are concerned about the reverse.) In the manufactures sector, however, even if producers are persuaded to look, the costs of finding new markets, especially for exports, may be high in learning about tastes, procedures and standards, and may be a more serious barrier to entry than those who see unexploited price differentials may recognise. There may also be additional costs in a transition period from import substitution to exports. But there may be other good reasons for countries to reject the use of prices. The period of adjustment to opportunities required by the normal lags in market responses may be unacceptable to policy-makers who have a view about the appropriate development path, and no bias against using direct ways of influencing the structure of output.[1] Prices, particularly short-term changes in market prices, may not be the right signal if growth is not the only goal of a government: industrialisation or a particular pattern of industrialisation or distributive or regional goals may require modifying a direct response to prices, although, as growth is always one of the goals, this is at a cost. There is no simple answer to how far market solutions can or should be used.

The characteristics of individual countries have great weight in determining how they can and wish to respond to external conditions, and therefore our analysis of how they can apply the experience of successful countries. One important difference is in the alternatives a country has to development. A country with a successful primary export may be able to grow for long periods without structural change.[2] One of the problems identified for Colombia is that of convincing decision-makers that it is not possible to rely on coffee, joined now by coal and oil, to provide sufficient growth in the future. Malaysia and Peru also offer examples of relaxation of industrialisation policy or efforts to develop new exports when rising export prices relieved the pressure. This can be considered an extension of 'Dutch disease' arguments (presented in the Colombia study) to include an effect on policymakers. It points up the importance of determination, the wish to develop.

If response to external conditions is not mechanical, this means that the present and expected state of world demand cannot be used directly to project the growth of exports or of a country. But this does not mean that it is irrelevant. What emerges from every issue examined in this study is the complex interaction between the state of the world economy and the rate and pattern of growth within developing countries. The change in the external economic situation, as identified in Chapter 2, is a significant common influence. The slow growth assumed here reduces the returns to exporting, and therefore to investment in aggregate, with direct consequences for growth and on development. It also reduces the returns to learning to respond to markets, and to adapting, because slow-growing markets are also slow to change. External difficulties can also make it more difficult to achieve distributional goals, and increase the pressure from domestic problems of political and social unrest; growth may fall back in a country's priorities. By slowing down development, slow growth makes it necessary to maintain the 'determination to develop' for longer periods, with poorer returns. In the past, industrialising countries' growth has usually come in short periods of rapid growth (cf. UN, 1987: 156).

It is not only the rate of growth that has changed. Technological changes, and changes in taste, are reducing the share of natural resources and labour inputs in final demand, thus removing the traditional comparative advantages of developing countries. This may increase the pressure for development, but only by reducing the opportunities for growth.

There has also been a change in the treatment of developing countries within the international system of trade and financing, away from emphasis on 'special and differential treatment' towards 'reciprocity'. On trade, this further reduces the expected returns to exporting. But in this study it is the change in financing whose effects are most striking. Although finance is still available as aid for the poorest countries, the other traditional motives for financial flows to developing countries now receive less weight. Public sector flows to increase the rate of investment, in order to permit accelerated growth, are restricted and, at present interest rates, less attractive than in the past. The slow growth expected in developing and developed countries alike deters private foreign investment, as it does domestic investment. Bank finance for investment led to high long-term servicing costs, and the OPEC surpluses which provided its base have diminished. Thus, the supply of new finance is expected to be low, and more of it will be official. At the same time, the need is greater because the cost of servicing existing debt is a much greater burden than it was for earlier generations of industrialising countries.

A second critical change in financing is the lack of balance-of-payments finance for temporary difficulties. Reserves and official sources of liquidity were inadequate for the expansion of trade and the increased fluctuations in income and import prices of the 1970s. Bank finance proved an imperfect and costly substitute, and for most countries is now unobtainable.

These changes affect potential investment and therefore growth directly. But direct experience of the cost of loan finance, and fears from observation of the consequences for the heaviest debtors, now mean that countries feel that they cannot choose to run a deficit as a permanent supplement to investment and should avoid the risk of having to finance even a temporary deficit. This increased aversion to risk means that the strategies with potentially the highest returns, including concentration on a limited range of targeted industries and exports, are less open to them. At a time when the sluggishness of external demand means that more weight needs to be put on supply factors including country initiatives, they are less able to risk such initiatives.

To describe this as 'only a liquidity problem' is to ignore the central role of liquidity in a situation of uncertainty and risk-taking. Investment and finding new opportunities are by their nature risky; very constrained ability to take risks, therefore, makes even growth difficult; development requires a higher rate of investment and a heightened degree of structural change.

Looking at the successful NICs, it is difficult to know *ex post* how much of a deterrent not being able to finance temporary difficulties might have been.[3] Some have developed with interruptions for external constraints, while others have had a steadier progress, but in the variable conditions of the 1970s it is not clear how far the differences were due to luck. The differences between those that were successful in the early part of the period and those later (UN, 1987: 156) imply that it is impossible to be confident of continued success. The Colombia study suggests that a strategy of avoiding large policy changes and risks can give a successful long-term growth path, but this is tempered by its recommendations that policy must now be changed to less dependence on natural resources because the risks are becoming too much of a danger.

THE LINK BETWEEN COUNTRY İNITIATIVES AND GENERAL CONSTRAINTS

Development is more than growth. In terms of the issues discussed in this study, it requires structural and behavioural changes: not merely diversification of output and markets by copying the patterns of others, but the ability to diversify in a way that gives a long-term growth path; not merely efficient responses to price or other incentives, but the ability to do so while pursuing a long-term structural transformation. It is thus essential to analyse the role of the external sector in terms of supply and demand and the nature of the interactions between them. Country initiatives, including the choices of product and industry which make economists feel uncomfortable, are an essential element in success, but external demand and financing determine the conditions in which they operate. The relationship between them is complex and dynamic, and cannot be described by treating either as a constraint on the other. It is not sufficient to treat the system as basically determined by demand, and then introduce some modifications of supply and response as efficiency effects of certain types of demand, such as exports.

One element of the influence of supply and national initiatives can be government policy, and market prices are one way of transmitting demand, but it is more useful to treat both planning and prices as operating to relate supply and demand. The countries in the case studies (like the NICs) take a pragmatic view of the role of government. It should intervene to achieve non-economic results, as in any model; to improve market functioning, and some of the authors would include here developing the ability to respond to prices; and also to achieve structural, non-marginal changes in the economy, for which prices do not offer an efficient guide. It should participate directly in areas like infrastructure, and also where the risks or size of an investment are too large for the private sector. In a strategy of choosing certain industries, it should participate in the initial choice, and perhaps operational decisions because the risks are high and wrong decisions may affect the whole economy.

It is difficult to distinguish the role of government, and harder to judge its past success, relative to prices, because of the extent of any government's activities in the external sector and in political relations with other countries and also because intervention and prices serve different purposes. Nor is it easy to judge whether the role of government is likely to increase or diminish in the new NICs. It may be more important in an export strategy than in import substitution because the choices are more difficult, and a country may have an increasingly complex set of goals which cannot be reconciled using only prices, but in the economy as a whole the number of new industries, and the need to make structural rather than marginal choices, may diminish. At the stage of development of the new NICs, with their objectives, there is a substantial area where government participation is important; the new constraints on its sources of finance are therefore a further significant influence from the external sector on development strategy. These fall on general revenue through trade taxes; on investment finance through the fall in total external finance; on stabilisation finance through the liquidity collapse.

COUNTRY RESULTS

For *Malaysia*, the role of national policy in creating the present problems and in alleviating them is seen as crucial. The main prospects are in increasing exports, but also in increasing the use of foreign finance. Import substitution should be given less importance, and in the conflict between economic performance and the social changes required by the NEP more weight should for the present go to growth. The conclusions are not optimistic.

In *Colombia*, foreign exchange is potentially the bottleneck, but what is needed is to reduce dependence on the traditional primary exports and to build up non-traditional exports. In the long run, import substitution will be important. Echavarria takes a cautious view of the government's ability to influence the structure of development: it can and should control inflation, and prevent external shocks from damaging domestic development. The need for it to concentrate on domestic regional and military problems limits its role in industrial restructuring.

The *Thailand* study emphasises non-traditional exports, not import substitution, under present conditions, because of the need to encourage efficiency and reduce the role of government investment. This is putting growth as the central objective. As in Colombia, the performance of the economy has not been seriously unsatisfactory.

The *Zimbabwe* study sees little scope for increases in traditional exports, but some for temporary gains in new exports. Foreign finance is not expected. In the medium term, import substitution and an autarkic solution offer the best prospects as preparation for eventually opening the economy. This is principally because of the type of development and regional equity which the country is seeking, but also because of its external vulnerability at the present time. The external situation is at present a basic constraint, in both economic and political terms. In these circumstances, avoidance of exposure to risks from its further deterioration is a crucial element of the strategy. Robinson sees the situation as 'bleak', but also emphasises that there is an opportunity to repeat the determination to develop the economy seen during the UDI period.

The external sector is clearly a constraint for *Peru*. The study and the Garcia government describe its removal as central to permitting the country to move to the alternative pattern of development which they, like Zimbabwe, are seeking. The external debt position is a more serious immediate problem, and external finance less likely to be available for liquidity in the future, than is the case in Zimbabwe. The programme was therefore to alleviate the immediate financial burden (the 10% limit), and then to avoid future liquidity problems (rebuild reserves). In order to obviate the need for future long-term financing, the strategy in 1985–6 was to balance the rapid expansion of the economy with a sufficient transfer of income to lower-income consumers in order to reduce imports and, in the long run, to increase foreign investment and reduce import elasticities. This can work only if the costs of past debt are eliminated and no short-term finance is required. Neither of these held in 1987. It is difficult to see any viable external strategy.

All the country studies regard establishing a new structure of production as essential to development, with import substitution and export promotion appropriate at different stages of industrialisation. The particular recommendations for promoting different types of exports or restraining imports are made in the light of more general objectives. They do not take either type of trade policy as an objective in itself, and describe the damaging consequences of regimes which appear to have done so, whether import substitution in Malaysia or liberalisation in Peru.

All the countries include finding and promoting new exports in their strategies. There is a general interest in finding agricultural (and for some, marine) exports as well as manufactures, and an emphasis on resource-based exports. These have been used by some of the NICs, but were not identified as a principal reason for their development, and do not contribute directly to the industrialisation patterns found to be characteristic of NICs and developed countries.

In spite of their differences, the studies show some common results. All emphasise the uncertainties of the external situation. Only Zimbabwe and Peru look explicitly at a longer-term path with a substantial change in their countries' domestic and external orientation, and try to find a transition to it. This may reflect the greater consensus in other countries, particularly in Thailand, on present goals, so that a new long-term development strategy is not on the agenda. They all assume that national goals should be set, and accept government intervention, but the external situation is in present circumstances a serious constraint. All four countries for which external borrowing could still be an option take a cautious view of it in practice (too cautious in the views of the Zimbabwe, Malaysia and Thailand studies); Peru, in contrast, is unlikely to receive external finance, but would still consider it an acceptable part of a strategy.

The studies all saw reasons why their countries could take the situation in 1986–7 as a turning point towards faster development: the opportunities offered by low energy costs for Thailand and Malaysia to improve their external positions; the cushion of reserves from the high coffee price to permit Colombia to restructure; the political strength derived from unity in the military crisis in Zimbabwe; and the support for the Garcia government in Peru. The fragility of such starting points can be seen in the changes between the first and second halves of 1987: the external prospects for Malaysia and Thailand fell with the outlook for growth in the industrial countries; the coffee price fell; instability in Colombia increased; support for Garcia, and quite specifically confidence in his programme, weakened. But confidence is probably as difficult for economists to explain, and allow properly for, as industrial choices; the test is whether confidence falls (notably in Peru) or the justifications for it change (Malaysia).

POLICY IMPLICATIONS, INTERNATIONAL AND NATIONAL

The external situation does matter, so the actions of the rest of the world are important. The conventional recommendations stand.[4] More rapid growth would improve trading prospects, confidence and the possibilities for structural change. Lower protection, or even standstill, would reduce the risks for any long-term industrial strategy as well as offering direct benefits to trade.

Increased external financing, most urgently greater liquidity to make temporary financing possible and affordable, could increase investment directly and by lowering risks. Financing would reduce the urgency of the need for greater trade growth by increasing the scope for domestic initiatives.

If it were permanent and low cost, it could permit the 'delinking' of developing countries from the performance of the developed which bank lending was expected to achieve in the 1970s. It might affect the balance of risk between primary and manufactures production. The combination of vulnerability to fluctuating interest rates and to prices gives an abnormal incentive to reduce dependence on primary goods. Reducing the cost of servicing past borrowing would also reduce vulnerability to risk. The combination of high real interest rates and depressed export revenues has raised the consequences of 'mistaken' financing decisions to unprecedented levels; some reduction in rates could therefore help to restore the balance in attitudes to borrowing, without tipping it too far the other way (the 'moral hazard' problem). It would need to be accompanied by re-establishment of confidence that temporary borrowing would not impose such extreme costs again. An increase in liquidity would need to be lower in cost, and not as subject to large changes or fluctuations. In practice, this probably means official reserve assets. For longer-term finance, changes in lending instruments (to fixed interest loans or forms which have some relationship with the performance of the debtor), with an institutional change to impose limits on debt enforcement at the international level comparable with those at the national, could restore attitudes to risk in investment to pre-debt-crisis levels.[5]

Unlike the literature of the 1970s, recent comparative studies of the NICs have reached hesitant conclusions, emphasising areas of ignorance and the limits of economic analysis[6] rather than firm policy recommendations for the NICs' successors. The different types and sources of uncertainty and the potential conflicts among ways of reducing risks suggest that no policy is likely to be so universally superior that an unequivocal recommendation is possible. In current conditions, which appear to present a high risk of making wrong decisions and more serious consequences for errors, the successes may be at least as small in number as they were in the 1970s. They may also be less spectacular, if higher risks or greater risk-aversion militate against specialisation in high-return paths. They must certainly be different at least in detail from those of the 1970s.

Emphasis on the role of the external sector and the implicit assumption that policies to implement a strategy for trade have predictable results created a presumption in the past that some set of policies would, if a country could be persuaded to accept them, promote development. Once the importance of a country's commitment and the possibility of unpredictability of behaviour are accepted, it is no longer possible to have simple confidence that policy imposed from outside will have the same effect as one adopted by national initiative, or that there is always some policy that will work.

Caution about policy in the countries themselves is understandable, but there is the risk of its leading in turn to greater pessimism about growth prospects (particularly if it is difficult for policy-makers to see industrial possibilities). This should not lead to inaction. The earliest recommendations, that development required industrialisation and began with production for domestic demand, still come out rather well from studies of successful countries, although the reasoning may now be different.

With the objective seen in terms of supporting the growth of industrial sectors, the question of how to overcome the initial disadvantages of home-produced relative to foreign products in the home market, and then in meeting the barriers to entering export markets, becomes a conventional one to which the conventional answers, to use domestic subsidies rather than trade measures, remain valid. The efficiency costs of intervention are reduced, however, as long as large changes are being made for structural objectives rather than minor ones to promote growth. But developing countries face practical difficulties. Some, as has been seen in the country studies, depend heavily on import tariffs, or already have instruments to collect export levies in place, like the coffee fund in Colombia. In general, the instruments to manage trade flows, through taxes or licensing, or exchange controls or multiple exchange rates, are available; difficulties in establishing new institutions in developing countries are not confined to the private industrial sector. Two other difficulties in moving to less distorting policies derive from the shift away from allowing developing countries differential treatment. First, subsidies make their exports more open to restrictions in export markets, directly through anti-dumping and countervailing actions; indirectly through increased pressure to remove any special privileges, such as the Generalised System of Preferences, and through pressure in trade negotiations. Second, if they must avoid allowing their current deficit to exceed a fixed amount, and if they also require tight control of their fiscal balance, and therefore of tax revenue and subsidy costs, only direct controls can be sufficiently precise. This is an additional inefficiency resulting from the reduction in liquidity.

The question of how to achieve (or even recognise) determination, or readiness for development, is one of the most traditional in the literature. The experience of the NICs, and of other examples such as Japan, suggests that it requires an ability to ignore existing economic interest groups, or to mobilise all interests behind structural change and growth, in contrast to the need to satisfy them which is assumed in some of the country studies, particularly Peru, Colombia and Zimbabwe. This seems at present characteristic of the successful Asian NICs, but it is probably related to the period of development, rather than specifically to Asian countries. The surges of export growth and industrialisation do not suggest that it is a permanent trait, and although South Korea is often cited as an example of successful resistance to protectionist demands, it may now be facing interest groups among those competing with importers. Successful development will itself create interest groups. Slow, interrupted growth may have disadvantages. The conflict between concern for distribution and concern for growth is a more difficult issue. If the pressures create an absolute political (or military) barrier to concentration on industrial structural change, and if growth is too slow (perhaps because of the external situation) to alleviate the pressures, then it may not be possible to develop until the conditions change.

Development is a complex change in the structure of a society of which the economy is only a part, and within that the external sector is only one aspect. One measure of the significance of the changes in the international economic environment is the fact that these are making that small part of countries' proper concerns govern the central choices of their development strategies.

NOTES

1. Cf. the Bank for International Settlements comment on relying on market forces to cure international imbalances: 'in the end, market forces would establish a new pattern of current-account balances. But when? With what risk of causing another round of exchange rate misalignments? What lasting damage would in the meantime be inflicted on the free trading system? And what price would have to be paid in terms of output losses and financial upheavals for this market-led adjustment?' (BIS, 1987: 194).
2. Taken to its extreme, the corollary of this argument is the view that countries like Singapore (or Switzerland) succeed because they do not have the cushion of natural resources.
3. Kubo et al. argue that 'an open development strategy, if successful, demands a difficult balancing of forces and careful timing. The gains from success are great, but the difficulties of managing the required structural changes and concomitant pressures on the balance of trade are also great' (in Chenery et al., 1986: 225).
4. In the context of the discussion of goals and constraints of this study: the failure to implement even those that would improve performance in the industrial countries must be accepted as another non-economic constraint on development.
5. The replacement of unlimited with limited liability is usually considered to have been an advance in company law.
6. Chenery concludes: 'Our analysis. . .does suggest that a certain modesty in claims made for particular policy choices is called for. Since our analysis of the shift from inward- to outward-oriented policies in the Korea-based model . . . succeeded in explaining only about half the actual acceleration achieved, it is likely that other important system effects are also involved' (Chenery et al., 1986: 359). See also Bradford (1986: 123).

BIBLIOGRAPHY

General

Anjaria, S. J., Iqbal, Z., Kirmani, N. and Perez, L. L., 1982. *Developments in International Trade Policy*, IMF, Occasional Paper 16.

Anjaria, S. J., Kirmani, N. and Petersen, A., 1985. *Trade Policy Issues and Developments*, IMF, Occasional Paper 38.

Ariff, Mohamed and Hill, Hal, 1985. *Export-oriented Industrialisation: ASEAN Experience*, Sydney, Allen and Unwin.

Bacha, E., 1985. 'Growth with unlimited supplies of foreign exchange: a reappraisal of the two-gap model', in Syrquin, M., Taylor, L. and Westphal, L., *Economic Structure and Performance: Essays in Honor of Hollis Chenery*, Academic Press.

Balassa, Bela, 1981a. *Adjustment to External Shocks in Developing Economies*, World Bank Staff Working Paper 472.

Balassa, Bela, 1981b. *The Policy Experience of Twelve Less Developed Countries 1973–78*, World Bank Staff Working Paper 449.

Balassa, Bela, 1982. *Development Strategies in Semi-industrialised Economies*, World Bank, Johns Hopkins University Press.

Bank for International Settlements (BIS) 1987. *Fifty Seventh Annual Report*, Basel.

Bhagwati, Jagdish, 1978. *Foreign Trade Regimes and Economic Development: Anatomy and Consequences of Exchange Control Regimes*, Cambridge, Mass., NBER.

Bradford, Colin, 1986. *East Asian 'Models': Myths and Lessons, Development Strategies Reconsidered*, Washington DC, Overseas Development Council, Oxford University Press.

Bradford, Colin (ed.), 1987. *Trade and Structural Change in Pacific Asia*, Chicago, NBER, University of Chicago Press.

Bradford, Colin, 1987b. 'Trade and structural change: NICs and next tier NICs as transitional economies', *World Development*, 15, 3, March, pp. 299–316.

Chenery, Hollis, Robinson, Sherman and Syrquin, Moshe, 1986. *Industrialisation and Growth: A Comparative Study*, World Bank, Oxford, Oxford University Press.

Clark, William, 1981. Book Review of *Official History of Colonial Development, ODI Review*, 2, p. 84.

Corden, W. M., 1971. *The Theory of Protection*, Oxford, Clarendon Press.

Corden, W. M. and Neary, J. P., 1982. 'Booming sector and de-industrialisation in a small open economy', *Economic Journal*, 92, December.

Cutajar, Michael Zammit and Franks, Alison, 1967. *The Less Developed Countries in World Trade*, London, Overseas Development Institute.

Dell, Sidney, 1982. 'Stabilisation: the political economy of over-kill', *World Development*, 10, 8, August, pp. 597–612.

Dornbusch, R., 1974. 'Tariffs and non-traded goods', *Journal of International Economics*, December.

Dornbusch, Rudiger, 1980. *Open Economy Macroeconomics*, New York, Basic Books.

Eshag, E., 1983. *Fiscal and Monetary Policies and Problems in Developing Countries*, Modern Cambridge Economics, Cambridge University Press.

Fields, Gary S., 1985. 'Industrialisation and employment in Hong Kong, Korea, Singapore and Taiwan', in Walter Galenson (ed.) *Foreign Trade and Investment: the Newly-Industrialising Asian Countries*, Madison, University of Wisconsin Press.

Finger, J. M. and Olechowski, A., 1986. *Trade Barriers: Who Does What to Whom*, Kiel, Conference, June, Washington, World Bank Paper.

Fishlow, A., 1985. In Inter-American Development Bank, *Economic and Social Progress in Latin America*.

Havrylyshyn, Oli and Wolf, Martin, 1981. *Trade Among Developing Countries*, World Bank Staff Working Paper 479.

Hiemenz, U. and Langhammer, R. J., 1986. *Efficiency Pre-conditions for Successful Integration of Developing Countries into the World Economy*, 2–246/Working Paper, Geneva, ILO, WEP.

Hughes, G. A. and Newbery, D. M. G., 1984. 'Effect of protection on manufactured exports from developing countries', London, CEPR, Discussion Paper.

Inter-American Development Bank (IDB), *Economic and Social Progress in Latin America*, published annually.

IMF, *Exchange Arrangements & Exchange Restrictions*, published annually.

IMF, *World Economic Outlook*, published annually. (Reference given as 1987b, etc.)

Krueger, Anne O., 1978. *Foreign Trade Regimes and Economic Development: Liberalisation Attempts and Consequences*, Cambridge, Mass., Ballinger for NBER.

Krueger, Anne O., 1983. *Trade and Employment in Developing Countries 3: Synthesis and Conclusions*, Chicago, University of Chicago.

Krueger, Anne O. (ed.), 1982. *Trade and Employment in Developing Countries 2: Factor Supply and Substitution*, Chicago, University of Chicago.

Laird, S. and Finger, J. M., 1986. *Protection in Developed and developing Countries*, Washington, World Bank Paper.

Lee, J., 1987. 'Domestic adjustment to external shocks in selected Asian developing countries'. Paper prepared for EADI conference, Amsterdam.

Llewellyn, John, Potter, Stephen and Samuelson, Lee, 1985. *Economic Forecasting and Policy – the International Dimension*, London, Routledge & Kegan Paul.

Lorenz, Detlef, 1986. 'New situations facing the NICs in East Asia', *Intereconomics*, December, pp. 263–8.

OECD, 1985. *Costs and Benefits of Protection*, Paris, OECD.

Page, Sheila, *Economic Prospects for the Third World*, London, Overseas Development Institute, published annually.

Page, Sheila, 1984b. 'Forecasting for the developing countries', *Development Policy Review*, 2, 1, May, pp. 13–34.

Page, Sheila, 1986b. *Relocating Manufacturing in Developing Countries: Opportunities for UK Companies*, London, NEDO Working Papers, EWP 25.

Page, Sheila, 1987b. 'The rise in protection since 1974', *Oxford Review of Economic Policy*, Spring, pp. 37–51.

Pazos, Felipe, 1985. 'Have import substitution policies either precipitated or aggravated debt crisis?', *Journal of Interamerican Studies*, 27, 4, Winter, pp. 57–72.

Puyana de Palacios, Alicia, 1982. *Economic Integration Among Unequal Partners. The Case of the Andean Group*, New York, Pergamon Press.

Reynolds, L. G., 1983. 'The spread of economic growth to the Third World: 1850–1980', *Journal of Economic Literature*, September.

Roy, Donald J., 1987. 'Size and wealth in perspective: their effect on economic structure and poverty', *Development Policy Review*, 5, 4, December, pp. 349–59.

Schmitz, Hubert, 1984. 'Industrialisation strategies in less developed countries; some lessons of historical experience', *Journal of Development Studies*, October.

Streeten, Paul, 1982. 'A look at "outward looking" strategies for development', *The World Economy*, 5, 2, September pp. 154–70.

Streeten, Paul, 1985. 'A problem to every solution', *Finance & Development*, June, pp. 14–16.

Taylor, L., 1983. *Structural Macroeconomics*, New York, Basic Books Inc.

Thirlwall, A. P., 1983. 'A plain man's guide to Kaldor's growth laws', *Journal of Post-Keynesian Economics*, Spring.

UN, 1987. *World Economic Survey 1987 Current Trends and Policies in the World Economy*, New York.

UNCTAD, 1987. *Trade and Development Report*.

UNIDO, *Industry and Development Global Report*, published annually.

Wilkens, Herbert, Petersen, Hans J. and Schultz, Siegfried, 1986. 'Economic, social and political prerequisites of development', *Intereconomics* 21, 2, March–April, pp. 86–93.

World Bank, *World Development Report*, published annually.

Malaysia

Ali, Syed Husin, 1985. *A Study of Malay Peasants*, quoted by Zawawi Ibrahim in 'Rich man, poor man – the NEP equation', *Far Eastern Economic Review*, 20 June.

Ariff, M., 1975. 'Protection for manufactures in peninsular Malaysia', *Hitsosubashi Journal of Economics*, 15, 2, February.

Ariff, Mohamed, 1984. *Constant Market Share Analysis of Malaysian Exports and Imports*, Kuala Lumpur.

Ariff, Mohamed, Chee, P. L. and Lee, D., 1984. 'Export incentives, manufactured exports and employment, Malaysia', Manila, Council for Asia Manpower Studies (unpublished).

Chee, Peng Lim, 1981. 'Changes in the Malaysian economy and trade trends and prospects', Washington, for Brookings Institution Conference, (mimeo).

Datta-Chaudhuri, M., 1982. 'The role of Free Trade Zones in the creation of employment and industrial growth in Malaysia', Asian Employment Programme Working papers ILO-ARTEP, Bangkok.

Hock, Lee Keong, 1984. 'Structure and causes of Malaysian manufacturing sector protection', ASEAN–Australian Joint Research Project, Canberra.

Institute of Strategic Studies, 1985. 'The management of the Malaysian ringgit', (mimeo).

Lim, Lin Lean and Chee, Peng Lim (eds), 1984. *Malaysian Economy at the Crossroads*, Kuala Lumpur, Malaysia Economic Association.

'Malaysia; Economic Planning Unit (EPU)', an unpublished study.

Power, J. H., 1971, 'The structure of protection in West Malaysia', in Balassa, B. (ed.), *The Structure of Protection in Developing Countries*, Baltimore, Johns Hopkins University Press.

Van Dijck and Verbruggen, H., 1983. *Export-oriented Industrialisation and Economic Development in Developing Countries*, Amsterdam, Free University.

Young, Kevin, Bussink, Willem C. F. and Hasan, Parvez, 1980. *Malaysia: Growth and Equity in a Multiracial Society*, World Bank Country Economic Report, Baltimore and London, Johns Hopkins University Press.

Thailand

Ajanant, Juanjai, Chunanuntathum, Supote and Meenaphant, Sorrayuth, 1984. *Trade and Industrialisation of Thailand*, a Report prepared for International Development Research Centre, March.

Akrasanee, Narongchai, 1973. 'The manufacturing sector in Thailand: a study of growth, import substitution, and effective protection, 1960–1969', PhD Dissertation, Johns Hopkins University.

Bank of Thailand, *Annual Economic Report*, Bangkok, various issues.

Bank of Thailand, 1978. *Analysis of Import Structure of Thailand*, Bangkok.

Chunanuntathum, Supote, Mongkolsmai, Dow and Tambunlertchai, Somsak, 1985. *Fiscal Implications of Investment Incentives and Promotion Efficiency*, Volume I, an unpublished report presented to the Fiscal Policy Office, Ministry of Finance.

Chunanuntathum, Supote, 1980. 'Development of selected commodity exports to Japan', in Krongkaew, M. (ed.), *Current Developments in Thai–Japanese Economic Relations: Trade and Investment*, Bangkok, Thammasat University Press.

Sakurai, Makota, 1984. 'Industrialisation in developing countries and industrial adjustments of industrialised countries', Research Institute of Overseas Investment, the Export–Import Bank of Japan, October.

Suwankiri, Trairong, 1970. 'The structure of protection and import substitution in Thailand', Master's Thesis, University of the Philippines, April.

Tambunlertchai, Somsak and Ippei, Yamazawa, 1981. 'Manufactured exports and foreign direct investment: a case study of the textile industry in Thailand', Research Report Series 50, Faculty of Economics, Thammasat University.

Tinnakorn, Pranee and Pathamasiriwat, Direk, 1985. 'External debt of developing countries: a case study of Thailand's external debt' (in Thai), a paper prepared for the Symposium on the Debt Crisis of the Thai Government, Thammasat University.

Watanabe, Toshio and Kajiwara, Korikazu, 1983. 'Pacific manufactured trade and Japan's options', *The Developing Economies*, December.

Wattananukit, Atchana, 1985. 'External debt of Thailand's state enterprises' (in Thai), a paper prepared for the Symposium on the Debt Crisis of the Thai Government, Thammasat University.

Wongwuttiwat, Pairote, 1975. 'The structure of differential incentives in the manufacturing sector: a case study of Thailand's experiences during 1945–1974', Master's Thesis, Thammasat University.

Colombia

Berry, A., 1971. 'Some implications of elitist rule for economic development in Colombia', in G. Ranis, *Government and Economic Development*, New Haven, Yale University Press.

Berry, A. and Thoumi, F., 1985. 'Colombian economic growth and policies. 1970–84' (mimeo).

CEPAL, 1986. 'Preliminary overview of the Latin American economy', *Notas Sobre la Economia y el Desarrollo*, No. 438/439, December.

Cuddington, J. T., 1986. 'Commodity booms, macroeconomic stabilization and trade réform in Colombia' (mimeo).

Davis, J., 1983. 'The economic effects of windfall gains in export earnings, 1975–78', *World Development*, February.

Echavarria, J. J. and Garay, L. J., 1978.'El control de importaciones en Colombia', *Coyuntura Económica*, October.

Echavarria, J. J., 1979. 'Subcontratación y ensamblaje en Colombia' (mimeo).

Echavarria, J. J., 1982a. 'Trade prospects for Latin America. The case of Colombia' (mimeo).

Echavarria, J. J., 1982b. 'Subsidios y tasa de cambio. Análisis de las primeras medidas del nuevo gobierno', *Coyuntura Económica*, October.

Echavarria, J. J., 1982c. 'La evolución de las exportaciones Colombianas y sus determinantes. Un análisis empírico', *Ensayos Sobre Política Económica'*, 2, September.

Echavarria, J. J. *et al.*, 1983. 'El proceso Colombiano de industrializacion. Algunas ideas sobre un viejo debate', *Coyuntura Económica*, September.

Echavarria, J. J., 1986. 'Auge, estancamiento y crísis en la industria Colombiana. 1970–85' (mimeo).

Edwards, S., 1985. 'The interaction of coffee, money, and inflation in Colombia', in Thomas, Vinod, *Linking Macroeconomic and Agricultural Policies for Adjustment with Growth*, Baltimore, Johns Hopkins University Press.

Edwards, S., (forthcoming). 'Commodity export prices and the real exchange rate in developing countries: coffee in Colombia', in *Macroeconomic Adjustment and Real Exchange Rates in Developing Countries*, National Bureau of Economic Research Conference Volume.

Edwards, S. and Aoki, M., 1983. 'Oil export boom and Dutch-disease: a dynamic analysis', *Resources and Energy*, 5, September.

Edwards, S. and Teitel, S., 1986. 'Introduction to growth, reform and adjustment: Latin America's trade and macroeconomic policies in the 1970s and 1980s', *Economic Development and Cultural Change*, April.

Fernandez, J. and Candelo, R., 1983. 'Política monetaria y movilidad de capitales en Colombia', *'Ensayos Sobre Política Económica*, April.

Furtado, C., 1976. *Economic Development of Latin America*, 2nd edition, Cambridge, Cambridge University Press.

Gomez, H. *et al.*, (eds), 1976. *Lecturas Sobre Moneda y Banca*, Bogota, Fedesarrollo.

Grunwald, Joseph and Flamm, Kenneth, 1985. *The Global Factory; Foreign Assembly in International Trade*, Washington, The Brookings Institution.

Harberger, A., 1983. 'Dutch disease: how much sickness, how much boom?', *Resources and Energy*, 5, March.

Jaramillo, J. C., 1982. 'La liberación del mercado financiero', *Ensayos Sobre Política Económica*.

Junguito, R. *et al.*, 1977. *Economia Cafetera Colombiana*, Bogota, Fedesarrollo.

Kamas, L., 1986. 'Dutch disease economics and the Colombian export boom', *World Development*, 14, 9.

Leiderman, L.,1984. 'On the monetary-macro dynamics of Colombia and Mexico', *Journal of Development Economics*, 14.

Martinez, A., 1986. 'Historia de la Protección en Colombia', CID, Universidad Nacional.

McCarthy, F. D. *et al.*, 1985. 'Fuentes de crecimiento en Colombia', *Revista de Planeación y Desarrollo*, June.

Ocampo, J. A., 1984. 'The Colombian economy in the 1930s', in Thorp, R., *Latin America in the 1930s. The Role of the Periphery in World Crisis*, London, Macmillan.

Ocampo, J. A., 1986. 'La política macroeconómica en el corto y en el mediano plazo', *Coyuntura Económica*, December.

Ocampo, J. A. (ed.), 1987. *Historia económica de Colombia*, Bogota, Fedesarrollo.
Ocampo, J. A. and Reveiz, E., 1979. 'Bonanza cafetera y económica concertada', *Desarrollo Sociedad*, July.
Ocampo, J. A. *et al.*, 1985. 'Ahorro e inversión en Colombia', *Coyuntura Económica*, June.
Ocampo, J. A. and Lora, E., 1986. 'Economic activity, macroeconomic policy and income distribution in Colombia, 1980–1990' (mimeo).
Perry, G. and Cárdenas, M., 1986. *Diez Años de Reformas Tributarias en Colombia*, CID, Fedesarrollo.
Ramirez, J., 1985. 'La bonanza cafetera de 1986', *Debates de Coyuntura Económica*, 1.
Rodriguez, Luis Hernando, 1985. *Análisis Descriptivo de las Exportaciones Colombianas 1950–1980*, Bogota, CEDE.
Ruiz, H., 1979. 'La producción y el comercio de la marihuana en Colombia', ANIF, *Carta Financiera*, Enero-Marzo.
Ruiz, H. and Lopez, A., 1981. 'Economias clandestinas, economia subterranea y las perspectivas del sector externo', ANIF, *Carta Financiera*, Enero-Marzo.
Sarmiento, E., 1984. *Funcionamiento y Control de una Economia en Desequilibrio*, Contraloria General de la República, CEREC.
Silvani, L., 1983. 'El fondo financiero industrial', *Ensayos Sobre Política Económica*, April.
Syrquin, M., 1986. 'Economic growth and structural change in Colombia: an international comparison', (mimeo).
Syrquin, M., 1986. 'Growth and structural change in Latin America since 1960: a comparative analysis', *Economic Development and Cultural Change*, April.
Thomas, Vinod, 1985. *Linking Macroeconomic and Agricultural Policies for Adjustment with Growth*, Baltimore, Johns Hopkins University Press.
Thorp, R. and Whitehead, L., (eds), 1987. *Latin American Debt and the Adjustment Crisis*, London, Macmillan.
Urrutia, M., 1985. *Winners and Losers in Colombia's Economic Growth of the 1970's*, Oxford, Oxford University Press.
Villar, L., 1984. 'Determinantes de la evolución de las exportaciones menores en Colombia, 1960–81', *Coyuntura Económica*, October.
World Bank, 1986. 'Economic growth and resource mobilization, an overview' (mimeo).

Peru

Abalo, Carlos, 1978. 'Sistematización de los problemas actuales del subdesarrollo', *Comercio Exterior*, 28(1), January.
Abel, Andrew B. and Beleza, Luis, 1978. 'Input–output pricing in a Keynesian model of the Portuguese economy', *Journal of Development Economics*, 5, pp. 125–38.
Alarco, Germán (ed.), 1985. *Desafios Para la Economia Peruana, 1985–1990*, Lima, Centro de Investigación de la Universidad del Pacífico (OIUP).
Alarco, Germán (ed.), 1987. *Modelos Macroeconométricos en el Perú: Nuevos Aportes*, Lima.
Arellano, José Pablo, 1985. 'Aspectos macroeconómicos de la balanza de pagos. Una nota docente', *Notas Técnicas*, 75, CIEPLAN, July.
Benetti, Carlo, 1974. *La Acumulación en los Paises Capitalistas Subdesarrollados*, Mexico, Fondo de Cultura Económica.
BCR, 1984a. *Perspectivas del Sector Externo: 1985–1989*, Lima, Banco Central de Reserva del Perú, Subgerencia del Sector Externo, December.
BCR, 1984b. *Memoria*, Lima, Banco Central de Reserva del Perú.

BCR, 1987. *Análisis de largo Plazo del Sector Externo de la Economia Peruana, 1975–1986*, Lima, Banco Central de Reserva del Perú, Gerencia de Investigación Económica, Subgerencia del Sector Externo, June.

Canitrot, Adolfo, 1975. 'La experiencia populista de redistribución de ingresos', *Desarrollo Economico*, XV, 59, October–December, pp. 331–51.

Cardoso, Eliana, 1987. 'Payment crisis and inflation: The IMF in Latin America', *Discussion Paper Series*, 70, Center for Latin American Development Studies, Boston University, May.

Cardoso, Fernando H., 1971. *Ideologia de la burguesia industrial en sociedades dependientes*, Mexico, Siglo XXI.

Cardoso, Fernando H., 1974. 'Las contradicciones del desarrollo asociado', *Desarrollo Económico*, 14, 53, April–June.

Cardoso, Fernando H. and Faletto, Enzo, 1969. *Dependencia y Desarrollo – América Latina*, Mexico, Siglo XXI.

Cardoso, Fernando H. and Faletto, Enzo, 1977. 'Estado y proceso político en America Latina', *Revista Mexicana de Sociologia*, 39 (2), April–June, pp. 357–87.

Cline, William R. and Weintraub, Sidney (eds), 1981. *Economic Stabilization in Developing Countries*, Washington, The Brookings Institution.

Daly, Jorge L., 1983. *The Political Economy of Devaluation – The Case of Peru*, Boulder, Colorado, Westview Press.

Dancourt, Oscar, 1984. *Precios Relativos, Distribución del Ingreso y Demanda Efectiva*, Lima, PUC, unpublished thesis.

Dancourt, Oscar, 1986. 'Sobre las políticas macroeconómicas en el Perú, 1970–1984', Lima, Instituto de Estudios Peruanos (IEP), *Documento de Trabajo*, 12, March.

Dancourt, Oscar, 1987. 'Deuda versus Crecimiento: Un Dilema Político', *Documentos de Trabajo*, 71, Lima, Pontificia Universidad Catolica, Departamento de Economia, March.

Diaz-Alejandro, Carlos, 1963. 'A note on the impact of devaluation and the redistributive effect', *Journal of Political Economy*, 71, pp. 557–80.

Dos Santos, Theotonio, 1979. 'The structure of dependence', *American Economic Review*, 60(2), May, pp. 231–6.

Ferrer, Aldo, 1978. *Crisis y Alternativas de la Política Económica Argentina*, Mexico, Fondo de Cultura Económica.

Foxley, Alejandro, 1982. *Experimentos neoliberales en América Latina*, Santiago, Colección Estudios CIEPLAN, 59.

Garcia, Alan, 1985. Speech to UN General Assembly, 23 September.

Godelier, Maurice, 1970. *Racionalidad e Irracionalidad en la Economia*, Mexico, Siglo XXI.

González Casanova, Pablo, 1971. 'Las reformas de estructura en América Latina (su lógica dentro de la economia de mercado)', *El Trimestre Económico*, 38(2), 150, April–June, pp. 351–88.

González Vigil, Fernando, 1985. 'Reestructuración internacional y perspectivas para la industrialización de América Latina', in Alarco, 1985, pp. 9–34.

Guisinger, Stephen, 1981. 'Stabilization policies in Pakistan: the 1970–77 experience', in Cline and Weintraub, 1981, pp. 375–405.

IMF Institute, 1984. *Programación financiera aplicada: El caso de Colombia*, Washington, DC, International Monetary Fund.

Kisic, Drago, Danino, Roberto and Morales, Raymundo, 1985. *El Perú y América Latina frente al Club de Paris*, Lima, CIUP and CEPEI.

Krugman, Paul and Taylor, Lance, 1978. 'Contractionary effects of devaluation', *Journal of International Economics*, 8, pp. 445–56.

Malloy, James, 1974. 'Authoritarianism, corporatism and mobilization in Peru', *Review of Politics*, 36(1), January, pp. 52–84.

Malloy, James (ed.), 1977. *Authoritarianism and Corporatism in Latin America*, University of Pittsburgh Press.

O'Donnell, Guillermo, 1973. *Modernization and Bureaucratic Authoritarianism, Studies in South American Politics*, University of California, Berkeley, Institute of International Studies, Politics of Modernization Series 9.

O'Donnell, Guillermo, 1977. 'Corporatism and the question of the state', in Malloy, James (ed.), *Authoritarianism and Corporatism in Latin America,* University of Pittsburgh Press.

Porto, Alberto, 1975. 'Un modelo simple sobre, el comportamiento macroeconómico argentino en el corto plazo', *Desarrollo Económico*, 15, 59, October–December, pp. 353–71.

Prebisch, Raul, 1976. 'Crítica al capitalismo periférico', *Revista de la CEPAL*, Semestre 1, pp. 7–73.

Sagasti, Francisco and Garland, Gonzalo, 1985. 'Algunas perspectivas sobre la evolución reciente de la economia mundial y de los cambios en la ciencia y la tecnologia a nivel internacional', in Alarco, 1985, pp. 35–56.

Santa Maria, Hugo, 1987. 'Perú', *Coyuntura Económica Andina*, Fedesarrollo 17, 2 June.

Schuldt, Jürgen, 1981. 'La trama invisible de la politica económica actual: algunas hipotesis', in G. Pennano (ed.), *Economia Peruana, Hacia Dónde?*, Lima CIUP.

Schuldt, Jürgen, 1985. 'Los Acuerdos Recientes con el FMI en Perspectiva', in Alarco, 1985, pp. 97–114.

Schuldt, Jürgen, 1986. 'Desinflación y reestructuración económica en el Perú, 1985–86: Modelo para armar', in Persio Arida (ed.), *Inflación Cero*, Bogota, Oveja Negra, pp. 119–203.

Schuldt, Jürgen, 1987.'Desinflación selectiva y reactivación generalizada en el Perú, 1985–86', *El Trimestre Económico*, special issue, September, pp. 313–50.

Schydlowsky, Daniel, 1979. *Containing the Costs of Stabilization in Semi-industrialized LDCs: A Marshallian Approach*, Boston University, CLADS.

Schydlowsky, Daniel and Wicht, Juan J., 1979. *Anatomia de un Fracaso Económico: Peru, 1968–1978*, Lima, CIUP.

Schydlowsky, Daniel, Hunt, Shane and Mezzera, Jaime, 1983. *La Promoción de Exportaciones No Tradicionales en el Perú*, Lima, Asociación de Exportadores del Perú (ADEX).

Sheahan, John, 1978. 'Market-oriented economic policies and political repression in Latin America', *Research Memorandum Series*, 10, The Center for Development Economics, Williams College, June.

Thorp, Rosemary, 1983. 'The evolution of Peru's economy', in Cynthia McClintock and Abraham F. Lowenthal (eds), *The Peruvian Experiment Reconsidered*, Princeton, NJ, Princeton University Press, pp. 39–61.

Torres, Jorge, 1985. 'Estrangulamientos de la economia peruana 1985–1990', in Alarco, 1985, pp. 57–74.

Ugarteche, Oscar, 1986. *El Estado Deudor, Economia política de la deuda: Peru y Bolivia, 1968–1984*, Lima, Instituto de Estudios Peruanos.

Vuskovik, Pedro, 1979. 'América Latina ante nuevos terminos de la división internacional del trabajo', *Economia para América Latina*, Semestre 2, March, pp.15–28.

Webb, Richard, 1987. 'Distribución del Ingreso Nacional 1–1 1986', Lima, Instituto Nacional de Planificación; internal document.

Weffort, Francisco C., 1968. *Classes Populares e Desenvolvimiento Social* (Contribuçao ao estudo do 'populismo'), Santiago, ILPES.

World Bank, 1981. *Peru: Major Development Policy Issues and Recommendations*, The International Bank for Reconstruction and Development, Washington, DC.

Zylberberg, Jacques, 1977. 'Estado–Corporativismo–Populismo: Contribución a una Sociologia Política de América Latina', *Estudios Sociales Centroamericanos*, VI, 18, 1, September–December, pp. 77–115.

Zimbabwe

Amin, Samir, 1983. 'Is a self-directed development strategy possible in Africa?', UNESCO Meeting of Experts, Libreville, Gabon, 19–22 December.

Clarke, D. G., 1980. *Foreign Companies and International Investment in Zimbabwe*, Gweru, Mambo Press.

CZI Export Directory, 1986.

Dairy Marketing Board, 1983. 'Milk collection in Chikwaka'.

Dairy Marketing Board, 1986. 'Masterplan for the dairy sector'.

Davies, Rob, 1986. 'The macroeconomic consequences of redistribution policies in Zimbabwe', ODI working paper.

Davies, Rob, 1987. 'The transition to socialism in Zimbabwe: some areas for debate', Manuscript.

Girdlestone, J., 1982. *Trade and Investment in Zimbabwe*, Whitsun Foundation Project 1.07, Harare.

Gray, Simon, 1985. 'A critique of manufactured exports', Paper presented at Ministry of Industry and Technology Workshop on the 1985 UNIDO study of the Manufacturing Sector, Confederation of Zimbabwe Industries, December.

Green, R. H., 1985. 'Parameters, permutations and political economy: Zimbabwe 1973/83–1986–96', Paper 20, Conference on Economic Policies and Planning under Crisis Conditions in Developing Countries, University of Zimbabwe, Harare, September.

Jansen, Doris J., 1983. 'Zimbabwe: government policy and the manufacturing sector', Larkspur, California.

Kadhani, X. and Green, R. H., 1985. 'Zimbabwe: transition to economic crises 1981–83. Retrospect and prospect', UNDP/UNCTAD Project INT/84/021 Studies on International Monetary and Financial Issues for the Developing Countries.

Lively, Jack, 1977. *Democracy*, New York, Capricorn Books.

MacDonald, Ian and Robinson, Peter, 1986. 'A multisectoral dynamic optimisation model for energy/petrochemical decision making in Zimbabwe and the SADCC', ZEAP Working Paper, Beijer Institute, Stockholm.

Mandaza, Ibbo (ed.), 1986. *Zimbabwe: The Political Economy of Transition, 1980–1986*, Dakar, Senegal, Codesria.

Manungo, Willard L., 1986. 'Recent changes in the international monetary system and the implications on developing countries', unpublished MSc thesis, University of Zimbabwe, February.

Masaya, T. R., 1985. 'The response of agricultural output to external cyclical excitation', *Zimbabwe Journal of Economics*, 1, 2, January, pp. 31–8.

Michelsen Institute, 1987. 'SADCC intra-regional trade study', Bergen, Norway, January.

Mkandawire, Thandika, 1985. 'Dependence and economic cooperation: the case of SADCC', *Zimbabwe Journal of Economics*, 1, 2, January, pp. 1–10.

Moyo, Sam, 1986. 'The land question', in Mandaza, Ibbo, *Zimbabwe: the Political Economy of Transition, 1980–86*, Dakar, Senegal, Codesria.

Ndlela, Daniel B., 1984. 'Sectoral analysis of Zimbabwe economic development with implications for foreign trade and foreign exchange', *Zimbabwe Journal of Economics*, 1, 1, July, pp. 68–76.

Ranis, Gustav, 1974. 'Employment, equity and growth: lessons from the Philippine employment mission', *International Labour Review*, July, pp.18–24.

Riddell, Roger C., 1983. 'A critique of "Zimbabwe: Government policy and the manufacturing sector"', CZI mimeo, July.

Riddell, Roger C., 1987. 'Zimbabwe's experience of foreign investment policy', in Vincent Cable and Bishnodat Persaud (eds), *Developing with Foreign Investment*, London, Commonwealth Secretariat.

Stewart, Frances, 1974. 'Technology and employment in LDCs', *World Development*, March, pp. 21–3.

Stoneman, Colin and Robinson, Peter, 1984. 'Economic modelling for LEAP – background and methodology', ZEAP Working Paper 16, Beijer Institute, Stockholm.

Stoneman, Colin, 1985. 'Strategy or ideology? The World Bank/IMF approach to development', Paper 10, Conference on Economic Policies and Planning under Crisis Conditions in Developing Countries, University of Zimbabwe, Harare, September.

Streeten, Paul, 1975. 'Industrialisation in a unified development strategy', *World Development*, 3, 1, January.

UNIDO, 1986b. 'Study of the manufacturing sector in Zimbabwe', Vienna.

World Bank, 1985. 'Zimbabwe country economic memorandum – performance, policies and prospects', Washington, DC.

Zimbabwe, 1981. 'Report of The Commission of Inquiry into Incomes, Prices and Conditions of Service', under the Chairmanship of Roger C. Riddell, Harare, Government Printer.

Zimbabwe, 1986. *First Five-Year National Development Plan 1986–1990*, 1, Government Printer, Harare, April.

Zimconsult, 1984. 'The domestic demand for beef', Harare, May.

Zimconsult, 1984. 'Rural distribution of dairy products', Harare, October.

Zimconsult, 1985. 'An input–output projection for the Five Year Plan 1986–1990', Harare, November.

Zimconsult, 1986. 'Viability of the Beira Corridor', Harare, April.

INDEX